THE ANALYSIS, DESIGN, AND IMPLEMENTATION OF INFORMATION SYSTEMS

McGraw-Hill Series in Management Information Systems

Gordon B. Davis, *Consulting Editor*

Davis and Everest: Readings in Management Information Systems
Davis and Olson: Management Information Systems: Conceptual Foundations, Structure, and Development
Dickson and Wetherbe: The Management of Information Systems
Dickson and Wetherbe: The Management of Information Systems Casebook
Everest: Database Management: Objectives, Organization, and System Function
Lucas: The Analysis, Design, and Implementation of Information Systems
Lucas: Information Systems Concepts for Management
Lucas and Gibson: A Casebook for Management Information Systems
Meadow and Tedesco: Telecommunications for Management
Weber: EDP Auditing: Conceptual Foundations and Practice

THE ANALYSIS, DESIGN, AND IMPLEMENTATION OF INFORMATION SYSTEMS

THIRD EDITION

Henry C. Lucas, Jr.

Professor of Computer Applications
and Information Systems
Schools of Business
New York University

McGRAW-HILL BOOK COMPANY

New York St. Louis San Francisco Auckland Bogctá
Hamburg Johannesburg London Madrid Mexico Montreal New Delhi
Panama Paris São Paulo Singapore Sydney Tokyo Toronto

This book was set in Optima by Black Dot, Inc. (ECU).
The editor was Christina Mediate;
the production supervisor was Marietta Breitwieser.
Project supervision was done by The Total Book.
R. R. Donnelley & Sons Company was printer and binder.

THE ANALYSIS, DESIGN, AND IMPLEMENTATION OF INFORMATION SYSTEMS

2 3 4 5 6 7 8 9 0 D O C D O C 8 9 8 7 6

ISBN 0-07-038929-2

See Acknowledgments on page xii.
Copyrights included on this page by reference.

Library of Congress Cataloging in Publication Data

Lucas, Henry C.
    The analysis, design, and implementation of information systems.

    (McGraw-Hill series in management information systems)
    Bibliography: p.
    Includes index.
    1. Management information systems. 2. System analysis. I. Title. II. Series.
T58.6.L79   1984   658.4'038   84-11238
ISBN 0-07-038929-2

To Scott

CONTENTS

PREFACE

The purpose of this text is to provide students with an understanding of information systems, management, and the operation of the computer department in an organization. The text emphasizes both the tasks involved in system analysis and design and the relationship between the designers and the users of a system. The book is divided into four parts.

In Part One, system analysis, the nature of the organization, the role of management, and the role of computer-based systems in the organization are discussed. The purpose of this first section is to furnish perspective on information systems and on the approach to systems design advocated in the next section.

Part Two is an overview of system analysis and design and approaches to this task. This section is extremely important; it presents a number of alternative approaches to building a system.

Part Three goes into depth on systems analysis and design, one of the major creative tasks undertaken in a modern organization. Here we follow the systems life cycle and illustrate our approach with a case. Part Four of the book discusses some of the problems of managing the computer department to prepare the student to undertake information systems-related activities in an organization.

The book is designed for students who plan to become programmers, systems analysts, and/or managers in the information systems area. The text assumes that the student has completed a course on a higher-level procedural programming language such as COBOL, PL/I, ALGOL, etc. The text should fit the needs of a second or third course on computers or data processing at the undergraduate level. Although the book assumes no further background than a good programming course, some prior preparation on hardware, software, and data base technology will make individual topics more meaningful.

For schools with a limited number of information systems courses, the text is intended to follow an introductory programming course. For schools which are able to offer a variety of information systems courses, certain topics in the book can be used as either a review of a prior course (for example, Chapter 8 on files) or an introduction to a more specialized elective (for example, Chapter 22 on the management of the computer department.) The book encompasses almost all the topics for the ACM Curriculum Recommendation for Undergraduate Programs in Information systems course UD9, Systems Design and Implementation, and about 70 percent of the topics in UA8, Systems Concepts and Implications.

The book attempts to cover the broad field of systems analysis and design. The instructor can go into depth on the topics introduced here or additional courses may be taken. One of the best ways to appreciate the nature of systems analysis and design is to complete a course using the text and then to participate in an actual systems analysis and design project.

For the instructor who wishes to use the text in a class on systems analysis and design, there are several features of the text and supplementary materials that may prove helpful. First, there is an Instructors Manual available from McGraw-Hill. In addition, *The Casebook for Managment Information Systems* by Lucas and Gibson contains a number of substantial case studies that can be assigned for class or as term projects to an individual or group of students. (The *Casebook* is also published by McGraw-Hill.)

The text itself contains a series of Discussion Questions, File Problems and Systems Design Exercises. The Systems Problems are very important and the student should be encouraged to read and solve them. These problems are discussed in the Instructor's Manual; they either make a point to supplement the text or require the student to solve a problem by applying the material in the book. The Discussion Questions and File Problems can usually be answered with a few sentences. The Systems Design Exercises are major assignments; here the student reads about a situation and is asked to design some part of an information system. All of this material is intended to better prepare the student for a role in systems analysis and design activities.

ACKNOWLEDGMENTS

I acknowledge the permission of Columbia University Press to reproduce Tables 7-1 and 7-2 from my 1974 book *Toward Creative Systems Design,* and Figure 4-1 from my 1975 book *Why Information Systems Fail.* McGraw-Hill has also given permission to use parts of *Information Systems Concepts for Management* in this text. *The IBM System Journal* granted permission to reprint Figures 16-3, 16-4, 16-5 and *Management Science* granted permission to reprint Figure 16-6.

Prentice-Hall provided permission to reprint Figure 1-1 from *The Structure of Organizations* by Henry Mintzberg.

Professor Margrethe Olson developed some of the file design problems and Professor Jon Turner provided useful comments on the final edition of the text. I am also extremely grateful to my wife, Ellen, who managed to make a significant contribution to improving the original manuscript despite being in the middle of a coast-to-coast move!

Henry C. Lucas, Jr.

INTRODUCTION

CHAPTER 1

THE INFORMATION SYSTEMS ENVIRONMENT

INTRODUCTION

In the past three decades, a new and dynamic activity has developed in organizations: the design, operation, and management of computer-based information systems. While many organizational activities and resources have long been devoted to the acquisition and processing of information, the advent of electronic computers has greatly extended our information processing capabilities. Computer-based information systems have influenced organizations of all types and sizes. Many organizations own or lease computers; others obtain computer time from commercial service bureaus.

Organizations with their own computer equipment constitute the majority of computer users, and most of these organizations have established a computer department to design, operate, and manage computer-based information systems. In this text, we explore all the activities associated with a computer department except programming. (We assume the reader has been exposed to and written at least one program in a higher-level computer language such as COBOL, FORTRAN, PL/1, PASCAL, or BASIC.) In this first chapter we examine general systems theory and organizations that provide the environment for information systems. However, before we discuss systems theory and organizations, it is helpful to present an overview of computer department activities and of the remainder of the book.

OVERVIEW

What is an information system? For our purposes, we define an information system as a set of organized procedures that, when executed, provide information for decision making and/or control of the organization. Information is some tangible or intangible entity that reduces uncertainty about a state or event. For example, information that the weather will be good tomorrow reduces our uncertainty about whether or not a baseball game will be played.

We are surrounded by information systems, as we shall see in the examples in later chapters. Organizations use information systems to process transactions, reduce costs, and generate revenue as a part of their products or services. Banks use information systems to process customer checks and produce statements. Many firms use computer-based systems to maintain inventories at the lowest level consistent with the kind of service they want to provide in terms of available items. There are many services firms that sell particular programs or data to various users. In the rest of the text, we shall examine some of the characteristics of these information systems and learn how to design them.

Who uses information systems? There are many examples of information systems and many different types of users. In this text, we are primarily interested in computer-based information systems because of the special requirements necessary to develop and manage these systems. There are many non-computer-based information systems. However, these systems can be highly flexible, since manual processing procedures are relatively simple and easy to change. Computer-based systems are complex and are often seen as rigid and difficult to change. The presence of computer technology also occasionally intimidates users. For these reasons we are primarily interested in systems analysis and design for computer-based information systems.

Most computer-based information systems exist within an organization of some type. Members of the organization are the users of the information produced by the system. Because the organization furnishes the overall environment for systems, we discuss organizations in a later section of this chapter. Many users of information systems are managers, and managers are also responsible for allocating resources for the development and operation of information systems. Therefore, in the next chapter we discuss the role of management in the organization.

One of the most important activities of the computer department is the design of information systems. The systems designer works with users to create procedures, file contents and structures, and processing algorithms and conversion steps. The analyst and others manage the programming and implementation of a new system and prepare documentation describing the system. Because the design of a system is so central to the organization and the computer department, the second part of this text is devoted to it.

The entire collection of computer-based information systems in the organization is operated on a regular basis. In addition, both the systems design and operations function in a computer department must be managed. In the fourth part of the book, we explore these activities as they relate to a computer professional. At the completion of the text, the reader who has had some programming experience should have a good understanding of the activities and responsibilities of a modern computer department.

SYSTEMS THEORY

General Systems

The field of systems analysis and design for information systems has its foundations in general systems theory. General systems theory emphasizes the need to examine all parts of a system. Too often the analyst focuses only on one component of a system; he or she takes action that may be ineffective because important components were ignored.

As an example, the federal government mandated certain bumper strength standards for automobiles to reduce damage from slow-speed accidents. However, the system in this case was too narrowly defined; the attention of the regulators was on repair costs for slow-speed accidents. When the system is enlarged to include the automobile as a consumer of scarce fuels and to include accidents occuring at high speeds, the wisdom of the standards becomes less obvious. The impact-resistant bumpers are more complex and heavier than their weaker predecessors. Therefore the automobile consumes more fuel to carry the heavier bumpers. The bumpers are more expensive than their predecessors to repair or replace if damaged in a high-speed accident. Partly as a result of this analysis, bumper requirements were reduced.

In addition to focusing on all the parts of a system, general systems theory helps communications among specialists in different fields. One field closely associated with general systems theory is cybernetics, the field of communications and control in man-machine systems (including computer systems). Cybernetics represents a combination of the fields of physics, biology, electrical engineering, etc.

In the analysis and design of information systems, we also have to apply knowledge from diverse fields. An information system involves people at different levels of an organization, computers, programs, procedures, and personnel to operate the system. Fields such as management, organizational behavior, industrial engineering, computer science, electrical engineering, communications, psychology, and others all have important contributions to make to the study and design of information systems. For these reasons we shall briefly review the main elements of general systems theory to prepare for our study of the analysis and design of information systems.

A system is an organized, interacting, interdependent, and integrated set of components or variables. Churchman has defined basic considerations in systems thinking (Schroderbek, 1971). A system has objectives or goals, and often these goals are hard to observe. The goals of a machine are clear, but what are the goals of a social system? What are the goals of a group of interacting individuals?

The environment is external to the system; it encompasses everything that is outside the system's control. The environment also determines in some part the performance of the system, so the system and its environment are interrelated and interdependent. Resources are all the means available to the system to execute activities necessary for goal attainment. In contrast to the environment, resources are inside the system and are under its control.

A system is made up of components that are the jobs, activities, missions, or parts of the system that are performed to realize objectives. One should not look necessarily at the traditional components of a system such as a department; rather, one's focus should be on thinking of the entire system. A focus on missions or activities makes it easier to understand a system.

The management of the system consists of activities aimed at planning and control. Planning encompasses setting goals, the utilization of resources, and the development of a program for undertaking different activities and of a strategy for dealing with the environment. Control deals with the execution of plans. Associated with control is the flow of information and feedback so that a system can evaluate its plans. For example, a thermostat is a feedback control for a heating system.

The following list has been suggested by various theorists as the basics of general systems theory (Schroderbek, 1971).

1 The components of a system are interrelated and interdependent; unrelated and independent components do not constitute a system. In fact, one of the important tasks in studying a system is to determine the relationships among components.

2 A system is viewed as a whole; we do not necessarily break it down into constituent parts, particularly if it means that we lose sight of the entire system. In many instances we shall concentrate on subsystems that constitute a large system, but we do not want to ignore the overall framework provided by the larger system.

3 Systems are goal-seeking in some way; the interacting components reach some final state or goal, an equilibrium position of goal attainment.

4 Systems have inputs and outputs; they are dependent on some set of inputs to process to attain the system's goals. All systems produce some output needed by other systems.

5 All systems transform inputs into outputs; usually the form of the output differs from that of the input.

6 Systems exhibit entropy, a term borrowed from thermodynamics. Entropy describes the state of a closed system (no inputs from outside the system) where all elements move toward disorganization and the inability to obtain and process inputs so the system is unable to produce outputs. Information processing is critical to the survival of systems.

7 The system must have a way to regulate its interacting components so that its objectives will be realized. Planning, control, and feedback are associated with this regulatory function.

8 Systems usually consist of smaller subsystems. The nesting of smaller systems within larger ones forms a hierarchy that is a characteristic of systems theory.

9 We usually find differentiation in complex systems; that is, specialized units perform specialized tasks.

10 Systems generally exhibit equifinality: some final state that can be reached from several different paths or starting points. In other words, there are multiple ways to achieve the goals of the system.

Systems Analysis and Design

Systems analysis draws heavily on general systems theory as a conceptual background (see Table 1-1). The many approaches to systems analysis are all aimed at basically the same objective: understanding a complex system and modifying it in some way. The modifications may be a new subsystem, new components, a new set of transformations, etc. The objective is to improve the internal functioning of the system to make it more efficient, modify the goals of the system, change the outputs, achieve the same goals with a different set of inputs, or make some similar improvement.

Normally we will follow a number of steps including:

1 Define the problem. What is it about the system that is not satisfactory? Have inputs changed in form, cost, or availability? Is the output unsatisfactory for some reason? What is the objective of the systems analysis effort?

2 Understand the system and define it. Because systems are hierarchical (subsystems exist within larger systems) and are interrelated with their environments, it can be very difficult to define exactly what constitutes the system under study. This activity can be further subdivided; we ask the following questions to

TABLE 1-1
GENERAL SYSTEMS THEORY AND INFORMATION SYSTEMS DESIGN

General systems theory	Importance for information systems design
1 Components of a system interact.	Delineate components and their interrelation during analysis.
2 A system is a whole.	Be sure to define the entire system before examining subsystems.
3 Systems are goal seeking.	What is the goal of an information system?
4 Systems have input and output.	A major design task is to specify input and output.
5 Systems transform input to yield output.	A major design task is to specify processing to produce output from inputs.
6 Systems exhibit entropy.	Information processing is critical to an organization's success.
7 Systems must be controlled.	Information systems help control the organization; information systems have to have feedback on their own performance and be controlled.
8 Systems form a hierarchy.	Information systems design is a hierarchical task; systems consist of hierarchies of subsystems.
9 Systems exhibit differentiation.	Information systems have many specialized parts.
10 Systems exhibit equifinality.	There are many ways to design a system to achieve desired goals.

develop an understanding of the system:
  a What are the variables (components) of the system?
  b How are these variables related to each other and the environment?
  c What are the boundaries of the system of interest; that is, where does the system stop and what defines its extent?
3 What alternatives exist to achieve our objectives with respect to modifying the system? What choices are there to improve the system, what is their cost, and can they be implemented?
4 Choose one of the alternatives defined in the previous step.
5 Implement the alternative.
6 If possible, we should try to evaluate the impact of the changes we have made in the system.

An Example

In a highly readable and entertaining paper, Savas presents an example of systems analysis applied in a highly charged political environment (Savas, 1973). This example will help to show how the systems approach works and how it can be used with a minimum of mathematical sophistication.

The Problem   The problem that led to this systems analysis effort arose in New York City on a February Sunday in 1969; 15 inches of snow fell though none had been forecast. As one might expect, only a skeleton crew was on duty in the sanitation department, which is responsible for snow removal. By the time the reserves were called, they could not get to work. Those who managed to report to work found that the equipment could not cope with the drifts or that abandoned cars blocked plow paths. Some workers ended up plowing out isolated street segments because complementary plow routes could not be completed.

The mayor, facing reelection soon, was soundly booed at his public appearances shortly after the storm because of snow-removal problems. Many individuals representing special interest groups offered solutions to the problem. The sanitation workers felt that by having sufficient workers on overtime around the clock during the winter, the problem could be solved. Manufacturers of snow-removal equipment thought that the city should buy more equipment from them.

The mayor turned to the systems analysis unit in his office to undertake a thorough study of the city's snow-fighting capability. The purpose of the analysis was not to find a scapegoat or place blame; the objective was to find out what went wrong and prevent it from happening in the future.

Approach   The systems analysis group studied the literature and city snow-removal procedures. After a great deal of thought, they developed a series of questions that would help define the system and its variables. Their questions were:

1 How much snow falls on New York City; snowfall is the input to the system in terms of demand.

SYSTEMS PROBLEM 1-1

Mary Cohen is the lead systems analyst on a project to develop a new on-line system to be used for production control in a string of manufacturing plants. The system will be self-contained at each plant because the products and management style of each plant are different. The headquarters of the company has decided that monthly reports are sufficient for its purposes so that no on-line access to the system is necessary beyond the local plant.

The tradition in the firm was to develop a system for the largest plant and then install it at the others when it had been completed. Mary, however, believed in a more participative approach to systems analysis and design. She was concerned that if the system were designed without the input from more than one plant, it would be very difficult, if not impossible, to install at the others.

The user representative appointed to form the project team was more authoritarian in outlook: "They will adopt our system because it will be good and because headquarters will tell them to do it." This system worried Mary, and she resolved to discuss the problem with her superiors.

If you were Mary's supervisor, what advice would you give her? Is there any action you could take to help resolve this problem? Do you think the system can succeed if the traditional approach in the company is followed?

---

2 How much work has to be done to clean up the snow that falls? This question is related to the goals of the snow-removal system and hypothesizes that the amount of work is related to the amount of snowfall.

3 What is the city's capacity for cleaning up the snow? What resources exist within the system to transform input snow into output, i.e., cleared streets?

4 What improvements are needed? What alternatives exist to improve the operation of the system?

To answer the first question, the analysts searched U.S. Weather Service records back to 1910. These records showed that what happened in the February storm, an unforecast Sunday storm, would occur about once in 168 years on the average, assuming a 50 percent accuracy in weather forecasts! More usefully, the records showed that New York City averages about 33 inches of snow a year, that an average season has two storms greater than 4 inches, and six or seven storms of an inch or more. The rate of accumulation of snow during a storm was as high as 10.4 inches in 8 hours. These Weather Service data were cast into frequency distributions.

To clean up after a storm there are several sequential activities. Special-purpose vehicles spread salt as a first line of defense (approximately 12 times a year). Salt is spread when a storm appears threatening or for a freezing rain. Plowing is done only three or four times an average year as depths of snow approach 4 inches. Removal of snow by hauling is relatively rare and is reserved for 6 inches or more of snow when the temperatures are expected to remain below freezing for an appreciable period of time.

To answer question 2, the street system was carefully analyzed. The sanitation department used a priority scheme for primary, secondary and tertiary roadways. However, primary streets required approximately 50 percent of the snow-removal effort. The analysts felt that this percentage was too large for the highest priority category.

The analysts devised a new set of high priority streets that included all parkways and bus routes, and streets that connect hospitals, police stations, fire houses, bus garages, and fuel depots to these arteries. This new grid represented 1600 linear miles or 33 percent of the city's total plow miles; clearing these streets was the minimum work that had to be done to permit the city to function during a snow emergency.

To determine capacity for clearing snow, the equipment in the city's inventory was examined. The analysts assumed 40 percent of the equipment would be out of service for repairs. Productive time when in use was estimated by making allowances for reaching the assigned work area, rest breaks, refueling time, meal time, etc. It was concluded that about 12 hours of productive time on a route is available during a two-shift, 22-hour winter workday. An average of 1.25 hours would be needed to start up and reach the route, and a speed of 5 mph for vehicles while on the route was assumed. All these numbers were very conservative; any bias was toward underestimating the capacity of the system.

Solution   Comparing the productivity figures and the street mileages led to some startling conclusions: sufficient equipment was available to plow every mile of every street in the city in only 6 hours and to plow the high priority streets in less than 2 hours.

The comparable analysis for salt spreading, however, showed that capacity was inadequate because it would take 7 hours to spread salt on all primary streets, during which time over 9 inches of snow had been known to accumulate, a depth preventing the spreaders from completing their tasks.

Given this analysis, the question became, where is the problem? If there is adequate capacity, why can the streets not be kept clear of snow? Is it a management or planning problem? Is the equipment not available for some reason? The answer to these questions was "yes"; the problem was found with both planning and the geographical distribution of the plowing and salting equipment.

Most plowing vehicles are refuse-collection trucks fitted with plows. These trucks were distributed in boroughs for collecting refuse, not plowing. A table was developed comparing plowing work versus distributions of trucks needed to collect refuse. A densely populated block in Manhattan generated more refuse than an equally long block in Staten Island though both had the same plowing demands.

A solution to this problem was to increase capacity by mounting plows on special-purpose vehicles such as flushers, which can easily be reallocated during the winter to areas that are short of plowing capacity. Remaining disparities were eliminated by directing certain truck-rich areas to send a number of trucks to

SYSTEMS PROBLEM 1-2

The example of snow removal discussed in this chapter is but one of many efforts devoted to bringing systems analysis techniques to the public sector. There are many commonalities between private and public sector problems, but there are also many differences. For example the objectives of a private firm, such as making a profit, are often well known. In the public sector, there is often disagreement with objectives or with the propriety of a public sector organization becoming involved in certain activities. The public sector is also complicated by the large, nebulous set of interacting subsystems such as schools, uniformed services, various subgroups in the population, suppliers to the public organizations, etc. Some attempts have been made to perform benefit/cost studies and to apply systems anslysis tools to a very emotional problem: the question of attaining racial balance in public school systems.

Imagine that you have been asked to conduct such a systems analysis for a medium-sized town. What are the interacting variables in the "system"? What boundaries would you place on the systems analysis exercise? Consider the composition of a systems analysis team; how would it be formed and who would be represented? What data would you need? Identify any special implementation problems in obtaining acceptance of your recommendations. Do you think analysis in the public sector, in general, is easier or more difficult than in the private sector?

---

certain truck-poor areas at the start of a snowstorm.

In a similar way, spreaders were found to be distributed inappropriately. Since these are single-purpose vehicles, it was easy to reallocate them to areas where needed. In one area, it was also determined that start-up times were too great, and a new garage was eventually constructed there.

Finally, the analysts constructed a mobilization plan to be prepared for a storm at a reasonable cost. The recommendation was to mount plows on one-fifth of the trucks just before winter weekends. This approach provides a critical time advantage, since it takes almost 2 person-hours to prepare a truck in this way. Some spreaders are also loaded with salt just before winter weekends even though they must be unloaded on Monday to prevent flat tires and caking of the salt. The unions cooperated to develop a special Sunday roster for a snow emergency. Workers on this roster agreed to respond to a telephone call-up and report promptly in return for compensatory time off.

The plan was accepted immediately by the mayor, since he was campaigning for reelection. The effort was capped with a detailed briefing for the press along with a display of some of the new snow-fighting equipment because, as Savas put it, there was nothing very photogenic about the study or the plan.

Conclusions   This example demonstrates the activities of systems analysis. The analysts had to define the problem and establish boundaries for the system being studied. The environment was complex and involved many different components interacting with the snow-removal system. Should the system include the political considerations of elected officials? Are citizens, independent contractors, city employees, and others a part of the system or the environment?

This example also illustrates the inductive nature of reasoning about systems. As opposed to deductive problem solving, where we have a set of principles or theorems, inductive reasoning proceeds from the data and observations to the development of a hypothesis about the nature of the problem. In systems analysis, we usually observe certain characteristics and symptoms of a system. We must define the system and place boundaries on it as described above. Then we examine a pattern of data and generate ideas about the nature of the problem. In this example, the analysts asked a series of questions about the nature of the demand for snow removal and the capacity for performing the task. When it appeared that there was sufficient capacity, the analysis led naturally to the hypothesis that planning and/or geographic distribution of equipment was the problem. This hypothesis proved correct and turned out to be the key to a solution of the snow-removal problem.

The step-by-step analysis is another characteristic of systems analysis. The analysts asked critical questions about the variables in the system, the input, processing, and output of the current system and finally asked why the system was not working satisfactorily, that is, why it was not accomplishing its goals. Then various alternatives were considered to improve the system and a combination of strategies was selected for this purpose. Finally, the plan was implemented. During a later snowstorm, also on a holiday, the plan worked!

This example does not involve an information system, but many of the steps in solving the problem and preparing a plan parallel those in the design of an information system. We can view general systems theory as furnishing the principles for systems analysis in general, and systems analysis is one vital component in the development of information systems.

ORGANIZATIONS

Introduction

In the snow-removal example, the problem and its solution existed in the complex environment of a large city. Multiple interacting groups and organizations were involved. Information systems also exist in the context of an organization; they do not operate in isolation. An organization furnishes the environment for most information systems. There are several reasons why we need to understand organizations to work effectively with information systems.

First, the users of information systems are members of the organization. Behavioral factors arising from membership in an organization affect the way users respond to information systems. Technically elegant systems have failed because of inadequate user participation in design, poorly understood needs, or clumsy implementation procedures. Most, if not all, of these problems involve organizational behavior.

Second, the computer department is a department in the organization and will have to respond to various levels of management. To function effectively, a member of the computer department needs to understand the functioning of the organization and its management.

Finally, the computer department is an organization itself. Depending on its size, the department may have several levels of management and a number of subgroups. Organizational principles should be understood by each member of the computer department, so he or she can make the maximum contribution to the department and the organization.

In the remainder of this chapter we discuss a number of theories of organizations to place modern organization theory in perspective. Because organizational behavior is a field in itself, this survey must be somewhat superficial. However, even a survey of this material helps computer professionals, especially systems designers, understand more fully the organization in which they function. In addition, the writings of the more modern organization theorists have had a significant influence on our approach to systems design in the second part of the text.

Definition

There are a number of definitions of organizations. For our purposes, we define an organization as a rational coordination of activities of a group of people for the purpose of achieving some goal. This definition has been adapted from Schein (1970, p. 9).

This definition has several important parts. First, the activities of the group of people are coordinated; that is, there is a joint effort. Contrast this situation with the example of political candidates running for office. Many people do not have a political affiliation but vote for the candidates. They wish to see their candidates elected but are not coordinated in any way to achieve their election. On the other hand, the political parties to which the candidates belong are organizations whose efforts are coordinated to achieve the objective of election to office. In most organizations some division of labor and a hierarchy of authority provide for the rational coordination of activities.

The definition also includes the goals of the organization; there are many different types of organizations with different goals. For example, corporations may want to maximize profit, provide good working conditions, and/or fulfill a responsibility to society.

Formal versus Informal Organization

The formal organization is what appears on the organization chart, and usually there are standards and procedures that describe the structure of the formal organization. Social organizations, on the other hand, are patterns of coordination that arise spontaneously from the interaction of a group. Social organizations have no rational coordination and generally lack explicit goals. Consider a group of friends at a party who have the goal of relaxation and having a good time; this is not a formal organization because of the lack of rational coordination (Schein, 1970).

The informal organization is the pattern of relations and organization among members of the formal organization that is not specified on a formal chart; it represents social interaction. The informal organization is a more realistic portrayal of the formal organization, since it reflects how people actually interact. For example, there are a number of approaches to cutting red tape and bypassing standard procedures.

The lesson is that we must be careful to avoid designing information systems that follow unrealistic standards and procedures. We may find that these prescribed rules are not actually followed and that our system is unworkable because we have adhered too closely to formal organizational considerations. Unfortunately, it is hard to observe and describe the informal organization. The informal organization depends on the personalities of specific individuals and patterns of behavior that have developed over time. People may view the information system as something highly formal, and they may not reveal facts about the informal organization. We have to remember to differentiate between what should be and what actually is the case when asking questions about information systems. A user may respond with an answer based on the formal organization when in fact the informal organization is the most relevant for our purposes.

CLASSIC VIEW OF ORGANIZATIONS

We need to understand the various popular conceptions of organizations, because these influence the way people view their organizations. Some of these views may be outmoded, but many people subscribe to these classic models.

Frederick Taylor

In the late 1890s, Frederick Taylor introduced the concept of "scientific management" (Filley et al., 1976; March and Simon, 1958). Taylor's approach focused on the effective use of human beings in organizations; it is a rational engineering approach to work based on time and motion studies.

There are four main principles to scientific management (Filley et al., 1976). First, develop a best or ideal method of doing a task and establish a standard. The worker should be paid an incentive for exceeding this standard. Second, select the best person for the job and train him or her in the best way to accomplish the tasks. Third, combine the scientific method with well-selected and trained people. (Workers will not resist improved methods, since they receive more money because of them.) Fourth, cooperation should occur between managers and workers based on the division of labor. Managers have the responsibility for planning and preparing work.

Scientific management resulted in the precise measurement and intensive study of the activities of individual employees and answered many questions on human engineering. The aspects of scientific management relating to humans in organizations is basically physiological in nature (March and Simon, 1958). Taylor was most concerned with repetitive production and clerical tasks requiring little discretion on the part of workers. In general, these tasks are much easier to describe than other kinds of activities that occur within an organization.

The most important constraints on physical activities have to do with capacity; there is an upper limit to an individual's rate of production. Speed is also an essential part of productivity. Taylor tried to set time standards for complex tasks to obtain the highest speed consistent with quality requirements. Muscle fatigue also influences the durability of workers, and it is necessary to provide rest periods. Taylor showed that productivity can actually be increased by having the worker spend less time at work and more time in a rest break. Basically, the goal of scientific management is to minimize the cost of the job and the length of time required to perform it.

Departmental Approach

A number of theorists, including Gulick, Urwick, and Fayol, have described organizations based on the grouping of various activities into departments. These theorists looked at the organization as a giant machine and tried to develop principles or universal laws that governed the machine's activities (Filley et al., 1976).

The general problem addressed in their writings is, given an organization, how do you identify the unit tasks and organize these tasks into individual jobs? Then, how are the jobs organized into administrative units, the administrative units organized into large units, and finally, how are top-level departments established (March and Simon, 1958)? The result of this analysis is the structuring of departments within the organization; each department contains a set of tasks to be performed by workers in that department.

Different organizational units are related through authority, responsibility, and accountability (Filley et al., 1976). Authority is the right of command that is assigned to a job; that is, who are the subordinates and who are the superiors. Responsibility consists of the duties associated with the job, and accountability is the necessity to report to a higher authority on action taken and the results.

The departmental approach led to a concern with the bases for creating organizational units, such as geographical area, product, customer, etc. This approach led to the design of pyramidal organizations with authority flowing from the top level down through the organization. These early writers were also concerned with the span of control: How many people should ideally report to a single manager?

Problems with the Classic View

Numerous authors have pointed out problems with scientific management and departmentalization approaches to structuring organizations (March and Simon, 1958; Filley et al., 1976). First, Taylorism is basically physiological in nature and ignores psychology (we shall see the consequences of this in discussing the

Hawthorne studies later in the chapter). Taylorism applies to lower-level routine and repetitive tasks and says nothing about decision-making activities in the organizations. Furthermore, it assumes that monetary rewards are the primary motivators and that human beings always act rationally. Taylor also suggests that people do not want to work, so that close supervision is necessary.

The departmental approaches also tend to overlook individuals. It is very difficult to define the basis for departmentalizing, and this approach ignores the problem of coordination and interdependence among departments. There is also no consideration of human problem solving and decision making; the departmental philosophy also makes unrealistic assumptions about human motivation.

TRANSITIONAL VIEWS

Several authors can be categorized as having broken with the classic approach; their works form the basis for a more modern view of organizations.

Chester Barnard

Barnard's book entitled *The Functions of the Executive,* written in 1938, has formed the basis for some more recent theories of organization (Filley et al., 1976). Simon (1947) has expanded on Barnard's ideas and stresses the decision-making process as a basis for the study of organizations. Emerging from this work is a view that organizations are a system of coordinated activities; that they consist of a cooperative group working to achieve some purpose. The organization must balance the inducements offered to members to maintain their affiliation with the organization against the required contributions to the organization from these members. This approach also recognizes the importance of the informal organization and suggests that authority rests on the acceptance or consent of those who are expected to respond to authority.

Human Relations

We mentioned earlier that the human element seemed to be overlooked by some of the classic theorists. The human relations school of organizations studied individuals in the organization from a psychological point of view. This approach is based on a series of experiments conducted in the 1920s at the Hawthorne Western Electric plant (Schein, 1970; Filley et al., 1976).

The experimenters were interested in determining the effect of different physical conditions on workers. In one particular set of illumination experiments, women who assembled telephone equipment served as subjects. The objective was to see if increased levels of illumination would improve output. The experimental subjects occupied a special room with one supervisor and were carefully observed. At first, increasing the levels of illumination increased worker output. To check the results, the subjects were returned to their preexperimental conditions and output continued to increase!

The researchers tried to understand the reasons for this; clearly, physiology could not explain the increased productivity. Instead, the experimenters suggested that the subjects felt special because they had been singled out for special treatment (Schein, 1970). They developed good relations with each other and with the supervisor and had considerably more freedom than under preexperimental conditions. Social contact was easier and the relationships made the work more pleasant.

In a further experiment an observer watched men in a room who wired banks of equipment while another group soldered them. A group of inspectors also worked in the room. These observers found two cliques: men in the front of the room had higher status because they wired more difficult equipment. The observers found that each group had its own games and habits. The groups had developed norms on what should be produced, and the norms were sufficiently low that an individual worker could easily produce more without fatigue. These norms were established so that enough work was accomplished to satisfy management, and anyone exceeding the figure was considered a "rate buster." There was also a norm that one must not produce too little. Thus, deviation in either direction brought kidding, outright rebukes, and pressure to get back into line from other workers.

The groups did not adhere to company policy on a number of issues. For example, jobs were often traded between wirers and solderers against company

---

SYSTEMS PROBLEM 1-3

John Sheffield is the president and principal stockholder of Midway Manufacturing Company, a medium-sized firm specializing in the design and production of children's toys. The firm has grown informally over the years until it has now reached $20 million in sales. At this level, the information handling procedures in the office are being strained; in fact, the situation has become so serious that the president is worried about the ability of the firm to satisfy its customers and keep accurate records.

Though Sheffield is concerned about the ability of the organization to cope with computer technology, he has gradually come to accept the fact that something has to be done to improve the capabilities of Midway to process data. After talking with some of his friends at other companies, he decided to start an information systems department and to hire a department manager and a systems analyst at first, to be followed by a programmer or two.

Midway has very little formal structure; tasks are assigned but the department labels relate only to location, like the warehouse, shipping area, etc. Sheffield is trying to figure out how to organize this new department of information systems. He wants to have it relate successfully to other areas but wonders if he should break tradition and draw an organization chart. He is worried that others might resent the structure being imposed to bring in this new department and that this resentment could reduce the chances for success of the new group. What would you recommend to Sheffield?

---

regulations. The men also reported relatively standard output each day despite wide variations in the amount actually produced. The observers noted that members of the high-status clique had uniformly higher production. From this experiment, the researchers concluded that social factors are extremely important in affecting the way in which people work and have an important impact on their productivity.

MODERN ORGANIZATION THEORY

Unfortunately, we cannot point to one unified theory of organizations that has emerged from these various approaches to the study of organizations. We still are confronted with many different ideas about organizations and the way they operate. However, we do have a more sophisticated and realistic basis for the underlying assumptions behind these different theories. We shall try to identify some of these approaches and highlight the major problems in organizations that affect us in the design and operation of information systems.

Individuals

A number of writers focus on the psychological needs and wants of the individual in the organization. The original classic theorists ignored the psychology of the individual and instead looked only at the physical issues. From the Hawthorne studies and other work, several writers have developed psychological models of people. For example, the Hawthorne studies stimulated a view of people as social beings. Some of the reasons for working are to fulfill social needs.

A number of organizational theorists have adopted the need hierarchy proposed by Maslow to form a basis for understanding human beings in organizations (Schein, 1970). Maslow suggests five levels of human needs as follow:

1 Safety, security, and survival needs
2 Social and affiliative needs
3 Ego satisfaction and self-esteem needs
4 Autonomy and independence
5 Self-actualization

The theory proposes that lower-order needs must be satisfied before a human is interested in higher-order needs (Schein, 1970). For example, thirst and hunger needs must be filled before ego satisfaction becomes salient.

It is widely assumed that for most individuals currently employed in an organization, lower-order needs such as safety, security, and survival are met. For many people, one of the primary reasons for work is to satisfy social needs. Some workers also receive ego satisfaction from their jobs as well as the satisfaction of autonomy and independence needs. There appear to be very few individuals in society who have reached the level of satisfying needs for self-actualization. Possibly a few authors, artists, and others are able to operate at this level.

Douglas McGregor   McGregor was influenced by Maslow and the need hierarchy when he developed his theory of management. McGregor describes Theory X as the approach that governs most current thinking about work (McGregor, 1960). There are a number of assumptions in Theory X, including the idea that the average human has an inherent dislike of work and will try to avoid it if possible. Theory X is consistent with a belief that people must be coerced, controlled, directed, and threatened to put forth effort to achieve organizational goals. The average person prefers to be directed and has little ambition, wishing to avoid responsibility and being concerned primarily with security needs.

McGregor rejects the assumptions of Theory X and proposes an alternative called Theory Y, which features very different underlying assumptions. Theory Y suggests that expending physical and mental effort in work is as natural as it is in play. People will exercise self-direction and self-control to achieve a goal to which they are committed. Theory Y also suggests that commitment to an objective is related to the reward associated with achieving the objective. People will learn not only to accept responsibility, they will seek it. Many people in the population are capable of exercising a high degree of imagination, ingenuity, and creativity in solving problems. In most organizations the intellectual potential of workers is underutilized (McGregor, 1960).

McGregor develops an approach to leadership and management that is consistent with the assumption of Theory Y. In particular, he advocates something called the Scanlon plan in which workers are rewarded for the end product through cost reduction savings plans. Workers are rewarded monthly for reducing costs below an agreed-upon level. The plan features worker committees that participate in the planning and scheduling of activities and that suggest new ways to reduce costs. The plan has operated successfully in several small and medium-sized manufacturing companies (McGregor, 1960).

Likert   Many organizational researchers have urged worker participation, as does McGregor. The works of Likert and his associates at the Survey Research Center of the University of Michigan emphasize worker participation in decision making in the organization based on the results of a number of careful studies. This group has developed a typology of organizations that ranges from authoritative to participative. One of Likert's important ideas for our purposes is that management serves as a linking pin and that a supervisor must have influence at higher levels to function effectively. A manager acts to link a group of subordinates to the group of managers that are at higher levels in the organization.

Schein   Schein has combined a number of the different models and assumptions about individuals in organizations into a model he calls "complex man" (Schein, 1970). Basically, this model suggests that the individual is both complex and highly variable, and has many motives that may change over time. A person can learn new motives and will become productively involved in an organization for a number of different reasons, responding in different ways to different managerial strategies. Schein presents evidence to support this view; his more modern approach will be our model in future chapters, since it helps to explain how different people react to information systems.

Decision-Making Approaches

An approach to the study of organizations based on decision making developed from the research efforts at Carnegie-Mellon University by March, Simon, and their associates. We shall discuss some of these ideas in Chapter 2 when we look more closely at what managers do in the organization. However, we mention them here for the sake of completeness. The book *Organizations* by March and Simon is a classic and often-quoted reference in the field of management.

Organizational Structure and Design

A number of writers have studied organizations from the standpoint of their structure to understand how to design better organizations. These approaches help us to understand how information is used in the organization and to appreciate what kinds of changes might be created in the organization by the introduction of new information systems.

Uncertainty   One of the major variables influencing organization activities is uncertainty (Lawrence and Lorsch, 1967). Many authors have suggested that managers try to eliminate or reduce uncertainty. An organization and its managers are confronted with many different types of uncertainty. There are frequently technical uncertainties about whether a new product can be manufactured or whether or not it will work. Market uncertainties exist when the firm does not know how a product will be received, potential demand, response from competitors, etc. The internal management of an organization also creates uncertainty. Key personnel may leave; individuals may not adequately perform the tasks they have been assigned. Thus, the organization and its managers face a variety of uncertainty.

The importance of uncertainty can be seen by examining organizations that face differing environments. Consider the dynamic environment of a computer manufacturer confronted with technological change and an uncertain environment versus the staid, conservative atmosphere of a regulated utility facing virtually no uncertainty. In fact, one can view much of the anticompetitive behavior we observe such as price fixing, etc., as an attempt to reduce uncertainty. There is some evidence that uncertainty is most effectively handled by decentralizing decision making to a level in the organization that has the information to deal with it (Lawrence and Lorsch, 1967).

Specialization   Another major variable in organizational design is specialization. Are specialized skills or conditions required for some tasks? Consider the activity of running a complicated machine tool versus sweeping the building; certainly, the former requires a specialist. From our standpoint, the computer department is highly specialized and requires a level of technological proficiency on the part of its staff.

Other writers have developed an index that measures the degree of differentiation between groups in an organization (Lawrence and Lorsch, 1967). For our purposes, differentiation is almost identical with specialization. The differentiation index includes variables such as the time span for feedback, personal orientation of the people in various departments, etc.

Coordination   When there is specialization, one task of management is to coordinate the diverse specialties so the goals of the organization are achieved. Management must balance differing orientations and resolve disputes between specialized subunits. For example, the marketing department may want to produce a product in each style and color for every warehouse. This plan is best for reducing uncertainty and providing good customer service. On the other hand, manufacturing may want to make products of the same color and model since this procedure reduces the uncertainties in production; that is, there are fewer setups and smoother production runs.

Management must resolve these differences and coordinate the specialists. Lawrence and Lorsch refer to this resolution as integration and suggest a number of integrating mechanisms to reduce the effects of differentiation or specialization. We shall examine some special integrators for reducing the impact of specialization in the computer department in a later chapter.

Interdependence   The last factor we shall consider in organizational structure is interdependence; that is, how do different departments or subunits in the organization depend on each other? Thompson has described three types of mutual dependence (Thompson, 1967). Pooled interdependence occurs when two organizations depend on each other because they are all components of some larger organization. One unit does not depend directly on another; for example, the different divisions of a conglomerate exhibit pooled interdependence.

Sequential interdependence occurs when the output of one unit is the input to another. For example, the painting and finishing department is dependent on outputs from component assembly. We can view each succeeding station on an assembly line as an example of sequential interdependence.

Reciprocal interdependence occurs when the output of each unit becomes the input for the other. A good example is the computer department that depends on receipt of data from a user department. The computer department processes the data for the user, who depends on the output from the computer system.

Interdependence is an important variable in organizational design, as we shall see in Chapter 4. The type of interdependence affects the amount of power one unit has in the organization. In designing an organization, or modifying the design (for example, through the development of a new information system), we must coordinate various interdependencies. The easiest type of interdependence to handle is pooled, the next hardest sequential, and the most difficult is reciprocal.

In trying to design organizations, one usually attempts first to group units with reciprocal interdependencies together so that they can be easily coordinated, possibly by one manager. Then the designer works on sequential dependencies and finally considers pooled interdependencies. Often, we attempt to reduce interdependencies. For example, in a manufacturing situation we can use a buffer inventory to decouple two sequentially interdependent departments. One department manufactures for inventory. As long as adequate stock is maintained, it can vary production without affecting the department that is dependent on its output.

Organization Structure

Mintzberg (1979) has developed an elegant theory of how organizations are structured. First, he conceptualizes the organization as consisting of five major components (see Figure 1-1). The operating core carries out the basic work of the organization; in a manufacturing organization it produces the product. It also

FIGURE 1-1
The five basic parts of organizations.

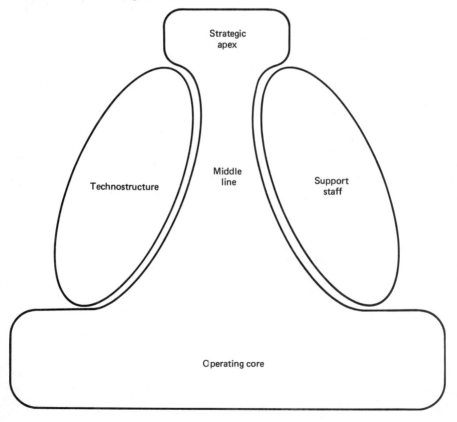

handles all the support tasks necessary for production.

At the next level in the organization is an administrative component that consists of three groups. At the top is the strategic apex, senior-level executives responsible for all the operations of the firm. Below the strategic apex, we find the middle line that joins the top group to the operating core. At the left of the middle line is the technostructure where analysts carry out the work of standardizing the work of others. For example, we would find operations research analysts in the technostructure.

The last group is the support staff on the right of the figure. This group supports the functioning of the operating core through indirect activities, for example, the research and development organization, legal counsel, and similar groups.

Using some of the coordination considerations discussed earlier in this chapter and further analysis, Mintzberg modifies the basic model of an organization to describe five typical structures: simple structure, machine bureaucracy, professional bureaucracy, divisionalized form, and adhocracy. In each of these types of organizations, one of the five groups in Figure 1-1 is dominant in importance. His theory is very appealing and provides a convenient framework for thinking about organizations.

It is interesting to note the role of information processing in the Mintzberg scheme (he does not discuss this activity in depth). For many organizations, basic information processing systems really belong in the operating core; the firm needs these systems to function effectively. The systems analysis and design activity, however, probably fits best in the technostructure, since this group concentrates on improving the work of others. Systems designers must develop a system, which is a form of research and development, and then must successfully transfer it to the operating core in many cases.

In other instances, a system is designed for middle management, the strategic apex, or even the support staff. The analyst's job then involves a great deal of boundary-spanning activity, integrating activities across a number of organizational boundaries. In fact, many systems are likely to involve information that flows across major organizational subunits. All these factors combine to make the implementation of a computer-based system an extremely important and challenging task.

MAJOR ORGANIZATIONAL CONSIDERATIONS

In this chapter we have reviewed general systems theory and different approaches to the study of organizations. For information systems, the organization furnishes the environment. Information systems relate to various subsystems within the organization. They derive their input from the organization and usually provide output for it. We will consider several important issues as we think about information systems in organizations.

First, what assumptions do we make about people and their reasons for working in an organization? Do we accept the ideas of Theory Y and Schein's complex man or are we predicting actions based on the classic views of people?

That is, do we assume that humans are only motivated by rational, economic self-interest?

Given a particular organization and its environment, the factors described as relevant for understanding organizational structure and design help explain why certain practices are followed. If an organization is highly centralized and conservative, is it because of a lack of uncertainty in its environment? Are departments given particular tasks because of specialization or because of difficulties in coordinating interdependencies?

We need to understand how people are likely to react when information systems are developed and implemented. If users do not cooperate, we are unable to design a system because we do not know what is needed. There will be problems in implementation because of human resistance if users do not cooperate. As a result of these difficulties the system will fail because no one uses it.

In designing systems, we also have to consider the structure of the organization and how a system might affect it. Are we changing interdependencies, or is the flow of information altered in such a way that the design of the organization needs to be changed? Finally, in operating information systems, we have claimed that the relationship between users and the computer department is one of reciprocal interdependence. How do we handle the coordination of users and the computer department given this most demanding kind of interdependence?

In Chapter 4, we consider some of these questions in more detail. We shall examine what is known about the impact of computers on individuals and the organization, and will speculate on the underlying reasons for different problems that occur. In Chapter 2, we continue our exploration of organizations and focus on the manager or decision maker. We are interested in the individual because information systems are designed to support decision making. To succeed in developing these systems, we must understand the needs of the user.

KEY WORDS

Authority	Hierarchy	Scientific management
Boundary	Human relations	Specialization
Departmentalization	Informal organization	Systems theory
Differentiation	Integration	Taylor
Entropy	Interdependence	Theory X
Equifinality	Linking pin	Theory Y
Formal organization	McGregor	Uncertainty
Hawthorne studies	Maslow need hierarchy	

RECOMMENDED READINGS

McGregor, D.: *The Human Side of Enterprise,* McGraw-Hill, New York, 1960. (This highly readable book presents compelling evidence why Theory Y should be preferred over Theory X management.)

March, J., and H. Simon: *Organizations,* Wiley, New York, 1958. (March and Simon present a thorough review of organization theory and present a number of propositions for serious students of organizations to consider.)

Mintzberg, H.: *The Structuring of Organizations,* Englewood Cliffs, N.J., Prentice-Hall, 1979. (A readable book presenting an appealing view of organizations.)

Ouchi, W.: *Theory Z,* Addison-Wesley, New York, 1981. (A book comparing Japanese and United States management practices with suggestions for changes in United States corporations.)

Schein, E.: *Organizational Psychology,* 2d ed., Prentice-Hall, Englewood Cliffs, N.J., 1970. (This short, readable book presents an overview of classic and modern organizational theory.)

Simon, H.: *Administrative Behavior,* Macmillan, New York, 1947. (Simon discusses the role of decision making as the unit of study for organizations in this classic book.)

DISCUSSION QUESTIONS

1 Why was general systems theory needed?

2 Is general systems theory really a theory, or is it more of an approach to problem solving?

3 Why is determining the boundary of a system so important and so difficult?

4 What are the major disciplines that are integrated to form the field of information systems?

5 Think of an example of a problem where the systems aspects of the situation were ignored. What happened when some part of the relevant system was omitted from the analysis?

6 What are the major subsystems of the system known as a university?

7 Think of a typical manufacturing company and identify the major subsystems within it.

8 Use the answer to the question above to prepare a chart showing the flows of information among subsystems in the manufacturing firm.

9 Why was the solution to New York's snow emergency planning relatively easy to implement?

10 Some experts in the field have suggested that systems analysis and design is like a research project in which one reasons inductively from the data to a model. Take a position on this proposition and defend it.

11 In mathematics we have the notion of optimality: The theoretical best solution to a problem. Is there a best information system for a problem?

12 Is there a theory of information systems? If so, sketch its major components. If not, why is there none?

13 One company tested a version of a new information system in a single department. A number of people from the computer department participated in the test. An outside consultant said that the test was not well designed because too many computer department people were involved and because the Hawthorne effect would influence the workers. What did he mean and what do you think the Hawthorne effect is?

14 One old management saying is that authority must equal responsibility. Is this always true? Is it always desirable for authority to equal responsibility?

15 An issue often raised by managers is their span of control; that is, how many people they supervise. Suppose that we determine that the effective span of control is no more than seven people. If an organization had five levels of management, how many employees could it have with this span of control?

16 A number of companies have opted for a flat organizational structure; that is, few levels of management. What do you think the advantages and disadvantages of this type of organization would be?

17 Leadership is a continuing topic of interest in organizations. Describe how you think the attitude and approach to leadership of a Theory X manager might differ from that of a Theory Y manager.

18 An organizational issue of interest to us is group processes. In many organizations, it has been found that suggestion boxes do not work; That is, workers never put useful suggestions in them. How would you contrast this situation with the heavy participation of worker committees under the Scanlon plan?

19 Why is the human relations approach insufficient when taken alone? (Hint: consider Schein's model of complex man.)

20 Where might scientific management principles be useful even today?

21 Consider an organization such as a school; describe the formal and informal organizations you would expect to encounter.

22 Why do departments become so central in an organization? Why do many people seem to exhibit more loyalty to their department than to the organization itself? (Hint: think about the Hawthorne experiments in answering this question.)

23 How does the presence of an informal organization affect the design of an information system?

24 Interdependence exists when one subunit in an organization depends on another one in some way. What are the interdependencies between the accounting department and other subunits? What are the intercependencies between the computer department and other departments?

25 Suppose that a new information system is being planned that will eliminate the need for five or six positions in one department. How would a Theory X manager approach this potential problem? What would a Theory Y manager do to ease the implementation of the system?

26 Many organizational theorists suggest that most workers in the United States are operating at the social need level. That is, most of the lower-order needs described by Maslow are met because of the general affluence of the country. If this is true, why are lower-order needs so often emphasized in labor negotiations (for example, wages, seniority, job security)?

27 In one company, a new factory floor data-collection computer system was implemented. Workers in the plant had to enter data using a terminal. The workers were paid on a piece-rate basis and no allowances were made for reporting time at the terminals. What do you think the results were? How could the system have been implemented more successfully?

28 When two departments in the organization differ in function and orientation but have the need to interact, special integrating devices are often employed. For example, there may be a person in each department who has been designated as a contact with the other department. Is there sufficient difference between computer department activities and other departments to warrant these special integrators? If so, what types of integrating mechanisms can you suggest?

29 What is the impact of information processing by computer on uncertainty? How does the development of a computer application change the level of uncertainty in an organization?

30 One of the problems in organizational design is to balance the need for specialization against the costs of coordination. As units become more specialized, they have to be better coordinated. How specialized is the computer department? How are the activities within this department best coordinated?

MANAGERS AND DECISION MAKING: KEY COMPONENTS OF INFORMATION SYSTEMS

MANAGERS AND DECISION MAKING: KEY COMPONENTS OF INFORMATION SYSTEMS

INTRODUCTION

We study managers because they are frequent users of information systems and are usually heavily involved in their design. Even the most routine information system has to be implemented, and the management of the areas affected by the system will be confronted with change. It is also helpful to develop an understanding of managerial activities and information requirements to design high-quality management information systems. Since information systems are designed to support decision making, we also need to study the decision process.

Figure 2-1 presents an overview of the topics covered in this chapter. First, we describe the different roles filled by managers and common managerial activities. Two classes of roles, informational and decisional, are most amenable to support by an information system as shown in Figure 2-1a. Since our definition of an information system stresses decision support, we look further at the decision process and the types of decisions made in an organization as shown in Figure 2-1b.

CLASSIC VIEWS

Basic Functions

Much of the literature about managers is normative rather than descriptive: writers prescribe what managers should do. However, few studies of managers have been conducted to see if they actually follow any of these prescriptions. The early

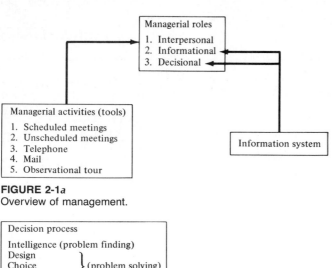

FIGURE 2-1*a*
Overview of management.

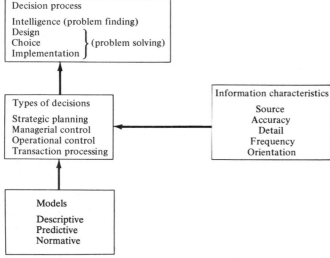

FIGURE 2-1*b*
Overview of decision making.

views of management were set forth in the 1900s by Fayol, who suggested five basic managerial functions: planning, organizing, coordinating, commanding, and controlling (Mintzberg, 1973). In the 1930s, Gulick coined an acronym to describe management. "POSDCORB":

P stands for *planning,* that is, developing an outline of what has to be done and the methods used to achieve these objectives;

O is for *organizing,* which is setting up the formal structure of authority in the organization;

S is for *staffing,* which refers to the personnel function;

D stands for *directing,* which refers to making and carrying out decisions;

C is for *coordinating,* that is, interrelating various components of work;

R means *reporting,* which is keeping superiors and subordinates informed of relevant activities;

B is for *budgeting,* which encompasses the financial, planning, accounting, and control tasks of managers.

Unfortunately, this early normative view is not very helpful; the activities are too vague and all that is described is the objective of managerial work, not the work itself (Mintzberg, 1973).

Other Approaches

Another attempt to describe managerial work has been labeled "The Great Man School" by Mintzberg (1973). This method of approaching a manager's job is typified by stories of successful managers in popular journals and magazines. The stories contain a wealth of detail, but little is generalizable from each case study. A number of books also concentrate on an individual and his or her personality; however, all they tell us is that one person, in a certain situation, had a series of impressive accomplishments.

On a more scientific basis, economists and management scientists have tried to describe how managers should perform. Unfortunately, these researchers have to assume that managers are rational and profit maximizing, and that they should make certain mathematically specified choices. Decision theorists base their approach on the identification of probability utility functions and use Bayesian statistical procedures to recommend optimal decisions. These approaches are not really descriptive; instead, they suggest how the rational manager should act. In the last chapter we saw that human beings are too complex for the simple assumptions of these models. These authors may feel that managers should act in the way specified, but their writings do not help us see how managers actually do act.

MANAGERIAL ROLES

The Studies

Mintzberg (1973) has discussed the small amount of relevant literature available along with his own observational study of the activities of five top managers. He has identified ten roles played by managers and divided them into three basic categories. A role is a position that a manager finds himself or herself in and that can be identified by a set of activities. For example, a television actor may portray a Western cowboy in one show and a modern detective in another. His activities and style, along with his dress and surroundings, let us know which role he is playing.

These roles are defined by grouping managerial activities together and assigning descriptive labels. The most support for these roles comes from Mintzberg's own study, and thus the discussion may be somewhat biased toward top managers, since they were the only people involved in his research. However, Mintzberg feels that the results are applicable to all managers, and that only the proportion of the time spent in the different roles varies between a president and a foreman. Several other studies are cited that provide evidence to support these observations.

Interpersonal Roles

There are three interpersonal roles that are characterized by their involvement with people, both inside and outside the organization. The first is a figurehead role; the manager is required to perform social or symbolic duties such as visiting a sick employee or working on a charity drive. The second interpersonal role is as leader; the manager must try to motivate subordinates and see that the organization is staffed and the work force trained. In this interpersonal role, the manager acts as a change agent. As a leader, he or she must bring change to the organization and convince members of the organization to adopt change. The last interpersonal role finds the manager acting as a liaison, maintaining contacts who furnish information from both inside and outside the organization.

Informational Roles

Managers have two major informational roles that clearly are important for information systems design. In the first role, the manager acts as a monitor, observing and processing a variety of information. Most of this information is current and has been developed from the organization and the surrounding environment. The top manager emerges as a nerve center for organizational information.

The next information-handling role finds the manager disseminating data. Information is transmitted to relevant colleagues including subordinates, superiors, and those outside the organization. Finally, the manager plays a minor role as spokesperson in which comments are directed to people outside the organization and company policies and actions are explained.

Decisional Roles

The set of four decisional roles is also important for us in thinking about the design of information systems, because information systems can possibly support some of these decisions. First, the manager functions as entrepreneur searching for and initiating improvement projects to bring about positive changes in the organization. The manager is also a disturbance handler, taking corrective action when the organization faces some unanticipated consequences. The manager is also a resource allocator, as decisions must be made on the allocation of resources in his or her area of responsibility. Finally, the manager is a negotiator, trying to adjudicate disputes.

Managerial Activities

Before we discuss the role of information systems in managerial activities, it is helpful to see how managers actually spend their time in the various activities making up these roles. Again we draw on Mintzberg to see how managers spend time. First, a manager's work consists of primarily verbal and written contacts. Many efforts are fragmented and many interruptions are experienced. The manager's work frequently is never completed because of an awareness that something overlooked, some new idea, could improve the situation. A manager appears to be much like a student preparing for final exams, never confident that one more hour of study is actually wasted, because that hour could uncover the answer to a key question on an examination. Because the work is never done, most managers seem to work at a vigorous pace.

Five main tools used by managers in their work include mail, the telephone, unscheduled meetings, scheduled meetings, and observational tours. The managers observed appeared to favor verbal media and spent much time in contact with other individuals. Scheduled meetings consumed the greatest percentage of managerial time and external contacts made up a third to one-half of the time spent on interpersonal activities.

Applicability of Findings

Since there is little evidence, much of which deals only with top management, how applicable are the roles and work activities described above to other individuals in the organization? Even though few data exist, the results seem intuitively appealing. Until further studies appear, these studies offer the best evidence on which to proceed.

Can we generalize from top executives to supervisors, and clerical workers in the organization? First, some of the results described above were found to hold when studies of supervisors were reviewed. Second, it does appear that various roles are descriptive of different levels of management; however, we might find that the activities differ in importance between, say, a supervisor and the president. For example, the figurehead role is played more often by the president than by the supervisor.

We also expect the situations surrounding the roles to differ. The president acting as a figurehead may be in contact with comparable leaders of other organizations and government. The supervisor, on the other hand, may be a figurehead for a company bowling team or may preside over a retirement dinner for a subordinate in the department. We also expect the tools of management to differ for top-, middle-, and lower-level managers. Our supervisor probably

SYSTEMS PROBLEM 2-1

Dorothy Norris is the controller for Housewares, Inc., a distributor of a number of homemaking devices ranging from cooking utensils to small appliances. The firm does not manufacture the items but instead purchases them for distribution and resale in its series of boutique cookware shops.

The company has grown rapidly during the last decade; approximately 5 years ago a small computer system was acquired. There is now a systems department with 15 individuals and a new inventory control system is currently being developed. As controller, Dorothy will be involved in some of the reports the system produces. However, her role in design has been minimal because of other commitments.

"I am controller, but there are only a few officers in the firm," she explained. "I have to spend a lot of my time on affairs having nothing to do with the direct operation of the firm. We really do not have a vice president of finance, so I wear that hat as well. I have to spend a lot of time with bankers, securities analysts, etc."

Dorothy is puzzled over the specifications for the reports she has just received from the systems group. One of the reports is a detailed status report on the contents of inventory at each warehouse in the country. The systems group maintains that this report is important for the controller since she is responsible for inventory control. Dorothy feels uneasy about the report and wonders how best to use it. What is your analysis of the situation? Is the report suitable for Dorothy? If so, how can she use it best?

spends more time on observational tours and less time answering mail than the chief executive of the company.

DECISION MAKING

One of the major roles of a manager is processing information and making decisions. We have suggested that information systems can help in this process, and now we explore decision making in more depth to see how systems can support decisions.

Problem Finding and Solving

Before a decision can be made, a manager must be aware of a problem. A problem exists when the decision maker's ideal situation differs from reality, for example, when profits are below expectations. This example corresponds to disturbance handling in which the manager discovers a discrepancy between the ideal model and reality and attempts to find some way to handle the disturbance.

After noting that a problem exists, a decision maker must decide what caused it. Are sales down or inventories up? Is advertising too low? After determining the cause or causes, the decision maker must work to solve the problem, having to develop some approach to remedy the situation. There is also another type of problem-finding activity undertaken by the manager who is looking for improvement projects. In this sense the problem can be defined, "What else can we be doing now?" Here, the manager is trying to anticipate problems and plan for them.

Stages in Decision Making

In finding and solving a problem, a decision maker faces a great number of decision cycles. What is the problem and what is the cause of the problem? What further data do we need now and how should we implement the problem solution? Each of these major steps in solving a problem involves a solution of subproblems, and many decisions have to be made.

Simon (1965) has suggested a series of descriptive stages for decision making that are helpful in understanding the decision process. The first stage is defined as *intelligence,* which consists of determining that a problem exists. The decision maker somehow becomes aware of the problem and gathers data about it. We described this stage above as problem finding or identification.

During *design,* the problem solver tries to develop a set of different alternative solutions, asking what approaches are available to solve the problem. In the *choice* stage, the decision maker chooses one of the solutions that has been delineated. If all the alternatives have been evaluated well, the choice stage is usually the simplest one to execute. We should add a stage to Simon's descriptive model called *implementation,* in which we ensure that the solution is carried out.

Types of Decisions

To complete our discussion of problem solving and decision making, we relate different types of solutions to the type of problem involved. A framework proposed by Anthony (1965) offers an in-depth view of the three types of decisions made in an organization.

The first decision area is *strategic planning,* in which the decision maker develops objectives and allocates resources to attain these objectives. Decisions in this category are made over a long period of time and usually involve a substantial effort and investment. For example, the development and introduction of a new product is a strategic decision.

Decisions that are classified as *managerial control* in nature deal with the use of resources in the organization and often involve financial or personnel considerations. For example, an accountant may try to determine the reason for a difference between budgeted and actual cost. In this sense he or she is solving a managerial control problem.

Operational control decisions deal with the short run that affects the day-to-day operations of the firm. What should we produce today in the factory? What should we reorder for inventory?

Given the three types of decisions above, we can ask who makes the preponderance of each type. Anthony does not really specify what types of decisions are handled by different decision makers. However, we suspect the top managers spend more time on strategic decisions than supervisors, while the reverse is true of operational decision making.

Another useful way to think about decisions is according to their degree of structure (Simon, 1965). A structured decision is one in which the decision process is well understood; these decisions are routine and repetitive. Often some specified procedure may be applied to reach a decision each time the situation arises.

Unstructured decisions are novel and do not have easily described procedures for solution. Frequently the problem has not appeared before. Of course, few decisions are at one polar extreme or the other; they range from structured to semistructured to unstructured.

Different types of decision-making technology are suitable for attacking each type of problem. Structured decisions have traditionally been made through habit, by clerical procedures, or with other accepted tools. More modern techniques for solving programmed decisions involve operations research, mathematical analysis, modeling, and simulation.

Unstructured decisions tend to be solved through judgment, intuition, and rules of thumb. Modern approaches to unstructured decisions include heuristic techniques and computer programs. Over time we expect to see new technology providing more support for unstructured decisions.

MODELS

A model is a representation and a simplification of reality; models are used in a number of fields to help in decision making. Architects frequently construct models of proposed buildings to help clients visualize the design more easily than they can from sketches or blueprints. We have many informal models in our heads; in this section we discuss more formal decision-oriented models.

Types of Models

In management science we discuss three general categories of models. The architect's model is descriptive, as is an organization chart that describes the formal relationships among individuals and/or departments in an organization. Descriptive models can be extremely helpful in facilitating understanding. In many instances, the systems analyst constructs a descriptive model of some organizational process in the effort to build an information system. Information systems can be thought of as a type of abstract model of information processing procedures.

Predictive models attempt to forecast the future and are very important in planning. Most organizations make some type of sales forecast to plan production, employment levels, etc. A predictive model, of course, will have an error component, since future events have some degree of uncertainty associated with them.

Another useful category of models can be considered normative or optimizing in nature. These models suggest the best action to be taken. Optimization is a field studied by operations researchers. Examples of optimizing models include economic order-quantity calculations and the class of problems that can be solved by linear programming.

Optimizing models can be further classified into deterministic models, models under risk, and models under uncertainty. Deterministic models do not have probabilities associated with them; parameters can be assumed to be known. The typical linear program assumes that the coefficients and constraints are deterministic.

Models under risk assume that while there is uncertainty, the probabilities of events occuring are known. The models then use the probabilities to suggest the optimum action given the existence of risk. If the probabilities are correct, then over a large number of trials, one should follow the recommendations of the model for optimum results. Actuarial tables represent one type of model that supports insurance decisions made under risk.

In models under uncertainty, we do not know the probabilities associated with different events, and this type of situation is the most difficult to model. One approach is game theory, which has been developed to formulate strategies to deal with uncertainty. What will a competitor do about a new product we want to introduce?

Frequently we encounter situations where it seems almost impossible to construct a valid model. It may be that the variables in the model are related in too complex a manner to be expressed mathematically. Perhaps a mathematical solution is available but when tested against real data, the model does not appear valid. Sometimes, we may wish to construct a model to test the quality of an optimizing model. It is often difficult, for example, to model the operation of a computer system mathematically. Instead we might try to simulate its operations by building a simplified model of the computer.

In these circumstances, the model builder often turns to simulation. A simulation is an abstract version of some process or situation just as any other model is. In a simulation the modeler constructs a simplified version of the actual process and runs the model under various conditions. The simulation does not purport to produce an optimal solution. Instead, the simulation allows the model builder to change various input parameters and assumptions and determine their impact on the output of the process being modeled.

The suggestions are made to improve the process being simulated based on the different input parameters and their impact on the output of the model. The simulation may be constructed using one of a number of special-purpose computer-simulation languages. Building a simulation model is a difficult undertaking, and expert advice is usually needed if a simulation model is to be employed as a part of a systems analysis and design effort.

SYSTEMS PROBLEM 2-2

John Robinson is the executive vice president of Landtrans, a major distribution firm. The company has a fleet of trucks and containerized ships that transport goods around the world. John has just finished reading an article in a magazine about operations research and how it contributed to a competitor's operations.

After finishing the article, John became very enthusiastic about applying operations research techniques to his firm. He made this suggestion at a meeting of the executive committee, which consists of the top officers of Landtrans. His first suggestion was for starting an operations research department with a broad charter to look at interesting problems in the firm.

The executive committee was less enthusiastic than John. They were not sure what the operations research group would accomplish, and they were concerned about what it would cost. They suggested that John contact a consulting firm and hold preliminary discussions with them about what operations research techniques might accomplish for Landtrans.

John got in touch with three consulting firms and asked them for proposals on problems where operations research could make a contribution for Landtrans. Two of the firms proposed to undertake studies of possible operations research projects within the firm. The third consulting company agreed to talk with John but said that the kind of study he proposed was probably not the best way to proceed.

What do you think was the reasoning behind the response of the third consultant? How would you help Landtrans?

Model Building

There are a number of ways to approach model building; for example, see Wagner (1969) or Murdick and Ross (1975). The first step is formulating the problem. What are the controllable or decision variables and what variables cannot be controlled by the decision maker? Just as in systems analysis, it is necessary to define the boundaries or constraints on the problem situation.

Usually, we try to develop a simple model. Given a set of variables, what are the relationships among them? Can we determine the most parsimonious interpretation of these relationships, that is, the simplest explanation for what we have observed? Try to state a verbal representation of the relationships among the variables.

Next, construct the model by developing a symbolic statement of the relationships among variables. These symbolic relationships are then turned into a mathematical model of some type that can be manipulated or solved.

After the model has been constructed, it should be tested with real-world data and evaluated. How does the model compare with previous approaches to solving the problem? Can it be used and is it reliable? The final step, one that is not often successful, is to install the model and to use it for making decisions.

Models in Systems Analysis and Design

During systems analysis, if we are designing an information system, we build a model of some information processing procedure. During the analysis stage and the construction of a system, we might employ a simulation model to determine how the input for a proposed computer application will function.

In addition to being an integral part of the systems analysis activities, models may be included in a system to help support decision making. Most operations research models are solved using a computer system. Some systems, such as those for inventory control, frequently employ operations research models to recommend economic order quantities and reorder points. For systems of this type, it helps if the analyst has some background in operations research. If the development of a model is a serious possibility, it is worth adding someone with this background to a design team.

THE ROLE OF INFORMATION SYSTEMS

Now that we have explored managerial work and decision-making activities, including the types of decisions, their information requirements, and modeling, we can think more about the role of information systems in the organization. For the most part we are interested in formal information, that is, information that can be processed on a computer in some way.

Managerial Roles

The relationship between formal information and managerial roles is summarized in Table 2-1. For interpersonal roles, probably little formal information can be used directly by the decision maker. Managers may relate the results of formal information processing to some of their contacts when acting as figureheads. They may also, for example, use personnel data in acting out their leadership roles. Formal information is used in the liaison role with outsiders; however, the most likely use of formal information by the decision maker is in informational and decisional roles.

In the informational role, managers have to monitor conditions; they can use a formal information system that supplies data on both the external environment and internal operations. The decision maker is looking particularly for problems at this stage and exception reporting is very useful; that is, reporting conditions that differ from the decision maker's expectations. As an example of this kind of information, consider the forecast of a leading economist who suggests that a strong upturn will lead to heavy, unexpected demands for a firm's product. Such information could cause the manager to revise production plans.

Acting as a disseminator, the manager may use a formal information system to process data and prepare various financial statements for company employees and stockholders. As a spokesperson, the manager may use the output of a

TABLE 2-1
THE ROLE OF FORMAL INFORMATION IN MANAGERIAL WORK

Role	Activity	Information
Informational roles		
Monitoring	Seeks and processes information from environment	External and internal data, exception reports
Dissemination	Transmission of information to colleagues	Processing of data, formal reports
Spokesperson	Dissemination to outsiders	Processing of data, formal reports
Decisional roles		
Entrepreneur	Defines and initiates improvements	External and internal data, processing of data, simulation, models
Disturbance handler	Resolves problems	Exception reports
Resource allocation	Distributes resources	Use of resources, models calculations, simulation
Negotiator	Resolves conflict	Processing of data

financial system to produce information for external consumption; for example, for stockholders or the financial community.

An information system also can be helpful in supporting the manager in various decisional roles. When acting as entrepreneur, the manager needs external data such as information on the market for a new product. In this situation, the decision maker may need to process large amounts of data—for example, by simulating the production of a new product. Another information system might be used to control a project and to monitor costs and revenues as a product is introduced. A decision model may be employed to help in an analysis.

Firms are also using information systems to gain a competitive advantage and to offer new services. One stockbroker developed a new type of account in which a customer's idle cash in a brokerage account was automatically invested in a high-yield money-market account. This firm increased the level of service to customers and the size of its money-market account dramatically; the service was possible only because of computer systems. Other firms exist just to sell information using computers to process and present the data to customers. One can purchase the ability to access various news articles, stock market results, economic models of the economy, and many other data bases.

We mentioned earlier that the manager's role as a disturbance handler corresponds closely with problem-finding activities. Here, the information systems designer can provide exception reports that clearly point out to the manager when existing conditions differ from desired conditions.

Formal information is also helpful in the resource allocation role because the decision maker needs to know how resources have been allocated in the past. An information system can monitor and report data, such as budgeting information.

The system can also perform calculations for the purpose of comparing different resource allocation alternatives.

Even in a negotiator role in which the manager is trying to resolve conflict, data processing may be necessary. For example, there is widespread use of information systems in collective bargaining to project the costs of union and management proposals.

Information Requirements

In any of these roles, the manager is called upon to make decisions, and we can classify these decisions according to Anthony's framework (1965). Table 2-2 shows the characteristics of information associated with different types of decisions. For example, strategic decisions tend to require external data; accuracy is not vital in this area and the data do not need to be up to the minute. We are generally interested in long-range considerations for strategic decisions.

Operational control decisions have information requirements at the other end of the spectrum: Here we use primarily internal data, and we need a high degree of accuracy and more detailed information. Frequent reporting is necessary because of the short range of the decisions involved; the data are used to take action. Managerial control information requirements fall between these two extremes of strategic planning and operational control.

In designing information systems we have to consider carefully the role of the manager when using information, and the nature of the problem. (We shall return to this topic later when we discuss systems design.) We also have to think about the kind of decisions supported; many information systems have failed because they overlooked the nature of the decision involved. For example, one system sent detailed information on the status of a large inventory to a top manager; this manager was interested in the managerial aspects of inventory control and turnover, not in the detailed balances in the current inventory. A more suitable report for this manager would have been summaries of inventory turnover by class. By not providing information suited to the decision maker's task, the information system designers failed in their attempt to support decision making.

There are many ways in which systems can aid the manager and the

TABLE 2-2
TYPES OF DECISIONS

	Informational characteristics	
Strategic planning	**Managerial control**	**Operational control**
External environment	Internal records	Internal records
Accuracy unimportant	Accuracy vital	Accuracy vital
Summaries	Detailed data	Detailed data
Periodic	Frequent	Frequent
Long range	Medium range	Short range
Predictive	Control	Action

organization. One purpose of this book is to prepare the reader to design, operate, and manage successfully a computer department that develops a full range of information systems from transactions processing to strategic planning for all levels of users in the organization.

KEY WORDS

Choice stage	Informational roles	POSDCORB
Decision roles	Intelligence stage	Predictive model
Descriptive model	Interpersonal roles	Problem finding
Design stage	Leader	Problem solving
Disseminator	Liaison	Resource allocator
Disturbance handler	Managerial control	Spokesperson
Entrepreneur	Monitor	Strategic planning
Exception reports	Negotiator	Structured
Figurehead role	Normative model/Optimization	Transactions processing
Implementation	Operational control	Unstructured

RECOMMENDED READINGS

Anthony, R.: *Planning and Control Systems: A Framework for Analysis,* Division of Research, Graduate School of Business Administration, Harvard, Boston, 1965. (A short, readable book presenting a framework for managerial decision making.)

Lucas, H.C., Jr.: *Toward Creative Systems Design,* Columbia, New York, 1974. (See especially the early chapters of this book.)

————: *Implementation: The Key to Successful Information Systems,* Columbia, New York, 1981.

Mintzberg, H.: *The Nature of Managerial Work,* Harper & Row, New York, 1973. (An extremely insightful book that should be read by all information systems students.)

Simon, H.: *The Shape of Automation for Men and Management,* Harper & Row, New York, 1965. (A short book containing several good essays on decision making and computer systems.)

DISCUSSION QUESTIONS

1 Describe your own activities according to the categories presented by Mintzberg. That is, keep a diary for a day or two, noting what you have done, and then assign these activities to Mintzberg's roles.
2 How would the techniques that Mintzberg used in his study be helpful in designing an information system?
3 Several authors have suggested that computer-based information systems can never support top management decision making. State your reasons for agreeing or disagreeing with this contention.
4 Why are there so many transactions-processing information systems?
5 Does all management information come from the data developed for operational-control and managerial-control decision making? If not, what are the other sources of management information?

6 Do you think computer-based information systems can ever be developed that process informal information?

7 Given our discussions about departments in Chapter 1, where should the computer department be placed in the organization? Should it be a part of accounting?

8 Simon suggested a distinction between structured and ill-structured problems. Structured problems are well defined, while ill-structured problems are novel and usually one-shot decisions. How does this scheme relate to Anthony's framework discussed in this chapter?

9 How would your design approach differ for a transactions-processing system versus a strategic planning information system?

10 Why are there so few computer systems today that serve top management?

11 Assume that you are the manager of some functional department (for example, marketing or accounting) in an organization. Make a list of the important decisions you would expect to make. Then classify each of these decisions according to Anthony's framework. What type of information would you need for each decision?

12 Suppose that several managers in an organization each want different information on a report. All the data each needs are on a single file. How could you provide each manager with a custom-tailored report at a reasonable cost?

13 Is there a relationship between the type of computer system involved and the type of decision in the Anthony framework? That is, would you expect an on-line computer system to be most useful for strategic planning or operational control decisions?

14 Mintzberg studied a group of five managers individually for one week. How could his method of observation and the structured approach he followed in data collection be applied to the design of an information system?

15 Information was characterized in several dimensions in this chapter, such as source, accuracy, detail, etc. What other dimensions for information can you suggest? How do they apply to the information needs for different decisions in the Anthony framework?

16 Take a decision problem you have recently faced and analyze it in terms of Simon's stages of *intelligence, design,* and *choice.* Also describe how the chosen alternative was implemented.

17 In this chapter, we distinguished between problem-finding and problem-solving information. What kind of information do you think most information systems produce? Why?

18 What type of computer system would you expect to have the greatest potential for aiding decision makers in problem-solving activities and why?

19 One management scientist has recommended that we reduce the amount of information produced by computer systems. He feels that managers receive too much irrelevant information; that computer systems need to provide more filtered data. Do Mintzberg's results agree or differ with this observation?

20 Given the observation that most computer systems are in the operational control or transactions-processing categories, why should managers be involved in computer-related decisions?

21 It has been suggested that an information system is really a model of some information processing procedures. Do you agree or disagree? What are the similarities between a system and a model?

22 Compare the process of building an operations research model with the activities involved in building an information system.

23 Why do most model-building efforts involve the use of a computer?
24 What are the responsibilities of management in the development of information systems?
25 The explosion of low-cost hardware has led to the development of inexpensive, small computers that can be used by an individual. What functional areas of management do you think would be most assisted by a personal computer?

AN OVERVIEW OF
COMPUTER APPLICATIONS

AN OVERVIEW OF COMPUTER APPLICATIONS

In this chapter, we discuss the general structure of information systems and look at examples of different kinds of systems. Our purpose is to gain an appreciation for the many different applications employing computer-based information systems.

TYPES OF SYSTEMS

Figure 3-1 is a simple illustration of the basic components of a computer-based information system. A system processes input that is provided by a user, for example, a list of hours worked by employees. The input is first edited for errors and corrected, if necessary, through manual intervention. An entry that indicates someone worked 120 hours in a week is probably incorrect and should be questioned. The input becomes immediate output (a check) or is used to modify the files (pay records) of the system. Input can also be used to request the retrieval of information stored in the system, such as the names of all employees who worked overtime last week.

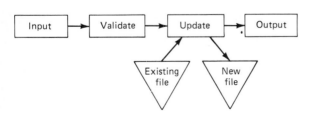

FIGURE 3-1
Components of a computer-based information system.

Files containing data are a major component of the information system. The files correspond to the information kept in folders, file cabinets, or notebooks in a manual information system. Information may be retrieved from a file or the file contents may be altered by modifying, adding, or deleting data in the file. We are also interested in some type of output from a system that may be a short response to an inquiry request for information from a file or the result of elaborate computations. Output is produced in many different formats and modes of presentation such as a printed report, a display on a televisionlike screen, or a verbal response.

It is helpful to distinguish among the types of information systems according to the technology employed. In a simple batch system, all input is processed at one point in time to produce the desired output. The input data are collected and used to update the files periodically, for example, daily, weekly, or monthly. The data are frequently out of date in this type of system because updating is periodic, but batch processing is very economical. A payroll system is an example of an application that is usually operated in batch mode, because paychecks are issued periodically.

A simple inquiry system features on-line retrieval of information from files that are updated in batch mode. A system for production control might be updated overnight and have its files available for inquiry using a terminal during the day.

An inquiry and post system is similar to a simple inquiry system in processing retrieval requests for information. However, it also accepts and edits input on-line for later updating in batch mode. This input is saved on a file and is used to update the system later. The production control system above could be operated in this manner to accept input from factory-floor data terminals during the day. Then in the evening, when the computer schedule is less heavy, the files could be updated in a batch processing run.

An inquiry and on-line updating system actually makes modifications to files as the information is entered from terminals. These systems require more complicated technology and are exemplified by on-line reservations systems.

A command and control system or real-time system is one in which information has to be fed back instantaneously to control an operation. For example, sensors on a missile feed information to a computer that must process the data in time to provide guidance control for the missile.

The applications above run on mainframe or minicomputers, computers that allow multiple users accessing shared data and programs. The fastest-growing area of the computer industry, however, is the microcomputer sector. These computers can be used for entirely personal work, for example, financial analysis or word processing. Most personal computers can also be turned into terminals to connect with mainframe or minicomputers; the user extracts data from the larger system and downloads it to the personal computer for processing.

Table 3-1 summarizes the types of systems and their characteristics, and provides an example of a typical application employing each type of technology.

TABLE 3-1
CHARACTERISTICS AND APPLICATIONS OF VARIOUS TECHNOLOGIES

Type of system	Characteristics	Example
Mainframe and minicomputers		
Simple batch system	Updating at one point in time	Payroll
Simple inquiry	Update in batch, retrieve on-line	Inventory status
Inquiry and post	Update in batch, retrieve on-line, enter and edit data on-line	Production control with factory-floor input
Fully on-line	All input, output, and updating done on-line through terminals	Reservations system
Command and control	Fully on-line and instantaneous feedback to control some process	Missile launching and guidance
Personal computers		
Local	No shared data, private analysis	Spreadsheet analysis
On-line	Access to corporate data	Extracting sales data

APPLICATIONS

In the rest of this chapter, we present a survey of various computer-based information systems to illustrate the diversity of situations in which these systems have been used. Our vehicle for presentation will be to follow a hypothetical user through a day's activities. We shall discuss the information systems encountered and briefly describe their characteristics. These information systems do not necessarily exist in exactly the form described here. However, all the applications areas suggested have been supported by computer-based information systems similar to the ones encountered below.

The Manager

Our hypothetical user is Martha Johnson, the executive vice president of Diversified Products, Inc. Diversified is a medium-sized conglomerate whose major operation is the production of automobile parts for new car and replacement markets. Several smaller subsidiaries manufacture parts for other consumer durable products.

Martha has an M.B.A. from a leading business school and has been working for Diversified for about 5 years. She began as controller, having majored in accounting and finance. Martha was recently promoted to executive vice president, a position with major operating and financial responsibilities.

The Morning

We join Martha on her way to work in the morning. She lives in a townhouse near a rail line serving the central city where Diversified's headquarters and main production facilities are located. This morning she listens to a weather forecast and decides to drive to the railroad station because showers are predicted.

A Weather System   Behind the forecast is a huge system of reporting stations and computer equipment: Data from all over the world are collected and processed to study and predict the weather. Some of the largest computational programs for modern computers were developed for the task of weather forecasting. However, the general public rarely glimpses the people or machines monitoring the weather and generating these forecasts.

A Police System   While driving to the station, Martha encounters a radar speed trap, though fortunately she is heading in the opposite direction! She notices that immediately after stopping the offending motorist, the police officer does not leave the patrol car but instead speaks on the car radio. Had she been able to overhear the conversation, Martha would have heard the officer checking with the dispatcher to get information about the automobile to be cited. What kind of data would the officer receive and how?

At the heart of this police information system is a computer-based file containing information on wants and warrants, and these data can be retrieved from the file on-line for an inquiring officer. The police officer in the field radios the command center and requests information on a given license number. At the center an operator, using a terminal connected to an on-line system, enters the license number. The computer is programmed to search for any information on the file about a car with that license plate or the person to whom it is registered.

Typical questions would be, "Are there any outstanding tickets or warrants for the car or driver? Is the automobile stolen?" Information is retrieved and radioed back to the police officer. If the driver is wanted, the officer takes special precautions or calls for assistance in approaching the automobile. Such information has greatly increased the safety of the police officer.

However, as with any benefit, there are costs connected with such a system. Police systems have raised issues of invasion of privacy over the records of data maintained on them. These systems also can result in abuses to citizens if not updated properly. For example, in one city, some stolen cars were recovered, but the computer system was not updated. Several rightful owners of the returned automobiles were arrested later because the information system was not kept up to date!

A Sales Application   After arriving at work, Martha receives a summary management report on sales in Diversified's major division. Diversified employs about 150 sales representatives nationwide. Twenty-five of these representatives call on Detroit manufacturers to sell new car parts, while the others concentrate on sales of auto replacement parts through chain stores and other retail outlets.

SYSTEMS PROBLEM 3-1

The chief executive of a small firm specializing in the acquisition of cable TV companies feels that the major reason for the firm's success is its ability to perform an economic evaluation of a proposed acquisition in two or three days. Larger competitors, because of standards and bureaucratic procedures, are not able to move as rapidly.

However, there are several problems with the analysis conducted by the firm. Because of the computational complexity of financing arrangements and depreciation schemes, very few possibilities are computed. The controller of the firm uses a pocket calculator for the computations; there is not sufficient time for a complete analysis of the myriad possibilities available.

The chief executive thought that a computer might be able to help, but he is unsure of how to proceed. Clearly a number of alternatives are available beyond the simple hand calculator used now. The choices appear to be either a small computer for the firm or the use of a time-sharing system.

Although the chief executive and the controller have narrowed the choices to the two above, they would like some help in making a final decision. What criteria should they use? Having chosen a processing alternative, how do they develop a system to assist in making decisions about acquisitions? (What type of information system is this?)

The company has developed a fairly elaborate batch sales-information system as an outgrowth of its order-entry computer system. Sales force members complete orders and send them to the data processing center, where they are transcribed into a machine-readable medium. The orders are summarized by type and product and printed by due date for production-control scheduling purposes. The orders are also analyzed to extract sales information; past sales history is kept on a computer file. Each sales representative receives a monthly report showing his or her accounts and 12 months of historical sales data. The reports also contain this-year-to-date and last-year-to-date figures on sales by unit and dollar volume.

There is a goal or quota for each sales representative that is also shown on the report. This system has eliminated much of the sales representatives' bookkeeping and allowed them to concentrate on sales. The sales information system also produces a summary report by territory and by product for management. A batch retrieval program allows managers to select different types of information based on their needs. Martha Johnson, for example, likes to receive a report of sales by product and sales by product within each geographical region. She uses this information to obtain a feeling for how different product groups are doing and to compare sales with inventories in different parts of the country.

The Production System   A 10 A.M. meeting is scheduled to discuss a request for a new production control system. Most of the operations of Diversified are classified as job-shop as opposed to assembly-line production. There is a series of manufacturing operations on each product, and a number of different machines can be used for these operations; there is no one sequence of steps. Scheduling job shops is difficult because of the combinatorial number of paths through the shop for a given product.

Early in the days of computer use, Diversified developed a timesharing simulation model to help in the scheduling process. A production control scheduler inputs the jobs to be completed to a terminal connected to a commercial firm selling timesharing services. A model developed by a consulting firm simulates the flow of orders through the shop and prints the best schedule. The simulation program has a table showing all machinery requirements for different orders. Various scheduling rules are tried and the best scheduling rule for time and cost is selected.

The purpose of the 10 A.M. meeting is to discuss a proposal for installing factory-floor data-collection terminals to record the status of production. Several managers in the company have questioned the advisability and need for such data, and the meeting continues until 11:30.

Microcomputers   Before lunch, Martha returns to her office and has a chance to meet with her secretary. The secretary has just finished making the corrections to a report Martha has written. The secretary uses a microcomputer with a word-processing package for this type of report.

Martha dictates the report based on an outline, and the secretary types from the dictation on the microcomputer keyboard. The system features a cathode-ray tube (CRT) display and a letter-quality printer to run off the final document. The secretary enters the report and then uses an editing program to make changes and corrections. The secretary also types in special commands to the word-processing program so that different headings are centered and/or printed in a different typeface than the rest of the paper. There are a variety of these special commands to allow for underlining, boldface print, and so on.

Martha also has a microcomputer in her office that she uses for various tasks. She can connect her microcomputer to the company's mainframe system and extract data from its massive files. Her extracted data are stored on small floppy diskettes or on a small hard-disk drive in her microcomputer. Then, disconnected from the mainframe, the microcomputer is used to process the extracted data using special, powerful software packages.

Of course, the microcomputer can also be used in the "stand-alone" mode for data that Martha enters herself. An example is an analysis she just performed of budget variances for two departments. Her secretary entered some of the data in an electronic spreadsheet program. This program provides the user with a spreadsheet with addressable rows and columns on the screen. Algebraic relationships between the cells defined at the intersection of a row and column are defined. Then, if the user wants to change a number or an assumption, the entire spreadsheet is recalculated. This package makes it very easy to try a number of different assumptions or pieces of data; the results are recalculated automatically. This kind of application is a good example of a simple decision-support system in which the user is interested in "what if" kinds of questions.

The word-processing example is a part of a larger trend called "office automation." The idea is to use computers to support office workers. Martha has been investigating the possibility of buying an "electronic mail" system for Diversified. This application uses a computer to set up electronic mailboxes for each user of the system. Users work with terminals to access the messages in their mailbox whenever they wish to review them. The advantages of this type of system make it very attractive; individuals do not have to be interrupted by phone calls or play "telephone tag" (it is estimated that fewer than 30 percent of phone calls actually reach the other party the first time dialed).

The major problem with the system is that it requires discipline on the part of users. Each person must have easy access to a terminal and be willing to use the computer. Although Martha knows that she and some of the other executives will work with it, she also believes that there are several who are quite opposed to computers. "This is a difficult implementation problem," she thought after reading the latest magazine article about electronic mail. "Maybe in a few years, but Diversified is just not ready yet."

Lunch

Computer-Aided Design   Martha lunches with the head of engineering for Diversified; they discuss a recent demonstration at a customer's location. The customer, one of the major automobile manufacturers, had showed them its engineering research center. The manager of engineering was fascinated by the customer's computer-aided design system. Automobile designers sit in front of CRT terminals, which resemble a television set, and work interactively with the computer to design new products. An engineer uses a light pen to indicate changes on the screen, and the computer system makes the changes on-line instantaneously. Several complete cars had been designed in this manner.

The system at the auto firm was custom-designed by the company's own engineering and computer staff. Since that time, a number of vendors have developed special software packages for their computers; independent software firms have also put together computer-aided design systems on different kinds of hardware.

Based on the demonstration and what had been appearing in the trade press, Martha and the manager of engineering agree to begin a project to evaluate the various offerings. Within a year, they would like to have a computer-aided design system working at Diversified.

The engineering manager is particularly enthusiastic, since not only does such a system help in design for new products, it stores all existing designs (once they have been entered) so that a minor change needed for a new customer does not require a complete redrafting of the part.

Two Customer-Oriented Systems   After lunch, Martha has a few minutes to conduct two items of personal business. First, she wishes to see if a check has been credited to her bank account. She stops at a branch of the bank and keys in her account number on a standard Touch-Tone phone. She receives a response giving the balance of her checking account: "four two oh one dollars and seven five cents."

This bank system is basically a batch on-line application. The telephone is an inexpensive terminal; computer output is produced by an audio-response unit. Numbers are prerecorded on this device and the computer program accepts the account number, locates the balance on file, and gives instructions to the audio response unit on what numbers to "play" for output.

Back at the office, Martha decides to try another letter to *Modern Living* magazine (earlier she had resolved to cancel her subscription). First, her subscription was not renewed as requested. Then two copies of the magazine started arriving each month. Several letters also came demanding payment even after Martha sent a copy of her cancelled check. This time Martha is writing to the publisher in hopes of obtaining satisfaction.

At the magazine, chaos had prevailed since a consultant had designed and programmed a new subscription system. For some reason, unknown to the magazine staff, the new system did not work. The computer cancelled subscriptions after the magazine sent two copies each month. Customers cancelled other subscriptions because they were not receiving copies. Circulation dropped and the magazine had to resort to costly overprinting to be sure enough copies were available. Because of the decline in circulation, advertising revenue also decreased. Finally, after the magazine hired some staff members with computer experience and turned to another consultant for help, the situation is improving. However, *Modern Living* was very close to bankruptcy at one point because the subscription system failed so badly.

Afternoon

Marketing Research   After lunch, Martha attends a meeting with the marketing department. This department is looking at marketing models to see how they could be used to assist the company. The department requested more funds in its budget to hire an operations research staff member and for time-sharing services. Several models were available to help in advertising decisions; there were also models to suggest strategies for new product selection and introduction. In addition to the models already available, a number of statistical techniques to answer different marketing questions could be applied to sales data already collected by the sales information system.

The marketing department also wants funds to use an existing information storage and retrieval system. Several vendors offer very large data bases of information useful for such research. For example, one company has much of the information for over 300,000 National Aeronautics and Space Administration (NASA) citations in a data base that can be accessed by customers for a fee. The user of these services dials a computer in California and employs a simple language to submit retrieval requests. A computer program searches for abstracts fitting the key words entered by the user. Abstracts can be printed at the computer center and mailed to the requester if a large number of citations is found.

Planning Systems   Later in the afternoon, Martha receives the output from the latest run of Diversified's planning model. Using a specially developed language for planning, a staff member constructed a model of the firm. Simple equations are used to express basic relationships among demand, production, sales, and inventory. The staff develops various scenarios and compares the output to predict the results of different courses of action.

Economic data obtained from a firm selling time-series data on the economy supplements the planning model. The vendor of economic data has a large computer model of the economy, constructed with sophisticated regression techniques. Information developed from this model is made available to customers; Diversified uses these data to provide information on general economic conditions for its own model.

Martha is particularly interested in a cash flow forecast for the next 4 or 5 years for a new subsidiary under consideration for acquisition. On the next run, she asks the analyst to show what would happen to cash flow projections if the new subsidiary is acquired this year and an existing, unprofitable subsidiary is sold in 3 years.

Airplane Reservations   Before leaving work Martha calls an airline to make a reservation for a trip the following week. The passenger agent who answers the phone converses with an on-line reservation system through an alphanumeric CRT terminal (unlike the graphics terminal for automated design, this terminal prints only letters and numbers). The agent obtains information on what flights are available from the computer system; a computer program checks the file of flights and times and displays them on the agent's screen.

Based on the schedules, Martha requests a round-trip flight. The agent enters her request; the computer system checks a file for the flight requested and indicates that space is available. The agent enters Martha's name, and the computer program places it on a file. Later, plans can be changed easily. Martha's record can be consulted by the agent when she appears for her ticket and proceeds to the gate to board the plane.

A Supermarket System   On the way home, Martha stops at a supermarket that is experimenting with a new automated checkout system. The system appears fast to Martha, but she wonders if it is economical. Each grocery item is coded with something called the Universal Product Code, and this code can be read by an optical scanner in the counter when the item and code are passed over the scanner. Price information is retrieved by a computer program, which also maintains a running total of the groceries purchased by the customer. The clerk no longer has to operate a cash register. By knowing every item sold, the store can keep track of inventory and place appropriate reorders. However, these point-of-

TABLE 3-2
SUMMARY OF SYSTEMS

System	Decision type	Technology
Weather	Operational	Batch, on-line
Police want/warrant	Operational	On-line
Sales, order entry	Transactional, operational, management	Batch
Production control	Operational	On-line (timesharing)
Microcomputer	Decision support	Personal computer
Microcomputer	Word processing	Personal computer
Automobile design	Operational	On-line
Account inquiry	Transactional	On-line inquiry
Subscription	Transaction	Batch
Marketing models	Managerial and strategic	Time sharing
Planning model	Strategic	Time sharing
Reservations system	Transactional, operational	On-line
Supermarket system	Transactional, operational	On-line

sale systems have aroused the fear of many consumer groups opposed to the lack of price information marked on grocery items, even though the price is marked on the shelf.

IN CONCLUSION

In this brief sketch, we observed a number of different information systems. These systems employ different types of computer technology and support different kinds of decisions (see Table 3-2). Some of the systems have problems, while others appear to work well. In later chapters, we shall explain some of these problems and try to suggest how to design successful computer systems.

We should emphasize that the scenario described in this chapter is hypothetical; however, applications such as these do exist. It should be obvious that computer-based information systems have been applied to many diverse situations. While we always are constrained by cost and technology, to a great extent we are limited only by our imagination, creativity, and ability to deal successfully with the changes created by computer-based information systems.

KEY WORDS

Alphanumeric	Graphics	On-line
Audio response	Edit	Output
Batch	Electronic mail	Posting
Command and control	Inquiry	Simulation
Computer-aided design	Microcomputer	Update
CRT	Models	Word processing
Files	Office automation	

RECOMMENDED READINGS

Business Week. (See section on information systems for current applications.)
Byte and other popular computing magazines. (Frequent articles on microcomputer applications.)
Time. (See section on computers.)

DISCUSSION QUESTIONS

1 What are the advantages and disadvantages of batch computer systems?
2 Do you expect input editing to be easier for a batch or for an on-line system?
3 Why do you suppose inquiry and post systems were developed instead of fully on-line applications?
4 What are the advantages and disadvantages of fully on-line computer systems?
5 How do backup requirements differ between batch and on-line systems?
6 What applications, if any, exist for command and control systems in business?
7 How does timesharing differ in its use from both batch and on-line systems?
8 What are the drawbacks to mathematical models applied to management problems?
9 What are the problems with simulation as a tool in business analysis?
10 Why do so many batch computer systems exist?
11 What factors inhibit the development of on-line systems? (Hint: think of the major components of such systems.)
12 What are the social issues involved in having massive files of personal data available on-line?
13 Computer-aided instruction has been suggested as one way to improve education. What do you think its limitations are?
14 Why are so many timesharing applications developed in user departments rather than under the control of an internal information systems department?
15 One critic has suggested that management information can never be automated. What is your reaction to this statement?
16 Examine a computer application with which you are familiar. Describe its purpose, input, output, processing, and files.
17 Inventory control is one of the most popular computer applications. Why? What has its impact been on the economy?
18 An entire industry exists for selling information. Make a survey of some of the data for sale and classify it by functional area, for example, marketing, finance, economics.
19 Why is it useful to have interaction capabilities when working with a computer-based model?
20 What factors from a user's standpoint are different in the design of a batch versus an on-line system?
21 What are the major advantages and disadvantages of inquiry and post systems where data are captured on-line but files are updated later, say, at night?

CHAPTER 4

THE IMPACT OF COMPUTERS

Many times information systems have failed because the impact of the system on the organization or individuals was ignored. People must use a system for it to be successful, and to design successful systems we must understand the impact of computers on users. Unfortunately, early studies of computer impact were not oriented toward the design of better information systems. Instead, most of these studies were conducted by researchers interested in broad questions of how computers affect employment or what effect computer systems have on the overall structure of an organization.

IMPACT ON THE ORGANIZATION

Early Predictions

Probably the best-known set of predictions for the impact of computers on organizations can be found in a paper by Leavitt and Whisler (1958). They suggested that firms would become recentralized as a result of computer technology; the availability of information would allow managers to centralize. The trend until the development of computer systems had been toward decentralization because centralized management could not cope with the amount of information and the number of decisions required in a large organization. Now, the computer offered the power to make centralized management possible so the organization could be tightly controlled by a small group of top managers.

Little evidence supports this early prediction (Lucas, 1973). In a few cases researchers have found examples of recentralization after computer systems were installed, but certainly there is no overall trend. Occasionally a system has replaced a level of management; for example, a military command and control system. The difficulty is that there have been too few studies; research in this area is hard to conduct because so many other variables besides computer systems affect the structure of an organization.

Another problem in validating these predictions occurs in trying to define centralization and decentralization. No one has developed an acceptable definition of centralization or a technique to measure it. Also, these early predictions assume that decentralization was negatively motivated. There are often other reasons to decentralize, such as to train managers and to provide more autonomy for lower-level supervisors.

There seem to be no real reasons why computer systems should lead naturally to centralization. In fact, we should consider centralization and decentralization as a variable in the systems design process. Centralization is not something to be measured after a system has been implemented. Management should specify the goals for the organization and the degree of centralization desired. Given sophisticated communications capabilities, on-line computer systems, and large data bases, we can design a system that provides information for decision making at any level or geographical location in the organization.

The Distribution of Power

The early studies of computer impact on organizations are not too helpful to us; they have not provided a basis for designing computer systems. The real problem with the impact of information systems on organizations is concerned with a subject not covered in past work: *Information systems affect the distribution of power in the organization.* Power is the potential to influence others to act according to one's wishes. In organizations, different departments have differing levels of power; a theory proposed by Hickson et al. (1971) offers some insight into these power relationships. These authors suggest that four major conditions, described below, result in a department having a high level of power. As we shall see, the computer department meets almost all these conditions for high power, and by its activities the computer department alters the distribution of power in the organization.

One determinant of power is the extent to which a department copes with uncertainty for other departments. Uncertainty is a lack of information about future events that makes their outcomes less predictable (Hickson et al., 1971). The computer department copes with a great deal of uncertainty for user departments. First, when it designs a new information system, the user often yields some control over an operation to the computer department. For example, consider a department that prepared budget statements manually, but that has just implemented a computer system to process budgets.

When a group of clerks and analysts prepared the budget before the computer system was developed, the manager of the department had control. If the manager was behind schedule, overtime could be arranged to see that the job was completed. A solution to most problems could be found within the manager's own department. With a computer system, the manager now has added uncertainty as to whether the computer department will finish processing on time and with acceptable accuracy. The development of the computer system has created uncertainty for the user where none existed before. Only the computer department can cope with this new uncertainty.

The computer department also supplies information, and one of the major uses of information is to reduce uncertainty. Thus, the computer department is in the business of supplying a product that reduces uncertainty. Finally, in the operation of systems there are many uncertainties: Will the job be finished on time? Will the output be satisfactory? Will the computer system malfunction or be down?

The second determinant of high power is whether or not a department can be replaced easily. There are not really many alternatives to the computer department. Dissatisfied company management could hire an entirely new computer staff, but there is likely to be chaos during the transition. One can also turn to a service bureau for processing, but it would be difficult and expensive to convert all present applications. Another alternative to the computer department is a facilities management arrangement in which a consultant contracts to run the computer department. However, most facilities management contractors hire a significant proportion of the people currently working in the department. The facilities management alternative also meets much resistance from management, which may be uneasy about having another organization responsible for a department that processes information vital to the company. Thus, for the mature computer department, there are not too many possibilities for completely replacing the department, or its personnel.

A third determinant of high power for a department is based on the number of links between other departments and the department in question. The larger the number of links to a department, the greater its power. Clearly, here is another case where the computer department has the potential for becoming quite powerful. The computer department may accept input from 90 percent of the departments in the organization and provide them with some type of service. In addition to the number of links, the importance of each link must be considered in assessing a department's power. If a link were cut, how long would it take for the organization to stop? For example, the janitorial department has a large number of links to each department. However, the lack of janitorial service would be only an inconvenience; in most organizations the final output would not be drastically affected.

For the computer department, the number of links and the importance of the output depends on the type of application developed. More transactional and operational control systems probably mean greater power, since these systems tend to have an immediate impact on work flows in the company. For example, most organizations become heavily dependent on on-line systems that process transactions.

The final condition for high power in the organization is related to the degree of interdependence between the department of interest and all other departments in the organization. The greater the dependence of department A on department B, the greater is department B's power. In the discussion of interdependence in Chapter 1, we pointed out that the computer department exhibits reciprocal interdependence with user departments. That is, the computer department and the department it is serving are mutually dependent on each other to process work; this type of mutual dependence is the most demanding. In designing a system, the computer department depends on users to supply information and to provide an understanding of what is needed. The user is mutually dependent on the computer department for the technical aspects of design and for seeing that the system is implemented. During operations, the user must supply input and help maintain the data base; the user in turn is dependent on the computer department to provide processing services.

On all these conditions for power, the computer department has a very high score, particularly on coping with uncertainty. The evidence suggests that coping with uncertainty is the most essential condition for high power (Hennings et al., 1974). As a computer department develops systems for different departments, it becomes more powerful in the organization. However, this trend often is not realized because no one stops to look at the department as a whole and consider the sum total of all applications.

When there are significant power shifts within the organization, users can become resentful of their dependence on the computer department, possibly without even knowing the real reason for their dissatisfaction. As a result, users may stop using systems or not seek added computer help when it could be of great assistance. Discomfort over the change in power relations also can lead to personal conflict, which we shall discuss below. In thinking of how to design systems and procedures for operating them, we should keep the problems of power in mind and try to find ways to reduce the transfer of power from users to the computer department.

IMPACT ON INDIVIDUALS

Early Predictions

Many of the early studies of the impact of computer systems focused on the reaction of individual users. Some of these studies were concerned with the psychological reaction of workers, and others concentrated on overall changes in employment levels. Although isolated changes in employment occurred—for example, personnel reduction in one department—it is difficult to find an overall trend. It is safe to say that the impact of computers on employment levels has been no greater than any other technological change. This lack of an adverse impact is particularly significant considering the short period of time that has elapsed since computers were introduced (the late 1940s and early 1950s) and the rapid development of computer systems.

In addition to employment levels, early writers were concerned with the impact of systems on jobs and job content. They suggested that computers would assume more of top management's innovative activities and lead to a managerial elite; that is, computers would accentuate the difference among levels of management (Leavitt and Whisler, 1958). Middle managers were expected to suffer the most; it was predicted that there would be fewer middle managers. Those holding middle management positions would need fewer skills and would receive lower pay; they would have less status in the organization and much lower mobility. The predictions also suggested that many nonmanagement employees would be replaced. For those remaining, jobs would become more boring and the worker would have less self-determination. (See Lucas, 1973 for a summary of some of these studies.)

The few studies undertaken failed to confirm these predictions. It is hard to define middle management, but the drastic changes that were forecast do not appear to have occurred. It does seem that clerical personnel occasionally have been replaced by a computer system, but the effect is not necessarily widespread. What often happens is that more work is done by the same number of workers than would have been possible before a computer system. There is some evidence that nonmanagement employees have found an increase in the number of deadlines and a reduction in the flexibility of their jobs as a result of the implementation of the computer systems. However, these results are old and correspond to the exclusive use of early batch computer systems.

SYSTEMS PROBLEM 4-1

Barbara Jackson is the supervisor of customer service for the Western Gas Company, a large utility in a Pacific Coast city. The group she supervises consists of about 50 customer service representatives who answer telephone inquiries from customers about their gas bills. The employees are all members of a union and are relatively well paid. The position is one of the most sought-after clerical jobs in the company.

A new computer-based inquiry system is about to be installed in Barbara's department. Under the old batch system, service representatives answer the phone and determine the customer's name, complaint, and, if possible, their account number. Then the service representative unplugs his or her headset and walks to a central printout of customer records. Either an alphabetical list is used to obtain the account number, or the account number provided by the customer is used to look up the customer's most recent billing history. The representative then copies onto a pad the important information and returns to the desk, plugs in the headset, and tries to solve the customer's problem.

Under the new system, each operator will have a CRT (televisionlike) terminal on his or her desk. By entering the account number or last name, the representative can view 4 months of bills without having to leave the desk.

Barbara feels a little uneasy about the new system, but she is not sure exactly why. Can you help her define the possible problems in terms of impact on the service representatives and their work group? What can be done to alleviate possible negative aspects of the new system?

Conflict

The studies that have been conducted in the past on the impact of computers on individuals also are not too helpful in the design or operation of information systems. With individuals, the real problems occur when conflict arises between users and the computer department staff. Conflict can be caused by a number of conditions, one of which is the fact that power is transferred from users to the computer department. If a system does not fit a user's needs or is not implemented on schedule, there may be conflict. Conflict is also likely to occur if the system is not operated according to specifications.

In addition to these problems, a number of conditions have the potential to create conflict in an organization (Walton and Dutton, 1969). We do not expect each computer department to fulfill all these conflict conditions, but the potential is there for these problems to arise.

The first condition is mutual dependence, which increases the potential for conflict because a failure to perform by one party can cause serious problems for the other. We have discussed the fact that dependence develops between the computer department and user departments, so there is a high potential for conflict here.

Task differences can also create conflict. Computer work is highly specialized, and there are many differences between the tasks of a programmer or analyst, the operations staff, and the average user. Uncertainty can also lead to frustration and conflict. We have seen that a large amount of uncertainty surrounds computer work. Ambiguities can also lead to conflict; in computer activities, who is responsible for a problem? Was the system designed badly or did the operations staff make an error in processing? It is possible also that the error was made by the user in submitting input data.

Occasionally when people depend on common resources, conflict arises. For example, conflict may occur if computer systems are seen as taking limited funds from a fixed budget in a user department. Several departments also may compete for limited computer resources. Job dissatisfaction is another condition that leads to conflict. Users or the computer department staff may be unhappy in their work or jealous of other workers in the organization. Computer jobs often pay more highly than other positions because of the skill levels required. If a user feels service is bad, the fact that computer people seem to be paid more may be resented. Also, computer staff members often keep rather strange hours: a user seeing a programmer arrive at 2 P.M. may not realize that the programmer worked all night.

Communication obstacles are a major problem in the computer area, and these obstacles can easily lead to conflict. The computer field has developed a special jargon, and many computer professionals do not realize that they are using a strange and unfamiliar terminology. Terms such as "core, so many K, dump, bugs" all have special meaning, and the user may feel that the computer staff is trying to demonstrate superior knowledge. In certain situations, the computer department staff also may be confused by special user jargon.

Performance rewards differ drastically among the computer department staff and users, and these differences have a potential for creating conflict. Few companies pay for harmonious relationships among users and the computer staff or for successfully designing and implementing systems. Personal characteristics and traits may differ among computer department staff members and users, and these differences also can lead to conflict. Computer work is very demanding technically and the staff member is usually committed to his or her career. Computer professionals may not empathize with and understand user problems, which can create conflict.

Again, let us emphasize that not all the conditions described above exist in any one organization. However, the relationship between the computer staff and users has the potential for leading to disruptive conflict. What are the likely results of this conflict? First, it is easy for a user to sabotage the computer department by withholding data or providing incorrect input. Because of the dependence of the computer department on users, it is easy for users to make the computer department appear in an unfavorable light.

The computer department also can sabotage users through delays in processing and by withholding service. The computer department can relax its controls, which introduces more errors into processing. If this type of warfare exists, users may refuse to cooperate in the development of new systems, systems that might have a significant payoff for the organization. As a result, the computer staff tends to become discouraged and the department experiences high turnover. New systems are not designed at all, or they are not designed as well. As these conditions continue, we face a continuing spiral of poor performance and increasing levels of conflict.

In our discussion of systems design and the operation of systems, we shall try to develop an approach that minimizes conflict and the transfer of power from users to the computer department. Surely, these unfavorable aspects of the impact of computers must be overcome if we are to succeed in the development and operation of information systems.

Reactions at Different Levels

Our discussion above has not differentiated among the levels of personnel in the organization. We have found that upper levels of management, middle management, and other employees in the organization react differently to computer systems. At the clerical level, the interface of the system with the user is very important. How easy is it to input data, locate and correct errors, and use the system?

Managers tend to be more concerned with the quality of the data and its timeliness. Critical management reports must be accurate. In one situation, the budgeting system was so inaccurate and had so many delays that key decisions were made in the belief that the firm had a deficit, when in fact it had shown a profit. A bypassed opportunity could have been capitalized on because the funds were available. Unfortunately, the key decision makers had received information that misled them into making a decision not to take advantage of the new opportunity.

Higher levels of management tend to receive complaints from others in the organization about the quality of service and the satisfaction with systems. Top-level managers also learn quickly when systems development efforts are exceeding cost and time estimates. Their concern with information systems is one of whether the organization is obtaining a satisfactory return for its investment in information processing.

INFORMATION SYSTEMS IN THE CONTEXT OF THE ORGANIZATION

Organizational factors can be equally as important as technical details in the design and operation of computer-based information systems. The problem with the studies described earlier is their lack of emphasis on how we can develop successful systems. The power and conflict models help to develop a model of computer-based information seytems in the context of the organization presented below. The purpose of this model is to help understand the organizational impact of systems and to predict the results of implementing a system. The model, when validated, can help suggest ways to increase the probability of the successful design and operation of information systems.

A Descriptive Model

Figure 4-1 presents a descriptive model of information systems in the context of the organization. Boxes represent important components of information systems activities, and arrows between the boxes indicate predicted relationships.

The numbers on the arrows in the figure correspond to relationships stated formally as propositions in Table 4-1. Although some of these relationships may appear to be self-evident, they are included to make the model complete. Experience has shown that it is important to subject even the most obvious relationship to scrutiny. Several times we have been confronted with counterintuitive results that required the revision of an "obvious" relationship.

The first part of the model deals with user attitudes and perceptions of information systems. Attitudes and perceptions are important in determining user reactions to systems and in influencing the use of the system. We expect that systems design and operations policies of the computer department influence user attitudes and perceptions directly and indirectly through the technical quality of systems. By technical quality we mean features of the system that are important to users such as input medium and requirements, output contents, medium, format, system accuracy, timeliness, etc.

User attitudes should also be influenced by management action, for example, management support for the design of new systems and membership on steering committees. User attitudes and perceptions should also be influenced by contact and involvement in the design of systems.

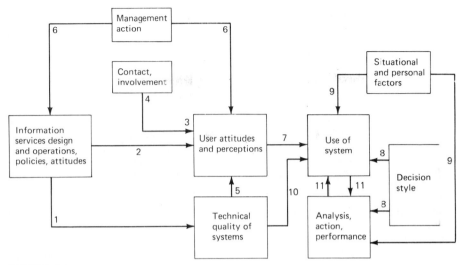

FIGURE 4-1
Information systems in the context of the organization. (*Adapted from Lucas, H.C., Jr.:* Why
Information Systems Fail, *1975, courtesy Columbia University Press.*)

Proposition 7 is based on the expectation that favorable user attitudes and
perceptions lead to high levels of system use, especially if a system is of high
technical quality. High technical quality should lead to more favorable attitudes
and perceptions since a high-quality system provides a better user interface and
better output than a low-quality system.

The use of an information system is a very complex phenomenon. Different
situational and personal factors should influence use; a supervisor with 20 years
of experience would probably not use an inventory reorder report as extensively
as one with 6 months on the job. Decision or cognitive style also can be expected
to influence the use of the system. Quantitatively trained individuals may wish for
different types of information than their counterparts who have a more intuitive
decision style.

The relationship between the use of an information system and performance by
the decision maker is very complex. High levels of performance depend on
analyzing the output of an information system and taking action consistent with
that output. On the other hand, low performance may stimulate the use of the
system to determine the nature and cause of problems. It appears that different
types of data are needed to support these different aspects of managerial decision
making.

A manager is frequently concerned with problem-finding activities, that is,
determining that a problem exists. Most computer-based information systems
address this aspect of decision making through exception reports, comparisons of
this year versus last year, or comparisons of budgeted with actual performance.
Under these conditions, low performance would be associated with high levels of

TABLE 4-1
THE FORMAL PROPOSITIONS OF THE MODEL

Proposition
1 The systems design and operations policies of the computer department and the execution of these policies influence the technical quality of information systems.
2 The systems design and operations policies of the computer department influence user attitudes and perception of information systems and the computer staff.
3 User contact with computer department staff members under adverse conditions leads to unfavorable user attitudes and perceptions of information systems and the information services staff.
4 User involvement in the design and operation of information systems results in favorable user attitudes and perceptions of information systems and the computer department staff.
5 Systems with higher technical quality result in more favorable user attitudes and perceptions of the computer department staff.
6 High levels of management support for and participation in information systems activities result in favorable computer department staff attitudes toward their jobs and users, and favorable user attitudes and perceptions of information systems and the computer staff.
7 Favorable user attitudes and perceptions of information systems and the computer staff lead to high levels of use of information systems.
8 Individuals with differing decision styles have differing levels of use of information systems, perform different analyses of data, take different actions based on information, and have differing levels of performance.
9 Different personal and situational factors lead to differing levels of use of an information system and different actions.
10 High levels of system use result from a system with high technical quality.
11 High levels of use of an information system make it more likely that a user will take action based on the information provided. Depending on the nature of the analysis, the problem, and the information, high levels of use may lead to high or low levels of performance or may be caused by low performance.

use of an information system as a decision maker tries to determine the reasons for poor performance.

After problem definition, the decision maker enters the problem-solving stage. We expect the use of problem-solving output from a system to be associated with high performance if the decision maker takes action consistent with the information. A problem-solving information system may provide such features as computational facilities and simulation of different alternatives.

Research studies have demonstrated that at least in some organizations, the

SYSTEMS PROBLEM 4-2

Harold Miller is the manager of information services for the National Insurance Group, a large insurance firm with worldwide offices. He is currently wrestling with a problem assigned to him by his superior, Marty Shapiro, the vice president of administrative services at National.

Harold has been asked to develop a 3-year and a 7-year plan for information systems and processing at National. The president of the firm finally exploded 2 months ago about the frequency and severity of the complaints he received about information systems. He moved Harold into the manager's position and changed his reporting relationship from the controller to the new position of vice president for administration.

Miller is trying to determine what type of information systems should be developed for National and what kind of physical computer systems would be best. Since the firm has fairly autonomous regional offices in the U.S. and abroad, he feels that highly centralized computer processing might not be the most appropriate. However, there is a real absence of input so far from other managers.

The only clear choice is to make plans. Miller recognizes that the firm has finally realized that a significant component of its business is information processing, and that a major investment will be needed to support its business during the next 5 to 10 years.

What kind of organizational structure do you think the firm should try to develop? How can Miller maintain control of information processing under the structure you have suggested? How should Miller go about the process of planning?

---

model is a valid way to describe the interaction of information systems and the organization (Lucas, 1975). These studies in actual organizations and in a laboratory setting have also produced findings of interest beyond the predictions of the model.

First, there are multiple roles for information provided for decision makers; the same information may have a different use for different individuals. A manager concerned about investment levels will respond differently to a report showing high levels of inventory than a warehouse manager concerned with service levels and stockouts. The same information, in fact, often plays different roles for the same individuals at different points in time. Historical data showing a trend toward decreasing sales may alert a decision maker to the existence of a problem. These same data may be used to develop a forecast to solve the problem of how much to produce for the next month.

Another finding is that we need more flexible information systems and the ability to custom-tailor output. Such flexibility can be provided through report-generator packages, different report formats, and the inquiry-answering capabilities of on-line systems. The technological capability to provide flexibility exists, but the user will have to provide guidance for the information services department to acquire and utilize the available technology.

Existing computer-based systems often provide too much data; users frequently have felt overloaded with information that could not possibly be analyzed. We need to concentrate on selecting the information necessary for decision making rather than on just providing more data. The user frequently is guilty of requesting large volumes of information just in case it is needed. Much information can be processed and saved for reference in archival form while only salient output is provided on a routine basis.

Implications for Systems Design

If we accept the model and results, what are some of the implications? From a systems design standpoint, the analyst should consider the following action steps, which are intended to produce high levels of systems use and successful implementation.

1 Urge the formation of a steering committee of users and information services department staff members to determine priorities for the development of new applications.

2 Encourage training sessions for the computer department staff to help its members adopt a role as catalyst in the development process.

3 Insist that a user be placed in charge of the design team for a new system.

4 See that management provides sufficient resources so that the user staff can spend time on systems design.

5 See that decisions and not just data flows are considered in systems design.

6 Ask probing questions to see if the design team has considered the multiple roles of information for the organization and different decision makers.

7 Review all proposed output from a new system, be selective, and avoid information overload.

8 Examine the user interface with the system; see that users have experimented with the input and output and find it acceptable.

9 Plan for implementation for all users, consider different personal and situational factors, and prepare for changes.

10 Ensure that adequate resources have been devoted to training and user documentation.

IMPLEMENTATION ISSUES

Our discussion of the impact of computers has been intended to encourage the designer to set a broad boundary in the analysis and design effort. Too often, a system has been viewed as consisting only of computer processing or input preparation and output reporting. Systems interact with the organizations; it is the responsibility of the designer to be certain that all aspects of a system will work. We must not only ask if input forms or displays are easy to use, we must be certain that users can and will provide that input.

Unfortunately, a number of problems with information systems have been reported by users. We have found systems in which excessive input error rates have rendered the output of the system useless. Some reports are discarded without being consulted. Voluntary systems exhibit low levels of use. These problems appear to come from four major sources:

1 The original design of the system
2 The interface of a system with the user
3 The process of design and implementation
4 The operation of systems

The original design of the system may have been faulty; for example, some systems do not provide the information needed by the decision maker. As we have seen, different information is required for different tasks. Other systems do not work technically; for example, there may be so many errors that no one trusts the output from the system.

SYSTEMS PROBLEM 4-3

The Hopkins Company manufactures a variety of sporting clothes and sells them through most major retail outlets throughout the United States and Europe. The company has used computers for 15 years in a variety of applications ranging from accounting through production control and sales analyses.

Because the firm is sales-oriented, the sales analysis and reporting system is one of the most important computer applications. Several years ago, the firm decided that the system was too slow and unresponsive to customer needs. The major bottleneck appeared to be in order entry. The processing of orders provided the basic input for sales statistics and reporting and also fed the stock distribution system that dispatched merchandise to customers.

To speed order entry, the information systems department developed a new order form to be completed by sales representatives when they booked customer orders. This new form would be read by optical character recognition (OCR) equipment and would not have to be transcribed through any kind of keying operation. OCR input required the sales force to print more carefully and to use a newly designed order form. The system was tried experimentally in a small sales division before it was suggested to the company as a whole.

The system was explained to the sales staff, and they were asked to use it even though it would slow the order preparation process at first. The sales representatives were told that customer service would improve as a result of the system. However, since the system was experimental, the test version did not really improve customer service.

When the sales staff was queried about the new input procedures several months after they had begun, their reaction was negative. The sales force was not satisfied with the new procedures and they felt that neither the customers nor the sales force gained anything from them.

What is your analysis of the reasons for this less-than-successful implementation effort? What should the firm have done differently? How should they proceed in installing the system for the other divisions?

The interface of the system with the user refers to the way in which we come into contact with the system, for example, through printed input forms, terminals and their associated input language, or batch reports. In one system, terminal input was so complicated that no one submitted data and the system had to be discontinued.

Implementation refers to the entire change effort associated with a new system. We design a system to improve information processing, and improvement implies that we must change existing information processing procedures. The operation of a system involves longer-term issues after a system has been designed and installed. If the operation section of the computer department does not provide good service (for example, meeting schedules for batch systems and having on-line systems available as needed), systems will not achieve their potential.

Definition

What is implementation? Implementation is part of the design of a system and is an organizational change process. We develop a new information system to change existing information processing procedures. Implementation as we use the term should not be confused with a step in systems design. This definition, frequently used by computer professionals, is too narrow. Their definition generally refers to the last steps of systems design, which we shall refer to as conversion and installation of a new system.

Our definition stresses the long-term nature of implementation: it is part of a process that begins with the very first idea for a system and the changes it will bring. Implementation terminates when the system has been successfully integrated with the operations of the organization. We expect most of implementation to be concerned with behavioral phenomena, since people are expected to change their information processing activities.

Success or Failure

How do we know that we have successfully implemented a system? Researchers have not really agreed on an indicator for successful implementation. One appealing approach is a cost-benefit study. In this evaluation, one totals the costs of developing a system and compares them with the dollar benefits resulting from the system.

In theory, this sounds like a good indicator of success, but in practice it is difficult to provide meaningful estimates. Obtaining the cost side of the ratio is not too much of a problem if adequate records are kept during the development stages of the system. However, an evaluation of the benefits of a computer-based information system has eluded most analysts. How do we value the benefits of improved information processing? With transactions processing and some operational control systems, we can usually show tangible savings. For example, many transactions systems have resulted in increased productivity in processing paperwork without a proportional increase in cost. Operational control systems, such as those used to control inventories, may reduce inventory balances, saving storage and investment costs while maintaining existing service levels. For systems that aid a decision maker or provide customer service, it is much more difficult to estimate the benefits, and there are few examples of any such attempts.

In lieu of the more preferable cost-benefit analysis, we can adopt one of two indicators of successful implementation, depending on the type of system involved. For many information systems, use of the system is voluntary. A manager or other user receives a report but does not have to use the information on it or even read the report. Examples of such reports are summary data on sales for sales management and a forecast for the marketing manager. Systems that provide on-line retrieval of information from a data bank can also often be classified as voluntary; the use of such a system is frequently at the discretion of the user. For this type of system where use is voluntary, we shall adopt high levels of use as a sign of successful implementation. We can measure use by interviews with users, through questionnaires, or in some instances by building a monitor into the system to record actual use.

For systems whose use is mandatory, such as an on-line production control system, we shall employ the user's evaluation of the system as a measure of success. For example, one can examine user satisfaction, although it will probably be necessary to measure several facets of satisfaction such as the quality of service, the timeliness and accuracy of information, and the quality of the schedule for operations. An evaluation might also include a panel of information processing experts to review the design and operation of the system.

RESEARCH ON IMPLEMENTATION

Unfortunately, there has been little research on the implementation process for computer-based information systems, although in recent years, some work in this area has been undertaken. Since the implementation of computer-based information systems is very similar to the implementation of operations research or management science models, we can also learn from studies of model implementation. For summaries of some of this research, see Lucas (1976) and Schultz and Slevin (1975).

Most research on implementation has been an attempt to discover factors associated with success; that is, what independent variables are related to successful implementation as defined by the researchers? If there is any basis for believing a causal connection exists between independent and dependent variables, we can then develop an implementation strategy around the independent variables. For example, suppose we found in several studies using different research methodologies that top management's requesting a new system and following through with participation in its design is associated with successful implementation. If there were sufficient evidence to support this finding, we might develop an implementation strategy that emphasized top-management action.

Although individual studies of implementation have addressed a number of independent variables, there is no real consensus in the field on an explanation of successful implementation or on a single implementation strategy. Table 4-2 contains a list of some of the variables in past implementation studies. The dependent variables used to measure implementation success generally can be classified as measures of usage, intended use, and/or satisfaction with a system. The independent variables fall into several classes, as shown in the table.

TABLE 4-2
VARIABLES ASSOCIATED WITH IMPLEMENTATION STUDIES

Independent variables

Computer department
  Policies
  System design practices
  Operations policies

Involvement
  User origination of systems
  Involvement and influence
  Appreciation

Situational and personal factors
  Personality type
  Business history
  Social history
  Structural factors
  Past experience

User attitudes
  Expectations
  Interpersonal relations

Technical quality of systems
  Quality
  Model characteristics

Decision style
  Cognitive style

Management
  Actions
  Consultant/client relations
  Support
  Location of researcher
  Managerial style

User performance

Dependent variables

Implementation
  Frequency of inquiries
  Reported use
  Monitored frequency of use
  User satisfaction

Although researchers have different methods of applying the variables in each study to operations, the variables can be placed into classes similar to ones contained in the descriptive model of information systems. One of the central variables in our model is the use of the system. We are concerned with factors leading to high levels of use, which we have also adopted as a measure of successful implementation. Thus, we can use the model we have already developed to help us to understand the implementation process.

Favorable attitudes on the part of users should be extremely important in implementation; attitudes have an action component, and favorable attitudes are consistent with high levels of use and satisfaction with a system. The technical quality of systems is important; it directly affects our attitudes as users and also makes it easier to use the system physically. For example, a system with difficult input requirements or a difficult language for user input will be used less than one with a good technical design.

As we have seen in our discussion of information, personal and situational factors make a difference in an individual's approach to an information system. We can predict that the new manager will be more interested in an acquisition planning model than the 20-year veteran. Decision style is also important in determining system use: Does an analytic decision maker use the same information as a heuristic one? The future use of an information system is also influenced by past experience in analyzing the information and in taking action. Successful use of information will make it more likely that a decision maker will use the system when faced with a similar problem in the future.

AN IMPLEMENTATION STRATEGY

The research and model described in this chapter suggest an implementation strategy based on our view of information systems design as a planned change in activity in the organization. We stated earlier that the reason for developing a new computer-based information system is to create change. Dissatisfaction with present processing procedures stimulates the development of a new information system. However, change can create almost insurmountable problems in the development of a system if only technical factors are considered by system designers.

What do we predict will happen as a result of the major changes undertaken during the development of a new information system? The model in Figure 4-1 helps to forecast the results. Suppose that change is attempted through a rational engineering approach. People are expected to cooperate with the design of a system because it is in their best interest to do so; we make no special efforts to ease the change process.

We predict that forcing change on a potential user of a system will create unfavorable attitudes; change is always difficult and threatening. If users develop negative attitudes and are afraid to cooperate with the systems design staff, the technical quality of the system will suffer, because the input of users is needed to design a good system from a technical standpoint. Poor attitudes and low technical quality are likely to lead to underutilization of the system—a state we defined as implementation failure.

In the remaining chapters of this book we shall present a design strategy that is intended to maximize the chances of successful implementation. Our approach stresses the process of systems analysis and design, especially the relationship between the analyst and the user.

From an organizational perspective, the following steps are recommended:

1 Identify the key departments and individuals affected by a proposed system.

2 Form a design team of users representing the departments and individuals defined above. The design team should include managers, users, and systems analysts.

3 Form a steering committee of the most senior managers involved. The steering committee reviews system plans and requests for resources; it serves an overall leadership role on the project.

4 Place a user in charge of the full design team.

5 Have the analyst act as a resource and a guide; we discuss this role more completely in Chapter 6.

6 Where appropriate, assign particular subtasks to smaller groups formed from the design team.

7 Hold frequent review meetings to discuss progress and resolve any problems with the design.

8 Evaluate the system after it has been installed.

In the next chapter we present an overview of systems analysis and design. The successful analyst must have a knowledge of the technology, the tools and methodology of systems analysis and design, and an understanding of users and the organization.

KEY WORDS

Action	Design policies	Operations policies
Ambiguities	Failure	Power
Analysis	Implementation	Situational and personal
Attitude	Management action	factors
Centralization	Mutual dependence	Success
Common resources	Performance	Task differences
Communications obstacles	Performance rewards	Uncertainty
Decentralization	Personal characteristics	Use
Decision style	and traits	

RECOMMENDED READINGS

Gilchrist, B., and A. Shenkin: "The Impact of Success on Employment in Supermarkets," *Communications of the ACM*, Vol. 25, no. 7, 1982, pp. 441–445. (A good assessment with reasonable estimates of the workers affected by the technology.)

Leavitt, H. J., and T. L. Whisler: "Management in the 1980's," *Harvard Business Review*. November-December 1958, pp. 41–48. (A historic article presenting many of the early predictions of the impact of computers on the organization and individuals.)

Lucas, H. C., Jr.: *Why Information Systems Fail*, Columbia, New York, 1975. (This book presents in detail the model of information systems in the context of the organization discussed in this chapter and describes the research findings that test the propositions of the model.)

————: *Implementation: The Key to Successful Information Systems*, Columbia, New York, 1981. (A summary of much of the research on implementation and a framework for the analyst.)

Walton, R. E., and J. M. Dutton: "The Management of Interdepartmental Conflict: A Model and Review," *Administrative Science Quarterly*, vol. 14, no. 1, 1969, pp. 73–84. (An academic paper describing the theory of conflict presented in this chapter.)

DISCUSSION QUESTIONS

1 It has been argued that computer department staff members are more highly specialized than others in the organization. Take a position on this issue and defend it. Are there characteristics of computer department jobs that make them more highly differentiated than other tasks?

2 How would you go about measuring the level of power held by a department in an organization?

3 What signs would you look for if you suspected that conflict existed between two departments in an organization?

4 Are there any situations in which conflict in an organization is good? Under what circumstances should conflict be discouraged?

5 Can you think of an example of an organization that is completely dependent on computers for processing? What kind of computer systems are these in terms of the characteristics described in this section of the text?

6 Why have clerical workers not been replaced on a massive scale by computer systems?

7 As the manager of the computer department, how would you handle the perceptual problem with users described in the text when programmers arrive at 2 P.M. because they have worked all night?

8 What reward structure would you design for users and the computer department staff? What behavior would you try to motivate with the rewards?

9 We suggested a change strategy in this chapter based on participation. How would you encourage participation by users in systems design activities?

10 What are the disadvantages to user participation in systems design as far as the computer department is concerned? Are there similar disadvantages for users?

11 Much early research on the impact of computers on the organization focused on the question of increased centralization. Do you think that computer systems create centralizing tendencies in organizations? Why or why not?

12 If centralization is an issue in the organization, how should it be resolved when a new computer system is being designed?

13 Why should a computer system have any impact at all on the organization?

14 How would you recognize a successful computer system in an organization? For what signs of success would you look?

15 How can an information system be designed to be successful according to the criteria you defined in problem 14?

16 Where should the computer department report in the organization and why?

17 How could you reduce the communications obstacles that exist between computer staff members and others in the organization?

18 Is there any way to reduce the mutual dependencies between other departments and the computer department?

19 How could conflict develop among different users of computer facilities? (Hint: think of the type of conflict that can be created by a dependence on common resources.)

20 Why do so many users turn to outside computer services, for example, to acquire timesharing or special packages?

21 Early forecasts suggested that middle managers would be reduced in number and stature as a result of the computer systems. Has this prediction been fulfilled? Why or why not?

22 Do computer systems have an impact beyond the organization, for example, on stockholders or customers? What kinds of impact and what problems are created for these groups?

23 Why should users be involved in the design of systems? How much influence should they have?

24 What will happen to information systems if users have negative attitudes?

25 How are attitudes formed? How can they be changed?

26 What does the model of information systems, in the context of organization discussed in this chapter, suggest will be the result of an unresponsive computer department?

PART **TWO**

SYSTEMS ANALYSIS AND DESIGN: OVERVIEW AND TECHNOLOGY

CHAPTER 5

SYSTEMS DEVELOPMENT OVERVIEW

INTRODUCTION

Systems designers are confronted with a challenging task; they must create a new system and plan a major change in the organization. What are the tools and activities of the systems analyst/designer in executing this task? For the most part, the designer is involved in a human, intellectual activity and the tools available are in the form of procedures, methods, and graphical aids to the design process.

Systems designers are like architects; they must work with users to identify the goals and shape of a new system. Then they create various plans that are reviewed and modified until a final version is chosen for development. The architect works with building materials and user needs for space; the systems designer examines decisions and information flows. Steel, concrete, bricks, and wood form the structure of the architect's building, whereas computer files form the basic structural component of the information system. Various tradespeople and supervisors construct the building, whereas programmers construct and test the new system.

The job of the systems designer is an active one, with much personal contact between the designer and others in the organization. In this chapter we shall review some of the conventional approaches to systems analysis and design as a preview to our new approach to systems design presented in Chapter 6.

THE SYSTEM'S LIFE CYCLE

A computer-based information system has a life cycle, just like a living organism or a new product. The various stages in the life cycle of a system are shown in

Table 5-1. The idea for a new information system is stimulated by a need to improve information processing procedures. This need leads to the preliminary survey to determine if a system can be developed to solve these processing problems. If the results of the survey are positive, it is refined to produce a more detailed feasibility study. Based on the outcome of the feasibility study, a decision is made whether to proceed with the design of a system. One of the alternatives sketched in the feasibility study is chosen for development if a positive decision is made.

In systems analysis, the existing information processing procedures are documented in detail. During requirements analysis, designers attempt to learn what

TABLE 5-1
THE SYSTEM'S LIFE CYCLE

Inception
  Preliminary survey

Feasibility study
  Existing procedures
  Alternative systems
  Cost estimates

Systems analysis
  Details of present procedures

Requirements analysis
  User needs
  Collection of data on volumes, input-output, files
  Boundary setting

Design
  Ideal system unconstrained
  Revisions to make ideal acceptable

Specifications
  Processing logic
  File design
  Input-output
  Programming requirements
  Manual procedures

Programming

Testing
  Unit tests
  Combined module tests
  Acceptance tests

Training

Conversion and installation

Operations
  Maintenance
  Enhancements

users expect a new system to do. One major task during this phase is to define the boundaries of the system. Does the problem just concern inventory control, or should any new system also consider the problems in purchasing when inventory has to be replenished? Data are also collected during analysis on the volume of transactions, decision points, and existing files.

The most challenging and creative part of the life cycle is the design of a new system. One approach to this task is to develop an ideal system relatively unconstrained by cost or technology; this ideal system is then refined until it becomes feasible. Detailed specifications must be prepared for the system just designed. The exact logic to be followed in processing and the contents and structure of the files must be specified. Input and output devices are selected, and the formats for input-output are developed. These requirements for processing, files, and input-output activities lead to the specification of programming requirements; these requirements can be turned over to a programming staff for coding.

In the programming stage, the actual computer programs necessary to perform the logic operations of processing are written. In some organizations this task is done by a separate group of programmers; other organizations use analyst-programmers. The same individuals who perform the systems analysis and design also code the resulting programs. Programs have to be tested carefully, first as units and then in combined modules. Usually a programming task is broken down into a series of smaller subtasks or modules; all the individual modules must operate together if the system is to work properly. During the final stages of testing, there will be some type of acceptance test in which users verify that the system works satisfactorily.

Since one purpose of the new information processing system is to change existing procedures, training is crucial. All individuals have to understand what is required by the new system. When training has been completed, it is possible to undertake conversion; it may be necessary to write special programs to convert existing files into new ones or to create files from manual records. Finally, after all these stages, the system is installed.

After the problems of installation have been resolved and the organization has adjusted to the changes created by the new system, the operational stage is begun; that is, the system now operates on a routine basis. However, this routine does not mean that it remains unchanged: there is a constant need for maintenance and enhancements. Maintenance is required because programs inevitably have errors that must be corrected when they appear. Because of the creative nature of design, users and the computer staff may not have communicated accurately, so that certain aspects of the system must be modified as operational experience is gained with it. As users work with the system, they will learn more about it and will develop ideas for change and enhancements. It is unreasonable to consider a computer-based information system finished; the system continues to evolve throughout its life cycle if, in fact, it is successful.

NEW APPROACHES TO DESIGN

In the early days of computers, almost all systems analysis and design was conducted (loosely) following the system's life cycle. Of course, many shortcuts were taken, particularly with documentation. Also, in most organizations the analyst performed the bulk of the work.

Unfortunately, the design process has not been an outstanding success. There are a number of problems, including late systems that do not meet their original specifications, systems that are not used, and systems that are heavily criticized by users. We shall explore the many reasons for these problems in later chapters.

Some recent trends, new approaches to design, attempt to solve some of the problems with the traditional methods of building a system. In later chapters, we shall discuss these alternatives in detail and try to suggest under what conditions they can be applied.

The first new approach is to use an applications generator, a language often referred to as nonprocedural. The purpose of the generator is to reduce programming·time and to allow a user to see quickly what the system actually does.

Another approach that is not new, but has matured to the point of being a more viable option, is the use of an applications package. The package consists of program code and possibly hardware that accomplish some part of a desired application. For example, we might buy a package to maintain an employee benefits system and produce various government reports.

A prototype is a model of the final system. The purpose of a prototype is to allow the user to see something concrete; it is very difficult to conceptualize the features of a system from a set of written specifications, particularly for the user. The prototype shows the user how some part of the system will look and may even be continuously modified to evolve into the final application.

Finally, a number of organizations are encouraging end users to write their own programs. Special languages and tools make this more appealing than it would be using procedural languages such as BASIC or COBOL. Users can obtain reports and data they desire much more quickly if they have the facilities and support to do some of the work themselves.

Figure 5-1 shows how these various techniques can contribute to the development of a system. The life cycle is still a good model for the development process; these alternatives contribute to improving our execution of various steps in the cycle.

RESOURCES FOR NEW SYSTEMS

Originally, in many organizations, the computer department had to search for new computer applications. Now, for most mature computer installations, there is more demand for services than resources available to satisfy the demand. Typically, the budget for developing new computer-based systems is only one part of the total budget for the computer department.

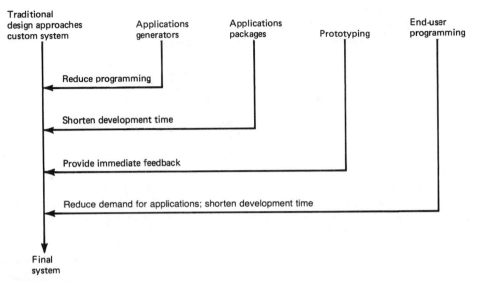

FIGURE 5-1
Improvements in development.

Demands and Resources

What are the demands on the computer department? A typical department has a number of responsibilities:

1 One of the first concerns is operating existing systems; that is, the information systems developed in the past must be executed on a routine basis.

2 Maintenance also requires resources. Where many existing systems are in operation, it is necessary to make repairs and to maintain computer programs. In some installations, 50 percent of the programming effort is devoted to maintenance.

3 Enhancements to existing systems are frequently requested by users; if a system is used, individuals will make suggestions for improvements. These modifications entail programming changes and sometimes even require new computer equipment.

4 The development of a new information system requires a major commitment of resources.

Many individuals outside the computer department see only the operation of existing systems and the development of new ones. However, maintenance and enhancements require considerable effort.

What are the resources available to the computer department? There are two major categories of resources: people and machines. Machine capabilities are necessary to develop and operate computer-based information systems. Different types of information systems require different equipment; for example, an on-line

SYSTEMS PROBLEM 5-1

The president of Farway Manufacturing Company was pondering the firm's recent disastrous attempt to develop a computer-based system for factory-floor data collection. The company wished to improve scheduling and control over work-in-process inventories. A consultant was hired who recommended the development of a computer-based production control system.

The recommendations of the consultant were accepted, and he was hired to design the system. It turned out that the consultant had designed a similar system for another manufacturing company and proposed to transfer it to Farway. This approach seemed very economical, so the president quickly agreed.

The consultant set about his task with zeal; within 6 months the necessary programming changes had been made, and the system was ready to begin operation. Over one weekend, terminals were installed in all departments and on Monday morning, workers were supposed to begin using the new system to report production. The workers are paid on piece rate and are unionized.

For reasons not completely understood by the president, the system failed completely. No one provided input, and the few data collected were all erroneous. What happened? Why did the systems development effort fail so miserably?

---

system necessitates equipment for communications and terminals. A large data-base application makes demands for data storage devices.

On the human side, many of the resources of the computer department are not interchangeable among jobs. We can identify a number of positions in this department.

1 Operators are trained to operate the computer and its peripheral equipment.

2 Clerical personnel manually process input and output; they may separate copies of reports and prepare output for distribution and may also check input and output for accuracy.

3 Input specialists transcribe data to machine-readable form by, for example, keying information onto a magnetic tape or disk or into a CRT.

4 Maintenance programmers repair errors in the programs that direct the computer. These individuals may also be responsible for enhancements to existing systems.

5 Systems analysts work with users to define specifications for a new system.

6 Applications programmers convert system specifications into the computer programs necessary to process data and produce the desired output.

7 Systems programmers are found in large installations; they work with the control software of the computer.

8 Managers of various functions such as operations and systems design are also employed by a computer department, if it is large enough.

We shall discuss the computer department further in Chapter 22.

A Resource Allocation Problem

The basic allocation problem is to match demands for services against limited resources; see Table 5-2. How much discretion do we have in this process? Unless some applications are to be eliminated, the computer department has to maintain equipment and needs operators, clerical personnel, control, and maintenance programmers to operate existing systems. (Some installations also need a systems programmer for this purpose.) Discretionary resources can be used for enhancements and the development of new information systems. Systems analysts, applications programmers, and necessary managers, plus machine capacity, constitute the discretionary resources available to the department.

How easily can these resources be increased? Machine capacity can be enlarged, although usually it takes many months to obtain and install new computer equipment. New personnel can, of course, be added; however, there is a limit to how rapidly new employees can be integrated into the organization and become productive. Thus, in the short run, probably little can be done to increase the resources devoted to the development of new systems within an organization. However, added resources can be used to purchase applications packages and/or consulting services from outside the organization. In the long run, if users are dissatisfied with the amount of resources devoted to the development of new systems, an effort to increase the discretionary portion of the computer department budget will be required. The largest constraints on systems development remain the availability of qualified systems analysts and time from users to work on systems design.

THE PRACTICE OF SYSTEMS ANALYSIS AND DESIGN

Discussion of the stages involved in systems analysis and design cannot do justice to the actual process of design. The designer is faced with several crucial

TABLE 5-2
DEMANDS AND RESOURCES OF THE INFORMATION SERVICES
DEPARTMENT

Demands	Resources
Operating existing information systems	Equipment
Maintenance	Human
Enhancements	Operators
Development of new information systems	Clerical personnel
	Input specialists
	Maintenance programmers
	Systems analysts
	Applications programmers
	Systems programmers
	Managers

problems that must be solved; just following a series of stages will unfortunately not result in success. Systems analysis and design is a creative activity, and creativity cannot be achieved by following a "cookbook" procedure.

We have discussed the problem of placing boundaries on a system and the need to define the system itself. This definition of a system and its boundaries is an extremely difficult task. We are trying to place an artificial conceptual structure on an inherently unstructured situation. The analyst must build an abstract model of some information processing procedure in such a way that it can be viewed as a system; in most cases no obvious system exists at present.

What the analyst is constructing is artificial; it is a representation of some processing procedures and decision-making processes. There are many possible models for the analyst to consider. By employing an iterative process of successive refinements to the model of a system, the analyst should be able to achieve consensus on a reasonable conceptualization of the system from other analysts and users of the system. There is no one correct model or one system, and that is why we usually employ a design team so that many views and diverse experiences can be brought to bear on the analysis and design task.

In the process of developing a model of the existing system and especially in the design of a new system, the analyst is faced with a continuing series of trade-offs that have to be considered. The analyst must delineate different alternatives for all parts of a system, establish the relevant criteria for choosing among the alternatives, and work with the user to make the final choice.

What are typical trade-offs? A trade-off exists when there is more than one way to accomplish some objective and one way is not clearly the dominant choice. An example might be the choice between keying information directly into a system from a terminal or the use of a written form read by a scanner. Here the trade-off might be between convenience and cost.

There are many criteria to be considered in choosing among alternatives. One of the most frequent considerations is cost versus performance. Usually, but not always, higher levels of performance are more costly. Other criteria include ease of use, interface of the system with the user, speed, reliability, etc. Each step in the design process raises a new set of trade-offs, even for the programmer who also makes countless design decisions at the coding stage.

One important skill of the analyst is the ability to determine which design alternatives exist, then to delineate the alternatives, eliminate some, develop relevant evaluation criteria, and work with the user to choose the most satisfactory alternative.

Because of these numerous trade-offs, often we find design is an iterative process. Decisions made at a later stage in design may force revisions of plans made earlier. A decision may have been made early in the design process not to include the purchasing function in an inventory control system. However, as analysis and design proceeds, it becomes increasingly apparent that purchasing is a major problem area and that a new system should contribute to alleviating the problems in this department. Once the decision is made to extend the boundaries of the system, prior work will have to be examined and probably much of it will be changed. The adoption of a new function for an on-line system may be the final element that makes the communications network unable to cope with the processing load. This new function then necessitates redesign of the communications network.

At times design will seem discouraging because new revelations and demands may push the designer back to what seems like ground zero. However, the design of a system can only proceed in this way. We again stress that design is creative; it is almost impossible to create a finished system with the first plan. We must expect to go through what seem like endless versions before the system we are finally going to install is constructed. Even after installation we must expect changes as users finally see in reality what has been rather abstract until the system is operational.

CONVENTIONAL SYSTEMS ANALYSIS AND DESIGN

Most current thinking in systems analysis and design views the design process as best being conducted in a top-down fashion. We begin at a high level of abstraction; for example, the first conceptualization of the system may be as general and broad as saying that we are dealing with inventory control. At each subsequent stage more and more details are developed. The lowest level of detail is the computer program and manual procedure level.

Top-down design prevents too early a concentration on details, which become overwhelming in a complex system. This approach helps develop an understanding of each successive level of detail. We focus first on the general problem of inventory control at a high level. Then we can break this overall model into a series of more refined subsystems such as the ones that present demands on the inventory, those that provide inputs, and a process that manages the inventory itself. Each of these components is then refined in successive stages to a greater and greater level of detail.

At each more detailed stage, however, a higher level at less detail provides order and logic to the entire system. A top-down approach greatly facilitates accomplishing tasks in an unstructured environment. Eventually, of course, we must reach a very detailed stage. Top-down design helps us to do that by providing an overall conceptual model of the system to guide us at each succeeding level of greater detail.

Goals

There are several major goals in a systems design study, and these are summarized in Table 5-3. First, we want to understand the problems that led to the systems analysis and design study, along with the present solutions to these problems. Here we familiarize ourselves with current processing procedures: Why is it desirable to consider improving them? How are the procedures accomplished now, and why is there dissatisfaction with them?

Next, it is necessary to see if we can improve present processing procedures.

TABLE 5-3
GOALS OF SYSTEMS DESIGN EFFORT

1 Understand the problem and the present solution
2 Suggest improvements to present procedures
3 Assess the feasibility of using a computer system
4 Design the best possible system within the limits of
   cost and technology
5 Program and test the new system
6 Implement the system

This is somewhat of a delicate problem; we must avoid falling into the trap of suggesting solutions that are too easy. Instead, we should spend time thinking about present methods before suggesting ways to alter them. At this stage the major question should be, is a computer system needed? If not, can changes be made to existing procedures to eliminate problems without undertaking the extensive development effort required to process information on a computer? If necessary, we assess the feasibility of using a computer system for processing the information. What are the costs of different alternative systems and what kind of benefits would we expect? Should a systems design effort be undertaken, and if so, at what level of effort?

If the answer is to develop the system, we have to undertake the actual design. Our goal at first is to develop the best possible system given limitations on cost, personnel, and technology. Then we have to program and test the new system. Our objective is to accomplish this task in the minimum effort consistent with high quality. Finally, the last goal of the systems analysis and design activity is to install the system successfully; that is, to produce a system that is used and makes a positive contribution to the organization.

Output of Systems Design Study

The various stages in Table 5-1 lead directly to the output from a systems design study shown in Table 5-4. (Of course, all these outputs are produced only if the systems design study is carried to completion, that is, if it passes the feasibility stage and is implemented.)

The preliminary investigation should result in an informal report on present processing procedures: this report may take the form of a short memorandum describing the analyst's understanding of a problem and the objectives for improvement. The survey will result in a more formal report. (We shall discuss the information to be included in this survey in a subsequent chapter.) The feasibility study has more refined data than the survey but covers most of the same topics. The feasibility study also sketches computerized systems that accomplish various subsets of the goals of a new system.

Detailed design specifications must be prepared if the system is to be developed. We have to specify file contents, linkages, program details, input-output forms, manual procedures, etc. Also, we must prepare training forms and manuals for users.

SYSTEMS PROBLEM 5-2

Mary Archibald is a systems analyst with the *Weekly News,* a national news magazine. She has been working as the lead computer department staff member on a design team to develop a comprehensive subscription, billing, and accounts receivable system. Currently, parts of this system—some of which are computer-based and some of which are manual—exist. The computer components of the system are executed on the computer at the *News,* and one part of the system runs on a local service bureau.

Mary has spent a great deal of time with Harry Gold, the controller of the *News.* His input has been influential in shaping the system, and Harry has helped pull together a design team to work on the project. However, Mary is becoming increasingly uncomfortable with the design team; she feels that morale is quite low. Recently several members of the team have complained about how long it seems to take to design a system and how they seem to cover the same ground over and over again. They think a professional computer department staff should be able to complete the system without requiring so much help from them.

Mary does not feel that the amount of time required of users has been inordinate; she has discussed her approach with the manager of the computer department several times, and he has encouraged her to continue. However, Mary wonders how to deal with the design team. The system has been sketched in broad terms, and the boundaries are established. However, a great deal of additional work is needed to complete the specifications, particularly since the new system will feature on-line input and updating, and the computer-based part of the old system was all in batch.

What advice can you offer Mary for dealing with this design team?

When the programs themselves are completed, they must be documented to help in finding errors and making subsequent program changes. Systems docu-

TABLE 5-4
OUTPUT OF THE SYSTEMS DESIGN EFFORT

Output	Inception	Design	Implementation	Operation
		Used during		
1 Report on present procedures	X	X		
2 Preliminary survey	X	X		
3 Feasibility study		X		
4 Detailed design specifications		X	X	X
Input-output forms		X	X	X
Programs		X	X	X
Files		X	X	X
Manual procedures		X	X	X
5 Training documentation		X	X	X
6 Program documentation		X	X	X
7 System documentation		X	X	X
8 User documentation		X	X	X

mentation serves this purpose, whereas user documentation helps the user answer questions about the system. All these outputs will be discussed in later chapters in much greater detail.

Problems with the Checklist

Some designers attempt to treat the stages in Table 5-1 and the output in Table 5-4 as a checklist. The task of systems analysis and design then becomes one of checking off each stage and accomplishment. Unfortunately, there are a number of serious problems with a checklist approach, even though these stages in Table 5-1 are widely recommended. First, the stages tend to focus attention on a particular type of application, and second, they mislead analysts as to their role in the systems design process.

The first problem with the checklist is the orientation it suggests toward transactions systems and paperwork automation. Notice the complete lack of mention of decisions in the checklist. This approach grew historically from tabulating operations conducted on punched cards, and the list was probably developed long before electronic computers. These card systems were directed at transactions processing, and hence the systems design stages reflect this bias. Certainly, there are good reasons to develop this type of system; transactions-processing information systems can save large amounts of money. However, if we have faith in the potential of information systems to improve managerial decision making, then we should also focus on decisions as well as document flows in designing systems.

The second problem with the checklist is even more serious. These stages suggest that the systems analysis and design activity must be carried out by an analyst; the analyst alone has the tools and techniques for designing a system. Any mention of the user or the relationship between users and analysts is conspicuously absent from these design steps. In Chapter 4 we discussed some of the organizational problems with systems and the fact that systems can affect power relationships and create conflict in the organization. We need to develop an entirely different role for the analyst to overcome these problems. This role will be the topic of Chapter 6.

Before exploring this new role of the systems analyst, we shall discuss different processing alternatives in systems design and introduce the example that will be used to illustrate systems design points in the rest of the chapters of this part of the text.

PROCESSING ALTERNATIVES

A number of alternatives is available in designing systems because of the wide range of computer and peripheral equipment available. For most applications, existing equipment offers sufficient flexibility to develop a wide variety of systems. Clearly, some applications will not be cost-effective, but within broad cost constraints we can design very flexible and user-oriented information systems.

In Chapter 3 we described some of the different types of computer systems that are available, including simple batch, inquiry, inquiry and post, on-line, and command and control. These alternatives are for a single computer system, though many organizations have multiple computers, each of a different type. For example, some firms have a batch processing machine and a separate timesharing computer. In addition, most modern computers are designed to handle batch processing and at the same time support multiple on-line applications. In addition, there has been explosive growth in the installation of microcomputers.

Toward On-line Processing

For all the systems that are on-line (anything beyond a simple batch processing system), there are several alternatives for the underlying computer system. We can have a dedicated system, that is, an operating system and applications program designed only for that application. A good example of this type of system is one used to make reservations for airlines, rental cars, or hotels. Many computers today also support mixed on-line and batch processing. For some applications that are on-line but do not have such severe processing requirements, we can use a commercial timesharing service bureau or even an in-house timesharing system. One automobile manufacturer uses a commercial timesharing system to process certain information for its dealers. In using this type of system, we take advantage of an operating system that already supports terminals and timesharing, and only program the application. The advisability of using this type of processing depends on costs and security considerations.

The availability of low-cost hardware and the explosion in the availability of very powerful processors and mini- and microcomputers, have provided a major impetus to on-line systems. Communications costs have been dropping as this industry becomes more competitive and technological advances occur.

Originally on-line systems were justified because of the need to coordinate actions at different geographic locations and to have fast response. These applications began with reservations systems and spread rapidly to applications such as on-line credit verification. Today costs have been reduced to the point that on-line systems can often be justified simply because they provide accurate input, and because error messages can be generated and the input corrected at once. On-line systems are also installed because in most instances the user interface with the system is much more pleasant than with batch processing applications.

Even if files are not updated on-line, the tedium and clumsiness of batch input can be eliminated if the data are captured and edited on-line and posted for later updating of master files. We expect the quality of input data to be significantly better with on-line input than with a batch system. Clearly a few applications will probably remain batch because of their inherent nature, such as payroll, but an analyst in today's information processing environment should seriously consider on-line features for almost every system under consideration.

Patterns of Processing

The rapid advances in technology and the reduced cost of hardware discussed above have created a variety of possible patterns for computing. In the early days of information systems, batch computers were installed in various parts of the organization to handle processing, often to process transactions in the accounting area. During the second generation of systems, which used transistorized circuits, the first-generation vacuum-tube machines were replaced, but the pattern of processing remained about the same.

Improvements in integrated circuits in the third generation of computers encouraged centralized computing sites. The increase in processing power exceeded the additional cost; that is, a large centralized computer operation exhibited significant economies of scale. During this time we saw the expansion of on-line systems to allow multiple access to a common data base; these systems usually operated from a single, centralized site.

Our ability to fabricate logic cheaply through Large Scale Integration (LSI) has dramatically reduced the cost of central processing units and memory, making it economical to install local or distributed intelligence. At first this trend toward distributed processing began by placing logic in terminals; one could edit some data locally and collect it in a buffer to be sent to the main computer, thus reducing the processing load on the central processor.

Patterns Now a large number of alternatives is available for providing computer services. Table 5-5 presents a continuum of possibilities, though there are many variations on these alternatives.

We have already discussed the totally centralized pattern where all processing is accomplished at a centralized site; there are no external input-output devices or terminals. This type of configuration represents one point on a continuum and is rare in a large organization. We might find this type of processing in a small company where there is only a single computer dedicated to a few applications.

From a totally centralized system, we move to remote input-output to a central

TABLE 5-5
PATTERNS OF PROCESSING

Totally centralized
Batch centralized with remote input-output
Some local processing, batch centralized, some on-line applications, remote input-output
Sophisticated local processing, remote input-output, interactive capability
Totally decentralized

TABLE 5-6
CRITERIA FOR PROCESSING ALTERNATIVES

Physical location of data base
Location for updating and accessing the data base
Costs for equipment and communications
User reactions
Management considerations
   Control of applications
   Control of processing
   Communication
   Coordination

---

site. The input-output is done through remote batch or on-line terminals. The next step toward more decentralized and distributed processing is to add a local processing capability but to maintain a centralized site running batch applications. There may also be a few on-line applications and remote terminals for on-line interaction. There are communications between local sites and the central site.

In a fully distributed system we expect to find extensive local processing, remote input-output, and an interactive capability. Retail point-of-sale systems are a good example of this type. Local store processors accept data from a centralized host computer, disconnect themselves, and function locally all day to register the purchase of merchandise and to control store inventory. Later the local computer is reconnected to the host to send summary data on the day's activity at the local store.

Finally, one can have a totally decentralized system; all processing is local, and there is no data communications directly among systems. (Some individuals refer to this type as one type of distributed processing, since there is no more central site; technically, distributed processing describes a situation in which there are communications among several computer systems.) Total decentralization might be found in various subsidiaries of a large organization.

Evaluating Alternatives One problem with this wide range of options is deciding on what pattern is best for a given situation. Table 5-6 suggests some design criteria for this decision. Is there a compelling reason for the data base for the application to reside in one location? If all data are generated in one location, then it may make some sense to locate the files and processing there.

Where is the data base to be updated? We may find that the transactions to update the files originate in a few highly clustered locations. If others need limited access to these data, then consider distributing the data base and processing to each of these clusters.

One motivation for distributed processing is cost; large computers have overhead and are complex. Some experts argue that because of low-cost

SYSTEMS PROBLEM 5-3

The National Insurance Company offers a full line of personal insurance, including auto, home, liability, and life coverage. The firm has been in existence for over 100 years and is licensed in all 50 states in the United States. Since the insurance business is information processing, National has long been a user of computers. During recent cost-cutting drives, however, the computer area had been severely impacted. Now officials of the firm recognize that this cost cutting has not been wise and that the capability of the firm to process information has not kept pace with the demands of the business.

National has greatly expanded the size of its systems staff, hired outside consultants, and increased the size of its computer budget. The company has also announced its intentions to employees to begin the development of major new systems. The statement from the chairman of the board said in part: ". . . to continue to grow and service our customers in the decade ahead, National must increase its ability to process information successfully. In the future, success in this industry will depend not only on innovative insurance products, but also on the ability to service customers by processing information quickly, inexpensively, and with high levels of quality."

A consulting firm has been given the responsibility of developing a 10-year processing strategy for National. The firm first visited a sample of National's agents and brokers throughout the United States and learned about their information processing needs. It appears to the consultants that a tremendous amount of data about policies needs to be available locally while only summaries of that information must be transmitted to headquarters. What type of processing pattern does this need suggest? What are the pros and cons of different approaches to developing a computer plan for National? What does centralization and decentralization of computer hardware imply about the availability of data and information?

hardware, we can dedicate small, inexpensive computers to each application. However, if the distributed computers must communicate, there are communications costs to consider. Often these costs are less than the communications cost of a central on-line system, since access to local data for a distributed system requires less data transmission. Also, we must be sure that the computers are capable of exchanging data easily with each other.

Another major reason for distributed processing has been responsiveness to users. Many users feel that large, centralized systems are unresponsive to their needs, especially when located some distance away. Distributed computers mean that the user may have more control and influence over computer decisions, though we will want to explore this belief more in Chapter 21. Distributed processing also is reliable and provides backup, since multiple computers are available.

There are management considerations in making decisions to distribute or decentralize computing. If the applications/development effort is not coordinated, each location may develop new applications that are almost identical and incur high costs and duplication of effort. The same logic applies to control of processing; there are strong arguments for some overall coordination of machine acquisition and operations policies.

In addition to considering machines, the computer department staff and users must also communicate. How do processing patterns affect human communications? How do they impact management control and coordination? Unfortunately, no one formula gives the best pattern of processing for an organization. There will probably be a mixture of different patterns for most large organizations, and each application will have to be evaluated to determine what type of processing is best.

We anticipate in the future that organizations will be moving to more networks of computers. Each user is likely to have a powerful work station that consists of a CRT, personal computer, local disk storage, and possibly a printer. The user will connect to the network with the work station and will obtain data from one of the many computers on the network. The user may also run specialized programs on other computers and have the results returned to the work station. Finally, there will be extensive local processing of data on the work station.

Input-Output Alternatives

Input The internal processing speeds of modern computers are extremely fast, in the range of 100 or less nanoseconds (100×10^{-9} seconds). Unfortunately, input-output is a major bottleneck because it cannot take place at anywhere near these speeds. Input-output devices are often mechanical and some rely on human processing to enter the data.

For computer input there are a number of alternatives; trends in recent years

TABLE 5-7
SOME INPUT/OUTPUT ALTERNATIVES

Input	Output
Terminals	Printers
Punched cards	Line printer
Key to magnetic medium	Nonimpact printer
Mark sensing	Remote printer
MICR	Microfilm
OCR	Terminals
	Hard copy
	Impact
	Nonimpact
	Alphanumeric CRT
	Graphic CRT

have been to move data collection closer to the source of data and to avoid as much transcription as possible to reduce errors and to eliminate delays in processing (see Table 5-7).

The classic form of computer input is a punched card. Forms containing data are keypunched and verified (a process in which a separate operator rekeys the information on a similar machine that indicates an error if the new keystroke does not match the punches in the card). There are also many key-to-magnetic tape or key-to-disk replacement units. For the most part, organizations are moving away from the use of punched cards.

There are also some small, portable key-to-tape or key-to-cassette units that can be held in one hand. Using one of these devices, for example, an inventory clerk could enter inventory data while taking stock. It is possible to transmit data collected on one of these devices over the phone to a central computer system. Clearly, such an approach is much faster than sending a paper form to be keypunched; also, the original source provides the data, which usually reduces the opportunities for transcription and transmittal errors.

Mark sensing also allows the direct input of data. Mark sensing is similar to machine-scored tests given in school in that the user has to mark a designated place on the form. Generally, the forms become quite large and unwieldy if there are a large number of alternatives, and the trend seems to be to replace mark sensing with OCR applications.

OCR (optical character recognition) devices read source documents at a very high speed. Because the source usually is not controlled, there is a possibility of a high reject rate. Most OCR applications use hand-printed numbers and a few special characters such as "X." OCR machines are available to read larger numbers of characters and more styles of type, although these machines tend to be more expensive. It is even possible to read typewritten information with a scanner if the typewriter has been given special care. There are a number of diverse applications of OCR input; one dairy uses it for records kept by milk deliverers, and an apparel manufacturer employs OCR for order entry.

Finally, the last input alternative is the use of on-line terminals; the terminal field has been one of the most rapidly developing in the computer industry in the past several years, and a variety of terminals are for sale or lease. There are many examples of on-line systems using terminals; most major airlines and many hotel and rent-a-car firms use on-line reservations systems. Input using a terminal is generally the preferred choice where possible.

Output   A wide variety of output alternatives are available. The most conventional form for output is the impact line printer (a type slug comes in physical contact with the paper like a typewriter). The major advantage of the line printer is the fact that it can make multiple copies of the same report using carbon paper. There are also a number of nonimpact printers that operate at much higher speeds, some at 8000 to 10,000 lines per minute, compared with the 1500 to

2000 lines per minute for an impact printer. These nonimpact printers often use heat-sensitive paper or some other medium and a matrix of styluses to create a mark. A nonimpact printer can also plot more realistic diagrams because of the much finer resolution provided by its matrix printing unit. However, usually these systems require special paper, and to get multiple copies it is necessary to reprint the report or photocopy it. There are also page printers based on photocopy technology. These devices take a computer tape off-line as input and produce entire pages of output at high speed.

The newest printers use lasers and a process similar to that of a photocopier to print very rapidly. These devices allow for variable type fonts and sizes. The quality is so excellent that the output would, in many instances, be suitable for publication as a book! Laser printing does not produce multiple copies but is extremely fast and attractive to read.

Microfilm is an output medium that has been used increasingly for data that have to be kept for historical purposes. Computer output to microfilm equipment is expensive, but some service bureaus take a computer output tape and produce the microfilm so that the average installation does not need to invest in computer-output-to-microfilm equipment. Examples have been given that show extensive savings in operating expenses using microfilm, particularly where reports have to be distributed to a number of locations. One state's unemployment services use microfilm output that is updated daily for job openings. The major disadvantage with microfilm is that a special device is needed to read it and special attachments must be used to photocopy one frame of the film. However, output occurs at much higher speeds than printing; output rates in the hundred thousand characters per second range are possible, and some computer-output-to-microfilm devices actually develop the film as it comes from the film-producing unit.

A large number of output terminals can be used in a computer system. A number of these feature hard copies through either an impact or a nonimpact printer. Nonimpact printers can run at higher speeds and are generally much quieter than impact terminals. Cathode-ray tube (CRT) devices are silent, but where hard copy is needed a special device is required to make the copy. CRTs print at high speeds, in the range of hundreds of characters per second. Alphanumeric CRTs have only the capability to print alphabetic characters and are used as a replacement for a printing terminal. On the other hand, a graphics CRT actually plots lines and figures on the screen. Several major companies use this type of display for data analysis; for example, in market research.

SUMMARY

We have presented a great deal of material in this overview of systems analysis and design. The following table is a summary of the stages of the systems life cycle and the tasks of the systems analyst during each stage:

Stage	Task
Inception	1. Respond to idea for a system
	2. Sketch outline of system, output, input, and files
Feasibility study	3. Describe existing methods of processing information (if they exist), output, input, file processing
	4. Delineate software and hardware alternatives
	5. Determine feasibility
	6. Choose an alternative software and hardware combination
Systems analysis	7. Complete analysis of existing system and document it. Collect data on transactions and file volumes
Requirements analysis	8. Repeated meetings with users to determine their needs and to review design to date
Design	9. Develop design from user requirements
	10. Choose strategy: packages, generators, nonprocedural languages, prototyping, end-user development or some combination
Specifications	11. Develop specifications as far as needed for chosen design strategy
Programming	12. Develop program specifications, modules, schedule, and work plan
Testing	13. Conduct unit, combined module, and acceptance tests
Training	14. Plan and conduct
Conversion	15. Plan, collect data, convert
Operations	16. Routine maintenance and enhancements

In the rest of the book we shall discuss the steps, tools, and approaches to the tasks above in detail. The large number of tasks that must be done well for a system to succeed make systems analysis and design a complex activity. However, the development of systems is crucial to the organization, and it is worth an investment of time and effort to see that systems succeed.

AN ILLUSTRATIVE EXAMPLE

For many of the points discussed in this part of the text, it will be helpful to refer to an example. The rest of this chapter introduces this hypothetical case study.

Hardserve is a company that specializes in the wholesale distribution of merchandise to retail hardware stores. Hardserve buys goods from the manufacturer and stocks them in a warehouse. Retail hardware stores order merchandise from Hardserve, which ships it from inventory. If Hardserve does not have the goods requested by the retail store, the store will go elsewhere. Hardserve has usually been the first choice for retail stores trying to find an item. Because of its efficient operations it has been able to keep prices slightly lower than its competitors. Naturally, the demand for goods fluctuates drastically by season. For example, tree stands are a big item just before Christmas, but there is very little demand for them in July. By the same token, lawn mowers move very rapidly during the spring, but only a few Western stores need them in stock all year around.

Until recently, Hardserve was a family-owned business that had been growing at the rate of about 10 percent per year compounded; sales are currently running at $150 million a year and about 60,000 different types of items are in inventory. The family recently sold the firm to a company that controls a small group of

FIGURE 5-2
Organization chart for Hardserve.

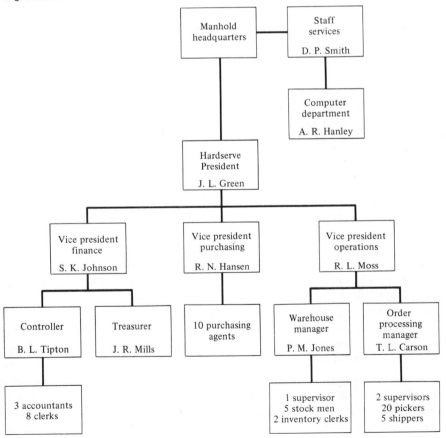

manufacturing companies. This firm, named Manhold, maintains a centralized computer department staff to serve its various divisions.

The sale of Hardserve occurred under happy conditions; the family wanted to retire. They felt the company had grown too fast and needed new management methods. Manhold retained all the existing employees and brought in several new managers to replace the family members who retired. The basic organization was left virtually unchanged. An up-to-date organization chart is shown in Figure 5-2.

Manhold headquarters views its primary duties as making gross resource allocations and providing staff services; divisions are left primarily up to their own devices as long as operations proceed according to plan. Within Manhold, the head of staff services, Dan Smith, is a graduate of a business school and has a background in operations research and management science; he has also been involved in some computer work. The computer department at Manhold is headed by Art Hanley, who has been in computer and systems work for the past 15 years; he has a B.S. in mathematics.

The president of Hardserve is Jim Green, who had been with a competitor before being offered his current position when Manhold bought Hardserve. Jim has 25 years of experience in the hardware business and has just completed a management training course for 2 months at a major university.

The vice president of finance for Hardserve is Steve Johnson, who has been with the company for 5 years; before that time he worked for an apparel manufacturer. The controller is Ben Tipton, a CPA who was hired from an accounting firm 7 years ago. The treasurer, Jane R. Mills, has worked her way up through the company and has been at Hardserve 25 years.

The vice president of purchasing, Dick Hansen, had been a purchasing agent for 16 years. A staff of buyers reports to him; their function is to keep the desired merchandise in stock. In this organization, the purchasing department also functions as the sales department.

The vice president of operations, Bob Moss, began with the company 30 years ago and has worked his way up to this position from a stock picker in the warehouse. (Employees in the warehouse who remove stock to fill orders are called "pickers.") Paul Jones supervises the warehouse and keeps track of inventory.

Terry Carson was hired 7 years ago to supervise order processing. His responsibility is to be sure that incoming orders are filled and shipped on schedule. He gives instructions to the scheduling crew that breaks the orders down into the various areas of the warehouse where the items are found. The individual items are scheduled for picking on the ship date. Finally, Terry has to coordinate these activities so that all items ordered by the customers are sent together in one shipment. He has a B.S. degree in physics and has recently attended a computer manufacturer's 1-week course for executives.

All the top management of Hardserve felt that action was needed to help improve operations; the following areas seemed to create special problems: sales forecasting, inventory control, order processing, and scheduling. Jim Green contacted Dan Smith and requested that an analyst look into some of these problems. Art Hanley, interested in starting off relations well with this new subsidiary, assigned his senior analyst, Tom Roberts, to work with Hardserve. In subsequent chapters we shall observe the results of the efforts of Manhold and Hardserve to improve information processing activities in the subsidiary.

KEY WORDS

Analog	Iterative
Batch system	Impact printer
Baud	Inquiry system
Centralized	Maintenance
Command and control system	Mark sensing
Control	Microfilm
CRT	Modern
Decentralized	Modulation
Dedicated system	Network
Digital	Nonimpact printer
Distributed	OCR
Documentation	On-line updating
Error checks	Processing alternatives
Feasibility study	Remote batch terminal
Hard copy	Survey
Ideal system	Trade-offs

RECOMMENDED READINGS

Burch, J. G. , F. R. Strater, and G. Grudnitski: *Information Systems Theory and Practice,* 3d ed. Wiley, New York, 1983. (A useful text on design and analysis.)

Jackson, M.: *System Development,* Prentice-Hall, Englewood Cliffs, N.J., 1983. (Jackson proposes a special approach he has developed for design.)

Martin, J.: *Application Development Without Programmers,* Prentice-Hall, Englewood Cliffs, N.J., 1982. (An approach that runs counter to tradition.)

Sprague, R., and E. Carlson: *Building Effective Design Support Systems,* Englewood Cliffs, N.J., Prentice-Hall, 1982. (A good book on building systems to help key decision makers.)

DISCUSSION QUESTIONS

1 What are the advantages of on-line data collection from a systems design standpoint?
2 How might an automobile manufacturer save money by using a timesharing system instead of developing a dedicated on-line system to provide information to its dealers? (*Hint:* Think about communications costs.)
3 Why is it more desirable for a user to request a system than for a computer department to suggest it?
4 Why are we moving away from punched cards as an input medium?
5 Describe the disadvantages of source data collection.

6 Is there any reason why we should not be enthusiastic about the development of higher-speed printers?

7 Who should review the results of a survey and feasibility study and make the decision to develop a new application?

8 Suppose, in gaining an understanding of a computer system, you as a systems designer observe a very clumsy procedure that could be modified easily without a computer. Describe the advantages and disadvantages of discussing your observations immediately with the users involved.

9 How would you handle the problem of rejecting a suggested system at the survey stage? What undesirable long-run implications could this rejection have?

10 What kind of a charging mechanism should be used for developing new systems; that is, should the user department or overhead be charged with development costs?

11 If systems analysts have the tools and training to conduct a systems design study, why should they not be in charge of the effort? What aspects of organizational behavior suggest an alternative approach?

12 Why has it been easier to concentrate on information flows and transactions-processing systems as opposed to decisions? What problems would you expect to encounter in adopting a decision-oriented design approach?

13 What criteria can be used to determine which of the many processing alternatives is best for a given computer system?

14 From the standpoint of developing a user-oriented system, what kind of input and output equipment would you select? Rank-order the various I/O alternatives according to their desirability from a user's standpoint (independent of cost). Next to this ordering, rank the same alternatives on their cost, from lowest to highest.

15 Most modern computers allow for a number of nearly simultaneous operations. It is possible to operate a batch processing system, an on-line application, and even a timesharing service on the same computer system. What are the pros and cons of such an installation?

16 Are there any commercial applications either in existence or proposed where the response time and reliability of an on-line command and control system would be necessary?

17 What do you see as the major advantages of optical character recognition input?

18 What reasons exist for an organization to use an outside service bureau for processing instead of an in-house facility?

19 Do the responsibilities of the systems designer stop at the input and output stages of a computer system? What other aspects of information processing are involved in a complete information system?

20 Is systems design more of an art or a science? What aspects of systems design influenced your answer?

21 What kind of computer system, based on the hierarchy of systems presented in this chapter, is the most flexible in meeting user needs when in operation? What type of system is the most flexible when it comes to making changes after implementation?

22 Why should on-line data entry provide more accurate input data? What steps must be undertaken to change input that is in error during batch processing?

23 What are some of the problems in on-line data entry? Can the analyst and user design edit checks that are as comprehensive as in batch data entry?

24 What kinds of edit checks are possible in on-line data entry that may not be available at least during an input edit for a batch system?

25 What are the major advantages of distributed processing?

26 In a distributed system, often one central computer is considered a superior in the hierarchy. Other computers communicate with this system but not directly with each other. In a ring configuration, all computers can communicate with certain other computers at their level. What are the advantages and disadvantages of each configuration?

27 Why have computer hardware costs been reduced so dramatically while communications costs have been decreasing much more slowly?

28 What advantages would a digital transmission network have over the more familiar voice-grade analog phone system? Why was the analog system developed to begin with?

29 What are the reasons for centralized processing?

30 What are the advantages of decentralized processing?

31 How would you evaluate competing alternatives for a communications network?

32 Does the type of computer system, for example, centralized, distributed, or decentralized, make any difference in where information can be provided for a user? Which is likely to be perceived as more responsive by users?

33 When computers were first installed by businesses in the 1950's and 1960's, most processing was decentralized because of the limited power of the computers. When the third generation of computers appeared in the early 1960's, the industry urged centralization of processing because of economies of scale; a computer that cost twice as much as another could do about four times the amount of processing. Thus, by centralizing one could accomplish the same processing at a lower cost on a few machines when compared to the alternative of many small computers. What is behind the trend to distributed computing?

34 Suppose that further advances in computers lead to supercomputers that are extremely inexpensive by today's standards. Do you think the trend to distributed processing would be reversed? If so, would it be as difficult a transition as the move from decentralized to centralized and then to distributed processing?

35 Place yourself in the position of a user interested in a new computer application. What would be your concerns about requesting a new system?

36 Some people have suggested that the task of systems analysis and design is one of the most creative in a modern organization. Do you agree or disagree with this observation? Why?

37 Why is systems analysis and design an iterative process? Compare and contrast this activity to other design tasks.

38 Many inexpensive computer terminals have small computer processors built in. What kind of applications can you think of for such a terminal?

39 As hardware becomes increasingly less expensive, it becomes easily affordable for the home. What home uses of computers can you envision?

40 Low-cost computers make it possible to have a personal computer in the office or at home. What are the advantages and disadvantages of personal computers in the office? What types of applications are good candidates for home computers? What types of applications probably should not be placed on a small personal computer?

CHAPTER 6

THE ROLE OF THE SYSTEMS ANALYST

If a systems design project is to succeed, the analyst must gain the cooperation and enthusiastic support of users. In this chapter we advocate a new and radical approach to systems design: we argue that the user should design the system with guidance from the systems designer (Lucas, 1974).

THE ROLE OF THE ANALYST

A Conventional View

In Chapter 5 we described the standard steps in systems analysis and design; this approach pictures analysts as skilled leaders interviewing users, collecting data, and returning to the computer department, where they and their associates create a new system. The systems designer plays a role similar to that of an architect or artist who receives a commission, talks with the client, and returns to a studio to create the desired product.

In recognition of the fact that this approach usually does not work in system analysis and design, numerous periodicals suggest that user participation is needed to ensure success. The writers in these journals suggest that the analyst spend more time with users and show them report formats, etc. However, in their viewpoint, the analyst is still clearly in charge. We label this "pseudopartici-pation"; users are consulted, but few changes are made in the system on the basis of their suggestions. The analyst and the computer department are still in charge of the project.

The Process of Development

Before we present our approach to the development of systems, it is useful to consider the process itself. In the last chapters we discussed the tasks involved in systems analysis and design, and we mentioned several times the relationship between the designer and the user.

What is the motivation for a system: Why is a new system desired? Whatever the specific reasons for a new system, in every instance there is some dissatisfaction with present information processing procedures or there would be no need for a new system. Either current or expected demands for information processing cannot be met, so that some new system is needed. Thus, we are trying to change existing information processing procedures and improve them in some way by designing a new system.

When we take a systems view, existing information processing procedures encompass not only forms and information flows, but also decisions, individuals, and the organization. A key point to remember is that *systems analysis and design is one type of organizational change effort. Since organizations are composed of people, a new system will almost always require individuals to change their behavior in some way.*

As we saw in Chapter 4, our failure to recognize the need for behavioral change in addition to procedural changes in systems analysis and design is the reason so many systems have failed. In addition to the mechanics of systems design, we also must consider the process of design—the way the relationship between the designer and the user develops.

There are many different approaches to effecting organizational change and to implementing new technology. One general model of organizational change has been applied several times to guide the implementation of information systems and has proved quite helpful (Kolb and Frohman, 1970). See Figure 6-1.

The focus of this model is the relationship between the change agent, in this case the systems analyst, and the client or user. The model recognizes that systems exist in the context of an organization. It focuses on two key ideas: the relationship between the designer and users and the nature of the implementation task itself. The stages in this model are not distinct; some stages will be encountered several times, as the feedback loops imply. The model deals with the design process and is parallel with the systems life-cycle stages.

The first stage of the Kolb-Frohman model is scouting, where there is really no

FIGURE 6-1
A process model.

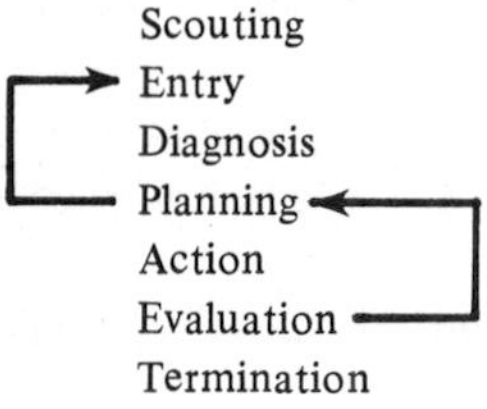

```
      Scouting
  ┌──► Entry
  │    Diagnosis
  └─── Planning ◄──────────┐
       Action              │
       Evaluation ─────────┘
       Termination
```

SYSTEMS PROBLEM 6-1

Jerry Levine has just joined the First National Bank as vice president of information services. During his first month on the job, he has been trying to assess the status of information processing at the bank. The first task he asked his staff to undertake was the preparation of an inventory of current computer applications and a report on the progress of all applications that were under development.

From this list, he determined the names of the major users of existing applications and the potential users of the new systems that were under development. Jerry then interviewed each supervisor in charge of areas making use of the computer. This ended up including almost all the functions in the bank.

The conclusion reached from this effort was disturbing. Jerry found numerous complaints about the quality of service and the demands that information processing placed on the user. There were reports of massive error listings, which users were asked to correct on each processing cycle. The bank had only one on-line system, and it had both response time and reliability problems.

Finally, the users working on the development of new applications did not seem enthusiastic about the systems. Most of them felt that the system had been mandated, and they did not know all its features. The users apparently understood the reports they received but had very little knowledge about the total system. When Jerry inquired about the process of design, he found that the systems analysts interviewed users and then returned with specifications for them to examine and approve. Most of the users reported spending no more than a few hours to a few days on the design of a new system.

Jerry is concerned about the status of systems design and operations at First National Bank. What would you recommend he do to improve the situation?

---

commitment on the part of the analyst or the user. Each party is trying to assess the motives of the other. A number of factors influence scouting, including the resources available, the motivation of the other party, and various organizational constraints. The analyst may not want to try developing a system if there are too few resources and too many constraints.

A formal entry point is defined from this initial relationship between the analyst and the user. What is the main point of contact with the user organization? Who will be the primary user?

Typically this primary sponsor is a manager at some level of the organization. The manager may be an actual user of the system, or various individuals working for the manager will constitute "users." Now the analyst and the user develop an informal, psychological contract that shows the expectations and goals for a new system. Agreement is needed on the scope and goals of a systems design effort. We should attempt to develop a broad definition of the project, the available resources, the method of approaching the design, the expected benefits, and the relationship between the designer and user.

The initial relationship between an analyst and the user is undoubtedly based on the expertise of the designer. It is important during the design process to change the expert power base to a relationship based on mutual trust and collaborative problem solving.

During diagnosis the user should help define the system in more detail. The feasibility study for a new system should be a part of the diagnosis stage. The designer is also thinking about his or her relationship with the client and assessing the client's readiness to develop a system. What is the nature of the information processing problem? What subunits of the organization are involved and who are the users? What resources are available to undertake the system? Is the organization ready for the changes that will be required to install a new system? Instead of a new information system, an organizational change program may be necessary.

Planning encompasses both the development of the technical details of a new information processing system and the relationship between the user and the designer. Schedules must be prepared and the final design team formed. Both the user and the designer plan for the impact of the system on potential users and try to prepare for successful installation of the final system. Here it is necessary to identify and list the changes envisioned in the new system.

The project is actually developed during the action stage. Users begin to work with new forms or terminals and start to change their behavior. Testing brings the user into contact with a physical system for the first time. During this stage, we often think of behavior as becoming unfrozen; that is, an individual is willing to change attitudes and behavior.

After unfreezing, the user moves to a new form of behavior. The designer must work carefully with users to make the change as easy as possible. Finally, success with the new behavior should lead to refreezing at the desired level of performance.

This view of change, unfreezing, change, and refreezing is attributed to Kurt Lewin, a well-known psychologist. He hypothesized that behavior could be represented by an equilibrium, a balance between forces inhibiting change and encouraging change. The designer, then, can work to decrease inhibiting forces or to increase forces favorable to change.

In the evaluation stage, the analyst and the user should examine the results of the project honestly. Were the initial goals achieved? Was the project completed on time and within budget? Try to evaluate the change process itself to determine if implementation was successful. This evaluation may lead to changes that can be suggested in the present system, and it certainly should contribute to our understanding of how to achieve greater success for the next system we design.

The final stage in the model is possibly the most important—termination. We must end successfully what has been a temporary relationship between the implementer and the user. We feel that the most successful termination of an information system project occurs when the user has developed psychological ownership of the system. To develop this transfer of ownership from the designer to the user, we must consciously consider termination and the relationship between the analyst and the user from the beginning of the systems life cycle.

A New View

Consistent with the problems of the conventional approach to design and the process model discussed earlier, we recommend a new approach to systems analysis and design, an approach that is intended to result in a successful relationship and a successful system. Instead of viewing the analyst as the designer of the system, we recommend strongly that *users should design their own systems*. Does this mean that the user actually does some of the tasks normally carried out by the analyst? The answer is definitely "yes." This approach raises two questions: First, why should users assume this role, and second, how can they do so? Our experience indicates that users are capable of responding to this approach and that successful results can be achieved. In the rest of the chapter we shall describe how this approach works and why we think it is advisable.

USER DESIGN

Motivation

There are a number of good reasons for participation and the design of the system by users. We do not mean to criticize suggestions of user involvement, only the way in which involvement had been attempted in the past. Real involvement requires time; users must understand the system, and their recommendations have to prevail. A number of beneficial results from participation have been summarized by Lucas (1974):

1 It is ego-enhancing and builds user self-esteem.
2 Participation can be challenging and intrinsically satisfying.
3 Participation usually results in more commitment to change.
4 As a part of the planning process, participation means the user becomes more knowledgeable about change and is better trained in the use of the system.
5 We can obtain a better solution to the problem because participants know more about the present system than computer department staff members.
6 Participation means the user has retained much of the control over operations.

Predicted Results

User participation eliminates many potential difficulties of an organizational nature in system design. Participation particularly helps to reduce problems created by power transfers and conflict. By having users in charge of the systems design activity, they retain control. All these factors combine to reduce the amount of power transferred from users to the computer department and the potential for conflict. Owing to participation the user is not as dependent on the computer department. Knowledge gained through participation and having an influence on the new system means the computer department copes with less uncertainty for the user, reducing the amount of power the user surrenders in developing a system. Mutual dependence is actually changed to cooperative effort to accomplish a common goal of developing and implementing a successful system. The user understands the system better by being in charge of it, and therefore the amount of uncertainty associated with the project is reduced.

Performance of some of the computer department tasks also reduces task differences between the computer department and users. By working together, both the computer department and users develop more understanding of each other's problems, helping to reduce ambiguities. Heavy participation by the user also leads to more understanding of computer department staff members' jobs, and vice versa, which reduces job differences. The user also becomes more familiar with computer jargon; close work together reduces communications obstacles between the computer department and users.

Is heavy user participation always necessary or advisable? Some systems have been successfully designed with limited or no user involvement. For systems in the transactions-processing and operational control areas, it is possible to design a system with less user input because the application is highly structured. However, user involvement can still help in creating acceptance of the changes produced by the new computer system.

As the trend in information systems design moves toward more managerial and strategic planning applications and less-structured systems in general, we predict that user participation will become more important. These less-structured applications need more input from users and also user enthusiasm to succeed, since the use of many of these systems is voluntary. Although a certain amount of user participation in the design of any system is important, the nature of the application influences the extent to which users need to be involved.

How can we have participation where conditions are not favorable; for example, for a single application to be used by many different individuals? Imagine a chain grocery store planning to install point-of-sale terminals for the check-out operation. If the chain has several hundred or thousand checkers, all of them cannot participate in the design of a system. In this situation, representatives of the checkers could participate in the design. These representatives would work with their co-workers at each store as the system is implemented. Any questions or problems during the design process could be explored with the checkers using the checkers' representatives as liaison agents.

There can, of course, be problems with full user participation to the extent advocated here. If an individual's ideas are rejected by the group, he or she may become alienated. It also may not be possible to satisfy expectations raised about future participation, for example, in the operation of the system. Participation is also time-consuming; usually users request a system because they are already under time pressure. We now have to ask for more of their time and the time of people working with them. Finally, we have discussed the dangers of pseudo-participation. Where the user does not have a real say and the motions of participation are evident, frustration will increase.

STEPS TO FOLLOW

In previous chapters we have described the stages in the systems life cycle, and we have just discussed the process of design. Conceptually, the stages in the life cycle and the process model cut across each other. We have associated certain life-cycle stages with certain stages in the process model, but the assignments are not exclusive or complete. The important thing to bear in mind is that we must simultaneously consider the process and the task of design as represented by life-cycle stages.

Operational Procedures

How might we implement user design in practice? User design is a process approach that is consistent with the Kolb-Frohman model; how does it fit into the life-cycle stages? Following we present one way to actually carry out user design in practice.

Inception   The designers meet with a large group of potential users to discuss the general boundaries of a system. What areas of information processing should be considered? What are current information and decision problems? Management sets the stage by emphasizing the need for the system and encouraging users to participate.

Preliminary Survey   A design team meets individually with users to develop an understanding of present information processing procedures. Some of the aids to understanding, such as flowcharts and decision tables discussed in the next chapter, are completed jointly, designers preparing some and users others. Management reviews the results and determines that work should continue.

Systems and Requirements Analysis   The designers solidify their understanding of the present system. Users are now asked to design the output they would like to have. At first, the user simply lists information that would be helpful, probably working with other users. Then, the information is shaped into different reports. Finally, the users work to develop a format for the output.

During this time designers and users meet in groups. At each meeting, some aspect of the system is discussed in detail in an attempt to solicit ideas from different individuals.

Feasibility   When the broad design of a new system is completed, the designers have to estimate costs, and the users help forecast benefits. Jointly, the user, management, and designers decide whether or not the system is feasible and if work should continue.

Requirements Analysis Again   Analysis activities never really stop. At each successive stage we perform more analysis work. Users are now working on almost final output specifications. The analyst begins to suggest what must be kept in computer files to support the type of output desired. Users respond to the file contents and describe the characteristics of the data, for example, its size in characters and its format.

SYSTEMS PROBLEM 6-2

Nancy Kennedy is the lead systems analyst on a project to develop an order-entry system for Designer Fabrics, Inc., a major supplier of materials to the garment industry. Nancy works for Systematics, a software and consulting firm that specializes in the development of turnkey systems. A turnkey system is one in which the consultant orders a computer, develops software for it, installs it for the client, and trains the client in how to use the system and apply it.

Nancy has found that her design effort works best when heavy user involvement is a part of the design process. Whereas this involvement may be time consuming, it seems to pay for itself in later training, as users are well versed in what the system can do. Also, she has found less need to modify programs if users are heavily involved in the development of system specifications.

Nancy has had several meetings with the executive vice president of Designer Fabrics to prepare for the systems design effort. She has requested that a design team of users be formed to work with her and two other staff members from Systematics. The response of the executive vice president has not been encouraging; he remarked, "What are we paying you for? Why should our people have to spend so much time working on the system? You are the experts; our staff certainly doesn't know anything about computers."

Could you help Nancy develop an approach to the vice president that will convince him of the importance of forming a design team and encouraging heavy user involvement in the design process?

At various stages, group meetings of the entire population of users and the designers convene to discuss the system and its features. At some point during this procedure, the designers present different processing alternatives to the group for consideration; for example, an on-line system, an inquiry and post system, etc. Jointly the group considers the options and makes choices. With output complete and file contents delineated, users can easily prepare input requirements.

Specifications   When the file contents have been completed and the reports are almost final, the designers turn the documentation to date into specifications that are detailed enough for programmers. To develop the processing logic, the users must indicate what transformations are necessary from the input and file contents to produce the desired output.

Programming   User involvement decreases during programming. The programmer and analyst will have to contact the user for certain detailed decisions, but this action will take little time compared to the original design effort.

Testing   The designer and the user work together to develop adequate test data. The user also has to review the test output to be certain that the system is operating properly.

Training   It is best if users actually conduct the training of other users. Full participation in design has a major payoff here because users will be quite knowledgeable about the system.

Conversion   The analyst plans detailed conversion requirements and prepares any special programs necessary. Users estimate the requirements of other users and try to predict the impact of the system on the organization and individuals in advance.

Operations   During operations, most design work ceases unless there are requests for major changes. Organizations expect routine change requests for new reports, minor enhancements, etc. for operational systems. A well-designed system will generate some requests for enhancements as users work with it. However, if our efforts at design have been successful, the system should not require major alterations in its first years of operations.

Trade-Offs

All during the design process, the analyst and user are making trade-offs among the various alternatives as we have discussed in the previous chapter. With user-centered design as advocated here, the analyst does not make all decisions unilaterally. The analyst can and should narrow the choices to a reasonable number, but the user and the analyst should jointly make final selection of design alternatives.

In one of the examples described later an incident occurs that illustrates this approach. In the design of a system to process accounts receivable on a minicomputer, a question arose as to how one could maintain an alphabetical sequence for a customer listing. Because the minicomputer had limited input-output capabilities and was slow in sorting, the analyst suggested that a numbering scheme be used to create the desired sequence.

By leaving a large number of digits between successive customers, the user could create a pseudoalphabetic listing. For example, if customer Adams were assigned number 1000, the next customer, Adamson, would be given 1010. If a new customer named Adamsen were to be added to the file, the number 1005 would be given. Over time, exact alphabetic order would be quite close. Certainly this process would be easier for the programmer and more efficient for the computer.

The user was presented with the trade-offs in nontechnical terms. The analyst explained the reasons for the programming choice, and the user was asked to think about how work could be done with the numbering scheme as opposed to the alternative of sorting the customer file alphabetically. The user indicated that a large number of new customers were added to the accounts receivable system each selling season. In addition, a large amount of work was involved in locating customers quickly on a printed report instead of one of the CRT terminals.

In this case, since alphabetic sorts are the most time-consuming, the trade-offs were between machine time and efficiency and programming ease versus user convenience. It was clear, when the analyst examined the cogent reasons of the user and empathized with her, that the trade-offs should be decided in favor of sorting the customers alphabetically as the user requested.

Although this detail is small, it could be an important one for the acceptance of the system. In the conventional approach, the analyst or programmer might have made the opposite decision unilaterally, and the results could have been disasterous. A large number of users would be inconvenienced; for them, the use of the system might constitute 40 to 60 percent of their daily activities. The out-of-sequence customer list would affect them every day in their jobs and would become a major irritant.

This one decision at a fairly late stage in the design process illustrates the kind of trade-offs that must be made continually during design. Our philosophy of user-centered design means that the analyst eliminates grossly inappropriate alternatives and presents the user with feasible choices to consider. Together the user and the analyst determine what the important evaluation criteria are. In our example, criteria were user convenience versus machine time and programming ease. The user makes the final choice given the pros and cons of the decision alternatives. It is important to emphasize that this trade-off activity is the essence of systems analysis and design; hundreds and even thousands of such trade-offs will be made during each design project.

Some Examples

Two examples illustrate further how we might have users design information systems. The first example is a labor union of farm workers. The union had a mission to improve the working conditions and lives of its members, many of whom were members of minority groups. A group of college faculty members and students became involved in designing a system for this union. The group did not achieve as full participation as desired because of heavy union-organizing activities. However, the design team did try to consult with union members from the beginning and planned carefully how to terminate the relationship with the union. Their goal was to ensure that the all-volunteer staff members of the union could develop and implement a system. The design group administered prelimi-nary attitudinal questionnaires and fed the results back to union members. These questionnaires indicated the degree to which different areas in the union were receptive to a computer system than were the clerical users who would have to work with it.

The design group first determined if computer processing was feasible for the union; was there any hope that it would be cost-effective? The answer to the question was affirmative, but the design group did not want to have the design belong to it. The union should clearly own the design. The designers asked to have a union member assigned full time to be in charge of computer activities. When this individual was appointed, the designers coordinated closely with this person and shared all documentation.

Even still, the design group performed most of the initial design activities. However, the design was presented to the union administrative staff in a review meeting. It was explained that the meeting would be a success only if 50 percent of the plan were changed. The system was presented, not "sold." Ideas were solicited from the audience and changes were made in front of the group

SYSTEMS PROBLEM 6-3

Shophere is a regional chain of discount department stores, primarily located in suburban shopping centers. The company has grown rapidly and owns all its stores. The firm currently has no single policy for data processing; each local store submits reports to headquarters monthly. Some of the larger stores have small computers, other stores use service bureaus, and some of the small stores prepare reports manually.

Shophere headquarters is concerned over the lack of timely reporting; there is a great deal of variance in the time at which reports are submitted. Despite efforts to create a common format for reports, the stores have not been able to comply with all the data requests from headquarters.

Shophere finally decides, after much deliberation, to start a corporate information services department; a manager and several staff members have been hired. Their first task was to visit a representative sample of the stores and study present information processing activities. The group then returned to headquarters and made a list of the individuals who should be involved in an attempt to develop some common systems for use in all the stores.

The problem confronting the design team is one of physical location of users and coordination of the design effort. Over 100 people should be involved in some way in the design process! The team would like your help in developing a strategy that will provide for adequate user participation in this decentralized, multiuser location environment while keeping the coordination problems of the design team to a minimum.

---

assembled. The group had a low level of formal education but was highly motivated and quickly understood the system. They suggested many changes that were incorporated in the plan. The team had designed a simple transactions and operational control system, and the leaders in the union saw the potential for added managerial reports. From this point on, the system was gradually turned over to the union, who began to develop a staff that was able to implement the system successfully.

The second example involves a small investment company buying and raising cattle as a tax shelter for its stockholders. A group of students in a course helped this small company develop a computer system as a part of a class project. The activities of the company were reasonably complex; there were production, accounting, and breeding considerations. The designers were separated from the organization by some 400 miles, and none of the employees had ever been exposed to computers before.

The students guided the users, who actually designed the system. The users described data for their areas of responsibility. The designers then combined these descriptions and eliminated duplicate data. A data file was constructed and different items in the file were assigned program-variable names.

The designers worked with the users and taught them flowcharting; users actually drew the logic flowcharts for their areas of responsibility. The president of the company established a prize. Each manager made up data for testing and tried to force other managers' processing logic to fail. The prize was given to the user whose own logic worked and who found errors in someone else's logic. The system was implemented gradually, and users have been very satisfied with the results.

The Design Team

The two examples described above are from highly diverse organizations; a relatively small number of users were involved in each case. However, the same principles can be applied in larger organizations. Our research activities have shown that users want to know more about information systems and computers and appear willing and eager to work on systems.[1]

To coordinate users and the computer department staff, we recommend the formation of a design team with a user as the head of the team. Placing a user in charge makes the user role apparent and ensures that time will be available from users. The user placed in charge of the design team should have normal job activities reduced. This structure for the design team demonstrates a strong commitment to users on the part of the computer department.

In cases where there are too many users to have them all involved, we can use liaison representatives. These people are users who interview other users and brief them on the system as it is developed. They are responsible for soliciting the participation of other users in the phases where it is meaningful.

Using this approach, the computer department systems designer guides the design team, teaching them the tools and techniques that are to be used in design and furnishing technical advice. The systems designer monitors the project, describes the stages, and helps to schedule them. However, the actual analysis and design work is done by users with the assistance of the analyst rather than vice versa as in conventional systems design approach.

Technology

Fortunately all the advances in computer technology of recent years contribute to the approach to user design advocated above. Very high level languages make it possible for the analyst to generate a portion of a system very quickly for user response. Parts of the final system can be programmed, and then completely redone if they do not satisfy the user. Through the use of some of these tools like applications generators, special development aids for formatting CRTs and producing reports, and through prototyping, we can use the technology to help the user take the kind of leadership role that is so important for the ultimate success of a system.

---

[1] We should point out that, of course, not all managers are eager to participate in systems analysis and design. For these individuals, we must demonstrate the importance of their participation to the ultimate success of the system.

THE HARDSERVE EXAMPLE

To illustrate our approach to systems design, let us join Tom Roberts (the systems analyst from Manhold) as he makes his first visit to Jim Green, president of Hardserve.

"Good morning, I'm Tom Roberts."

"How do do you do, I'm Jim Green, I'm pleased to meet you. We've been looking forward to your arrival—we hope the computer system can help solve some of our problems here. When do you begin?" said Green.

"Well," responded Roberts, "I certainly am encouraged by your optimism. However, I should point out some of the problems and the level of effort involved in doing a systems study. Have you ever been involved in one before?"

Green thought for a moment and replied, "Not very closely. At one place I worked, we had a tab card operation, but I didn't do much with it. Why is there so much effort involved? Don't you just look at our operations and then tell a computer what to do? What's that called—a program that you write?"

"Jim, if it were that easy you wouldn't need us at all," said Roberts.

Green laughed and said, "I guess that is a bit of an oversimplification. What's really involved in this?"

"Well," Roberts said, "our computer department has a bit of an unusual approach to systems design. We've learned the hard way that things don't go well when we design the system after interviewing a few users and then try to implement it. Many people are still threatened by computers and there is a lot of bad publicity."

"Yes," Green interrupted, "I've even been a little concerned myself. All these data banks; stories of people being bothered by police computers for a traffic violation that had been paid already."

"These are unfortunate examples of poor systems design," replied Roberts. "That's the thing we'd like to avoid; however, there is a higher price for doing the job right the first time."

"What do you mean, higher price?"

"The way we would like to approach a system takes a little longer than other designers and this runs up the initial investment cost. However, the real price of our activities is less tangible because much of it comes from the involvement of the people at Hardserve," explained Roberts.

"What kind of involvement do you need? You know we will cooperate and give you all the information you want," replied Green.

"We appreciate that," Roberts continued. "In fact, your personal interest will be a big help in getting that cooperation. However, with our approach we do more than just interview people. We would like to form a design team headed by someone at Hardserve. The design team would include several of your people, plus myself, and maybe another analyst."

"My employees are all pretty busy—why can't you design a system and take care of the interviews yourself?"

"Well," said Roberts, "there are two main reasons. First, we find that we can never understand the user's job as well as the user does; we really need that input in the design. Second, we find that when users have actually done the design themselves, they are much more receptive to implementation. This way the system isn't something forced on them. Also, because of their participation, the users are well trained before we even get the system working. It seems to create less resentment and fewer problems all around."

"That sounds fine," Green responded, "but there are a few problems you are overlooking. Number one, my employees have no experience in data processing except for maybe Terry Carson, who handles order processing. He went to some computer manufacturer's school for a short course. The second problem is, where do all these people find time to work on a system?"

"Your second point is the most crucial," said Roberts. "The big problem is getting enough user time, and this is where you come in. It may be necessary to hire some extra people, possibly on a temporary basis, and realign some of your present staff. A project leader should be a user who has 50 to 75 percent free time. Other team members will probably need from one-quarter to one-half of their time available. As far as having data processing experience, that's where we come in. Our job is to guide the analysis and design. We can show your staff everything they need to know and keep them moving through the various stages of design."

"It's hard to argue with what you say," Green conceded. "I hadn't realized we were getting into so much, but we really do need help. Let me think about who the best person for this would be, and see how I can shift work responsibilities around to free up his time. Right now, I would tend to choose Terry Carson since he has had some experience, but I want to see if he would like an assignment as head of a design team."

"That sounds great. Why don't I call you next week and see how things are coming?"

With that, the meeting was completed after Green asked Roberts about some problems at headquarters.

KEY WORDS

Action	Planning
Conventional systems analysis	Pseudoparticipation
Diagnosis	Scouting
Entry	Termination
Evaluation	User-designed systems
Participation	

RECOMMENDED READINGS

Lucas, H. C. Jr.: *Toward Creative Systems Design,* Columbia, New York, 1974. (The first part of this monograph is devoted to user-oriented design; it explains some of the reasons behind this approach in greater detail.)

————: *Implementation: The Key to Successful Information Systems,* Columbia, New York, 1981. (A collection of research results on implementation.)

McGregor, D.: *The Human Side of Enterprise,* McGraw-Hill, New York, 1960. (A review of Theory X and Theory Y in this book should help to understand the motivation for the systems design approach suggested in this chapter.)

Mumford, E., and D. Henshull: *A Participative Approach to Computer Systems Design,* Associated Business Press, London, 1979. (A good case study of user design.)

DISCUSSION QUESTIONS

1 How would you overcome some of the disadvantages of participation pointed out in this chapter?

2 Would you expect the approach to systems design advocated here to be more or less costly than the conventional approach? Why?

3 To encourage participation, what view or orientation is required of the computer department?

4 How is the approach to systems design presented in this chapter consistent with Theory Y and complex man?

5 What would your basic approach have been in designing a system for the cattle investment firm described in this chapter?

5 Make a list of different mechanisms that might be used to elicit user participation.

6 Design a questionnaire for obtaining both design and attitudinal data for a computer system for the registrar of a university.

8 If a preliminary survey showed that clerical employees are extremely worried about a computer system, what strategy would you as a systems designer develop for the design team?

9 The examples given in this chapter have been primarily small organizations; how would you generalize the participatory approach to systems design for a larger organization? Sketch the composition of the design team and describe how it would work in a larger organization.

10 Given a 2-hour class period, what topics would you cover to prepare users to participate on a design team?

11 Why is it important to find a "client" in making initial contacts about information systems development projects?

12 This chapter has described the process of systems design and focused on the critical relationship between the designer and the user. Later chapters will deal with the task of actually designing the system. Which of these is the most important? Why?

13 What does one expect to learn during the evaluation stage near the completion of a systems design project?

14 Systems analysis and design has been described as an iterative process. Compare this activity with other tasks that also require iterations. What is it about systems analysis that makes it iterative in nature?

15 What can management do to make it easier for users to participate in the design of a new information system?

16 The design of an information system is one of the few activities in most organizations that is best accomplished using a team approach. What problems might this effort create with other employees of the organization? How should this different organization structure be presented to ease these problems?

17 If users have difficulty explaining how they use information or what they would like to see in an information system, what alternatives are there to an interview?

18 Research in a number of organizations has shown that perceived levels of involvement are not consistently associated with more favorable user attitudes toward computer systems. Is this finding surprising and does it contradict the approach to systems design suggested in this chapter? How can this research result be reconciled with the suggested design philosophy presented here?

19 Why do you think conventional approaches to systems analysis and design have concentrated on information flows and transactions?

20 Many existing information systems serve to automate transactions processing. However, a trend has been also to use the computer for decision support systems. Typically these systems feature interactive computing and support decisions; they do not really make a decision in the sense that a transactions application often includes and executes decision rules. Are the techniques for systems analysis and design described in this chapter more important for transactions or decision support systems? Why?

21 How do the design techniques suggested in this chapter contribute to the implementation process?

22 We have discussed approaches to the design process that are intended to elicit user support for systems and result in systems that are used and contribute to the organization. Can you think of any ways that the technology can be used creatively to make systems more appealing to users?

23 Computer hardware is becoming less expensive and more capable; hardware devices are also shrinking in size. What are the implications of these changes for the computing environment seen by users?

24 Some organizations charge user departments for the development of new information systems and others charge off systems development to corporate overhead. What are the pros and cons of each approach? What incentives for user behavior are provided under each alternative?

25 What are the potential problems of developing an information system that will serve to coordinate activities among several departments?

TRADITIONAL TOOLS FOR ANALYSIS AND DESIGN

TRADITIONAL TOOLS FOR ANALYSIS AND DESIGN

In the past chapters we have been concerned with the stages and the process of systems analysis and design. Analysis and design is more an art than a science. The analyst must understand what alternatives are available and bring them to the attention of the user. The analyst identifies trade-offs and helps determine the relevant criteria for evaluating them.

Fortunately in the recent years some tools have been refined, and others have emerged to help the analyst in this task—tools that are particularly helpful for describing a system. In earlier chapters we discussed the demanding task of placing a boundary on a system and defining the variables or components of a system, such as inputs, outputs, and their relationship. Some of the tools discussed in this chapter help the analyst in several ways.

First, there are approaches to collecting data about how the current system functions. Then there are tools to help describe graphically the processing logic of a system; other techniques help to describe input, output, and processing in tabular and graphic formats. All these approaches, whether tabular or graphic, help us visualize and make concrete a system that is inherently abstract and hard to comprehend.

The analyst will certainly not use all the devices discussed in this chapter on any one project. However, the importance of these tools is their existence; they are available and each will fit a particular situation. An analyst with knowledge of these tools is also in a good position to develop a design aid of his or her own in a particular situation.

DATA COLLECTION

To analyze a system, we must collect data. Consider the example in the first chapter where extensive data were gathered to characterize the amount of snowfall in New York City, the city's network of streets, and capacity to clean away the snow. A variety of techniques are available for data collection. Primary data collection involves direct interaction; secondary data are collected from existing sources. Interviewing an individual or observing someone at work would be examples of primary data collection. An examination of company records concerning the volume of invoices or shipment would be an example of collecting data from secondary sources.

Data Collection Approaches

Observation   One technique for collecting data on a process is to observe that process. Frequently in systems analysis and design we will "walk through" a system observing crucial information flows and decision points. Then we may use one of the graphic techniques described later in this chapter to prepare documentation of our understanding of how the system functions.

Observations can also be quite structured; we may develop a rating form of some type to collect data on the frequency of inquiries, say, in a credit office. The analyst prepares a form showing the possible inquiries and then during a sample of different days and hours codes the actual inquiries.

Interviews   The systems analyst spends a great deal of time interacting with others, particularly in interview settings. Interviews have varying degrees of structure; for a first meeting there may be no structure at all. The analyst may be getting acquainted with the user and gaining a broad understanding of the problem area.

Often, as the project progresses, more structured interviews are conducted. The analyst may wish to prepare in advance an interview schedule containing the questions to be asked and the points to be covered. The main thing is to be prepared.

One of the most common problems in interviewing is probing for the answer. The interviewer, perhaps unconsciously, encourages the interviewee to give a desired response. Often people being interviewed follow these cues and try to help the interviewer. It is very important from the standpoint of systems design to be sure that the data collected are as accurate as possible.

Questionnaires   A questionnaire allows us to obtain data from a relatively large number of people at a reasonable cost. A questionnaire can be thought of as a structured interview form with questions designed so they can be answered without a face-to-face encounter. The design of a good questionnaire is a difficult task. While the idea is an extension of a structured interview form, the questionnaire is, in principle, capable of being completed by the respondent alone without an interviewer being present.

TABLE 7-1
SAMPLE INTERVIEW AND QUESTIONNAIRE ITEMS

Attitude Questions

Directions: Circle the number which best represents your opinion.

For example: The temperature inside today is:

Too cold _____ Too hot

1 2 3 4 5 (6) 7

The answer indicates that the temperature is hot.

1 My general impression of the data processing staff is that they

are uninterested _____ are interested
in the user   1 2 3 4 5 6 7   in the user

are not too   _____ are highly competent
competent technically 1 2 3 4 5 6 7 technically

are not too good in _____ are good in dealing
dealing with people   1 2 3 4 5 6 7 with people

do low-quality work _____ do high-quality work

1 2 3 4 5 6 7

2 How do you think a computer might benefit you? (You may answer more than one.)

1 Reduce the time I spend processing papers
2 Reduce errors
3 Make my job more interesting
4 Make it easier to find information
5 Make it easier to use information
6 I don't know specifically how, but feel it would help
   Comments _____

3 What do you think the major problems with a computer would be? (You may answer more than one.)

1 It would make things more complicated
2 It would make more mistakes
3 It would be harder to use
4 It would take more of my time
5 It would lose information
6 It would make our jobs boring
7 I don't know specifically what, but feel there would be problems
   Comments _____

4 If we use a computer here, the company will not need me anymore.

1 Strongly agree 2 Agree 3 Neutral 4 Disagree 5 Strongly disagree

Design Information

Please rate the following reports on the indicated characteristics

Inventory Status Report

1 Highly accurate _____ Highly inaccurate
                   1 2 3 4 5 6 7

2   Out of date _____ Timely
                   1 2 3 4 5 6 7

3   Useful _____ Useless
                   1 2 3 4 5 6 7

Sales Analysis Report

4 Highly accurate _____ Highly inaccurate
                   1 2 3 4 5 6 7

5   Out of date _____ Timely
                   1 2 3 4 5 6 7

6   Useful _____ Useless
                   1 2 3 4 5 6 7

Table 7-1 presents some examples of questionnaire and/or structured interview questions. (A questionnaire can also be completed in an interview setting.) The example illustrates several different types of questions. The questions with a 1 through 7 number scale assess subjective perceptions and attitudes; no real unit like dollars, degrees, etc. measures such variables.

Another type of question is open-ended. Here we simply ask the respondent to write a short paragraph to answer our inquiry. Such a question might be, "Please indicate the four most important pieces of information that you use in your work."

Fixed alternative questions are difficult to construct, because we must be sure to bracket the range of alternatives. For example, we might ask, "What is the average value of an invoice in your department?" and provide four choices:

1 Under $2000
2 $2000 to $5000
3 $5000 to $10,000
4 Over $10,000

This question looks all right; however, there may be a problem if the average value of invoices for the firm is $25,000. The answer would be 4 for virtually all respondents and we would get very little information. Most of the time in systems analysis and design, we are interested in more exact figures, so we would actually collect a sample of invoices and compute the average and variance, or we would ask a question and leave a blank so that users could provide their own estimate.

As a part of our effort to determine attitudes during the design process, we may also use questionnaires and interviews. Knowing attitudes helps us prepare for how different users will respond to a new system. In fact, we could use these attitudinal ratings to include some of the least receptive people who are important potential users on a design team.

Comparison   Both questionnaires and interviews are important for the analyst, though interviewing will probably be used more. The advantage of the interview is that a new tangent can be followed. The respondent is not constrained by the limitations of the questions but can expand in other directions. If the question is ambiguous, the interviewer can explain what is desired. Interviews are the best technique in an unstructured setting and when it is necessary to probe issues in depth.

Questionnaires offer the advantage of being relatively inexpensive to administer to a large group of respondents. They are well suited to expanding data collection beyond the interview. For example, assume that a system is being developed that will be used by a number of sales representatives nationwide. If the firm has 500 sales representatives, it is impossible to include all of them on a design team; instead we would use representatives chosen to be typical of the types of salespersons on the force. This group might assist in developing a questionnaire for the rest of the sales force that has, until now, been uninvolved in the design. The questionnaire could explain some of the chosen trade-offs and characteristics of the system to all potential users to obtain their input and

SYSTEMS PROBLEM 7-1

After a 6-month study, Johnson Sports has decided to develop a comprehensive administrative computer system for the company. Johnson manufactures a complete line of sporting equipment including baseball, tennis, football, soccer, and gym equipment. The company sells through retail sporting goods stores and bids on large contracts for schools and teams. Currently there are six warehouses throughout the United States and Canada and three manufacturing plants.

The proposed information system would tie together the plants, warehouses, and the headquarters location. Eventually it would be expanded to include certain major sales offices, as well.

Martha Weiss has been given the assignment to assess the readiness of the organization for such a system and to obtain a preliminary idea on what features it should indicate. The total number of potential users is about 1000 according to best estimates. Although Martha would like to talk to as many of them as possible, she recognizes that such a task would be impossible in the 2 months she has been given to complete the assignment.

Martha has been conducting research on methods for collecting data on both user attitudes and what features should be included in a system. She would like your help in assessing the pros and cons of questionnaires and interviews, or some kind of joint approach. Can you suggest what criteria should be considered in making a decision? How would you evaluate questionnaires and interviews on the criteria you have outlined?

---

feedback. Valuable attitudinal data could also be collected at the same time. Questionnaires are also a good way to obtain feedback in a postimplementation audit.

ANALYSIS AND DESIGN TOOLS

In the remainder of this chapter we present an overview of some of the tools that have been developed to assist the designer.

Flowcharts

Probably the oldest graphic design aid is the flowchart. Each organization may have its own standards for flowcharting; in addition, the American National Standards Institute (ANSI) has published a standard for flowcharts.

A flowchart consists of a series of symbols and connections among them. A chart can depict a number of information processing activities ranging from a computer configuration through the detailed steps of a program. (However, flowcharting of programs at a detailed level has been declining in popularity because of the effort involved and because of failure to update flowcharts when programs change.)

Figure 7-1 contains the basic symbols in the ANSI standard. Input and output

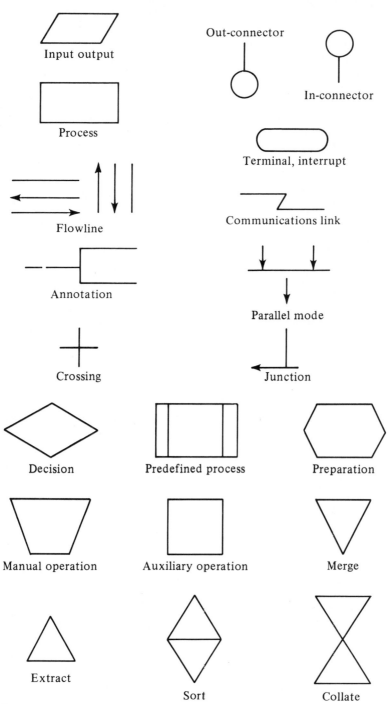

FIGURE 7-1
Basic and specialized symbols.

activities, irrespective of media or format, are represented by a parallelogram. However, specialized symbols may be used instead for punched cards or a terminal. The process outline is a rectangle and is used for any kind of data processing; it is the symbol to use when no other special one is available. This symbol can stand for data transformation, movement, or logic operations.

The flowlines show the sequence among steps and the transmission of information among operations. An arrow is used to specify direction when it is not implicit in the diagram. ANSI specifies that arrows are not necessary when the flow is from top to bottom and from left to right.

An open rectangle with a dotted line connecting it to the flowchart is used to annotate the flowchart. Because charts rarely fit on a single sheet, different pieces are cross-referenced. Out-connectors are used to indicate that the flow is to be continued on another page, and an in-connector shows that another page contains the preceding processing.

An interrupt symbol shows a beginning, an end, or a break in the usual line of flow. Communications links indicate the transmission of data from one location to another.

The next set of symbols in Figure 7-2 is specialized and augments the standard processing symbols. One of the most important of these is the diamond, which represents a decision point. Multiple paths representing possible outcomes of the decision exit from this symbol.

Figure 7-2 shows some of the input-output special symbols that represent various types of media. This figure also contains additional symbols that can be used to represent specific computer equipment such as a disk or drum.

Given these symbols, a wide variety of processes can be represented graphically. For the analyst, flowcharts of the existing system can be of great assistance in visualizing how it operates. We shall see many flowcharts of manual procedures in subsequent chapters. These charts can be used to communicate with users as well as within a design team; they also are valuable for training purposes.

Unfortunately, the many ways to combine these symbols into flowcharts can make it difficult to read and share charts among different individuals. We can offer some guidelines to facilitate the construction and the later readability of the charts (Chapin, 1970):

Use simple symbols where possible; avoid overly elaborate charts.

Try to maintain the same level of detail on the charts.

Consider using hierarchies of charts; one chart is at a high level and succeeding levels of detail are shown in charts that expand the symbols in the higher-level chart.

Develop the chart to suit the reader; if the chart is for communications with users, it should be annotated and clear.

Try to develop a standard or use the existing standard in the organization so that the charts can be more easily read by others.

Although the use of flowcharting is not being recommended today for

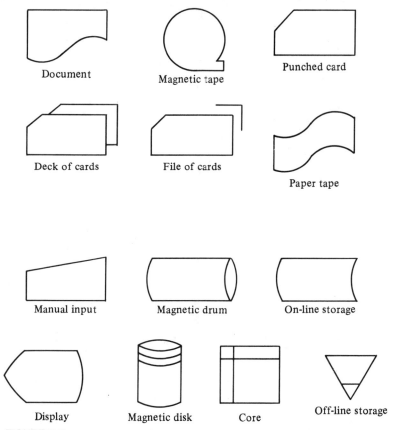

FIGURE 7-2
Input/output and equipment symbols.

programs, there are two places where we shall use flowcharts extensively. First, there are systems flowcharts that show all the inputs, major files, processing, and outputs from a system. This kind of a flowchart will be used for both the batch and on-line versions of the Hardserve example, though the on-line version will look more like a block diagram.

The other important use of flowcharts in analysis and design is for manual procedures. Particularly in transactions-processing systems, a large number of documents is a part of the system flow. The manual procedures chart shows the origination, processing, and final destination of these documents. It also shows the procedures to be employed by users. Since systems cannot function without human assistance, these charts are quite important.

Decision Tables

A decision table is another graphic technique to facilitate communications among users and analysts. As a side benefit, automatic decision table translators or

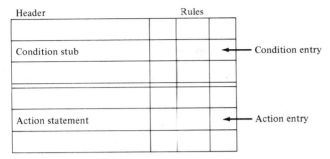

FIGURE 7-3
Decision table format.

manual algorithms exist so that a program can easily be generated from a decision table. The decision table expresses a series of conditions; when the conditions are fulfilled, then a rule associated with the condition is executed.

Figure 7-3 shows the basic decision table format. A header is used to identify the table, and condition stubs describe the various conditions. A rule is a procedure for checking the different conditions, and the action statement tells what action to take when a rule is true. The table is read until the conditions for a rule are met and the action described is taken. Then the next scan of the table begins.

The decision tables in Figures 7-4 and 7-5 represent the logic for a credit card purchase authorization. In this example, a purchase under $50 is approved automatically. Purchases between $50 and $100 are given an authorization number. Finally, for purchases over $100 we give an authorization number and place a "hold" on the customer's account for the amount of the purchase.

	Rules			
Credit card authorization	1	2	3	4
Is purchase less than $50	Y	N	N	N
Is purchase between $50 and $100		Y	N	N
Is purchase over $100			Y	N
Approve with no action	X			
Give authorization no.		X	X	
Place hold on account			X	
Error				X

FIGURE 7-4
Limited-entry example.

Rules

Credit card authorization	1	2	3
Is purchase p	$p > \$100$	$\$50 \leqslant p \geqslant \$100$	$0 < p < \$50$
Approve with no action			X
Give authorization	X	X	
Place hold on account	X		

FIGURE 7-5
Extended-entry example.

Figures 7-4 and 7-5 illustrate two different forms of decision tables. The first figure is a limited-entry table that allows only a "yes" or a "no" entry for the rules. In this type of a table, each possible condition has to be expressed in a statement. The extended-entry form in Figure 7-5 allows us to use logical conditions as entries and save space. Readers should assure themselves that these tables adequately describe the logic for the credit card example and that the two tables are equivalent.

Decision tables have a number of advantages. First, they can facilitate communications among analysts and users. In fact, users can often learn rather easily to describe the logic of their decisions using decision tables. Decision tables are compact and express far more logic in a small location than a comparable flowchart. They are a good form of documentation that can be updated easily (Murdick and Ross, 1975). Computer programs are available that translate decision tables into COBOL and FORTRAN programs automatically.

Some guidelines have been offered for table construction. First, avoid making tables too large; often several small tables are better than one. (A rule in one table can be to execute another table.) All possible rules must be presented and every rule must have an action associated with that rule. The action is to be taken if the set of conditions hold. (Tables can be action tables that consist of a single rule.)

Decision tables should be analyzed to be certain that they are complete and to avoid excessive rules, contradictions, and possible redundancies. See Fergus in Couger (1979). A table is complete if it accounts for the correct number of independent rules to cover all combinations of possible conditions. The number of rules to be accounted for is equal to the number of unique condition combinations possible. This number of possible conditions is the product of the values each condition might assume.

In the example in Figure 7-4 there are three conditions, each of which could be answered with two values, "yes" or "no." To be complete, the table should then have $2 \times 2 \times 2$ or 8 rules. However, note that the possibilities of having two "yes" answers for a rule would be contradictory; a purchase could not be less than $50 and greater than $100 at the same time. Therefore, there is no need for rules that would have all three "yes" values.

If all the conditions in a table have the same number of values, the number or rules needed to satisfy all combinations is the number of values raised to the power of the number of conditions. Figure 7-4 has three conditions, each of which has two possible values, yielding 2^3 or 8 possible rules. However, as mentioned above not all possible rules will make sense, and editing is necessary.

The rules themselves must be unique and independent; they cannot contradict one another, and only one rule can apply in a given situation. It does not matter in what sequence rules are presented, since only one set of conditions can be satisfied at a time.

The rules consist of relationships among the various conditions. That is, if there are three conditions in a rule—A, B, and C—then A and B and C must be true for the rule to be satisfied. Finally, if the rule is satisfied, then the logic of the table dictates that the action is to be executed (Murdick and Ross, 1975).

HIPO

HIPO stands for Hierarchy plus Input-Process-Output and was developed to display what a system or program does in a graphic manner. With a technique like HIPO the actual design process produces documentation as a by-product.

HIPO also facilitates a top-down design process; it concentrates on functions

---

SYSTEMS PROBLEM 7-2

John Kowalski is manager of systems and programming for the *Rocky Mountain News Courier*, which operates a chain of newspapers in the Midwest. He has had significant problems with the programming and systems staff in obtaining adequate documentation for systems.

When Kowalski first arrived at the *News Courier* he found that the only documentation in use was program listings; there were no file record layouts or descriptions beyond the programs themselves. John was quite worried by the absence of documentation. He then found that the maintenance budget was 85 percent of the total systems and programming budget. No wonder so few new applications were being developed! The lack of documentation hindered every aspect of maintenance. Not only was maintenance a problem, but the company was vulnerable to turnover by programmers and analysts. Since every employee held valuable information about a system in his or her head, their resignations created a major loss for the newspaper.

Traditional methods of flowcharting had proved unsatisfactory. It was possible to enforce flowcharting standards when programs were first developed, but there was no way to keep the flowcharts up to date. The firm had tried automatic flowchart programs, but the charts produced by these package programs were not that helpful.

For the long term, John is investigating the adoption of one of the structured design approaches discussed here. However, in the meantime he is concerned about the systems that already exist without documentation. How will a structured design technique help solve his problems? What can he do for the existing applications?

---

rather than immediate details. A function is a process that accepts inputs and produces outputs. HIPO usually consists of a visual table of contents describing the system, overview diagrams, and detail diagrams with extended descriptions. The table of contents is like an organization chart showing the major functions included in the system. Successive charts break down aggregate functions into more and more detail. See Figure 7-6 for an example of a HIPO chart for processing checks and deposits. This chart is at an intermediate level of detail.

HIPO is also a form of modular design in which parts of a system are broken into independent modules. The way in which functions are grouped within modules determines the strength of the module. The objective is to produce modules that have functional strength, that is, that contain all the steps necessary to perform a single function. If an upper-level module performs a single function and performs that function in its entirety, then the module has functional strength even though the lowest-level module may be called and used by several higher-level modules.

Module coupling refers to interactions between modules. We would prefer that this coupling take place through data coupling; each module simply passes applications data to the next-lower-level module. This way calling modules do not have to pass switches and control parameters to subordinate modules.

HIPO has been used successfully by some organizations and criticized by others. Canning (1979) suggests that one problem is that HIPO encourages the analyst to focus on one process at a time rather than several processes and the

FIGURE 7-6
A HIPO example.

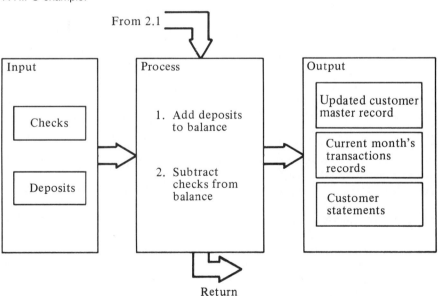

interactions among them. Also, critics contend that HIPO is really a programming aid rather than a tool for systems design.

It should also be noted that HIPO and some of the modular approaches discussed below present a picture of the structure of a system. However, these techniques do not usually provide information on the sequence or timing of events. Flowcharts or other representations are required to show when various events occur.

Pseudocode

Pseudocode is not a design approach as much as it is a way to communicate specifications to programmers. In fact, it might be used by the programmer as a first step before coding given specifications prepared by an analyst. An example of pseudocode is:

```
Begin Check__balance
     // Comment: Check inventory balance //
     For each item
             Retrieve item__no, EOQ, on__hand
             If on__hand is less than EOQ, Then place__order
     next item
End
Begin Place__order
     // Comment: Prepare order form //
     Retrieve vendor data for item__no
     Print purchase order
End
```

This particular example is in no known programming language. Instead, the pseudocode describes the logic of an algorithm in a pidgin-English programming language. It can be read by an analyst, a programmer, and possibly by a user. Its purpose is to replace the flowchart with text, but with a text that is not dependent on the peculiarities of a particular programming language.

Other Techniques

Several other techniques for systems analysis and design have been developed. Canning (1979) has revised two of these approaches, Information Analysis and Structured Analysis and Design Technique (SADT). There are reports that both of these approaches have been used successfully in systems design; the approaches have been credited with reducing costs and development time and improving the quality of the final system.

Information Analysis   Information Analysis involves the use of a simple, large form. A square on the form represents the bounds of what is being included in the system. The analyst constructs small boxes outside the square to represent documents or materials flowing into and out of the system. The analyst identifies three to six activities that constitute a function. The analyst describes the inputs and outputs and represents the actual activities by dots in the square.

The purpose of the dots is to force the analyst to refrain from thinking about the details of the activity at this point: he or she notes only that the activity exists. Such a technique forces one to use a level-of-abstraction approach where each step in design proceeds to a more detailed level of analysis.

Next the analyst connects input boxes to one or more of the activity dots. The analyst looks then at each activity dot in the square to determine what major types of information and output are produced by that activity. Information and/or materials flowing outside the function require lines drawn to boxes at the bottom of the square representing the output of the whole system.

A high-level diagram might have five or six information and material input boxes at the top of the square and five or six output boxes at the bottom with several activity dots. There are two types of diagrams: activity graphs and information analysis graphs.

Figure 7-7 is an example of how we might construct an activity graph for a simple inventory control system for a wholesale supplier. The wholesaler orders merchandise from manufacturers and stores it in a warehouse. The customer of the wholesaler orders merchandise, which is shipped to the customer from the warehouse.

The inventory control department receives shipments from suppliers and is responsible for seeing that there is enough merchandise available for filling orders. Incoming orders from customers enter the warehouse's order processing operation and a shipping order is written for their inventory control department. The inventory control department uses an inventory status report from the computer department to send reorder notices to the purchasing department. This department in turn generates purchase orders, which go to suppliers, an action that generates shipments from suppliers, which are placed in inventory.

As we might expect, the next step is to examine each of the activities in the high-level diagram and draw subsidiary diagrams. Through this process the system is decomposed into lower levels of detail. The entire process is known as activity analysis.

Following activity analysis is information analysis; each information-handling activity from the activity diagram is analyzed on a separate information flow diagram. The inputs are identified on the top of a square by boxes and the output similarly at the bottom as before. Now the analyst identifies the information processes needed to transform inputs into outputs; he or she also must specify the sequence required for processing.

Information analysis shows what information must be available at each processing step and what information is produced as output. Again, the information processes from a diagram are decomposed and shown on separate forms. At

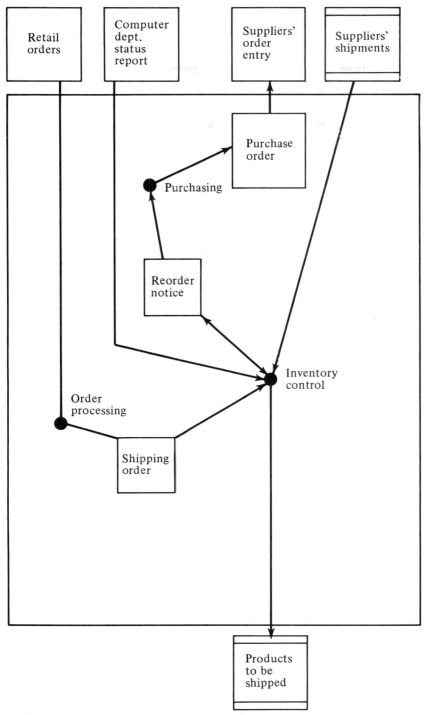

FIGURE 7-7
An example of an activity graph.

the lowest level of decomposition, the information is displayed with a listing of data types that make it up. Finally the data are broken down into fields and records.

Now the analyst is ready to develop a process table showing what inputs are needed, what calculations must be performed, and what outputs are produced. Detailed procedures have thus been postponed until this stage, which is consistent with the principle of levels of abstraction in design.

SADT Structured Analysis and Design Technique was developed by a private firm. This proprietary system consists of a graphic language for building models, a method for developing models, and management practices for controlling the development of the models. The SADT package is similar in concept to others that are offered; the objective is to force structure on the unstructured systems analysis and design task.

SADT seeks a top-down decomposition of a problem, using a graphic modeling language. The development of a typical system will involve a number of different models, such as functional models that define what the system should do, implementation models to tell how the system is to accomplish its tasks, conversion models, and so on. Both activities and data are modeled top-down using a graphic language. The technique is designed for large projects requiring 4 to 6 analysts and from 6 to 9 months.

Activity diagrams and data diagrams are used. The former use boxes to represent activities, and lines connect the boxes to show data interfaces. The rule is to keep the number of boxes between three and six on any diagram.

The approach emphasizes the concept of bounded context; each box and all its arrows must completely describe its activity and nothing outside that activity. Arrows on the left of an activity box represent data inputs, and arrows from the right side are outputs. Control arrows enter the top of the box and mechanisms exit from the bottom. Control arrows indicate the conditions under which an activity is to be performed. Mechanism arrows show resources used to perform activities, like an individual or a computer.

An output from one box can be a control or input to other boxes on the diagram. The top-level activity diagram represents the complete system being investigated; the boundaries of these diagrams are retained throughout the design process. The diagrams force the analyst to think carefully about the contents of the function boxes and how they are to be decomposed. The graphic technique helps guide the analyst in decomposing the system into lower levels of abstraction.

The boxes contain short statements about the activity. As with other techniques, higher-level boxes are decomposed at each step. The diagrams are a part of developing the specification; they are not necessarily intended to be used after the design is complete as documentation.

After the activity model is completed, the analyst undertakes a top-down decomposition of the data by drawing levels of a data model. The boxes in this diagram represent data classes at the current level of decomposition. This process frequently results in changes being made to the activity model.

The approach also involves individuals who read the various diagrams and

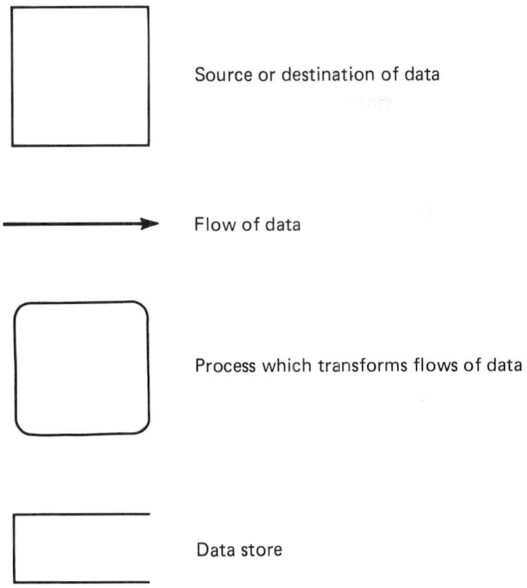

Source or destination of data

Flow of data

Process which transforms flows of data

Data store

FIGURE 7-8
Data flow diagram symbols.

comment on them. Design is not done in isolation; there is review and feedback. However, the role of users in this design process is not clear. For more details on information analysis and SADT see Canning (1979).

Data Flow Diagrams   Gane and Sarson (1979) have presented an extremely useful approach to systems analysis and design. Their technique requires only four symbols, making it very easy to apply. In Figure 7-8 open-ended rectangles represent stores of data, such as a file of items in inventory, their quantity and the Economic Reorder Quantity (EOQ). Rounded rectangles stand for some type of processing, and arrows represent the flow of data. Finally, a square is a source or destination of data. Data flow diagrams should also be prepared in a top-down manner.

An example will help to illustrate the use of data-flow diagrams. Imagine that a group of entrepreneurs has decided to open a mail-order business selling software for personal computers. A customer sends in an order form, and employees of the business ship software back to the customer. Figure 7-9 is a high-level data flow diagram for this firm. At this level, we see the basic flow of an order coming to the firm and a shipment going to the customer. We have to look at an inventory record and check the customer's credit.

Figure 7-10 presents the next level of detail. We see that the first action is to check the inventory to see if the software program ordered is in stock. If so, we place the order in a file "to be filled." The warehouse staff removes orders from this file, finds them in inventory, packages the program, and sends the shipment

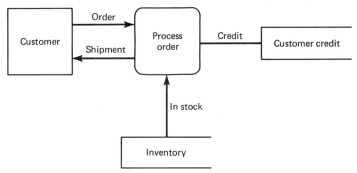

FIGURE 7-9
Overview of mail-order business.

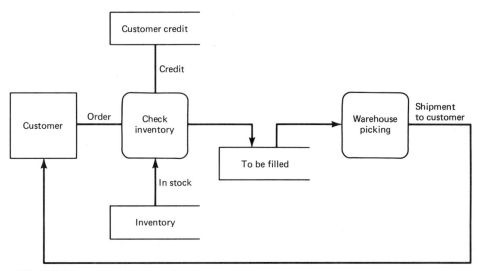

FIGURE 7-10
The next level of detail.

to the customer. If at any point one loses track of the process, it is necessary only to back up one or two diagrams to get an overview.

In Figure 7-11 the designer addresses the question of what to do when we are out of stock. Management has made the decision that backordering is probably not feasible; the customer will look elsewhere for the program rather than wait. However, it is important to reorder when stock is low or entirely gone. If we need more merchandise, an order must be placed with a supplier. There is also a path from warehouse picking to the reorder process in case the inventory records do not match the warehouse contents exactly. Here we would want to check the warehouse carefully and then reorder if in fact there is nothing in inventory.

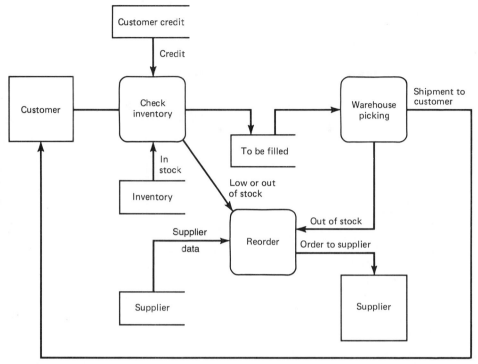

FIGURE 7-11
Reorder logic.

Figure 7-12 adds more detail to the reorder process and includes an accounts receivable process. We see that the firm must check in merchandise when it is received from suppliers; the goods eventually are placed in inventory. Accounts receivable are important if the firm is to stay in business! We must send an invoice with the shipment of goods to the customer and create a receivables record.

It would be possible to expand Figure 7-12 further, but the diagram is beginning to get cluttered. At this point, the designer would probably take each process and treat it as a subsystem for further explosions. For example, it would be possible to treat the accounts receivable process as a subsystem and generate several pages of greater detail on how receivables are created and processed in the firm.

The data flow diagrams and the top-down approach help the analyst and the user understand the design and cope with complexity. What of the elaborate flowcharting symbols earlier? These symbols can be used to describe different hardware configurations and for some kinds of manual procedures. The use of a particular set of symbols is not that important; rather, it is the concept of structuring the design and moving from lesser to greater levels of detail that contributes to the design process.

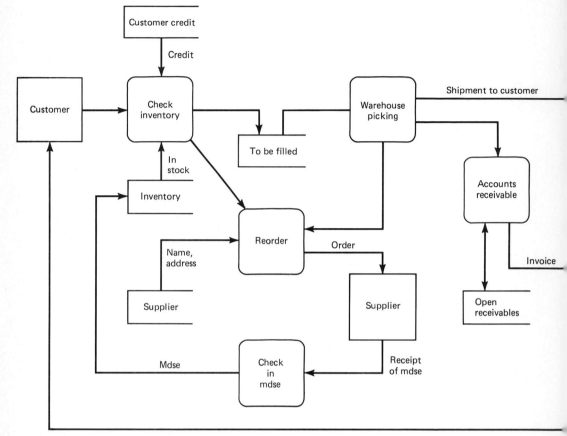

FIGURE 7-12
Receipt of goods and accounts receivable.

CONCLUSIONS

In this chapter we have discussed several aids to the design process. These tools can help structure the analysis process and communicate about a system. Their goal is to help produce structure during the creative process of systems analysis and design, a process we have described as requiring us to develop structure where little or none may exist.

The importance of these techniques is not just in the fact that we can master and use them. Rather, it is the idea that some kind of design tool is available and that we can significantly improve the quality of analysis and design by using one or a combination of these aids. It is quite likely that at some point none of these techniques will be exactly appropriate for the situation we face. In that case, the analyst may wish to design his or her own graphic or tabular tools to aid in the analysis and design task.

Canning (1979) has suggested a list of desirable properties for design aids:

1 The approach should encourage design through levels of abstraction. Higher levels of the system are decomposed to furnish more details; however, the analyst is concerned with just one level of detail at a time. Consideration of lower levels is postponed.

2 A small number of elements should be considered on one diagram, say three to six. The designer is forced to aggregate components and think about similarities and differences in data and functions, creating more understanding of the system.

3 Bounded context is helpful to see that all relevant data and processing are considered with a particular function and that irrelevant items are omitted.

4 A technique should emphasize the analysis of both data and activities.

5 It is helpful if the technique has some type of graphic representation; such presentations help convey information. The graphic display should be suitable for users both to view and help develop.

6 A technique should be simple for analysts and users to understand.

7 It should be easy to change the design as lower levels or successive stages of development show that certain design decisions have to be altered.

8 Frequent inspections and reviews should be a part of the methodology. As we stressed, design is a creative activity and many inputs and ideas are needed.

9 The analysis methodology should flow naturally into design. As much as possible of the work done in analyzing a system should be transferred into the design of a new system.

SYSTEMS PROBLEM 7-3

Sam Cameron is manager of systems development for Animal Foods, a major processor of food for farm animals and pets. He has been reading about different design techniques such as structured design, information analysis, etc. and is confused over the different approaches.

Animal Foods has been having significant problems in developing new systems. Three out of the five new development efforts are over 6 months behind schedule. The two projects that are on schedule are package programs that are being installed with only minor modifications at Animal Foods.

Sam feels that the unorganized and personalistic approaches used by each designer have led to some of the problems with these new systems. The philosophy behind more structured approaches sounds good; however, Sam sees two major problems in moving in such a direction.

First, he is unsure what approach to try. Should Animal Foods standardize on one approach, or should it encourage several? Second, what will be the cost to the organization aside from any requirements to purchase a special course? Finally, how can the new approach(es) be implemented? What problems are the analysts likely to present, and will they adopt new procedures? What suggestions can you make to Sam Cameron and Animal Foods? What approaches can be taken to install a more structured design methodology?

In summary, we expect to see expanded usage of techniques such as the ones described here. One way to make systems analysis and design work more productive is to provide tools or develop them where needed. Both the concepts and the methodologies discussed in this chapter are extremely important for the analyst.

KEY WORDS

Activity graph	HIPO	Observation
ANSI Standards	Information analysis	Open-ended questions
Bounded context	Inspection	Primary data
Data collection	Interviews	Pseudocode
Decision tables	Levels of abstraction	Questionnaire
Extended entry	Limited-entry table	Secondary data
Flowchart	Modular design	Structured analysis

RECOMMENDED READINGS

Canning, R.: "The Analysis of User Needs," *EDP Analyzer,* vol. 17, no. 1, January 1979.

Chapin, N.: "Flowcharting with the ANSI Standard: A Tutorial," *Computing Surveys,* vol. 2, no. 2, June 1970, pp. 89–110.

Gane, C., and T. Sarson: *Structured Systems Analysis,* Prentice-Hall, Englewood Cliffs, N.J., 1979. (An excellent book on a structured approach to analysis.)

Jackson, Michael: *System Development,* Prentice-Hall, Englewood Cliffs, N.J., 1983. (The Jackson methodology is presented for structured design.)

Katzan, H.: *Systems Design and Documentation: An Introduction to the HIPO Method,* Van Nostrand Reinhold, New York, 1976.

Stay, J.: "HIPO and Integrated Program Design, *IBM Systems Journal,* vol. 15, no. 2, 1976, pp. 143–154.

DISCUSSION QUESTIONS

1 What are the advantages of a questionnaire for data collection?
2 What are the advantages of interviews for data collection?
3 Explain the term "bounded context"; why is it important in systems analysis and design?
4 How should one choose among the different design tools and techniques discussed in this chapter?
5 Is there one design approach that is best in all situations?
6 What design approach would you choose for a system to process incoming orders for a manufacturing firm?
7 What design approach would you recommend for an interactive decision support system to be used by the treasurer of the firm to manage cash deposits?
8 What are the advantages of extended-entry decision tables compared with limited-entry tables?
9 Flowcharting has been falling into increasing disfavor as a way to document programs. Why?

10 If flowcharting is not used for program documentation, does it have another role in systems analysis and design? If so, what is that role?

11 Take a process with which you are familiar (for example, the solution to a mathematics problem), and flowchart the steps involved.

12 A department store follows the following rules for reordering merchandise. If it is less than 2 months before the end of the sales season, do not reorder an amount A when the existing stock reaches a level of r. The store also tries to avoid having excess stock and controls this problem by taking markdowns. If it is over 3 months before the end of the season and there are S units left, the price of the item is reduced 20 percent. If 1 month or less is left until the end of the season and there are T units left, the price is reduced 50 percent. Draw a flowchart that depicts these reorder and markdown rules.

13 For problem 12 above, draw a decision table and compare it with the flowchart. What are the major differences? Which method of representing the process do you prefer?

14 Using some higher-level language, write a program module that expresses the logic of the flowchart in problem 12. Do the same for the decision table in problem 13. How do the program modules differ?

15 Several approaches have been taken to automating part of the development of information systems. One effort, called ISDOS, uses a problem statement language to describe a new system. This language is eventually translated into a computer program automatically. At present, the feasibility of this approach is being tested. If this design aid comes into widespread use, how would it affect the systems design tasks we have discussed so far? Would there still be a need for design teams and user involvement?

16 It can be argued that the structured design approaches reduce the freedom and flexibility of the designer. Do you agree with this observation?

17 Which techniques in this chapter do you think would be most easily understood by a user?

18 What is the essential concept behind modular design? Can you think of other places where modular design is used?

19 Explain in your own words what is meant by the term "levels of abstraction." How does this concept fit with a view of systems analysis and design as an interactive process?

20 Some have argued that HIPO is really a program design rather than a systems design technique. Take a position on this issue and defend it.

21 There are many structured approaches to other design tasks, like the construction of a building. What is so different about systems analysis and design for a computer system?

22 What parts of the systems design process do you think could be automated?

23 How does one employ structured design approaches when considering an applications package?

24 What technological advances would help the systems analyst in developing a new application?

25 Take a problem with which you are familiar and draw a data flow diagram expressing the logic of information flows.

CHAPTER 8

FILE DESIGN

Before we can discuss detailed design specifications, it is necessary to understand files and data bases. Data storage and retrieval are the heart of a modern information system; both the analyst and the user must work together to define the data base.

File design considerations represent the most technical material we shall discuss in this text. A systems designer does not necessarily have to be an expert programmer but does have to understand files and file structures. Files are the heart of an information system, and the systems designer must define and structure files. If users are to work meaningfully on the design team, analysts need to teach them the basics of file systems. Although users do not have to understand the details of a direct-access directory, they should understand the basic difference in capabilities between direct- and sequential-access files. Since the systems analyst defines the files and teaches users about files, the analyst must have a thorough knowledge of files. Methods of file storage and access probably are the major technical constraint limiting the state of the art in developing information systems today.

FILE ELEMENTS

A file is a collection of data. A computer file is organized in some way; that is, there is some well-defined structure to the information in the file. A computer file consists of a collection of records, each of which is made up of fields. The various fields consist of groups of characters as described below.

Data

The smallest unit of storage of interest is the character, for example, the number 9 or the letter A. We generally do not work directly with characters, but rather with groups of characters that have some intrinsic meaning, for example, Smith or 599. These groupings of characters are called "fields" and we identify them with a name; for example, Smith is an employee's surname and 599 is Smith's department number.

Groups of fields are combined to form a logical record such as the one shown in Figure 8-1a. This logical record contains all the data of interest about some entity; in this example it has all the data in the file about an individual employee.

A key to a record is some field of interest. In many files, we organize the file in order on a key. Last name is the primary key for a telephone book; that is, the telephone book is arranged in alphabetical order based on telephone subscribers' last names. We also can have secondary keys: In the case of the telephone book, the secondary key is the first name or initial. The telephone book, then, is arranged in sequence on the primary key (last name) and within the primary key is arranged in order by the secondary key (first name). Fields designated as keys are also used as a basis for retrieving information from a file. For example, an inventory part number may be the key for retrieving information about the quantity of the part on hand from a computerized inventory file.

Storage Devices

Files of any size are usually stored on secondary storage devices. These devices are considerably cheaper than primary memory in the computer and have much greater capacity. We cannot expect to hold all the data in a file in primary memory. If we could hold these data in memory when the application is first installed, the amount of data processed for the application probably would expand over time beyond the capacity of primary memory. Therefore, most applications are designed so that any number of transactions can be processed and the files can expand in size.

Another reason for using secondary storage is that we probably do not want the data for an application to be available for computer access all the time. Secondary storage devices make it possible to store these data off-line at a reasonable cost. The off-line storage units can be mounted on a secondary storage device when we are ready to use them.

FIGURE 8-1a
A logical record.

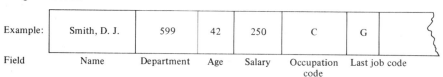

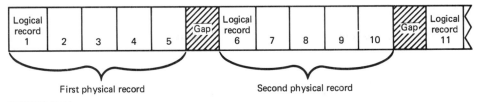

FIGURE 8-1*b*
Physical records (blocking factor = 5).

The mechanics of reading or writing data on secondary storage devices requires physical gaps between groups of characters. The number of characters actually transmitted between main computer memory and the file is called the physical record size. Between each physical record there is an interrecord gap, and we group logical records together to reduce the number of these interrecord gaps. For example, we might include 60 logical records in one physical record. This means that the blocking factor is 60; that is, there are 60 logical records blocked to form one physical record. See Figure 8-1*b*.

One reason for blocking records is to use space on the storage device more efficiently. Suppose the interrecord gap on a magnetic tape is 6/10 in. If we can record data at 1600 characters per inch, each gap could contain 960 characters if it did not have to be used as a gap. If a logical record were 500 characters long, grouping 60 together, we would have a physical record of

$$\frac{60 \text{ logical records} \times 500 \text{ characters/record}}{1600 \text{ characters/in.}} + 6/10 \text{ in. for a gap}$$

$$= 19.35 \text{ in. of tape}$$

If the logical records were unblocked—that is, if the logical record were the same size as the physical record—we would have a physical record of

$$\left(\frac{500 \text{ characters}}{1600 \text{ characters/in.}} + 6/10 \text{ in. gap}\right) \times 60 \text{ records} = 54.75 \text{ in. of tape}$$

since there is one interrecord gap for each logical record. We would have used 35.4 in. more tape to store the 60 logical records by not blocking them.

More efficient utilization of space on the tape also means more efficient input and output operations. Since one physical record is transferred to main memory with each read (and the reverse on writing), blocking results in transfer of more information at one time and fewer read operations on the secondary storage device. The transfer rates of such devices are very fast, particularly when compared with the time required to begin reading. Thus, reducing interrecord gaps by blocking increases both the utilization of the storage medium and the efficiency of input and output operations.

Record Types

Different applications require a variety of record types and file structures. One basic distinction is between fixed- and variable-length records. In a fixed-length record, we know the size of every field and the number of fields in the record in advance. We allow room for all the data that are of interest, as in the example in Figure 8-1a. A new hire will not have a last job code, and that field in Figure 8-1a would be blank. However, we do not expect many new hires compared with the total number of employees on the file, so that much wasted space is not a problem.

However, consider a system to keep track of patient visits to a medical clinic, type of test conducted, and results of the test. Assume that each test result can be described by 10 to 500 characters of data except for one test that requires 2000 characters of data. The patient also can have more than one test per visit. How could we possibly set up a fixed-length record for this system? Even if there were just one test per patient we could not afford to allow for 2000 characters of data in the record when only a few of the tests would ever need that much room.

The solution to this problem is a variable-length record; the number of fields and the length of a record do not have to be specified in advance. Of course, this adds to the complexity of our programs. Under a very general scheme for variable-length records, the program has to put a code in the record to identify what is there. In this example the record would have to specify what fields are present and the size of each field. We can carry either a single code at the beginning of a record or a code that indicates the contents of each field and its length before that field. In Figure 8-2 a code that precedes the record is shown. The first number in the code, 4, gives the length of the code in characters and the rest of the code tells what variables are present and how many characters were required to record each variable.

As an alternative, often we can specify several standard formats, each of a different length. That is, to avoid having to use codes, we may be able to establish three or four different formats of varying length, for example, 100 characters, 250 characters, and 2000 characters. Each of the formats for these records could be fixed in advance, but the combination of records for the file would be of varying length. There might be two records of 500 characters followed by one of 250 characters, etc.

FIGURE 8-2
A variable-length record code.

4N5T7	Allen	EK 61002	Data*
Code	Name	Test record	

Code length = 4
First name length = 5
Test name length = 7

*Another code could be used for the data on the test or there might be a standard format in the program for the data for each type of test.

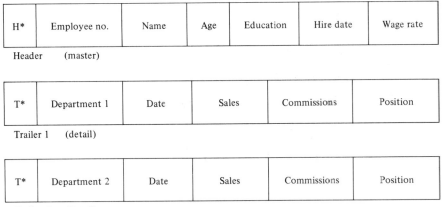

H*	Employee no.	Name	Age	Education	Hire date	Wage rate

Header   (master)

T*	Department 1	Date	Sales	Commissions	Position

Trailer 1   (detail)

T*	Department 2	Date	Sales	Commissions	Position

Trailer 2   (detail)

*Code identifying record type.

FIGURE 8-3
Header and trailer records of the same fixed length.

We can see that this type of record structure adds complexity to file design and programming, but it does save file space. In some systems we lose space on the physical record in blocking variable-length records. There may be leftover space; for example, if the physical record is 1000 characters long and the sum of the variable-length records is 950 characters, it would be possible to waste 50 characters of space in the physical record. (Some systems will break a variable-length logical record into pieces to fill two physical blocks.)

Fortunately, another alternative to fixed- and variable-length records can be used if a problem is structured so there is a varying number of fixed-length records. As an example, consider a department store that wants to keep track of the departments where a salesperson has worked, the length of time on the job, department number, gross sales, and commissions while working in that department. In this example we have the same information for each department, but a clerk could work in several departments. One solution in designing a computer file for this information is to use header and trailer records (sometimes called master and detail records). We keep the benefits of fixed-length record processing by having header and trailer records of the same size, although it may be necessary to put the data for several departments in one trailer record. The header and trailer records are identified by a single code in Figure 8-3. There will be one header record for each employee along with a variable number of fixed-length trailer records.

SEQUENTIAL FILES

The simplest kind of file is one in which all the records are in sequence according to some key, such as employee number, part number, etc. Many computer applications rely on sequential files, and although there is a trend to other types of files, sequential files will continue to be used heavily in the future.

Storage Media

Sequential files are most commonly associated with magnetic tape, but they can be supported on other file devices as well. In sequential files, the data are ordered on some key; for example, the telephone book is ordered on the last name, as we discussed earlier. It is also possible to have the file ordered on other keys, just as the telephone book uses a secondary key based on a subscriber's first name or initial.

A magnetic tape for computer storage is similar to the tape used on a home tape recorder. It has an underlying base that is covered with a magnetically sensitive coating. It is easiest to regard the tape as a matrix of bit positions, that is, nine rows or tracks of magnetic positions that can be either 1 or 0, stretching along the length of tape. Each character is represented by one column of bits:

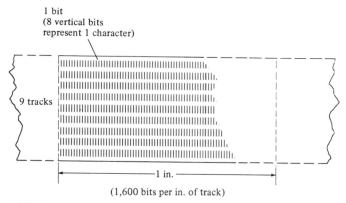

FIGURE 8-4
Schematic of a nine-channel tape showing capacity of 1600 bits per inch.

see Figure 8-4 (in this particular scheme eight bits are used to represent a character and one bit is used to check for errors). *Note:* Eight bits equal one bite.

The density of the tape is the number of characters that can be recorded in an inch, and is often referred to as bits per inch (which is really characters per inch). In the early days of computers, densities were quite low. In the late 1960s and early 1970s, 800 characters per inch was considered normal and 1600 characters per inch was classified as high density. Now tapes are available with densities of 6250 characters per inch.

Processing Sequential Files

Because sequential files are in a sequence (for example, numerical order) and must be kept in that sequence, much of sequential file processing involves sorting data on some key. For example, all subscribers must be sorted on their last name and first name before a telephone book can be printed. There have been numerous books and articles written on various approaches to sorting (for example, Martin, 1971). Fortunately, most computer manufacturers supply sorting packages as a part of their operating systems. These packages are very efficient and simple to use: All that is necessary is to indicate the fields, record sizes and sort key, and assign intermediate work areas for the sort to use.

Updating A schematic for updating a sequential file is shown in Figure 8-5a. Since the master file is in order, input transactions must be sorted into the same order as the file before being processed. Note that a new file is created in the update process, since it is not good practice to try to read and write from the same tape file. (In fact, how could you possibly insert a new record and keep the tape in sequence?) The old file in the sequential update provides backup. If we keep the input transactions and the old file, any errors or the accidental destruction of the new tape can easily be remedied by running the update program again and updating the old file with the transactions.

On an update there are three possible actions. First, we can modify a record; that is, we can change some part of the record read from the old file and then put it on the new file. Second, we can add a record by placing it in proper sequence on the new file. Third, we can delete a record from the old file by simply not writing it on the new file.

The logic of the sequential file update is complex, because we should be able to add a record to the file, modify the new record by processing transactions against it, and delete the record, all on the same update run. (Consider someone

FIGURE 8-5a
Sequential file update schematic.

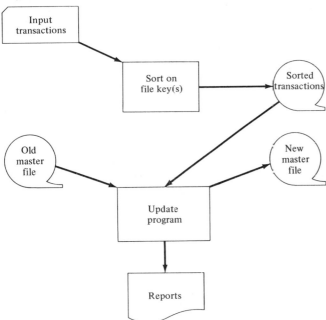

who on the same day opens a bank account, writes several checks, and then closes the account.) This objective implies that transactions affecting a single record should be sequenced in the order of (1) add, (2) modify, and (3) delete. If there are nine types of transactions, transaction type 1 should be the creation of a new customer record, types 2 through 8 might be various other transactions that can occur, such as (in banking) deposits and withdrawals, and type 9 should be the delete. The transactions are processed in sequence by type number for each account.

The logic of a sequential file update is determined by the sequential nature of the file. The file must be maintained in sequence according to some key or keys. Incoming additions, modifications, and deletions must be in the same sequence as the file being updated. In the above banking example, the transaction file containing additions, modifications, and deletions to update the master file in the bank would be in exactly the same sequence by account number as the master file itself. Account number 10054 would appear on both files before account number 10056.

All transactions affecting the record for account number 10056 would be grouped together in the incoming group of transactions. The transactions affecting the record of account number 10056 should also be in order by transaction type. That is, the first transaction affecting 10056 would be an addition if this account number were being added to the file for the first time. Then all transactions of types 2 through 8 would appear, followed by transaction 9 if this record were to be deleted. Using this sequence for transactions, we cannot delete and add a record with the same key on the same run. For example, we are unable to close one account and assign that number to a new account on the same run, since a delete has a higher transaction number than an addition and the transactions for each master file record are in ascending order by transaction number. Since the key is usually a field such as the account number or employee number, we would probably not want to reuse the deleted number immediately anyway.

SYSTEMS PROBLEM 8-1

A small, special-interest magazine wishes to increase the number of issues published each year. Currently, the journal appears quarterly, but the editors desire to publish every other month. The magazine uses a computer system to print mailing labels and renewal notices. This old system is written in assembly language and allows only for the existing four issues a year. There seems to be no way to persuade the program to allow more frequent publication.

What do you think the original designer did in constructing the system to produce such inflexibility? How could the files have been designed originally to allow for more issues? Should the editors of the magazine try to modify the old system or develop a new one? What type of file design would you recommend if a new system is developed? How would the file design differ if the magazine decided to integrate the subscription system with an accounts receivable application?

Old master file record number	Transaction				New master file
	Record	**Code**	**Meaning**	**New master file**
110	115	1	Add	110
130	115	2	Modify	115*
150	130	2	Modify	130*
170	131	1	Add	150*
200	131	3	Modify	165
	131	9	Delete	170
	150	3	Modify	200
	165	1	Add	

*Refers to a modified record, that is, a record which has been updated by some transaction.

FIGURE 8-5b
Sequential file update example.

An update program should be designed so that during the update, with proper authorization, it is possible to change any field in the record to correct errors. Of course, we cannot change the key field through a simple modification. Instead, if there is something wrong with a key, we delete the record with the wrong key and add a record with the correct key.

To place the transactions in the same order as the master file, we use a sort program as described at the beginning of this section. A utility sort program allows us to specify the keys and the order of the sort, either ascending or descending. Since we also want to have the transactions for each master file record in order by transaction number, we would specify a major and a minor (primary and secondary) sort key. For the above example, the major key would be account number and the minor key the transaction code. The sort program would produce as output a sorted transactions file with all transactions in the same order as the master file. Within the transactions affecting a single master file record, all transactions would be in order by transaction code.

An Example The example in Figure 8-5b should help to clarify the logic of a sequential file update. The left column contains the record number of each record in the old master file. The center column contains the sorted record numbers of transactions; these transactions are sorted on record number as major sequence and transaction code as minor sequence. Finally, the right column shows the new master file.

To begin the update, the program reads an old master record, 110, and a transaction record, 115. By comparing these two numbers, the program knows that record 110 has no changes. (There is no transaction record less than 115, and since the file and transactions are in sequence, there is no transaction to modify record 110.) Record 110 is written into the new master file and the program reads the old master record 130.

Because 130 is greater than the transaction record 115, the program knows that 115 must be the addition of a new record. (Any transaction with a key that does not match a key on the master file must be an addition or an error.) A check of the transaction code verifies that it is a new record, and the new record information is held in primary memory until there are no further transactions with the new record number 115. The next transaction is read and it does apply to the new record being constructed. The new record 115 is modified (indicated by an asterisk), and the next transaction is read.

This transaction is 130, so the program knows it can write the new record 115 into the new master file. Record 130 is already in memory, and so transaction 130 is used to modify it. The next transaction is read, number 131. Because 131 is greater than 130, the program is done with record 130, and it can be written into the new master file. The old master file record 150 is read next. Record 131 is an addition to the file; the next transaction modifies this new record, and the last transaction affecting record 131 deletes it. A deletion is accomplished by simply not writing the deleted record into the new master file. The next transaction, this one affecting record 150, is read and used to modify record 150.

The program reads the next transaction, which affects record 165. Now record 150 can be written into the new master file and record 170 read. The transaction for record 165 adds it to the new master file and an end-of-file mark is encountered for the incoming transactions file. Therefore, the program only needs to copy old master file records into the new master file to complete the update.

Retrieval Retrieval from a sequential file can be accomplished with a retrieval transaction request, and a retrieval report can be prepared during the update. If there is only one printer in the physical computer system, most operating systems allow multiple reports to be spooled for later printing, that is, to be placed on a secondary storage device and printed later. Even without this capability, one could put all the reports on a tape as the data are processed. If a report code is included on the tape, it can be sorted on the code and the different reports printed. Frequently, however, because we need complex retrieval logic that complicates the update program, or because we are using a file management package, we process the entire file to retrieve information. If only a few records are needed for retrieval, we still have to read the entire tape. Also, even if only a few records are changed during an update, it is necessary to update and rewrite the entire file.

DIRECT-ACCESS FILES

To overcome some of the problems above and to provide more rapid retrieval for on-line applications and more complex storage structures, direct-access files are used. These files allow more flexible file structures, but more work is required to use them.

Storage Media

The most common device for storing direct-access files is the magnetic disk (see Figure 8-6). One type of disk consists of a series of platters mounted on a spindle. The top and bottom of each platter (except for the very top and bottom ones) are coated with a magnetic material like that on a tape. Read and write heads are fitted between the platters. By moving the heads in and out we can access any track on the rotating disk. The maximum block size or physical record size for a disk file is limited by the physical capacity of each track. If the access arms do not move, each head reads or writes on the same track of each platter. Conceptually, these tracks form a cylinder, and, when using a disk file sequentially, we write on a given track of the first platter and then on the same track of the second platter and so on. This minimizes the access time since the heads do not have to move.

The total access time to read or write is made up of two components, seek time and rotational-delay time. Seek time is the time used in moving the read-write heads from one position to another. Rotational delay occurs because the data we want may not be directly under the read-write heads, even though they are located over the correct track. We have to wait for the disk to revolve to the beginning of the desired data.

There are also available a number of fixed-head disk drives often called head-per-track disks. Since the largest component of average access time for a movable-head disk is seek time, fixed-head disks are considerably faster. For example, the average access time for one movable-head disk is 38 milliseconds, and for the fixed-head counterpart, the average access time is 8 milliseconds. Recent trends in technology suggest that in the future we shall be moving more toward fixed secondary storage media and away from removable devices.

Each track on the disk has an address. Usually, manufacturer-supplied software lets us specify a file and record size and then retrieve a specific record. The records are numbered 1 through n, where n is the number of records in the file. Thus, we can treat a file as consisting of a group of separately numbered records

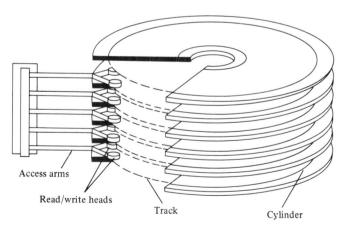

FIGURE 8-6
Magnetic disk.

Access arms

Read/write heads

Track

Cylinder

without concern over the physical track address where the record is stored. The software associates the track address with a logical record and finds the desired record for us.

Processing Direct-Access Files

Basics There is no reason why the direct-access file cannot be processed sequentially in the same manner described in the last section for tape files. In fact, in many applications we update sequentially and retrieve records by direct access.

When processing the files directly, how do we locate the record wanted? If we request a record number, the file management software will supply it for us. However, we must associate the logical record number with the information desired. For example, in an inventory application, how do we know where information on inventory part number 1432 is located? What logical record contains data on part 1432? One solution is to begin at the first record on the file and read each record until we find part 1432, but this is simply scanning the file sequentially, which has no advantage over tape processing.

To relate a key of interest (part number 1432) to a logical record on the file, a directory is used. The directory is like a map that tells us where a particular address is located in a city. The problem of finding the location of a record for a particular key is called the key-to-address transformation problem. We have the value of a field, the key (part number 1432), and we want the record number (address) where the logical record with this key is located.

Direct There are three basic methods or types of directories for transforming a key to an address. The first is called the direct method and is rarely applicable. Here we let the key be the address; for example, part number 10 is stored on record 10. It is not often that an application occurs where this approach is possible. Possibly in setting up an entirely new system we could assign a part number to the inventory and use the number as a record address.

Dictionaries The second method for key-to-address transformation, called the dictionary approach, is probably the one used most often. A dictionary (a table in memory) relates keys to their location, for example:

Key	Dictionary entry	Record address
1432	1432-312	312
4293	4293-137	137

We search the dictionary in primary memory (which is several orders of magnitude faster than searching the disk itself) looking for the key. The dictionary entry tells at what record that key is located. See Figure 8-7.

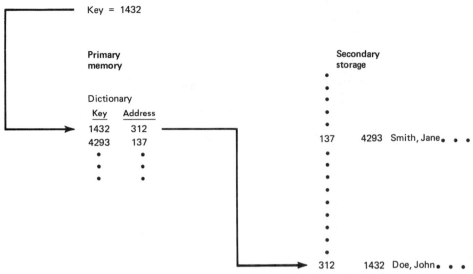

FIGURE 8-7
Dictionary lookup.

In the case of a very large file, the dictionary may become so big that it is stored on the disk file. Parts of the dictionary are brought into primary memory for searching. We usually try to keep dictionaries in order, so that it is not necessary to search them sequentially. A binary or some other rapid search is used to reduce search time.

In a binary search we divide the dictionary in half and compare the middle entry with the value of the key. If the key is in the bottom half of the table, then we divide the bottom half in half. A comparison of this entry and the key indicates in what quarter of the dictionary the key is located. With each successive comparison, we reduce the number of possible dictionary entries in half. By the third comparison we look at one-eighth of the dictionary. When there are only a few entries left it is possible to search sequentially. Remember that the key may not be in the dictionary because there is no record with this key in the file! (For example, information may be requested on a part number that is not stocked in inventory.)

When the dictionary is in order and we use a binary search, the need to store the dictionary on disk because it is so large is no problem. The various breakpoints—the value of the key in the dictionary at the ½, ¼, ⅛ positions, and so forth—are kept in primary memory. Then, the search key is compared with these numbers and the appropriate one-eighth, say, of the dictionary is brought into memory for searching. In this way, we have formed what can be considered a hierarchical directory. That is, a limited amount of information is maintained in primary memory as a directory to a more detailed directory on the disk.

Hashing   The final key-to-address transformation technique is randomizing or hash coding. Here we gain access speed at the expense of storage space. Randomizing refers to performing some calculation with the key and using the result of the calculation as an address. Clearly, there is no guarantee that the computation will not result in the same address for two different keys. Such an occurrence is called a "collision," and the keys with the same address are called "synonyms." In the case of collisions, we can recalculate the address or we can look for the next open record in the file and put the data there. For this approach to work we need a file with many open locations, or eventually processing will become sequential. Experience indicates that a file 50 percent larger than the total number of records is necessary for this approach to work.

Collisions or synonyms create a problem when hashed files are modified. Assume that we have a hashed file and are using the next sequential location that is available on the file for collisions. If two keys hashed to logical record 2365, and if record 2366 were empty, the second of the two incoming records would be placed at record 2366 on the file. Later, suppose that the first record, which was actually stored at file record 2365, is to be deleted. If we physically remove this record from the file, we shall "lose" the record at file location 2366!

This situation occurs because both records had the same address after hashing. The collision of keys forced us to put the second record in an adjoining location, 2366. When the second record is requested, it will still hash to 2365. When we examine location 2365 in the file, we find it empty and assume that the second record is not in the file. Thus, physically deleting the first record has destroyed the path to the second.

To solve this problem, we can simply use a delete indicator (a field we establish in each record) to signal whether a record is to be deleted. Periodically, the file is restructured physically, deleted records being dropped and all records being reassigned to new locations on the file. Now, when we try to retrieve the second record, we find the first record at location 2365 in the file. Since the key of this first record is not the one wanted, we look at the next sequential record at location 2366. Since its key matches the one for which we are looking, the desired record has been located. Later, when the file is restructured, the first record, with the delete indicator set, would be dropped and the second record would be stored at location 2365 on the new file.

One of the most frequent computations used in randomizing is to divide the key by the largest prime number smaller than the file size in records and use the remainder as the record address. The objective of any transformation technique is to have a distribution of addresses that results in the minimum number of collisions. As an example, if a file had 1000 records the divisor would be 997. A key of 3722 would give a quotient of 3 with a remainder of 731, and 731 would become the record address for storage purposes.

More Complex Access

So far in the discussion of direct-access files, we have talked about how to locate a unique primary key such as an inventory part number. (This key is unique because there would be only one part with a given number.) More complex structures are also possible with direct-access files. For example, we can ask

TABLE 8-1a
FILE EXAMPLE

Record no.	Part no.	Assembly	On hand	Vendor
1	4326	103	27	ACME
2	6742	607	51	JOHNSON
3	8137	12	100	DAWES
4	3218	103	13	FRAZIER
5	3762	607	43	ARMOR

questions about how many parts are needed for a particular assembly and obtain a response. Clearly, all the same things could be accomplished with tape files and sorting, but the time and processing required would be inordinate.

Consider an inventory example in which it is desired to keep track of what parts belong in what assembly. This situation is depicted in Table 8-1a, and we wish to define a file structure to answer questions such as what parts in inventory are used to build assembly number 103. To find all parts used in assembly 103 it is possible to read each record and see if the assembly field is equal to 103. In Table 8-1a we read record 1, which is used in assembly 103. We find it again at record 4, and so on. Clearly, this process is not very efficient; there could be a hundred records between each occurrence of assembly 103.

To avoid this reading time we use a pointer, which is a piece of data whose value points to another record; in this case it points to the next record where assembly 103 is found. The inclusion of pointers in the file is shown in Table 8-1b. The pointer in record 1 points to the next occurrence of assembly 103 in record 4. Now, when looking for assembly 103, we retrieve record 1 and examine the pointer field; it tells us that the next occurrence of assembly 103 is at record 4. We follow the chain of pointers through the file to answer the retrieval question of what parts belong in assembly 103. This type of file structure is known as a "linked list" or a "chained file."

How do we find the record of the first part in assembly 103? We could read the file sequentially, but there might be 500 or 600 records before the first part in assembly 103 is located. This problem is easily solved using a directory like the

TABLE 8-1b
FILE EXAMPLE

Record no.	Part no.	Assembly	On hand	Vendor	Pointer
1	4326	103	27	ACME	4
2	6742	607	51	JOHNSON	5
3	8137	12	100	DAWES	13
4	3218	103	13	FRAZIER	42
5	3762	607	43	ARMOR	106

TABLE 8-1c DIRECTORY FOR ASSEMBLIES		TABLE 8-1d INVERTED DIRECTORY FOR ASSEMBLIES	
Assembly	**Record**	**Assembly**	**Record**
12	3	12	3, 13 . . .
25	212	25	212 . . .
103	1	103	1, 4, 42 . . .
104	62	104	62 . . .
607	2	607	2, 5, 106 . . .

one in Table 8-1c. This directory simply points to the first part contained in assembly 103; first we retrieve this record and then follow the chain of pointers in each record through the file.

It is also possible to remove the pointers from the file and put them all in the directory, which is then called an inverted directory, as shown in Table 8-1d. If there are multiple chains, questions can be answered without accessing the file, just by processing the directory. Suppose that the file also has a directory for vendors, with the vendor ACME located in records 1, 16, and 42. By examining

---

SYSTEMS PROBLEM 8-2

Scientific Laboratories, Inc. is interested in developing a new computer system to aid its researchers. Most of the members of the company are natural scientists engaged in basic research; these individuals place heavy demands on the library and support services. Currently the company uses a service bureau to develop and print a KWIC (Keyword in Context) index of articles.

This rather simple approach takes each major word in the title and alphabetizes articles on it. Thus, the same article may appear many times in the listing, once for each keyword that is major. As an example, consider a paper "The Use of PVCs and Diseases of the Lungs, Pancreas, and Liver." This article would appear five times in the KWIC index under PVC, Diseases, Lungs, Pancreas, and Liver.

The company would like to develop a more sophisticated retrieval system for the research staff. They would like to have a system that allows Boolean retrieval requests. For example, a researcher could ask for all papers that discuss PVCs and diseases of the lungs, pancreas, and liver. Such complex logic makes it possible to formulate a very specific retrieval request. The system should also be able to retrieve on journal and author's name. The library staff would provide keywords and abstracts of the papers that would be stored on-line. Copies of the articles would be available in filing cabinets in the library, and their location would be referenced by the abstract displayed on a CRT for the user.

You have been asked to sketch the basic file structures for such a system. What kind of files and keys would you choose? Show how retrieval requests would be processed.

the directories for part and vendor, we see that Acme supplies two parts for assembly 103, since both ACME and assembly 103 can be found in records 1 and 42. All this processing can be done with the two directories without ever accessing the file! However, the price for this added flexibility is increased programming complexity and the need to create and maintain complex directories.

How are the directories and links built in the first place? One possibility is to use the program written to create the file originally. In creating the file, a program maintains a table in memory containing each part number. When the part number is encountered, the program places a pointer in the file to the last location in the file containing this part number and updates the pointer table. When the program is finished, the table becomes a directory and the pointers run backwards through the file.

In the example of Table 8-1a the program keeps a list of inventory part numbers in primary memory. On encountering part number 103 in record 1, the program places a 0 in the pointer field of the record and a 1 in the record address portion of the directory. Processing is done the same way for records 2 and 3 (assemblies 607 and 12). When the program encounters assembly 103 at record 4, it places the pointer from the directory (1) into the pointer field of record 4. Now, record 4 points back to record 1. Then the program updates the directory record address field to 4, and the directory points to record 4, which points to record 1. When finished, the record address field in the directory points to the most recent occurrence of assembly 103. That record points backward through succeeding records until the chain ends at record 1 with a pointer of 0. Another alternative to developing pointers in the file is to use a packaged software system. We shall discuss this topic later under data-base management systems.

Updating

Updating a direct-access file can be done randomly (direct) or sequentially. However, if we update on-line, then only the records that are actually changed need to be modified; it is not necessary to process the entire file. The disadvantage of this approach is that it is easy to lose an audit trail; records are changed and there is no backup copy as there is in the sequential update. To keep an old version of the file it is necessary to copy (dump) the file on some other storage medium, such as another disk file or tape.

What happens to pointers when records are added to, modified, and deleted from a direct-access file? Suppose part number 3218 in Table 8-1 is changed to assembly 607 from assembly 103. Can we just modify the assembly field in record 4? If it were not for the pointer chains running through the file, the answer to the question would be "yes." However, the modification would destroy the chain of pointers (see Figure 8-8). We could change the pointers, but in performing an update on record 4 we would have to know that the previous pointer was located at record 1.

There are three choices available. First, the program can look up assembly 103

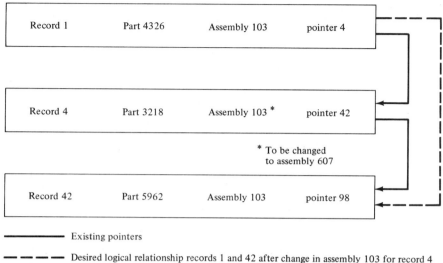

———— Existing pointers

— — — — Desired logical relationship records 1 and 42 after change in assembly 103 for record 4

FIGURE 8-8
Changing chained files.

and trace the chain of pointers through the file to find the one pointing to record 4. In this case, the program would change the pointer of record 1 from 4 to 42. Here we were lucky to find the record of interest on the first try; on the average, we would expect to follow a chain of pointers through half the file to locate the pointer immediately preceding the record to be changed.

A second alternative is to design the file with backward pointers for the assemblies; for example, a pointer from record 4 to record 1. Then, both sets of pointers have to be changed, but it is necessary only to access the three records that are involved for each change. This solves the problem of changing assembly 103. Here we save processing time at the cost of secondary storage and extra programming logic.

The third choice is to set a delete indicator and leave the record in the file just as we did with hash coding. In this case, we set a delete indicator at the old part number 3218 in record 4 and add a new record for part 3218 showing 607. Then we periodically restructure the file: The old file becomes input to the original file-creation program, which eliminates records with delete indicators and sets up new pointer chains and directories.

Any of these three choices solves the problem of modifying record 4 while maintaining the assembly 103 pointer chain. The last step is to modify record 4 and add assembly 607 to its chain. We can add assembly 607 to its chain simply by making the directory now point to it and letting its pointer field point to the old directory entry. That is, the directory record field for assembly 607 would now be 4 and the pointer in the new modified record 4 would be 2.

SYSTEMS PROBLEM 8-3

Betty Martin, marketing manager for Interland Express Company, was amazed at the memorandum she had just received from the information services department. She had asked to have sales information for the company available for inquiry. In particular, she had wanted to know the performance for each sales representative and to retrieve information on sales by customer.

The information services department said that they had all these data, but they were not available on the right files. Betty did not understand exactly what this meant. The computer group went on to say that the data on sales were stored on a "sequential tape file"; her request would require the use of several sort programs and would produce two massive reports.

Betty knew that the company had just installed a new on-line retrieval system and asked why the data she wanted could not be made a part of that system. The information services department responded that this addition could be done but would require the design of new files and retrieval commands. The new files would be on disk and would require two directories, one on sales representatives and the other on customers.

Betty Martin was now completely perplexed. Could you explain to her the alternatives available to the computer staff in meeting her request? What are the pros and cons of each alternative? Which do you expect to be most expensive? Which is most responsive to Betty's needs?

ERROR CONTROL

In any file operation, we should provide for some kind of backup. In a sequential or a batch system, backup is produced automatically. For an on-line system, we have to dump the files periodically if they are not updated sequentially.

Processing controls are also necessary to ensure the integrity of the file. An edit should be performed on each transaction to see if all numeric fields are filled with numeric data and to pinpoint transactions or data coding errors. It is also useful to include upper- or lower-bounds checks for reasonableness. Such a check specified by a user might be to determine if the number of items received is less than two times the number ordered. The program should keep processing but should issue notices that an error may have been made. Sometimes a record is flagged to ensure that a change is made on the next update.

For fields that are particularly crucial on the file, it may be desirable to verify all changes. For example, the program updating the file could carry a summary record at the end of the file with various totals on it. In the example used here, we could keep a total on the number of parts in inventory on a record at the end of the file. During file updating, the program would add all parts, keeping track of additions and usage. At the completion of the update, the summary record would be examined to determine if the old figure adjusted for additions and usage matches the new one.

FILE DESIGN CONSIDERATIONS

We have discussed a large amount of technical material in this chapter on file devices and logical file structures. However, we have not described how the systems designer should decide what kind of a file structure to use. Unfortunately, file design is more of an art at this time than a science. In this section, we attempt to provide some general guidelines for file design. However, much of the structure of the files for a computer system depends on the individual application, and the designer will have to make a number of decisions from the information developed during the systems analysis steps preceding file design.

Record Structure

The first file design decisions involve the data to be stored on the files. As the design for a new information system is developed, the requirements for information to be stored for subsequent retrieval will be specified. Related information is grouped into records, and several types of records may be in a single physical file. Record types must be defined, and so must the key fields for retrieval purposes.

Information in a file is typically updated in two ways. First, routine transactions occur that change fields in the file. For example, the receipt of a new shipment changes the balance due in an accounts-payable file and the quantity on hand in an inventory file. Other fields on the file are changed much less frequently—for example, vendors' addresses. The input for this type of change can be classified more realistically as file maintenance. In principle, it should be possible to change any field in the file with proper authorization, because errors can occur anywhere and provisions must be made to correct them. File maintenance input is usually processed by different users than in normal transaction processing, and the design of the input form and medium may differ for the two types of updates.

Having defined the basic information content of the files along with grouping of logical records, the designer approaches the problem of defining the record format. Fixed-length records are the easiest and simplest to use from a processing and programming standpoint. If there is a varying amount of fixed-length information, header and trailer records can be used. However, if the length of the record must vary, then variable-length records are necessary.

Response versus Cost

Having defined the contents and format of the file, the analyst next examines information on the nature, volume, frequency, and response-time requirements for retrievals and updates involving the file. We must balance response-time requirements against the costs of (1) creating the data base (including programming costs), (2) storing the data, (3) retrieving data, and (4) updating the data.

Some of the research on file design has resulted in the development of several models that aid the designer by forecasting the costs of alternative data-base configurations. Most of these models are in the research and development stage, but when they are refined, we hope that systems designers will be able to make routine use of them. In the future, the designer should be able to describe the physical file devices available, the structure of the data base, and expected activities, and be able to work with a timesharing computer system to compare different file design strategies. However, in the absence of these models or the time and resources to compute manually the trade-offs between response and cost for different data-base configurations, what guidelines can be offered?

Batch Files   If there is no need for immediate inquiry or on-line updating, then batch sequential files are the cheapest to develop and maintain for most applications. In addition, these files offer good error-checking and backup features. However, even for a batch application, with seemingly no need for on-line access, direct-access files may be necessary because of processing requirements. For example, if a direct-access file structure were not used in the application of Table 8-1 to produce a bill of materials for each assembly, it would be necessary to sort the file many times and undertake very complicated processing, which might not be feasible.

Direct-Access Files   If processing or access response-time requirements justify the added cost, direct-access files can be selected by the designer. In the simplest case, only processing logic demands direct access, as in the example for the bill of materials processing above. For this application, it is not necessary to process retrieval requests on-line. The next level of design effort and complexity is represented by allowing on-line inquiry but updating the files in batch mode. This alternative is less costly and complex than on-line updating and offers better error control. If the only need for access is on a single key, simple packages are available to maintain directories, for example virtual sequential access method (VSAM).

If the information to be retrieved on-line must be up to date instantaneously—for example, in a reservations system or stolen-vehicle law-enforcement application—then on-line updating will be necessary. Of the three directory approaches discussed in this chapter, the easiest one to program is a dictionary with a linked or chained list of pointers through the file. If storage space is not a problem but speed is important, hash coding is the fastest key-to-address transformation technique. However, remember that a significant amount of extra file space must be available to realize this speed advantage. Inverted directories should be used only where there are complex retrieval requests or where presearch statistics are needed before the data file is actually accessed.

Data-Base Management Systems   The acquisition of a data-base management system may be warranted if systems currently being designed and ones planned for the future incorporate direct-access files for any of the purposes described above. As discussed in the next chapter, these systems offer a number of advantages. Although they may require a substantial investment in capital and labor, subsequent applications should be more easily designed and implemented. There is clearly a growing trend in organizations toward the adoption of data-base management systems to facilitate file design for information systems.

KEY WORDS

Addition	Hierarchical
Average access time	Interrecord gap
Backup	Inverted directory
Batch processing	Key
Binary search	Key-to-address transformation
Blocking factor	Linked lists
Chained file	Logical records
Character	Magnetic tape
Data-base management system	Modification
Deletion	Physical record
Density	Pointer
Dictionary	Retrieval
Direct access	Rotational-delay time
Directory	Secondary storage
Disk	Seek time
Field	Sequential file
File	Trailer record
Fixed-length record	Transactions
Hash coding	Variable-length record
Header record	VSAM

RECOMMENDED READINGS

Dodd, G.: "Elements of Data Management Systems," *Computing Surveys,* vol. 1, no. 2, 1969, pp. 117–122. (An extremely well-written article describing possible file structures; read it several times to be sure you understand it.)

Martin, J.: *Computer Data Base Organization,* 2d ed., Prentice-Hall, Englewood Cliffs, N.J., 1977. (An excellent text on data files and their organization.)

Tsichritzis, D., and F. Lochovsky: *Data Models,* Prentice-Hall, Englewood Cliffs, N.J., 1982. (An advanced book about data structures.)

DISCUSSION QUESTIONS

1 Why is a new file written during a batch update?
2 What are the advantages and disadvantages of batch updating?
3 What are the advantages and disadvantages of direct-access updating?
4 Where do users encounter computer files? Why is an understanding of their structure and operations important?
5 Compression techniques are often used to reduce file-storage requirements and input-output transfer times. Various schemes are used to compress information and eliminate redundant data. For example, we might remove blanks from a file of text and replace them with a special character and a number indicating the number of blanks that were removed. What are the advantages and disadvantages of compressing a file key along with the rest of the record for a direct-access file?

6 Is there any advantage to blocking records for direct-access retrieval?

7 What procedure do you recommend for providing file backup for an on-line system?

8 For a file of 1000-character records that contains 20,000 records would a dictionary or hash coding be faster for retrieval on a single key? What are the advantages and disadvantages of each type of directory?

9 Why would programming for an inverted directory be more difficult than for a dictionary and a linked-list (chained) file?

10 What are the major capabilities a data-base management system should offer?

11 A relatively new mass-storage device was described in this chapter that is capable of holding hundreds of millions of characters. However, access to each record on a direct basis is relatively time-consuming. In what types of applications do you think such a mass storage device might be used?

12 It has been suggested that the difficulty of updating is inversely related to the difficulty of retrieval. That is, a file structure that facilitates retrieval is likely to be very difficult to update. Do you agree with this observation? Why?

13 Why is it undesirable to have the same data stored on more than one file?

14 Data-base management systems stress independence between data and access programs. To what extent is this possible; that is, can a program ever be completely independent from the data it uses?

15 How does a data-base management system contribute to the flexibility of information systems?

16 For a mature computer installation with 50 or 100 different applications, what problems would you envision in the adoption of a data-base management system?

17 If a dictionary is so large that it cannot be stored in primary memory but must be placed on a disk, would you recommend that it be placed all at one location in a separate file or that the directory be interspersed with the actual data records? Why? If the directory were to be interspersed, what criteria would you use to determine where to place it relative to the data in the file? (Hint: consider the average access time for the disk, which consists of seek and rotational-delay times.)

18 Does the use of accessing techniques such as VSAM or complete data-base management packages mean that the analyst and programmer do not have to understand how files are structured or how the packages work? What problems can be created if the programmer and analyst are unaware of the physical and the logical structure of the data?

19 What difficulties would be created by having to add data to a file on tape, for example, to print a new piece of information on a report? What would the problem be if the information is to be retrieved on-line from a direct-access file? Would your answer differ if the added information is to be a retrieval key?

20 Can a programmer really remain ignorant of the data-base management system when writing applications programs that use the system? Where might a programmer run into difficulties if he or she does not understand the retrieval logic of the data-base management system?

21 How is it possible for the logical view of data to differ from the physical storage layout of data? (Hint: consider the discussion of direct-access files in this chapter and how those files are stored on different devices.)

22 The acquisition of a data-base management system is a major undertaking. It is unlikely that its first application can cost-justify the effort; instead the acquisition is amortized over a number of applications. How can the organization justify moving into a data-base system, given this problem?

23 Take a system that is relatively well known, like an airline reservations system. Make a list of the major transactions processed by such a system and then use it to sketch the data structures necessary to support the system.

24 Why is it such a problem for many organizations to adopt common identifiers for names that will become data in a data-base system? Why is it necessary to do so?

25 Can you think of an example where different users of the same data would tend to view it differently?

26 If massive amounts of computer storage become available at a low cost, will there still be the need to design secondary storage structures?

PROBLEMS

1 Assume that you have been given the following information to be contained in a sequential tape file with fixed-length records:

Item	Size in characters
Social security number	9
Last name	15
Middle initial	4
First name	10
Address line 1	15
Address line 2	15
Address line 3	10
Zip code	5
Account number	7
Account balance	10

The file is used by a retail store for charge-account processing.

a On what key(s) would you organize this file if it is to be updated with purchases and payments?

b Given your file organization, how would you produce a report of customers by geographic area?

c If you have a tape 2400 ft long and can record on it with a density of 1600 characters per inch, how many customers could you get on a reel, assuming a blocking factor of 1?

d What would the answer be to c with a blocking factor of 10?

2 Given a sequential tape file, assume that it is desired to keep a record of each transaction during the year. Each customer may have 0 to an infinite number of these transactions.

a What are two possible solutions for including these data?

b What are the problems with each solution?

c Which do you recommend?

3 A direct-access file on a disk has been proposed for a police on-line system to locate (1) stolen vehicles and (2) cars with outstanding tickets. Officers in the field will radio inquiries to a terminal operator. The officer can inquire about (1) license plate number, (2) auto make, (3) color, or (4) make and color together. It is estimated that the proportion of inquiries will be 70, 15, 10, and 5 percent, respectively.

a Describe the organization of the file and the directory for your primary key.

b For the other two access keys, do you recommend a linked list or an inverted directory? Show how the file would appear under each alternative and explain the reasons behind your choice.

4 Consider the following job-matching system that is maintained on-line. A record consists of

> Social security number
> Employee's name
> Employee's address
> Salary requirements
> Skills code
> Area

The file is used for several purposes, and it was decided to keep it on a disk in social security number order. You may assume that record addressing is relative to the beginning of the file and is independent of the physical track address.

For one application, employer representatives call the employment office and a clerk enters their requests, which can be either by area, skills code, or some combination of the two.

a How would you update this file (remember an update includes adding, deleting, and modifying records) if the skills code and area are referenced by a directory showing their initial file location and a linked list of pointers through the file? Describe how your update plan would affect subsequent inquiry file accessing.

b What would your answer be to **a** if there were no points in the file and the area and skill codes were referenced through an inverted directory?

5 A request has just been made to include two additional fields in the file in problem 4. These fields would contain a code for the employee's last two jobs.

a What problems would this change create both for files and for programs?

b Would the change be easier with an inverted directory or a linked-list file organization?

6 An analyst has just recommended that your company invest in the development of a financial data storage and retrieval system. The plan calls for using the system inside the company and for sales to other firms. The system will operate on-line.

The major problem facing you is to evaluate the analyst's proposal for the file system. The use of a fully inverted directory and file—that is, inverted on every field—is recommended. The analyst feels that this file will enhance the marketability of the system, since it is difficult to anticipate all user requests.

Do you agree with the analyst? Why or why not?

The contents of the file are:

> For each Fortune 500 company:
> > For each of the past 20 years:
> > > Beginning stock price
> > > Closing stock price
> > > Average stock price
> > > Dividends
> > > Splits
> > > Sales
> > > Income
> > > Profits
> > > Number of shares outstanding

7 Anderson's is a chain of department stores in a large metropolitan area. There is one main department store downtown, and presently there are six suburban stores. Anderson's carries a full range of department store items from clothing to housewares to furniture. All merchandise is ordered centrally and distributed to stores from the central warehouse so that all stores carry approximately the same merchandise.

The company has a centralized computer located in their corporate offices near the main store. For customer billing and inventory, they are presently using a batch system and sequential files.

The inventory file contains fixed-length records in sequence by item number. Each record contains the following fields:

Field	Size in characters
Vendor number	10
Item number	10
Department	3
Quantity on hand	5
Quantity sold	5
Quantity on order	5
Wholesale price	7
Retail price	7

Anderson's keeps track only of total inventory; in other words, the "quantity on hand" field represents the total quantity of an item in all stores. Although they are considering ways to keep track of items by store, they presently do not have that capability.

The following three types of transactions may be included in an update run: (1) Orders of merchandise (remember that some items will be reorders but many items will be new merchandise never before ordered), (2) receipt of merchandise (do not worry about distribution to stores—all orders are received at the central warehouse), (3) sale of merchandise (for each item sold, part of the price ticket is sent to the central warehouse to be keypunched and entered into the system).

a Describe and illustrate with a flowchart the process for updating the inventory file. Show how the contents of the file will be changed by each transaction type.

b The company presently has a separate system for keeping information about customer credit and making it available to each sales clerk. Next to each cash register there is a small calculator-like terminal with a 10-key pad and a one-line screen for displaying a message to the sales clerk. The clerk enters the customer number from the charge plate and receives a message indicating how much above or below their credit limit the customer is or indicating that the customer cannot charge because the account is past due. The file for this system, which contains customer number, credit limit, amount due, and amount past due, is updated each night from the regular customer-billing file as part of the regular update run. What file organization would you suggest for this file with what key(s)? Justify your answer.

c Anderson does extensive mail advertising to its charge customers. Management wants a system developed that will select customers on certain criteria for selected mailings. For instance, they want to be able to select by geographical location, charge plan, age of customer, family versus single account, and credit limit. Using the customer master file (which contains all billing and address information for each charge customer) as a base, propose a file organization to accomplish this selection. Illustrate how your system works with a few records and one selection criterion.

8 General Products Corporation is a large company that produces, packages, and distributes a wide variety of grocery products nationwide. It has a customer base of about 3000 large grocery wholesalers and retail food chains. All ordering, shipping, and invoicing is coordinated through the central office. About 500 orders are received and processed per day.

The company presently uses a batch system to create customer invoices and to keep track of all payments to customer accounts. One daily processing run adds new invoices to a sequential file of outstanding invoices, and another program records all payments and removes paid invoices from the file.

a The invoice file includes, for each invoice, the following: invoice number, customer number, (unique for each customer), date of order, date of invoice, total amount due, and date due. Invoice numbers are assigned in sequence as orders are processed. If the invoice file is to be stored sequentially on magnetic tape, what field or fields should be used as keys? Why? Given your choice of key, simply describe the update procedure and logic (1) to add new invoices to the file, (2) to remove paid invoices from the file.

b A separate sequential file contains detailed descriptive information about each customer, including address information, outstanding balance, outstanding overdue balance, credit limit, and other credit information. Each customer record is about 300 characters long. About 20 percent of the customers have special credit allowances for which additional information is needed, and management wants to add this information to the existing file. There are three categories of special customer credit allowances for which are needed 40, 60, and 100 additional characters, respectively. Suggest and explain a method for incorportating these data into the file.

c Because of the high volume of customer inquires regarding their accounts and a need for better control of each account, the company wants to go to direct-access files for on-line retrieval and update of accounts receivable. Both the customer and invoice files will become direct-access files.

(1) For direct access to the invoice file, with invoice number as the key, what would be the most efficient direct-access method? Why?

(2) With direct access to invoice records, a customer may choose to pay on account by any of several methods: (a) by specific invoice number, (b) by oldest invoice first, (c) by most recent invoice first. Explain and illustrate, with a few sample records, how you would set up a linked list to process transaction types (b) and (c).

(3) Explain and show diagrammatically how the linked lists would be affected when a customer paid a specific invoice (not the oldest or the most recent).

CHAPTER 9

DATA-BASE MANAGEMENT

In the last chapter we learned the details of how direct-access files are created and accessed. The programmer must build and maintain complex directories to provide retrieval of data; these directories create problems for updating the files as well. Consider two different applications, one to inquire about parts in inventory and another about bank balances for checking account customers. Although the actual data themselves are different, each of these systems might feature a directory based on an identification number, for example, an inventory part number or a checking account number.

Why should each programmer develop separate directory and file management routines when the problems are so similar? This question led to the development of a type of systems software called a data-base management system (DBMS). One purpose of this DBMS is to automate the directory handling and accessing tasks in developing direct access files. We shall also see that a DBMS has many other purposes as we explore data management more in this chapter. We begin with a discussion of how different data structures can be created and then consider data-base management itself.

DATA STRUCTURES

Data structures are the physical and logical relationships among records in computer files. A physical data structure is simply the way data are actually found on a storage device. In a sequential file all records are located in a linear sequence; they are usually related logically according to a sequence based on some key field. On a direct-access device, the physical data structure might

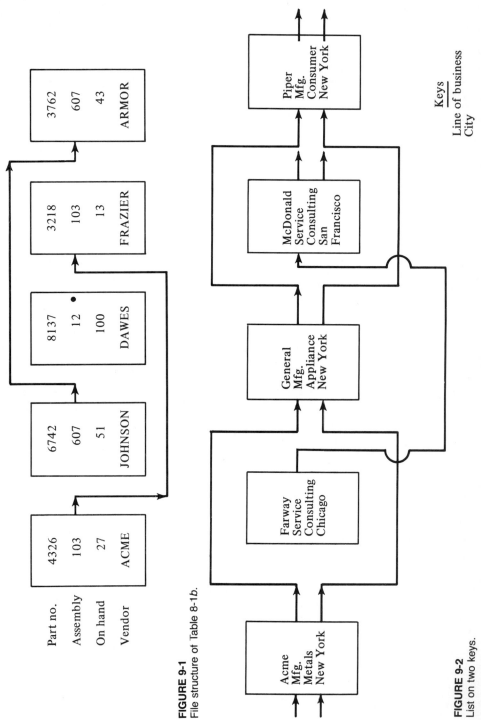

FIGURE 9-1
File structure of Table 8-1b.

Part no.	4326	6742	8137	3218	3762
Assembly	103	607	12 ●	103	607
On hand	27	51	100	13	43
Vendor	ACME	JOHNSON	DAWES	FRAZIER	ARMOR

Acme	Farway	General	McDonald	Piper
Mfg.	Service	Mfg.	Service	Mfg.
Metals	Consulting	Appliance	Consulting	Consumer
New York	Chicago	New York	San Francisco	New York

Keys
Line of business
City

FIGURE 9-2
List on two keys.

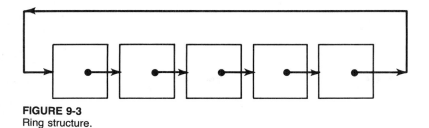

FIGURE 9-3
Ring structure.

include some directory records at the beginning of a physical location followed by portions of the record with data.

Of more interest to the analyst are logical data structures. We can develop many different logical structures to support different types of processing applications. In fact, we have seen several logical structures earlier in the chapter but have studied these primarily from the combined view of logical and physical structuring. For example, we indicated how we would include pointers and directories in a file. A completely logical view would simply have used arrows to show the connections among different fields. In designing physical data structures, we are concerned with how to best represent the desired logical structures on physical storage devices.

We have seen a list structure earlier in the chapter. We can redraw that structure as shown in Figure 9-1 to emphasize the logical relationship among records. The inverted list looks almost the same from logical considerations, but the actual implementation differs since the pointers are now in the directory rather than in the actual data records. A more complex structure with two lists is shown in Figure 9-2.

A list can easily be extended to become a ring as shown in Figure 9-3. In a ring the last record in a list points back to the first record of the ring, which contains a special symbol to show that it is first. One can follow the ring to find any record, for example, the preceding record, the next record, or the first record of the ring. One can also use a ring with connections in each direction (Dodd, 1969).

The three major types of data structures are generally defined in the literature today: hierarchical, plex or network structure, and a relational file.

A hierarchical file is a case of a tree structure as shown in Figure 9-4. The tree is composed of a hierarchy of nodes; the uppermost node is called the root. With the exception of this root, every node is related to a node at a higher level called its parent. No element can have more than one parent, though it can have more than one lower-level element called children. See Martin (1977).

A hierarchical file is one with a tree-structure relationship between the records, for example a master detail file with two record types. Such a representation is often very convenient because much data tend to be hierarchical in nature or can easily be cast into this structure.

A network or plex structure exists when a child in a data relationship has more than one parent. An item in such a structure can be linked to any other item. (See

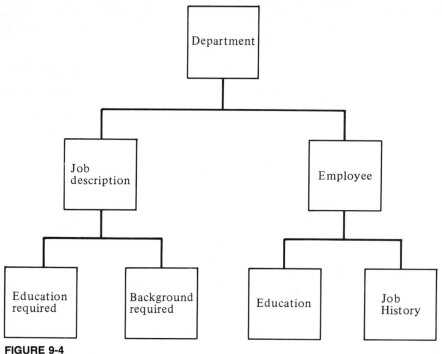

FIGURE 9-4
A tree or hierarchical structure.

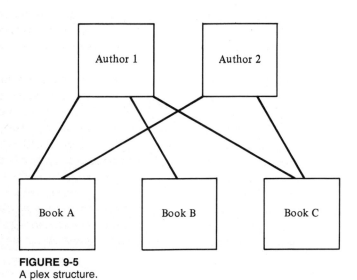

FIGURE 9-5
A plex structure.

Figure 9-5.) Martin (1977) discusses simple plex structures in which the child-to-parent-mapping is simple; that is, arrows do not go in both directions. The physical data structure to support complex plex structures is far more difficult to develop than for simple structures. An examination of Figure 9-5 should show the reasons for this difficulty.

There has been much research on yet a third type of data structure called "relational." The underlying concept of a relational file system is very simple; data are organized in two-dimensional tables such as the one in Figure 9-6. Such tables are easy for a user to develop and understand. One virtue of this type of structure is that it can be described mathematically, a most difficult task for other types of data structures. The name is derived from the fact that each table represents a relation.

Since different users see different sets of data and different relationships

FIGURE 9-6
A relational data base.

Name	Address	Zip Code	City	Department no.
Smith	16 Main	92116	New York	302
Jones	37 Spencer	07901	Chicago	161
Morris	19 Old Way	83924	New York	302
Able	86 Fulton	10006	Denver	927
Charles	19 Hunter	11126	Chicago	161

Name	Profession	Income
Johnson	Bartender	15,000
Martin	Programmer	14,000
Jones	Systems Analyst	18,000
Carson	Manager	17,000
Smith	Systems Analyst	19,000

Join:	Name,	Address,	Zip Code,	Profession,	Income
	Jones	37 Spencer,	07901,	Systems Analyst,	18,000

Project:	City,	Department
	New York	302
	Chicago	161
	Denver	927

between them, it is necessary to extract subsets of the table columns for some users and to join tables together for others to form larger tables. The mathematics provides the basis for extracting some columns from the tables and for joining various columns. Martin (1977) argues that this capability to manipulate relations provides a flexibility not normally available in hierarchical or plex structures.

The subject of data structures is extremely complex, and a number of good references are devoted entirely to this topic. The important thing for the analyst to realize is that there are many ways to represent different logical data structures. The flexibility and relatively low cost of direct-access storage make it possible to develop very complex logical data structures to support information systems. As we shall see in the next section, software exists to help implement many of these complex structures in a generalized manner.

SYSTEMS DESIGN

It should be apparent at this point that one of the major design tasks is to determine the contents and structure of the data base. The type of retrieval and reporting required by users and the availability of input determine what data have to be stored. However, it is a very complex task to specify these data, group them into records, and establish data structures for a system.

Schema

Some of the early work on data bases developed the concept of a schema that is the description of the logical data base (we can think of this term as synonymous with "model" as used in the last section). The schema shows the types of data and relationships among them. In data-base terminology, the data that are of interest are often called entities, such as student, class, major as shown in Figure 9-7. Entities also have attributes; a student has an identification number, age, sex, and date of birth.

For certain data-base types, especially those that follow the design created by the CODASYL task group, entities are grouped into sets. In Figure 9-6 there is a set of advisors, students, majors, biographies, and classes. The sets are joined together by relationships. In the figure, an advisor is related to students by the relationship *advises*. This is an example of a 1 to n relationship; a single advisor advises n students, but each student has only one advisor. A student has one biography and there is one biography per student giving a 1 to 1 relationship. On the other hand, n students can be enrolled in m classes. Finally, n students each have one major.

The schema in Figure 9-7 presents an entire, simple data base. However, there can be subschemas as viewed by different individuals. A professor might only care about a class list, not the major or advisor of a student. The department chairperson wants to know something about majors in the department.

Sometimes these differences are called logical views of the data. It is very likely

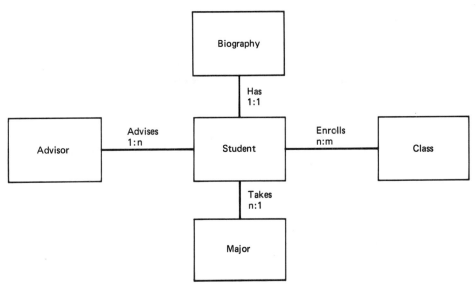

FIGURE 9-7
A schema.

that different users will have different logical views of the data; a key task of design is to integrate these different views and create a physical data base that is capable of supporting different logical views with adequate performance.

Data-Base Administrator

Many organizations using data-base software described in the next section have created a new position known as the data-base administrator (DBA); this individual has the responsibility for working with systems analysts and programmers to define the physical and logical views of the data to be manipulated by computers.

DATA-BASE MANAGEMENT SYSTEMS

The objective of a data-base management system is to facilitate the creation of data structures and relieve the programmer of the problems of setting up complicated files. Data-base management systems have developed from a concept of the data base as something distinct from the programs accessing it. In addition to easing processing, this approach has tended to highlight the importance of data as a resource in the organization and as something that has to be carefully managed.

Data-base management systems have grown from simple file-accessing aids and retrieval packages. The early file-management packages operated on sequential files. Users described the file records, and a retrieval language was used to express complex logical relationships among fields for retrieval. Many of these packages have been extended to include updating capabilities, thus eliminating the need to write a detailed program for retrieval and substituting a much higher-level, user-oriented language instead.

As direct-access files became more common, several vendors offered file-access packages for use in writing programs in computer languages such as COBOL. One of these accessing methods is known as the indexed sequential access method, or ISAM. This software package allows the COBOL programmer to develop a program to update and retrieve information from a direct-access file with a single access key without having to construct a directory or write search routines. The ISAM software maintains a directory (a dictionary in this case) for each record. The application program supplies a key, and the system retrieves the record. The current version of this package is called VSAM, and it represents a major improvement in the system.

The software maintains overflow areas and pointers to keep the file in order sequentially. Thus, updating can be done sequentially, and retrieval can be accomplished on a direct-access basis. This type of file has been very popular because it is possible to update in batch but inquire on-line. As a file gets out of order and the overflow areas are filled, it is periodically necessary to restructure the file. Statistics are provided by the software as to when this updating is advisable. Simple access methods such as this and file-management packages have evolved into much more complex data-base management systems.

Complete Data-Base Systems

A complete data-base management system separates the definition of data from the programs that access it. This concept of data independence is one of the key advantages of a data-base management system. When programs own all the data they process, it is quite common to have the same entity represented by different program variables in each separate program. As a result each application stands alone, and it is very difficult to answer inquiries across several applications.

The lack of data independence from traditional approaches to programming also creates a significant maintenance problem. As programs are changed to reflect changing conditions or requests from users, all the programs in a system that access the file have to be altered. At a minimum, the record descriptions in the programs will have to be changed; it also may be necessary to make modifications in the programs themselves to process added data.

With a data-base management system, only programs that access the actual fields altered are affected in general by a change. Programs that do not use the fields that have been altered do not have to be changed usually. As a result, we have gained some independence between the data and the programs that access those data. This kind of data independence is the essence of the data-base concept. Combined with the ease of access to data, data independence, and other features of data-base management systems discussed below, we have DBMS software available that can dramatically ease the tasks of developing a computer application and maintaining it after its completion.

SYSTEMS PROBLEM 9-1

Marvin Thompson is president of Midwestern Bank and Trust. He has just returned from a bankers' convention at which the major topic was data-base systems. Midwestern has been studying the problem of central files for several years. The idea of a central file is to consolidate all the information about a customer of the bank. Currently, one system maintains data on loans to commercial customers, another one keeps track of demand deposits, a third keeps track of savings and certificates of deposit, and so forth.

The major advantage of central files is the better service they allow. The bank knows the total business picture of any given customer. However, as with any new system, there are disadvantages. Several representatives at the convention indicated that data-base management systems were not a panacea for computer problems. Because so much data were resident on expensive direct-access storage, costs were very high for central files.

Marvin wondered what major factors to consider in deciding whether or not Midwestern should move toward a central file system. If the file system is to be developed, should the bank program its own data-base routines or acquire a commercial data-base management package? What factors should it consider? Can you help Marvin structure the bank's decision problem?

Components of a DBMS

Originally the DBMS was used to refer to two very specific functions in creating a data-base environment. At the core of such a system is a data-definition language for describing data structures and the programs that are used to build, update, and retrieve data from the data base. The trend is for vendors of data-base management systems to create integrated tools for building and operating data bases.

Figure 9-8 is an overview of an integrated-data-dictionary data-base environment. The data dictionary is used to store and define definitions of data, including identifiers, location, and format for storage characteristics. The data dictionary can be used to retrieve the definition of data that has already been used in an application so that standards for naming can be enforced across applications (see Allen, et al., 1982). Depending on the specific system, the data-base administrator might also store some of the description of the data structures in the dictionary, for example, entities, attributes, and relationships. The data dictionary must have software to update itself, produce reports on its contents, and answer queries. A complete system will also tie into the data-definition component of the DBMS.

The data-base administrator, or programmers, must use a special data-definition language with the data-base management system to describe the data and file structures to the system. Martin (1977) has described some of the characteristics a good data-definition language should have, which of course implies what characteristics a good data-base management system should include.

The language must identify various subdivisions of data, for example, items,

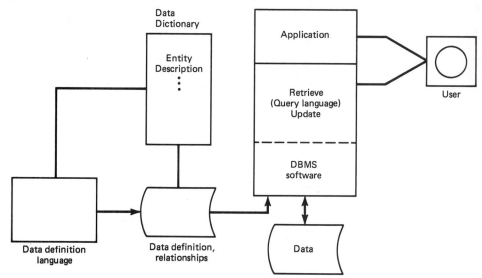

FIGURE 9-8
Overview of a data-base management system.

segments, records, and files. There should be unique names for each data-item type, record type, file type, data base, etc. The language should specify how data items are grouped in aggregates, records, or other subdivisions and show repeating groups of items. The language must make it possible to designate data items as keys. It is also necessary to specify how various subdivision or record types are related to make different logical structures, and it should be possible to give names to relationships among data groupings. Martin also describes additional capabilities that the language may possess, including the specification of privacy locks to prevent unauthorized reading or modifications. He also argues that the language should be concerned only with logical data description and not with specific addressing, indexing, or searching techniques or the placement of data on physical storage. These topics belong to the physical definition of the files, not the logical (Martin, 1977).

An integrated data dictionary (DD) at the least generates a file for the data-definition language (DDL) that it uses to generate the schema for the DBMS. Such an interface between the DD and DDL can be in batch mode; that is, the DD generates a file that is passed to the DDL. A dynamic interface involves the DBMS software actually consulting the DDL and DD during its execution. Although it creates overhead, such a dynamic link means that changes are automatically reflected in all components of the data-base environment as soon as they are made.

Given the data definition and the data base, the data-base management system constructs all pointers, linkages, and directories automatically. The applications program issues calls for the data it desires. The data-base management system examines the data request and determines where the records of interest are located; it returns the entire record or the field requested to the calling program.

Typically the programmer inserts some type of call to the DBMS to access the data base. The actual statements used in the program differ among DBMS vendors; the specific commands are also dependent on the underlying structure of the DBMS: hierarchical, network, or relational.

The DBMS does provide a great deal of assistance to the programmer, but this individual still must write programs to load the data, maintain it, and answer inquiry requests. A DBMS can contribute to productivity but will not reduce systems development time by a factor of 10 or 20.

Another component of the DBMS can reduce the need to program ad hoc retrievals: the query language. The user of this language must have some knowledge of the underlying data-base structure (the applications programmer can conceal this structure through menus and other approaches to retrieval programs that are written as a part of an application). The query language makes it possible to formulate requests for data without the need for a program to be written. For example, a retrieval language might allow us to say:

SELECT FROM student WHERE age GT 19

Using the schema of Figure 9-6, the lowercase words above represent entities, sets, and attributes. SELECT FROM, WHERE and GT are a part of the query language; "student" is the name of a set and "age" must be an attribute of records in the student set. The value of age is used to determine what records to retrieve, in this case records of students whose age is greater than 19.

In Conclusion

With a DBMS, it is possible to design file structures much more easily and to set up a data base that can be used by a number of different applications programs. As a result, the systems increase programmer productivity. These systems also try to avoid data redundancy; the same data are not maintained by a number of different systems, each having different files.

Data-base management systems can be very difficult to learn to use and install. As one can imagine, they are very complex programs and they tend to be inefficient in computer time and costly in storage. However, the importance of these costs is being reduced by the need for greater programming productivity. Machine costs are getting cheaper, and human costs are getting higher.

Many organizations have achieved impressive results using data-base manage-ment systems. However, it is necessary to study and evaluate the systems carefully. If you do not need the most complex system, do not acquire it. Clearly, the future trend is to use data-base management packages to save programmer, analyst, and implementation time. There is also an insatiable demand for on-line data access by users. Currently, there are few standards and there are wide differences among the packages. It is best to look at present and planned applications and then use references supplied by the package vendor to talk with other users. Try to determine the good and bad points of each package under consideration. For a discussion of various selection factors for data-base management systems, see Merten and Sibley (1973).

Two Examples

A Network The different data-base management systems offer a variety of file structures, though the same file problem can usually be solved with the structure of each system. One data-base management system features two kinds of files, a master and a variable file. The master is accessed on some key and linked to the variable file. Within the variable file, associations among entries are linked by pointers.

Figure 9-9 shows examples of different logical file structures represented with this plex scheme. At the top of the figure we see a master file of inventory parts and their quantities in stock. This master file is linked to a variable file containing a history of usage of each part issued from the inventory.

A master file can have multiple variable files in this system. In the example of Figure 9-9, we can add another variable file to keep track of receipts of each part. It is also possible to have two master files accessing a single transaction file as shown in the bottom half of Figure 9-9. The parts and inventory master file is the same as the example in the top half of the figure. The second master file, a list of projects, is linked to all transactions that took place for a particular project. There

FIGURE 9-9
A network data-base example.

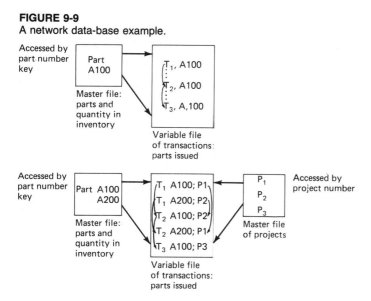

would be two types of linkage in the variable file—one for transactions for the same part and the other for transactions for the same project. This same logical structure could be represented by data-base management systems using other forms such as a hierarchical tree structure.

One major advantage is that data-base management systems set up all the directories and pointers automatically. The user specifies only the logical structure of the files; much of the complex programming for direct-access retrieval and updating is thus eliminated by the data-base management system.

A Relational System The system described in this section has been developed for a microcomputer and is based on the relational-data model. Table 9-1 shows two relations that could be defined using this system: STUDENT and CLASS.

To begin the development of the data base, the user would use the DEFINE command to describe each relation. The system helps the user define an input format on the computer's display device to enter data for each relation.

Once the data shown in Table 9-1 have been entered, the user can ask questions using the operations of the data-base system. For example, we could type:

SELECT STUDENT WHERE Year EQ 1

and obtain a list of students number 100 (JONES) and 155 (MURRAY).

To obtain a class list we could perform a join operation:

JOIN STUDENT CLASS MATCHING Student#

This operation would produce a new relation containing the columns (nonredundant) of the student and class relations. Student number 160 would appear in two places in the new relation, once for class B371 and once for class B600. We could print the results as a class list or just select one class and print the students enrolled in it.

TABLE 9-1
RELATIONAL EXAMPLE

Student relation				Class relation	
Student #	Name	Age	Year	Class #	Student #
100	Jones	19	1	B371	100
150	Smith	21	4	B371	160
155	Murray	18	1	B371	165
160	Berman	22	4	B400	150
165	Doe	20	3	B600	160

SYSTEMS PROBLEM 9-2

Marlyn Atkins is Vice President of Human Resources for Multinational Manufacturing, Inc. Her firm employs nearly 100,000 people around the world. A constant problem is filling vacancies when they arise; preference is given to existing employees. However, it is very difficult to know that an existing employee may have the skills needed for an opening so that they can be notified to apply.

Marlyn talked to representatives of the Multinational computer staff, and they indicated that a new, relational data-base management system they had acquired might help her. Currently there is a personnel system that is updated in batch mode once each month. It contains data on the employee, including header records with name, education, skill, salary, and similar data. Trailer records reflect job history—the positions the employee has held in the firm.

The new data-base system extracts data from sequential files like the ones used in the personnel system and then builds relations that are available for inquiry through a query language that is part of the package.

Can you help Marlyn define relations and formulate a few sample inquiries to extract the kind of information she needs from the existing personnel system using the new data-base manager?

CHOOSING A MODEL

The choice of a particular data-base management system is a complicated one. We should ask if the system is easy to use, understand, manipulate, and implement. Just as with any other package, the computer department will be interested in the quality of the computer code in the system and with its documentation.

There are advocates of all three major data models: hierarchical, network, and relational. Academically the choice is relational because of the many features it offers. Relational-data models can be analyzed formally, which gives them a strong foundation and some degree of standardization across implementations.

Relational models are also favored because the retrieval and data manipulation languages tend to be easy to understand and use. Also, relational systems tend to appear simple to the user, making retrieval and manipulation easier. Thinking of data in the form of tables is conceptually more simple than complex hierarchical or plex relations.

SUMMARY

In this chapter we have discussed data structures and data-base management. The simple techniques of the last chapter using pointers and directories can be applied to the creation of quite elegant data structures. To encourage data independence and to ease accessing requirements, the industry is moving to data-base management systems. A DBMS that is integrated features a data dictionary, data-definition language, data-base management routines themselves, and a query language. The definition of the data base is one of the most important activities in the technical component of systems analysis and design; data-base management systems can help accomplish this task and greatly expand the power of the computer.

KEY WORDS

Attribute	Logical view
Data-base administrator	Network
Data-base management system	Plex
Data-definition language	Query language
Data dictionary	Relation
Data independence	Relational
Data structures	Ring
Entity	Schema
Hierarchical	Tree
Key	VSAM
List	

RECOMMENDED READINGS

Allen, F. W., M. E. S. Loomis, and M. V. Mannino: "The Integrated Dictionary/Directory System," *Computing Surveys,* vol. 14, no. 2, June, 1982, pp. 245–286. (A good article on dictionaries and their role in design.)

Martin, J.: *Computer Data-Base Organization,* 2d ed., Prentice-Hall, Englewood Cliffs, N.J., 1977. (A classic text.)

Tsichritzis, D., and F. Lochovsky: *Data Models,* Englewood Cliffs: Prentice-Hall, 1982. (Advanced data structures.)

DISCUSSION QUESTIONS

1 Why do users have different logical views of their data requirements?
2 Which model, hierarchy, network, or relational do you think offers the most flexibility? Which would be easiest to explain to a user?
3 Explain the concept of data independence. Can programs and data ever be totally independent?
4 What advantages does a query language provide for the computer staff? What disadvantages for users?
5 Why do most organizations use a DBMS for specific applications rather than attempt to define a comprehensive data base for all applications?
6 How does a DBMS make it easier to alter the structure of a data base?
7 Does a DBMS completely isolate the user from the underlying structure of the data?
8 Why does it make sense to use a data dictionary and enforce common naming standards for data items in an organization?
9 Is a DBMS only useful for applications that run on-line as opposed to batch processing?
10 What complications are added to a data-base management system when distributed processing is involved?

11 What kind of security and controls are needed in a DBMS?

12 In an on-line environment, a common problem is the need to lock out access to a record while it is being updated. Why do you think this is necessary? What scheme can be used to lock the record?

13 Recovery from a computer failure or other interruption of a system is a major consideration for organizations. What problems do you see in recovering from such a failure when using a data-base management system?

14 How should one back up a data base used for on-line processing?

15 How can accessing data in relational tables be speeded over a straight sequential search?

16 What evaluation criteria would you recommend be applied to a decision as to what data-base management system to acquire?

17 Why is there a need for a data-base administrator in an organization using a DBMS?

18 How can the systems analyst use the facilities of a DBMS during the design process for a new system?

19 To what extent is performance (speed of access) a major consideration in data-base design?

20 In the schema of Figure 9-7, how would an advisor query the system to determine the major for a given student? How would the query language access the data base?

21 Under what conditions is it better to program a retrieval option into a system as opposed to providing a user with a general-purpose query language?

22 Are there any conditions under which it would be desirable to duplicate data in a data base? If so, what are they?

23 Think of an application like student registration, and design a relational data base for the registrar. Then, using the same data, design the system as a hierarchical data base. What are the major differences?

24 Under what conditions might an organization want to have more than one vendor's DBMS? What problems do you forsee if there are multiple data-base systems?

25 In the last chapter we discussed hash coding; do you see an application for hash coding in the design of a data base using a DBMS?

26 There has been discussion in the literature of a special computer that would operate as a data-base "backend." That is, the computer would handle only operations relating to the data base and would interact with a central computer. What advantages do you see for such an approach?

27 What major trends in the field make data-base management systems feasible?

28 What does a DBMS mean for users of systems?

29 Does a DBMS from a particular vendor mean that the organization is tied to that vendor for the forseeable future?

30 For any of the file problems in the last chapter, describe how your design would be different using a data-base management system.

DATA COMMUNICATIONS

DATA COMMUNICATIONS

Early computers processed data in batch mode at one point in time. Devices were soon developed to transmit the information on punched cards from one location to another over phone lines, marking the beginning of the communication of data through an existing telecommunications network. The operation took place off-line; the computers involved were not directly connected to the phone lines. In addition to card punches that could send and receive, there were devices to send the contents of magnetic tapes from one location to another.

In the early 1960s the first on-line systems were developed; these computers used for airline reservations served many terminals connected through various types of communications lines. (A few years earlier the first such on-line systems had been developed for defense applications.) At about the same time, terminals were attached to computers that were used for timesharing. The major difference between on-line and timesharing systems is that the former are dedicated to a single application. For example, an airline reservations agent can only make a reservation or inquire about the status of various flights; the agent cannot write a program from the terminal. With timesharing, the user of the terminal does usually have the ability to write programs.

The use of on-line systems has expanded rapidly; today a large proportion of new systems have some portion that is on-line such as data entry, update, and/or inquiry. At the same time, there has been an expansion in the number of alternatives available for establishing communications among computer devices. One has a choice from dial-up phone service to private networks using satellites for transmission.

In this chapter we cover the fundamentals of data communications. To develop

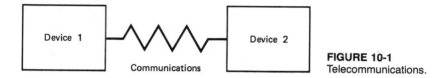

FIGURE 10-1
Telecommunications.

a major communications network, specialists are required because of the complexity of the problem and the large number of alternatives. However, it behooves the systems analyst to have a basic knowledge of data communications, given its importance.

BASICS

Figure 10-1 is a high-level diagram of data communications between two computer devices; we shall expand this very basic schematic further. The most familiar type of communications is probably the case in which device 1 is a terminal and device 2 is a computer of some type. The transmission line may be nothing more complex than a pair of twisted wires from the terminal to the central computer that offers timesharing services.

Codes

The data sent over the line is represented as some type of code; that is, the sending and receiving ends of the communications lines have to agree on how to represent symbols like the letter A, B, C, etc. For telex data the Baudot code is the most common; it uses 5 bits for each letter. (A bit is either 0 or 1.) The number of symbols that can be represented in binary by a code is raised to the power of the number of bits, e.g., $2^5 = 32$, a fairly small number of symbols when one considers the length of the alphabet!

The most frequent code for interchanging data is called ASCII (American Standard Code for Information Interchange), which is a 7-bit code (there is an eighth bit for error checking), and thus has 128 symbols. A code used with earlier computers was BCD (Binary Coded Decimal), which is a 6-bit code. Finally, there is a code that is primarily used by one manufacturer of computers known as EBCDIC (Extended Binary Coded Decimal Interchange Code), which is also an 8-bit code.

All codes, then, use sequences of 0s and 1s to represent different symbols; as an example the ASCII code for H is 1001000. On the sending end, an H is translated into 1001000 for transmission, and on the receiving end the string of bits is translated back into an H. (It should be noted that computers are designed to represent data in memory in coded form. However, there is no necessary relationship between the internal coding and the codes used for transmission between computers.)

Codes often feature extra bits or characters that are used to control transmission and to detect errors. A simple transmission scheme that sends one letter at a time might include a start and a stop bit to delimit the beginning and the end of the character for the receiving station. A basic error detection scheme is parity checking; the sending device checks to see that there is, say, an odd number of bits in each character; if there is an even number, the sending station makes the parity bit a 1, thus creating an odd number. Under this odd parity scheme, the receiving device also counts the bits; if there is an even number, then at least one bit has been lost in transmission. The parity scheme is rather simple; there are far more elaborate error-detecting and even error-correcting codes available.

Transmission Modes

There are a number of options for transmitting data over communications lines; the most frequently used approaches follow.

Character Mode   Data are transmitted as single characters as they are typed on a terminal. This technique is very simple and does not require complicated hardware or software.

Block Mode   In block mode, data are placed in a hardware memory on the sending device temporarily; the block is surrounded by appropriate characters for start and end of transmission. The data are then transmitted as a single block usually with some type of error-checking sequence at the end of the block to detect errors. If there are errors, then the two nodes arrange for a retransmission of the data.

Asynchronous Mode   Asynchronous transmission is associated with character mode operations, since the characters are sent when entered. A single bit is added to the front of each character and one or more bits at the end. These extra bits alert the receiving device to the existence of the character and delimit it.

Synchronous Mode   Block transmission features blocks that are of equal length, and one follows another. There is no need for start and stop bits that are associated with each character in asynchronous transmission; considerable overhead is saved using block mode. The beginning of each block is identified and the sending and receiving devices must be synchronized.

Direction

There are several ways to send data over lines. In simplex transmission the data are sent in one direction only, but this approach is rare. Using half duplex transmission, data travel in two directions, but not at the same time. Full duplex is the most convenient for interactive communications; here the data are transmitted simultaneously in both directions. Note that this approach will require two lines in general, since the same data path cannot carry signals in two directions at the same time.

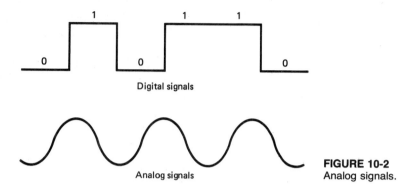

Digital signals

Analog signals

FIGURE 10-2
Analog signals.

Signal Representation

There are two basic ways to represent signals: in analog or digital form. These signals are shown in Figure 10-2; analog signals are used because the first data transmission took place over voice telephone lines that were originally developed to carry analog signals. Since computer devices communicate in digital form, the digital signal must be converted into an analog signal for transmission and then changed back to digital at the receiving end. A *modem* in Figure 10-3 places the digital code on an analog signal.

Figure 10-4 shows one approach to this modulation task. In the figure we see encoding done using amplitude modulation. The analog signal is continuous and has the form of a sine wave. By using different amplitudes to represent 0 and 1, the digital data can be encoded for transmission over analog lines. The device that actually accomplishes this modulation is called a *modem*. It is possible to modulate a signal using the amplitude of the sine wave as described above, varying the frequency of the wave or changing the phase of the sine wave to encode 0 or 1.

Owing to the explosion in data transmission that has occurred over the last two decades, the phone company and private communications carriers have developed digital transmission networks. Here there is no need for a modem; the only requirement is some kind of a line interface device to connect the sending or receiving unit with the transmission line. It is also possible to send analog signals (such as voice communications) over digital lines using pulse code modulation (PCM). The analog signal is sampled at a high rate, say 8000 times per second, and converted into discrete levels for transmission. A modulator at the receiving end then reconstructs the analog signal that was transmitted.

Speed

Transmission can occur at different speeds. The communications specialist uses a measure of speed called a *baud,* which is the number of times per second that the signal changes. For our purposes, it is easier to think in terms of bits per second or

FIGURE 10-3
Modulation and demodulation.

characters (bytes) per second. Subvoice-grade lines transmit at from 45 to 150 bits per second, and voice grade goes to a maximum of 14,400 bits per second, with 9600 being fairly common. Wideband goes up to 230.4 K (1000) bits per second.

PROTOCOLS

Transmission involves protocols that are sets of rules and procedures to control the flow of data between points. Both the sending and receiving stations need to follow the same procedures; for example, if blocks are being sent, then both stations must agree that the transmission is to be in block mode. A protocol can also increase the efficiency of transmission by reducing the amount of data that have to be sent for control purposes.

We must control:

1 Setting up a session
2 Establishing a path from node 1 to node n
3 Linking the devices together
4 The hardware sending and interpreting the data

Protocols are also used to handle:

1 Detection and correction of errors
2 Formatting
3 Line control
4 Message sequencing

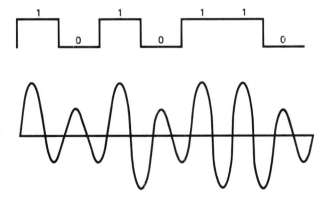

FIGURE 10-4
Amplitude modulation.

The International Standards Organization (ISO) has suggested a layered architecture to facilitate communications among different types of equipment. The seven logical layers are:

1 Application
2 Presentation
3 Session
4 Transport
5 Network
6 Data link
7 Physical

The highest levels should remain similar across equipment, but lower levels become more dependent on the devices and manufacturers involved.

Summary

A device sends out a code, for example ASCII characters, to some type of interface, which sends the message over a transmission line. For analog transmission the interface is a modem that one can use to transmit characters or blocks of data. At the receiving end, the interface unit must reconvert the code into the appropriate code for processing the transmitted data. See Figure 10-5.

TRANSMISSION NETWORKS

General Networks

A network connects a variety of terminals and computers together. The public switched telephone network is the same network used for carrying most voice traffic in the world. Here, one simply dials a number and establishes a point-to-point connection only when it is needed. In addition to telephone and telex, special private network services also provide switched connections.

Aside from the switched network, another transmission method is a simple connection between a computer and a terminal. It uses pairs of twisted wire that run directly between the two devices. One can generally use direct wire for a mile or two before the loss of signal (attenuation) becomes too great and modems are needed.

A line that is used intermittently can be shared by more than one terminal.

FIGURE 10-5
Some communications options.

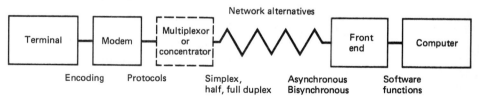

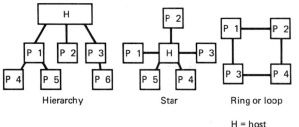

Hierarchy   Star   Ring or loop

H = host
P = processor

FIGURE 10-6
Examples of
computer-to-computer
connections.

With a multidrop line, the terminals each send and receive messages over the same line; a terminal identification must also be sent with the data.

Another way to reduce line costs is to have several terminals connected to a device called a multiplexer. The multiplexer combines the signals from various low-speed terminals and sends them over a higher-speed line. In time-division multiplexing the device samples separate incoming signals and combines them on the output line. At the receiving end the signals must be demultiplexed. With a multiplexer the speed of the output line must equal the sum of the input line speeds.

A concentrator is a small hardware device that collects messages from terminals and stores them if necessary. The concentrator sends the messages over a higher-speed line to the computer. However, unlike the multiplexer it can temporarily store the data so that the capacity of the high-speed line does not have to equal the sum of the capacities of the low-speed lines.

Network Configurations

Given the various communications options, one can configure a network of computers and terminal devices in any number of ways. Figure 10-6 presents some popular options. In a hierarchical scheme, one computer controls a series of subordinate computers; an example of this approach might be a central computer controlling local grocery store computers that, in turn, control point-of-sale terminals at checkout stands. The star scheme is similar, but here a single host or central computer can communicate with each remote processor. The local computers communicate with each other through the central system.

In a ring or loop configuration all processors can communicate with their immediate neighbors. This pattern can be extended to allow communications from any processor to any other processor. One major problem in connecting computers is the fact that they must all be able to accept data transmitted from other computers and send data to them. In theory this problem is trivial, but in practice it can be difficult to achieve satisfactory connections.

Since a large number of alternatives are available in configuring a computer network, we shall need the help of a communications specialist in many situations.

Local Area Networks

The local area network (LAN) is an important topic today; it is an approach to connecting various devices that need to communicate with each other and that are grouped closely together, such as in a single building. The devices are not necessarily all computers or terminals; they may include copying machines, communicating word processors, and similar devices.

One possible scenario for the computer configuration of the coming decades is a network of various devices consisting of a number of mainframe, mini-, and microcomputers. Essential to tying these diverse machines together is one or more local networks.

The usual structure of a local area network is a ring, in which a device communicates with its immediate neighbors only. Another possibility is a bus, in which all devices are connected to a single pathway. With either of these configurations, it is not necessary to have a central computer in charge. The LAN must, however, be able to handle the problem of contention, when more than one station is trying to send data at the same time.

One solution to the contention problem is called carrier sense–multiple access with collision detection (CSMA/CD). The transmitting station sees if a channel is clear by listening for a carrier signal. If the network is busy, the station waits until it is clear and then sends a message while listening for collisions with other stations that might have started to send at the same time. If a collision is detected, the station stops sending and waits a random time interval before starting to send again.

Another alternative scheme is to use a token that is passed along the network from node to node. A station with the token can transmit; this approach is more complicated than CSMA/CD to implement, but it reduces the collision problem.

An alternative to the local network is the private branch exchange (PBX). Originally these exchanges were developed for voice communication only, for example as the switchboard of a firm or university. Recognizing that most buildings already have phone lines installed, manufacturers of PBXs have developed units that handle both voice and data. The new PBXs feature digital transmission so that modems are not needed for data. Some units digitize voice at the PBX, and newer systems digitize voice at the telephone instrument so that the entire operation is digital. It is possible with these devices to avoid some of the expense of cabling, though cabling may be used to connect units with a high volume of traffic between them.

We expect that many new buildings will be constructed with cables for local area networks. Other sites will make use of PBXs that can carry both voice and data, and which of these technologies will dominate is not yet certain.

TRANSMISSION SOURCES

There is a large number of sources for communications services. We have discussed the public, switched network in which phone lines on the local level connect with AT&T Telecommunications. We can also pay to lease a line or pay

---

SYSTEMS PROBLEM 10-1

Global Manufacturing Company is considering a new computer application. The company wants to process orders in a central location, and then assign production to different plants. Each plant will operate its own production scheduling and control system; data on work in process and completed assemblies will be transmitted back to the central location that processes orders.

Global has small computers at each of the plants now that do routine applications like payroll and accounting. The production scheduling and control systems will be a package program running on a new computer dedicated to this application. Global has a high-level systems design for data transmission from the central computer to the plants and for the plant data to be transmitted back to central planning.

The systems staff at Global has retained you as a consultant to help them with further analysis. What kind of computer configuration seems most appropriate? What kind of transmission network do they need? What data should they collect? Prepare a plan showing the information Global must develop to plan this telecommunications system.

---

by the time the line is in use. The actual communications path may be through land lines, microwave communications, satellites, or some combination of the three.

Several firms offer packet-switching networks. These companies lease existing lines and enhance their value (value-added carriers). The customer sends a packet of information from a source to a destination and is likely to be charged by the number of packets rather than the distance traveled. Such a charging scheme is different from conventional charges, which are usually based on time and distance.

At least ten firms offer transmission facilities. In addition, one large, high-volume, transactions-oriented bank is using its own private communications network featuring a satellite transponder leased from a provider of satellite channels.

SOFTWARE

At some point the network must be controlled through a combination of software and hardware logic. There are several choices as to where this logic is located:

1 Intelligent terminals
2 Concentrators
3 Front-end processors
4 Computers (hosts)

Software must be used to control:

1 Network
2 Traffic flow
3 Speed conversion

4 Code conversion (e.g., terminal to internal computer code)
5 Error detection and correction
6 Formatting
7 Terminal polling

See Loomis (1983). Various equipment manufacturers provide different software packages for these purposes.

All these options must be considered by the network designer. It is important for the systems analyst to work with the communications specialist to determine where various functions are to be performed. We may want to have some data editing done at the terminal or store screen formats there to reduce the load on the host CPU and improve response times. The options available for communications networks contribute a great deal of flexibility to the systems design task.

THE FUTURE

Most experts in the field expect to see a greater integration of all communications, both voice and data. Office automation, conventional information processing,

FIGURE 10-7
A future computing complex.

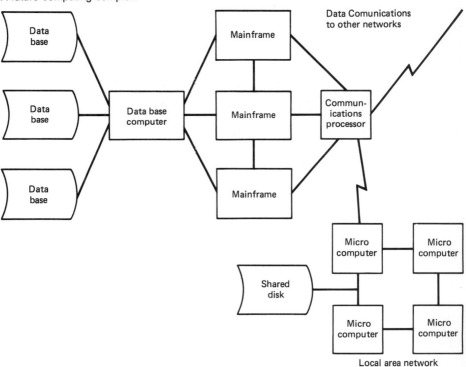

and voice communications will merge. There will be a standard series of interfaces, for example, common carriers that will interface different brands of computers and terminals so that the firm does not have to develop its own network.

The computer system of the future is likely to be a network with computers of varying capacities at different nodes. See Figure 10-7. There will be local work stations, terminals with significant logic, and built-in microcomputers. Communications networks will tie all the various devices together and help to interface dissimilar pieces of equipment. In Figure 10-7 we have a group of interconnected mainframes for transactions processing and large data file access. The mainframes access a large data base through a specialized data-base processor. A communications processor links the complex to remote work stations consisting of several microcomputers in a local area network. There is a connection to other networks as well. All these trends will lead to an increasing availability of computation and significant opportunities for systems analysis and design.

KEY WORDS

ASCII	Intelligent terminal
Amplitude	Line
Analog signal	Microwave transmission
Asynchronous transmission	Modulation
Attenuation	Multidrop line
Baud	Multiplexer
Baudot code	Network
Binary	Node
Bit	Packet switching
Block	Polling
Buffer	PBX
Byte	Protocol
CPU	PCM
Character	Response time
Code	Satellite
Demodulation	Simplex
Concentrator	Switched network
Duplex	Synchronous
Errors	Terminal
Frequency	TDM
Full duplex	Value-added carrier
Half duplex	Voice grade
Host	Wideband

RECOMMENDED READINGS

Housley, T.: *Data Communications and Teleprocessing Systems,* Prentice-Hall, Englewood Cliffs, N.J., 1979. (A good discussion of the basics of communications systems.)

Loomis, M.: *Data Communications,* Prentice-Hall, Englewood Cliffs, N.J., 1983. (A book that covers all the basics of data communications along with industry history.)

Data Communications Management, Auerbach Publishers, Pennsauken, N.J. (A loose-leaf service focusing on data communications.)

Data Processing Management, Auerbach Publishers, Pennsauken, N.J. (A loose-leaf service on information processing in general; a good overview of data communications.)

DISCUSSION QUESTIONS

1 Why were the first phone communications over analog circuits?
2 Define batch processing and contrast it with on-line systems.
3 What is the difference between timesharing and on-line applications?
4 How could a timesharing system be used to offer an on-line application?
5 Why are communications between computers digital in nature?
6 Why do we use an 8-bit code for transmission instead of one that is 5 or 6 bits?
7 Draw sine waves of differing amplitude, frequency, and phase.
8 For what is a protocol used in data communications?
9 What is the difference between sychronous and asynchronous transmission?
10 What is the advantage of using voice-grade lines for timesharing in a university environment?
11 Describe the steps involved in a protocol for communications between an asynchronous terminal and a host timesharing computer.
12 Describe at least one network configuration. For what applications do you think it is best suited?
13 Why are firms interested in local area networks?
14 What advantages do packet-switching services offer?
15 What are the major differences between a local area network and a PBX?
16 Why would a bank develop its own entirely private communications network using satellites?
17 What function does a multiplexer serve?
18 What is the difference between a multiplexer and concentrator?
19 What are the implications of work stations replacing terminals from the standpoint of systems analysis and design?
20 Why might a local area network not have a host computer?
21 Can you think of any disadvantages of satellite communications?
22 Why is it natural to think that office automation, information processing, and data communications are all likely to come together in the future?
23 Why is a communications specialist needed to design a large network?
24 Think of a business with which you are familiar; in what ways would a network and data communications aid this firm?
25 Why does the systems designer need to have some knowledge of data communications?

APPLICATIONS GENERATORS AND NONPROCEDURAL LANGUAGES

APPLICATIONS GENERATORS AND NONPROCEDURAL LANGUAGES

There are a number of problems with the development of custom applications following the systems life cycle. First, a long period of time usually elapses before the user comprehends all the features of a system. It is difficult to understand specifications; usually it takes a significant period to progress from specifications to the first tests the user sees. If the user did not understand the specifications to the point of being able to conceptualize all the features of the system, then it might be over a year from the time the application is first discussed until its characteristics become known through test results. In addition, the development of custom systems has been associated with routine cost and budget overruns, particularly during programming and testing phases.

BACKGROUND

History

In the early days of computers, programs were written in machine language, a series of numbers that were interpreted directly by the hardware to perform the operations indicated by the programmer. Programming using numbers is highly error-prone, and computer scientists have developed computer languages that are closer to natural languages.

The first advance was assembly language. Here mnemonics, easily remembered symbols, were developed for instructions to the computer like add, subtract, multiply, and so on. Symbolic names were also substituted for storage locations so that a programmer did not actually have to mention the address in memory where data are located; it is only necessary to give the data a symbolic name like X, or PAY. Instead of a series of numbers, one had programs that looked more like:

```
LDA X
ADD Y
STO Z
```

The program above adds X and Y and puts the result in a location called Z. Even though this program is an advancement over using numbers, it still requires one program instruction for each machine-language instruction executed. The next step was to develop languages of a higher level, that is, in which we could express the formula above as $Z = X + Y$. The first of these languages was called FORTRAN for FORmula TRANslation. A program called a compiler is used to translate FORTRAN statements into machine language. Today there are many higher-level or compiler-level languages, including COBOL, PASCAL, BASIC, PL/1, and ALGOL. Using these languages a programmer still must specify in detail how the computer is to perform a task.

Advanced Approaches

The need to improve productivity in developing systems has led to the development of new approaches to building applications. We shall define three broad categories of advanced development techniques:

1 Report generators aid in retrieving data and producing a report. These generators are probably the first example of a nonprocedural language and were developed originally for sequential files.

2 Query languages are languages that retrieve data from a data base. The language has access to data definitions so that it can map field names entered by the user to the structure of the data base. The languages provide the user with the ability to specify complex logical relationships among fields for retrieval purposes.

3 Applications generators and nonprocedural languages. Nonprocedural languages have commands that are at a higher level than compiler languages. A nonprocedural language may simply interpret a series of commands entered by the programmer and do what they indicate, for example, sort records, summarize them on a field, and print a report. Another approach is for a language processor to translate the commands into some intermediate language that then is compiled or interpreted for execution. An application generator is a complete system built around one of the nonprocedural languages and/or a data-base management system. The generator provides an environment for developing a complete application, from the definition of the data through all necessary procedures to update and retrieve information.

TABLE 11-1
A REPORT GENERATOR

File definition

F INVENT	ISFB02552025525	
D ITEM	00040005CA	04ITEM
D PACK	00170003CA	04PACK
D SLOT	01470005CA	04SLOT
D SIZE	00090008CA	04SIZE
D DESC	00200028CA	11DESCRIPTION
D VENDOR	01610004CA	06VENDOR
D NETCST	01650005CN2	08NET COST
D QUANT	00490005CN	13CASES ON HAND
D FAMILY	01230002CA	06FAMILY

Program

```
TITLE, GROCERY     PHYSICAL INVENTORY – CURRENT PRICE 'FIFO' RUN D
SELECT,ITEM.LT. ('27000').OR.ITEM.GT.('29999')
CALL, GETDATE
NEWFLD,EXT.FLO.2, 'EXTENSION'
SORT,SLOT
COMP,DT,EXT–NETCST*QUANT
OPTION,STDSP–1
PRINT,ITEM,SLOT,PACK,SIZE,FAMILY,DESC,VENDOR,NETCST,QUANT(S)EXT(S)
END
```

REPORT GENERATORS

Report generators provide facilities for use in extracting data from files and manipulating it. A typical language includes:

1 Statements to define the layout of the file

2 Statements to extract records based on logical criteria, for example SALARY GT (Greater Than) 10000

3 The ability to compare key fields of two or more files, for example matching a summary file to a file of details

4 Statements to manipulate the extracted data to compute new values

5 A method for specifying the format of a report

Some report generators also provide the ability to update files; theoretically one could develop an entire application using a report generator. See Table 11-1 for an example of a generator. Note the level at which the statements are entered; the SELECT command would require a number of lines in a compiler-level language. Instead, the user only has to use one word that expresses the logic clearly; we want to select records based on certain criteria. In a procedural language like COBOL a large number of statements would also be required to print the desired output report.

SYSTEMS PROBLEM 11-1

Martha Jackson runs a small investment firm that manages securities for a number of corporate entities and individuals. As an example, Martha has her own stocks in two entities, one as an individual investor and the other a trust established for her by a relative.

Each of the entities may own any number of different shares of stock. As shares are bought and sold, an exact record of the lot of stock, the number of shares, and the price at purchase and sale must be maintained. In addition, the bookkeepers at the firm must post all cash and stock dividends to each entity's records each time dividends are received.

All this processing is currently done on a manual basis. The staff is able to keep up, though it can take 4 to 6 weeks after quarterly dividends to finish posting. Closing the books at the end of the fiscal year and producing reports for the firm's accountants takes a great deal of time and work. Also, it is not easy to answer Martha's questions when she asks about various entities' stock holdings, for example, how much AT&T stock is managed in total across all accounts.

Martha is thinking about a computer system. However, she feels that the firm is unique and is not optimistic about finding a ready-made package. What advice can you give her? How should she proceed?

At first, report generators were used with sequential files. They are particularly helpful in amassing data from different files, for example, an insurance company with a master record of losses on a policy basis and another file of details for each claim. Using a report generator we could sort both files into the same sequence, for example, policy number, and produce a report of each policy's total losses and a detailed history of claims.

These generators have expanded with the widespread use of direct-access files and data-base management systems. Generators have interface routines that allow retrieval from the most popular DBMSs. The generators are sometimes called retrieval languages and are sold frequently to non-information processing professionals, users, auditors, and others who want to develop reports quickly and do not have the time or training to use compiler-level languages. These systems can be very useful for producing a printed report of an ad hoc nature. They are very attractive to users who do not want to wait for a programmer to be assigned to produce a new report. The languages are fairly easy to use; the computer staff must provide some support in the form of consulting help and must show users files where data are stored and the formats of files.

Although probably not the best approach for developing a totally new application, the use of these report languages can provide flexibility in creating output from a system and can improve the responsiveness of the computer department in satisfying requests for new reports. To the extent that users are willing to learn and use these languages, the user's efforts will supplement those of the computer department, in effect increasing the manpower devoted to systems work.

Summary

Report generators are very useful in extracting data from files, though they often have limited capabilities. For example, they often place restrictions on the order in which procedures are executed. However, newer versions of this type of software are far more capable than their predecessors.

QUERY LANGUAGES

Most data-base management systems have languages for retrieving data without writing detailed, procedural code. The statements entered by the user are interpreted by the query language processor. A typical statement for the microcomputer-based, relational data-base management system discussed in Chapter 9 would be:

SELECT KEYWORDS WHERE TERM EQ COMPUTERS, TECHNOLOGY

The query processor examines and interprets this line; the processor then does the processing of the line requests. The user is asking for rows from a table (relation) named KEYWORDS to be selected where a column in the table defined as TERM has an entry that is either COMPUTERS or TECHNOLOGY.

The query processor first looks for the relation KEYWORDS in the data dictionary and checks to be sure there is a field in it named TERM. Then it accesses the data and looks in each row for the word COMPUTERS or TECHNOL-OGY in the column labeled TERM. Records matching the request are moved to a temporary relation that becomes the result of the request. Finally, the user can print the temporary relation's values or process them further.

One important characteristic of a query language is that the user must have some knowledge of the contents and structure of the data base. Data structures designed for one type of query processing can make it difficult to answer other types of queries, at least for the novice user. It is fairly simple to select rows from a table based on values in various columns; joining and matching several different relations requires a different level of knowledge and understanding.

QBE

An interesting advanced application of a query language and a relational data-base system is Query By Example (QBE). QBE can be learned relatively easily and requires little data processing background. All the data are visualized as existing in a series of two-dimensional tables, that is, a table consisting of columns and rows.

To perform an operation, the user fills in an example of the solution in a blank skeleton table that is associated with an actual table. The user can input examples of the data required or actual data values. A series of retrieval examples will demonstrate some of the power of this particular system. The first inquiry is for a list of the names and departments of all employees in a simple personnel data base (IBM 5796–PKT).

EMP	NAME	SALARY	MGR	DEPT
	P.			P.

In a qualified retrieval, the user requests the name, salary, manager, and department of any employee who earns less than or equal to $16,000 and works for Morgan. The P symbol asks that the data be printed.

EMP	NAME	SALARY	MGR	DEPT
	P.	P.<=16000	P.MORGAN	P.

A more complicated example allows one to link multiple tables together. In this example the D1 used in the department column is an example element. It establishes a link between two or more entries in the same row or two or more rows of different tables. The same example, D1, must be used in both tables to link the tables together. This query says print the names of the employees that work in a department, D1, such that department D1 sells perfume.

EMP	NAME	SALARY	MGR	DEPT
	P.			_D1

SALES	DEPARTMENT	ITEM
	_D1	PERFUME

One advantage of this type of system is that the computer department can react to user needs immediately, not in several months. Also those needs can be met without writing extensive programs. The QBE system has cut programming requests at one firm and maintenance requirements over 30 percent and has eliminated many hard copy reports (*Data Processor,* June/July 1980).

Summary

Query languages are very effective, but they require some knowledge of the application and data-base structure. For the most part query languages are designed for the end user, not the computer professional. However, the end user needs training and good documentation and support to become facile with query languages. Research indicates that often queries are not successful. Either the query is formulated incorrectly, or more often, the data requested are not in the data base. Extensive documentation and support is needed to be sure that queries have a good chance of being answered and that user expectations are realistic about what data can be retrieved from a system.

APPLICATIONS GENERATORS

Report generators and retrieval languages are generally used with files and applications designed without the report in question as a consideration. Query languages help users access data that are already stored in a data base. Rarely with either of these tools does the user actually update the files or process transactions against them.

An applications generator, on the other hand, is designed to facilitate the development of a complete application including:

1 The definition of input transactions
2 Editing transactions
3 Creation of a data base
4 File updating
5 Report generation
6 Query processing

Most generators are built around data-base management systems, since the definition and creation of a data base is so critical in the systems design process.

From the standpoint of the systems life cycle, the generator attempts to reduce dramatically the time required in the programming and testing stages. This time savings in turn means users will see the results from the development of a system much more quickly than if a procedural language is used.

One should not, however, assume that the generator automates the systems design cycle; there still is a need to undertake a good systems analysis and design study. We still must have specifications before a generator can be used. A generator can help in developing specifications through prototyping, a procedure we shall discuss in Chapter 13.

Microcomputer Example

The relational data-base system for personal computers discussed in Chapter 9 actually has features that make it a type of applications generator. The data-base part of the system establishes relations. We could define a relation ARTICLES containing the following columns:

ARTICLE#, AUTHORS, TITLE, JOURNAL, VOLUME, NUMBER

Another relation might be KEYWORDS with fields:

ARTICLE#, TERM

Multiple entries for each article are possible in the KEYWORDS relation, e.g., computers and technology for article 85062901. Entries in the relation would then be:

85062901 COMPUTERS
85062901 TECHNOLOGY

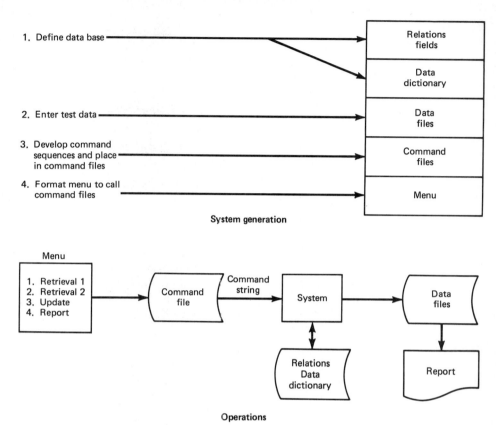

FIGURE 11-1
A microcomputer applications generator.

We could create the same type of relation for AUTHOR. We need ARTICLE# to link the various relations together. One approach to this number is to use the year, month, day, and a sequential number for each article entered on a particular day. From that point on the user does not have to be aware of the number; it will be used internally to match relationships.

We could stop at this point and use individual commands to access the data base. However, this strategy requires the user to know the structure of the data base and the commands to enter data, update the files, generate queries, and produce reports.

By including a menu builder and command files, the system makes it possible to generate applications. The menu program lets the designer construct a CRT menu, e.g. :

1 RETRIEVE ON AUTHORS
2 RETRIEVE ON KEYWORDS
3 UPDATE DATA
4 REPORT

The user enters a number and the system automatically invokes the appropriate command file. The designer creates the command file; it consists of a sequence of commands to carry out each function. For menu choice 1, the command file would ask for input of authors' names and then would SELECT the articles from ARTICLE where the author names, in the relation in the data base, match the names provided on input. At the end of the command file we return to the menu display again. See Figure 11-1.

Now the user sees a fairly conventional application; he or she does not have to learn much about how the data base is structured or how the command language works. The designer has generated an application without writing program code in a procedural language.

Mainframe Example

The same philosophy of the microcomputer example can be extended to larger mini- and mainframe computers. For a larger computer, the system will be more focused on processing transactions and updating the data base.

A system for mainframe computers is described by Tamir et al. (1981). This system is built around a hierarchical data-base management system. It includes a transactions processor that is quite sophisticated. The transaction is read from the input medium and checked for syntax plus the validity of its data fields. The processor checks the user's authorization to update the data and then updates the data base, creating whatever subsidiary transactions are required. Finally, successful transactions are recorded on a journal. Applications generators of this type may interpret input commands or actually generate code like a conventional compiler or translator. The generators that produce code are sometimes called "fourth generation languages" to indicate that source input statements are at a much higher level than those of procedural languages like COBOL.

SUMMARY

Applications generators and nonprocedural languages offer the organization a way to reduce the time required to develop information systems: They concentrate on improving productivity in programming and testing. The reports from developers of these tools claim reductions in time for development of from 5 to 10 times.

The designer or programmer must be trained to use these systems, and the organization must provide computer support. The systems are not terribly efficient, but the cost of computing is dropping and the cost of systems staff increases steadily. Some of the personal computer versions can be learned by a dedicated user. More capable and complex systems, however, will require the assistance of the professional computer staff.

These tools, if used well, can help improve productivity. However, we still must develop specifications for the system and determine the requirements for information processing.

KEY WORDS

Applications generators	Query by example
Assembler	Query languages
Compiler	Relations
Data-base management system	Report generators
Format	Retrieval
Generator	Source language
Hierarchy	Testing stage
Higher-level language	Translator
Interpreter	Transactions
Nonprocedural	Update
Procedural	User programming
Programming stage	

RECOMMENDED READINGS

Martin, J.: *Applications Development Without Programmers,* Prentice-Hall, Englewood
Cliffs, N.J., 1982. (An excellent book describing a number of languages and alternatives
to the traditional development approach.)

Tamir, M., et al., "DB1: A DBMS-Based Application Generator," *Proceedings of the Very
Large Data Base Conference,* Glasgow, 1981. (A description of a generator for a
mainframe computer system.)

Also recommended are various language manuals for report generators, retrieval
languages, and generators. For example, see articles on the systems described in Martin
like NOMAD, the DATA ANALYZER, MARK V, etc.

DISCUSSION QUESTIONS

1 What is the primary motivation behind applications generators and nonprocedural
languages?

2 How does a report generator differ from a query language?

3 What are the advantages of a system like QBE? The disadvantages?

4 What is the advantage of assembly language over machine language?

5 Should we be concerned if applications generators use the computer inefficiently? Why
or why not?

6 Why are some very high level languages called nonprocedural?

7 What distinguishes an applications generator from a query language or report
generator?

8 How can it be faster for a user to write a program using a report generator than to have
a professional programmer prepare the report?

9 Why must a user understand the structure of a data base to use a query language?

10 If applications generators become pervasive, will there be a need for applications
programmers?

11 Using a procedural language like COBOL or BASIC, code the logic required to perform
a record selection based on employee's salary greater than 10,000 and length of
service in the department over 2 years.

12 Why have some generators grown out of data-base systems?

13 Is there still a place for writing custom programs in applications development?

14 What are the functions of a transactions processor in an applications generator?

15 What are the trade-offs to be considered between a generator that interprets commands versus one that compiles code?

16 Using the microcomputer generator example, add a relation on AUTHORS and describe how the system would answer a request for papers written by three different authors. Remember that there may be more than one author for a single paper.

17 What is the advantage of the command file in the microcomputer generator in the example?

18 If we see substantial numbers of computer networks in the future, what role does the data-base management system for personal computers have in this environment?

19 How might an applications generator be used to help increase the users' understanding of a new system under development?

20 Why do tools like generators seem to help improve productivity more than approaches like structured programming?

21 What does the computer staff have to do to support users writing report requests using retrieval languages?

22 Where do the techniques described in this chapter have the greatest impact on the systems life cycle?

CHAPTER 12

PACKAGES

A package is one solution to the problems of custom systems design. We usually think of packages as software, but an increasing number of vendors sell software and the hardware on which the software is run. Thus a package can be thought of as a problem solution that is partially or completely ready to implement. The package almost always includes computer programs and may involve hardware as well.

The use of a package can dramatically reduce the time required to install a system by saving design time and the effort devoted to programming. There are, however, important considerations in purchasing a package. We can expect to spend far more than the cost of the package by the time it is installed, and it is unlikely that the package can be purchased one day and fully utilized the next!

GENERAL CONSIDERATIONS

Advantages

There are a number of advantages to packages.

1 A package should require less total development time, since detailed programming specifications are not needed, nor is as much programming usually required as with a custom system.

2 In total, a package should result in lower costs, though it is not always clear that lower costs result by the time one learns how to use the package and makes modifications to it.

3 We often find that a package has more functions or extra features that we might not have bothered with in a custom design.

4 If the package has been used in other locations, many of the programs included in the system have been debugged, or at least have run successfully in an operational environment.

5 From the standpoint of user understanding of a system, a package usually provides the opportunity to see what we are purchasing in operation before committing to its acquisition.

Disadvantages

Although there are a lot of advantages to packages, some counterarguments raise questions about this approach:

1 A package may not include all the functions we would like to have.

2 As a result, many packages have to be modified before they are acceptable to users. Modification is difficult; it requires changes to existing code and may only be possible through the vendor. Changing existing code can be expensive and is likely to introduce errors in the system. As with any programming endeavor, modifications also take time, reducing some of the benefits expected with a package that was intended to reduce development time.

3 To avoid making major changes in a package, we may elect to change procedures in the organization. Such changes are not always easy to accomplish and can be disruptive to the firm.

4 We become critically dependent on vendor support for the software. If the vendor is not viable, we may be left with software and no way to support it, that is, to have errors corrected, receive new versions, training, etc.

5 The package may necessitate the purchase of hardware, and that system may not be compatible with our existing hardware or our overall plan for information processing in the organization.

Package Design

The vendor wants to produce a general-purpose program, for example, to handle accounts-receivable processing in a large number of organizations. How can one build this generality into a system? There are four strategies.

1 Design the software with a lot of input parameters or tables; for example, an airline reservations package must have tables for city pairs between which flights operate. The input tables and parameters allow each user to tailor the system for his or her environment. ~

2 Provide different modules for different situations. Assume that a company is selling a registration package for universities. There must be a module that will handle grades; the vendor might have separate modules depending on the type of grades used, A through F, 100 to 0, and so on. It is unlikely that the same institution would use more than one grading scheme, so the appropriate module is included in each package.

3 Expect the organization to change its procedures to use the package. Often it is pointed out that a small procedural change to use the package is cheaper than the alternative of program changes. For packages that address very similar applications across companies or industries, the organization will seriously want to consider making some of these changes.

4 Plan for custom tailoring and modifications for each customer. With this in mind, the package might be offered with a very flexible report writer so that the desired reporting formats of each customer can be developed when the package is installed. One vendor includes as a part of the purchase price modifications to its package to print output on the preprinted forms used by its customers for invoices and statements.

Some combination or even all these approaches may be followed for any given package. Whenever a package is to be installed, the more dedicated it is to a given application, the more input that is required by users to describe their organization and environment.

At least one large services company offers standard packages that it will not change because of the operational difficulties changes create for its staff. A large number of firms have seen fit to change their procedures to avail themselves of the service bureau's systems.

Modifications may turn out to be the largest expense of the package, depending on how much programming is required. Some package vendors will not sell their source code; only the machine language is provided. Under these circumstances we are totally dependent on the vendor to make any needed modifications. Are modifications that run 20 to 50 percent of the cost of a package justified? In one situation the manager of a warehouse could not fill orders with the procedures included in a package. The package had to be modified so that he could use a procedure that had been followed for a number of years to allocate products to preferred customers and to ship only orders that were completely filled by available stock.

Regardless of whether the vendor, an in-house programming staff, or some third party makes package modifications, there are precautions that should be taken to minimize future problems. One good strategy is to try to confine modifications to certain modules. All changes should be carefully documented with comments on the modified programs and external documents detailing the changes. Most packages go through continual revisions and improvements. If changes have been made and not noted, the organization will be unable to install new versions, because the staff will not know what modifications to make to keep the new version compatible with custom changes in the earlier version.

TYPES OF PACKAGES

Packages are hard to classify; a large variety have been designed for different purposes and types of computers. See Figure 12-1. There is some debate as to what is a package and what is a language. We shall take a broad view and include a variety of candidates for classification as a package. Packages are often

Package type	Computer		
	Mainframe ⟶	⟶ Minicomputer ⟶	⟶ Microcomputer
Higher order language/ Applications generator	Natural Focus	Inform	Focus (version for micros)
Systems software	DBMS Total, IMS ADABASE	RIM	Condor, DBMaster, DBase II
Problem-oriented languages	SPSS, SAS	SPSS, Tel-a-graf	Visicalc, Multiplan, Lotus
Dedicated	Accounts receivable	Garment system	Accounting

FIGURE 12-1
Examples of packages.

developed for certain types of computers—mainframe, mini-, or microcomputers.

Higher-Order Languages

These higher-order languages are also sometimes called fourth generation languages. They can easily grow into applications generators with the addition of report generators and screen layout capabilities. There is a growing number of these languages for mainframe and minicomputers and at least one is available for a microcomputer.

These packages are languages; they are not dedicated to a particular application but instead require the user to apply them to a particular problem. Some of the languages are designed for specific problem areas like financial modeling, but a number exist that are really general purpose. A major advantage for the vendor is that, since the package is a language, there is little need to provide modifications for each user. Instead, the vendor concentrates on enhancing and refining the language.

Systems Software

Software packages also exist that are designed for a specific purpose, such as a set of programs to provide data-base management or programs to control the interaction of a computer with terminals. These packages can be quite general, but as an example, a data-base management system is usually built around one data model—hierarchical, network, or relational. These programs may also be designed for just one or a small number of computers.

Problem-Oriented Languages

Packages in this category are like higher-order languages in many respects but are aimed at a specific problem. A good example of this type of package is the

Statistical Package for the Social Sciences (SPSS), which is used by nonprogrammers to analyze data. The user does write a program, but the statements look very much like high-level commands:

```
FILE NAME        STOCK
VARIABLE LIST    INVINDEX,GNP,CORPROF,CORPDIV,YEAR
REGRESSION       VARIABLES=INVINDEX,GNP,CORPROF/
                 REGRESSION=INVINDEX WITH GNPR TO CORPDIV (1)
FINISH
```

Although a language, these statements are not difficult to learn, and many nonprofessional programmers use this package.

The most popular package in this category is Lotus 1-2-3, a spreadsheet program for microcomputers. This package makes it possible to construct elaborate models and test their sensitivity to changes. Figure 12-2 is an example of a simple spreadsheet. A firm publishes magazines and is concerned about whether its warehouses have enough capacity to stock the magazines before they are distributed to newsstands.

The spreadsheet appears on the CRT and is referenced through numbered rows and columns designated by capital letters. The cursor (a bright light) is on location F14; the formula at F14 is shown in the window at the top. We see that F14 is calculated by adding F7 and F13. If we were to change the data value in F7, the results would automatically be reflected in cell F14.

FIGURE 12-2
A spreadsheet example.

F14 (V)+F7+F13

	A	B	C	D	E	F	G	H
1								
2					Brevis Press		(1000 issues)	
3								
4			Boston	N.J.	Atlanta	Chicago	Denver	L.A.
5	Sales forecast		25	30	40	35	25	40
6	Price/1000 issues		2000	2000	2000	2000	2000	2000
7	Revenue		50000	60000	80000	70000	50000	80000
8	% in warehouse		.3	.5	.45	.35	.24	.35
9	Warehouse required		7.5	15	18	12.25	6	14
10	Warehouse capacity		6	12	20	8	5	12
11	Variance		−1.5	−3	2	−4.25	−1	−2
12	Cost/1000 issues		2000	1500	1800	1600	1400	2000
13	Overage costs		−3000	−4500	0	−6800	−1400	−4000
14	Revenue-storage cost	47000	55500	80000	63200	48600	76000
15								
16	Total rev							390000
17	Total overage							−19700
18	Margin							370300

This ability to relate rows and columns using formulas gives spreadsheet programs their power; a few data items can be changed and the results for the entire spreadsheet are shown automatically. Many of these spreadsheet programs are available and large numbers of microcomputers have been sold just to build models like Figure 12-2.

Dedicated Packages

The last category in Figure 12-1 contains dedicated packages, systems devoted to a particular application. This group is experiencing explosive growth as more and more installations look first to buy such a package rather than programming a custom system. This kind of package presents the most challenge for implementation. Examples of some of these dedicated packages include systems for making airline reservations, managing production, accounting, general ledger, accounts payable, accounts receivable, bank demand-deposit accounting, bank trust management, and so on.

These packages are most likely to require modifications or changes in the buyer's procedures, or both. They are not intended to be used as a language but as an off-the-shelf substitute for a custom-designed and programmed system. The fundamental choices are (1) live with the package as is or (2) pay to have the package changed or (3) change one's own procedures.

Packages have been around for a number of years, but three factors account for the increasing interest in this option for developing a system.

1 The cost of programming is rising, as are the risks of not completing a project on time and within budget. We now realize that specifications and features are often compromised in a custom design so that the user ends up not getting everything that was desired in the specifications.

2 The packages themselves are getting better, as many have been through several generations of improvements.

3 The declining cost of hardware means that we can afford to run a package that operates inefficiently on the computer to save development time and cost.

EXAMPLE

Accounts receivable is a common business computer application. Almost all firms that sell a product or provide a service have a need to send bills to their customers. The shipment of a product or provision of a service creates a receivable, that is, an asset that represents money due from customers. It is important to keep track of receivables, as this item appears on the balance sheet and because receivables have to be managed. As payments are received they must be credited against open receivables; if payments are overdue it is important to work on collecting them.

One services and consulting firm offers a complete package for a garment manufacturer. If the manufacturer is small, it can rent terminals and run the

SYSTEMS PROBLEM 12-1

Jack Robinson manages the computer department for Sports World Manufacturing Company, a full line manufacturer of sports equipment. He has just finished reading a proposal from one of the smaller plants for a complete inventory control and production-scheduling system that runs on a small minicomputer. The minicomputer would have to be acquired, as the plant has no in-house system at present.

Robinson is concerned because his department operates a large, mainframe computer that is not fully utilized. How can I be sure that the new system will work? Is the package proven? What about the money we have invested in the mainframe? Is it wise to buy another computer given the fact that we have a system now?

Jack feels that he must respond to the plant and he wonders what to do. He has asked your help in defining the issues. Should his staff undertake a study to evaluate the package? He could compare the package with the use of a custom system on the mainframe, or he could look for a package with the same features that would run on the larger computer.

In addition to this request, Jack feels this is an important issue that will come up again in the future. He would like to develop a way to handle the problem when it recurs. What is your advice?

---

package on the vendor's timesharing computer. A larger customer buys the package and a computer on which to run it. The package is quite comprehensive, and we shall concentrate here on the accounts-receivable portion of this dedicated application.

The package has the following functions, all of which operate on-line:

1 Initialization of master files, file creation, and maintenance
2 Daily entry of summary invoices and product returns
3 Daily posting of cash receipts
4 Daily sales and cash-journal processing
5 End-of-month aged accounts-receivable reports, customer statements, and commission reports for sales representatives
6 Information reports for credit and sales analysis

The system contains master files about the company, division, various codes, terms, sales representatives, buying office, and customer details. Master files are supplemented by transactions files. The first of these is accounts-receivable items, a file of all transactions and open receivables. An item record includes garments shipped, the quantity, and cost. A transactions file of cash receipts is also maintained with all customer checks and pointers to the invoices paid by the checks.

The last major category of files is that for posting totals. Here we find cash receipts control, a file of pointers to all open items for each customer. The customer credit file has totals owed that appears on the customer credit inquiry screen on a CRT. There is also a file of customer sales that has various totals of sales for each customer.

This package is dedicated, and all transactions are processed on-line from terminals. The software runs on a minicomputer under the control of a proprietary timesharing operating system and data-base manager. If the other modules of the system are purchased, they create the open receivable in the accounts-receivable file when merchandise is shipped from the warehouse. Basic information for the entire package begins at order entry when the customer's order is entered using a CRT.

When cash is received in the form of checks, a clerk working from a CRT enters the total amount and then applies the payment to open items. The clerk looks for invoices paid entirely by the check; if not obvious, then he or she must figure out what items are being paid by the check.

One firm bought the entire package including software and hardware. About 20 to 25 percent was added to the base cost of the software for modifications; in addition, the firm made some changes in the way it processes information to take advantage of the features of the package.

ACQUISITION

Choosing a package is not an easy task. First, we have an information processing problem. If it looks as if the application is dedicated, then we should perform a systems analysis and design study. The study should be carried through to a high-level design for a new system containing outputs, the contents of files, and inputs. This design becomes a benchmark against which to evaluate various packages.

In today's environment, we should not begin to look for hardware at the outset. Instead we should conduct research on possible packages. Trade journals in the computer field rank packages, and certain proprietary information firms keep listings of packages. Another good source of information is trade journals in the industry; the garment firm above found out about the system in a garment industry trade journal. Finally, for software for microcomputers one can visit various computer stores and look at their documentation on packages.

Evaluation of a package is difficult; it is important for users and the computer staff to understand the package in detail. We should be sure to see the package work and that users understand what it will and will not do. Then we should estimate the extent of modifications and determine whether the package will really work in our environment. A procedure for package purchase will be discussed in more detail in Chapter 23.

Some packages are executed on the computers of the package vendor; others are run on internal hardware. The declining cost of hardware and the advantages of internal control suggest that the trend is likely to be toward internal hardware for packages that can be operated in this manner.

IMPLEMENTATION

Package implementation is not a trivial task; it may be even more difficult in certain respects than the development of a custom system. See Figure 12-3,

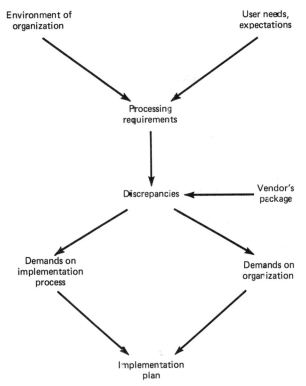

Environment of
organization

User needs,
expectations

Processing
requirements

Discrepancies

Vendor's
package

Demands on
implementation
process

Demands on
organization

Implementation
plan

FIGURE 12-3
Package implementation.

which is a framework for package implementation. The environment of the organization, user needs, and expectations about what the system should do combine to create processing requirements.

The package vendor offers a solution to these requirements. It is unlikely that the package will match exactly with the customer's requirements, giving rise to discrepancies between the two. As an example, the customer may use eight-digit part numbers although the package has provided for only six digits. During implementation we must resolve these discrepancies, either through making changes in the organization or through special considerations in the implementation process. Finally, an implementation plan should be the result of the effort.

The vendor can help in package modification by providing flexibility in the design of the system. Data-base management systems to support the package, good query languages, and report generators to custom-tailor the output all help. Good documentation is very important, as is consulting help in implementation. A number of vendors also offer telephone "hot lines" to answer calls from users who have problems.

It may appear to users that they do not have to become involved, since they are purchasing a package that has already been developed. In all likelihood, users will be more involved in the development of a package, or at least more intensely involved over a shorter period of time, than with custom development. One must be sure that the requirements analysis is complete, that users in fact define processing requirements. The users also must understand in detail how the package works and think about it in their present job environment. The users must provide help in outlining the discrepancies and in deciding how they are to be resolved, through package changes or changes in company procedures. There have been just as many examples of package implementation disasters as disasters with custom systems!

SUMMARY

Packages are increasingly important in systems development; it is too costly to develop systems with custom programming if a package exists that will work for a given task. Remember to develop specifications on requirements at least at a high level before talking to a package vendor. It is very important to have a basis for comparing all the different packages and to avoid being swayed by features that we really do not need or want.

In today's environment, we look first at the software and then the hardware, a complete reversal of the early days of the industry. A package is an important option for the analyst and can help reduce the time and cost of information systems development. Packages are no panacea, and they do require a great deal of input from users. Acquired and implemented intelligently, they can contribute greatly to productivity.

KEY WORDS

Accounts receivable	Packages
Applications generator	Parameters
Dedicated package	Problem-oriented languages
Discrepancies	Processing requirements
Expectations	SPSS
Evaluation	System software
Higher-order languages	User needs
Implementation	Vendor solution
Modification	Vendor support
Modules	

RECOMMENDED READINGS

Lucas, H. C., Jr.: *Coping with Computers: A Manager's Guide to Controlling Information Processing*, The Free Press, New York, 1982. (See the chapter on packages for a simple explanation of their key features.)

Martin, J.: *Applications Development Without Programmers*, Prentice-Hall, Englewood Cliffs, N.J., 1982. (A good description of a number of higher-order languages and generators.)

Martin, J., and C. McClure: "Buying Software off the Rack," *Harvard Business Review*, November-December, 1983, pp. 32–60. (A good article on purchasing and contracting for packages.)

Nie, N., et al.: *Statistical Package for the Social Sciences,* 2d ed., McGraw-Hill, New York, 1975. (An example of a problem-oriented language and an excellent set of accompanying documentation; a good model for user manuals for any package.)

See also various computer periodicals and trade journals that have annual ratings of packages to obtain an idea of what is available

DISCUSSION QUESTIONS

1 How do packages reduce development time for a system?
2 How can packages ower costs?
3 What are all the costs associated with a package beyond the purchase price?
4 Does one always get debugged programs buying a package?
5 Why should one insist on a demonstration of a package?
6 Why might a package not include some of the functions we want?
7 What services are included under vendor support? Why is it important?
8 Why do we advocate not looking first at hardware, but first at the software?
9 How does the vendor provide a package that will fit in a number of different organizations?
10 Why is it important to carefully control changes to a package?
11 Under what conditions might an organization be willing to change its procedures to use a package?
12 Is a large organization likely to change procedures or change a package? Why might the large firm have more need to modify a package than a small one?
13 Why do you think a vendor of services using packages might not want to make changes in a package that it operates for a large number of firms?
14 What are the advantages of a higher-order language from the vendor's standpoint? From the customer's?
15 How can a higher-order language be turned into a complete applications generator?
16 How does a data-base management package reduce one's flexibility in acquiring hardware or other software packages?
17 In what functional areas do you think problem-oriented languages might be most useful?
18 What are the differences in implementation strategies for a dedicated package versus the other types of packages in Figure 12-1?
19 Is accounts receivable likely to be the same type of application no matter what the firm? What characteristics might differ among companies?
20 Why do you think the accounts-receivable package described in this chapter uses a summary file for sales statistics instead of computing them every time they are required?
21 What is the cost of using the summary file above?
22 What is the user's role in determining whether or not to acquire a package?
23 What are good sources to find out if a package exists for a particular problem?
24 Develop an implementation strategy for the accounts-receivable example in this chapter.
25 How can discrepancies between user requirements and a vendor's package solution be resolved?
26 What is the user's role in resolving these discrepancies? What is the system professional's role?
27 Why is a package a more viable alternative to a custom system today than it was 10 years ago?

CHAPTER 13

PROTOTYPING AND
END-USER PROGRAMMING

PROTOTYPES

The objective of prototyping is to reduce the time needed to develop requirements for a system. The traditional design approach features an analyst who spends time with users to elicit requirements. The analyst prepares specifications that are given to the user to approve. Most users seem to have difficulty comprehending the specifications, and as a result, it may be during testing that the user first gains an understanding of how the system will work.

A prototype is a model of a system that will eventually be developed. Its purpose is to:

1 Reduce the time before the user sees something concrete from the systems design effort

2 Provide rapid feedback from the user to the designer

3 Help delineate requirements with fewer errors

4 Enhance designer and user understanding of what systems should accomplish

5 Bring about meaningful user involvement in systems analysis and design

A prototype does not have to be real; for example, the architect's model of a building made from card stock is a representation of the building. Part of a system can be "dummied" using sample data, and reports can be incomplete. The prototype may become a living specification that is constantly changed as the prototype is refined. In fact, the prototype may grow into the final system without the development of detailed specifications!

The external appearance of the prototype must be clear. As an example, the prototype for a transactions processing system is likely to provide a fixed set of CRT screens that accept input from the user, process it, and possibly return output (Mason and Carey, 1983). The full logic of the system has not been developed yet, so there will be restrictions. However, there should be enough of a system present so that users can understand how the final version will operate.

The Process

It is important that the prototype be developed quickly and that feedback occurs in a timely manner. The actual development process is likely to be a sequence of activities such as:

1 The designer meets with the user
2 The user describes the system
3 The designer builds a prototype
4 The user works with the prototype and critiques it
5 The designer modifies the prototype or starts again
6 Go to steps 1 or 4

Changes here should be encouraged, not discouraged! We choose the prototyping approach because a set of system specifications is usually very abstract to the user. The prototype makes the system come alive; we want users to interact with the system and make it into what they would like to have. To accomplish the objective of rapid development the designer will need to use one or more tools to develop the prototype.

Timesharing   One popular way to develop a model of a system or part of it is to use a timesharing computer. Timesharing gives the designer a tool for rapid development. Using a language like BASIC or APL, a prototype can be constructed quickly for review by the user; it can also be modified rapidly as the desired features of a system become clearer.

Personal Computer   A personal computer can be an effective approach to prototyping; there is no interference from other users. Many microcomputers offer special development software that is easy to use. The disadvantage is that for a large system, it is unlikely that the prototype could grow easily to the final application.

Software   Above we suggested high-level languages like BASIC or APL; the designer may also want to use an applications generator to develop a prototype. The ability to produce a system quickly is a major advantage of the generator. It is quite likely that the prototype will grow here into the final application.

Another possibility is to use a simple data-base management system to form the foundation for a prototype. These systems make the task of developing and modifying data structures much easier than is possible with most programming

SYSTEMS PROBLEM 13-1

Bob Jackson is manager of systems development for Atlantic Manufacturing Company. This firm makes a variety of tools for home craftsmen and professional carpenters, mechanics, and other tradespeople.

Bob is reviewing a request from one of the plants for an integrated production scheduling and control system for shop-floor control. This particular plant manufactures hand tools; the tools are relatively simple, ranging from 4 or 5 parts to 50 parts in a completed tool. Although the number of parts is relatively small, the volume at the plant is quite high, and scheduling is a problem because a tool can be made in a number of different ways. The plant is the classic "job shop" as opposed to an assembly line.

Jackson has just returned from a 2-day professional seminar on prototyping, and he is eager to try this new approach to systems development. The request in front of him raised the possibility of trying prototyping for the first time at Atlantic.

Jackson discussed the idea with two other analysts. They, however, are quite skeptical. "The system will be so large, that we'll need conventional specifications and design," one advised. The other said, "How can we build a prototype of a system this complex?"

Where do you think prototyping could be used for this suggested application?

---

languages. Retrieval commands from the DBMS may be all that is needed to develop the prototype.

Good programming and development tools are a requirement for prototyping. Remember that the prototype begins as a model; it does not have to include any of the editing and error checking of a finished system. The purpose of the exercise is to show what can be accomplished, not to demonstrate that a system is complete.

An Example

The firm that developed this system offers services throughout the world. The firm was investigating a change in its ownership; it is owned by its employees, but new United States legislation made some alterations in ownership structure potentially attractive. The vice-chairman of the board asked the manager of the computer department to develop a small system to project the financial position of the firm several years in the future if the new form of ownership were adopted.

The computer department operated batch, timesharing, and on-line systems on its computer; a data-base management system and various screen generators were also available. At first the computer department manager simply wrote a small program in BASIC to model the plan.

The output of the model formed one part of the recommendations made to the board of directors. After that meeting where the new plan was adopted, several managers noted the ability of the computer to forecast. One of them asked the computer department if it would be possible to forecast the benefits an employee would have several years in the future.

The industry is competitive and firms frequently hire staff from each other. Because there are a variety of stock and benefit plans, it is difficult to show an employee the total value of remaining with the company. The computer staff began to work on this problem with help from different personnel and financial managers. Various formulas were programmed and the results checked by different groups until the rules were regarded as satisfactory.

The manager of the computer department had a feeling that the system would grow, so he had the staff develop it using the data-base management software and CRTs for data entry. The treasurer kept most of the data needed on what benefits were available to each individual, and he became very interested in the system. Computing bonuses took a long time and required heavy overtime; in general, records for each employee were scattered over several files and reports were often inaccurate.

The treasurer asked that the system be made capable of maintaining all employee records and benefits. Because of the data-base approach and good development tools, it was fairly easy to meet his requirements. Over time, the system has evolved into a comprehensive personnel records and benefits application.

This system succeeded because it was able to grow and change over time. As users saw new features, they developed ideas for extending the application. The primary user changed from the president, who had originally requested the projection system, to the treasurer. The application had high visibility, and senior management provided extensive input.

The use of tools was also very important in the success of this effort. High-level languages, screen formatting aids, and a data-base management system made it possible for the system to evolve. The ability to program a BASIC model using timesharing for the first part of the system was also crucial.

In addition to heavy user involvement, the analyst working on the application listened carefully and followed the logic defined by the users. She brought the results back to them, and the managers actually debugged their own rules. By not trying to be in charge of everything, the analyst was able to develop a system with which users felt comfortable because they understood the details of how it worked.

Not every system could be developed in this manner. In other circumstances there might be a need for concrete specifications. However, the use of prototyping to show users what the system will do should be applicable across a wide range of settings.

Prototyping is a very effective way to improve the requirements definition phase for a system. The prototype may be a small model and often may evolve into the final system. The designer needs flexible tools to provide rapid responses to user inputs. The approach appears to be good for attracting users to the design process and obtaining their involvement and input. Done properly, it should result in systems that more closely fit user needs and that are completed more quickly with fewer operational changes required.

Mainframes / minicomputers

Terminal access	Query language	Modeling language	Generators	Procedural languages
Packages	Word processing	Electronic Spreadsheets	DBMS generators	Basic, Pascal

Personal computers

FIGURE 13-1
Spectrum of end-user computing.

END-USER PROGRAMMING

End-user computing is a very imprecise term. Many end users have worked with computers and written programs for a number of years. Engineers frequently use languages like FORTRAN to write programs for their own needs. Some actuaries in insurance firms use FORTRAN or APL to develop their own systems.

Who is the end user? We usually define this individual as a nonprofessional in the systems field. The end user is in a different function than information systems; he or she is a user in finance, accounting, production, etc. The computer is not the primary consideration of the user, so that a full-time systems analyst working in the accounting department would not be considered an end user.

Figure 13-1 shows a possible spectrum of end-user computing. The simplest form is a user working at a terminal using a predefined menu. The system might allow the user to access a high-level command language. One retrieval system features a menu to get the user started; then he or she "programs" requests and asks for statistical analyses of the data retrieved using high-level commands.

As we move along the spectrum we encounter query languages on mainframe computers. Here the user must have good knowledge of the data base and the language. He or she enters requests in the language and possibly processes the data retrieved as in the example above. At about the same level of user involvement in programming we encounter the personal computer. The user works with a number of software packages, but does very little coding.

A modeling language moves us more toward programming. The user of this language actually writes a program to model the phenomenon under study. See Table 13-1, which is an example of a model of a movie theater.

On the personal computer side, the user moves to word processing and spreadsheet packages. These packages present row and column coordinates that the user identifies for placing entries in each cell. See the example in Chapter 12.

Other languages are available for special purposes as we discussed in the last chapter, for example, SPSS for statistical analysis. The user defines the format of the data and writes a simple program to perform quite powerful statistical tests on data. A number of languages also exist for providing output in a graphic form on a CRT or plotting device. Each of these languages contains commands at a high level:

GENERATE A PLOT
X AXIS "DOLLARS (000)"
Y AXIS "SALES"
etc.

End users can also work with the generators discussed in Chapter 11. The simplest generators available use DBMS packages on personal computers. For mainframe and minicomputers there is a number of retrieval programs for sequential files, and there are query languages for data-base systems. The retrieval systems may require the user to construct something that looks a lot like a program, but at a higher level than a compiler language.

At the extreme, end users actually write programs in a procedural language like BASIC, PASCAL, or APL. At the present time it is not clear how many users will go this far. For the next few years, we would be surprised to see significant numbers of users writing programs in these languages.

Support

End-user computing cannot be the sole responsibility of the user; there must be support. The computer staff should help in selecting whatever tools are to be provided for the end user. Next the department should see that adequate training is available in the use of the systems acquired. Finally, the computer staff should provide ongoing consulting on the use of these tools.

There will be a need for consultants to help answer questions about the systems and languages with which end users are working. The computer staff also has to help the user locate data and may need to write programs to collect data from different files or process it in some way before the end user can access it.

Policy Issues

One policy for the computer department described above is to help and support the concept of end-user computing. A more difficult problem is to control the proliferation of hardware and software. Users conducting their own research may come up with a number of different approaches. Each new system, be it hardware or software, requires the computer staff to learn how to support it. Such an effort is costly and time-consuming. Thus, the computer department may establish a policy with support from senior management such that all software and hardware is purchased with the approval and through the computer department. Then the computer staff can evaluate the systems recommended and allocate its staff to become familiar with it. The computer department can keep control so that a reasonable number of different systems are acquired.

As users acquire terminals and local computers, the computer department will also have to coordinate acquisitions. Eventually the various pieces of hardware will probably be linked in some kind of a network. Compatibility among the different devices is of concern here. Again, multiple hardware vendors and different types of software place a heavy support burden on the computer staff. Coordination is vital!

The end user is, by definition, not a systems professional. For most applications the computer staff will allow access to data under its control but will not allow users to change these data. The systems professional must be concerned about error checking, editing, data validation, and the protection of the integrity of the data base. There is no reason to suspect that the user necessarily is aware of this aspect of systems analysis and design. The consulting staff can raise some of these issues, particularly when local, self-contained systems are being developed. However, for corporate data that have been entrusted to the computer department, the computer staff will have to establish controls on data access and updating.

Benefits

Users have already discovered the benefits of end-user computing; they are purchasing microcomputers and packages with great enthusiasm. Other users are demanding tools they can use to solve their own problems. To some extent, the computer staff has lost the initiative. To regain it, the computer department needs to coordinate the systems, and to avoid duplication and waste, it needs to establish a support center staffed with the kind of consultants described above.

End-user computing is another way to reduce the time required to develop an application. This approach provides immediate feedback; the user becomes the designer of the system. This strategy also adds to the total number of individuals working to solve systems problems. By increasing the number of individuals brought to bear on the problem, we should reduce the backlog of systems work. End-user computing, then, can result in better systems and can reduce the length of time the user must wait to solve an information processing problem.

SYSTEMS PROBLEM 13-2

Carole Carter is the vice president of finance for Rubon Cosmetics. The firm has grown rapidly in the last 10 years stressing natural cosmetics for the active woman. Several years ago she established a headquarters programming group that uses APL to help users quickly produce new applications.

Carole is currently confronted with the problem of what to do about personal computers. Already a number of users have purchased the computers from their own budgets and are using them for various kinds of analyses. Generally the applications are nothing more than simple spreadsheets using Lotus 1-2-3.

The president of Rubon recently came to Carole upset that he saw staff members writing programs. "I thought that's the reason you developed a central support group," he said. "I don't want expensive staff writing programs."

In general Carole agreed, but where do you draw the line? How can she tell someone with a personal computer that they cannot set up a spreadsheet, but must call in a consultant from her staff? Certainly users should not be writing major systems in a language like BASIC, but shouldn't Lotus 1-2-3 be available to them?

Carole has asked you to help her frame a policy for end-user computing in Rubon.

TABLE 13-1
EXAMPLE OF AN EMPIRE MODEL OF A MOVIE THEATER

```
 empire

-----------
E  M  P  I  R  E
 TRANSLATOR
    VER 2
-----------


ENTER COMMAND:    execute cinema

***TRANSLATING: CINEMA

     *MODEL *

***TRANSLATION COMPLETED***

FORTRAN: CINEMA
ADRSI
LINK:    Loading
[LNKXCT CINEMA execution]

-----------
E  M  P  I  R  E
 EXECUTIVE
    VER 2
-----------


YES... verify
THE FOLLOWING ITEMS FLAGGED "INPUT" HAVE NO VALUE SET:
EXPSAL
LAB
TPRICE
TCOST
YES... data
->expsal(cin1)2000,2400
->lab(cin1)450,550
->tprice 5.00
->tcost 3.50
->end
YES... run
YES... print from incsmt
ADJUST PAPER, THEN ENTER A CARRIAGE RETURN TO PROCEED=>
```

CINEMA ONE AND TWO INC.
PROJECTED INCOME STATEMENT

	CINEMA ONE	CINEMA TWO	TOTAL BOTH CINEMAS
EXPECTED # TKTS SOLD	2,000	2,400	4,400
TICKET REVENUE	$ 10,000	$ 12,000	$ 22,000
FIXED COST OF SALES	$ 7,000	$ 8,400	$ 15,400
LABOR COSTS	$ 450	$ 550	$ 1,000
GROSS PROFIT	$ 2,550	$ 3,050	$ 5,600
INCOME TAX			$ 2,688
PROFITS AFTER TAX			$ 2,912

```
YES... what is profat if tprice=6.00

PROFAT                 5200.000

YES... what is profat if tcost=3.75

PROFAT                 2340.000

YES... what is profat if tprice=3.85

PROFAT                 280.800

YES... what is prof if tcost=2.00

PROF    (CIN1  )       5550.000
        (CIN2  )       6650.000
        (TOTAL )      12200.000

YES... what is prof if tprice=5.5

PROF    (CIN1  )       3550.000
        (CIN2  )       4250.000
        (TOTAL )       7800.000

YES... exit


***E M P I R E  -  END OF SESSION***
```

TABLE 13-1 (*Continued*)
EXAMPLE OF AN EMPIRE MODEL OF A MOVIE THEATER

```
 ty cinema.mod
00100    column section
00300    CIN1  "CINEMA/ONE"
00400    CIN2  "CINEMA/TWO"
00500    total  "TOTAL BOTH/CINEMAS"
00600    row section
00700    expsal input "EXPECTED # TKTS SOLD"
00800    salr "TICKET REVENUE"
00900    csal "FIXED COST OF SALES"
00950    lab INPUT "LABOR COSTS"
01000    prof "GROSS PROFIT"
01100    scalar section
01200    tprice input "TICKET PRICE"
01300    tcost input "COST PER TKT"
01400    trate "INCOME TAX RATE" .48
01500    inctax "INCOME TAX"
01600    profat "PROFITS AFTER TAX"
01700    rules section
01800    for col=CIN1 to CIN2 do
01900    salr=expsal(col)*tprice
02000    csal=expsal(col)*tcost
02100    prof=salr-csal-lab(col)
02200    end
02300    total=CIN1+CIN2
02400    inctax=trate*prof(total)
02500    profat=prof(total)-inctax
@
```

```
 ty incsmt.rep
00100    select CIN1:total
00200    columnwidth 15
00300    title 1 center "CINEMA ONE AND TWO INC."
00400    title 2 center "PROJECTED INCOME STATEMENT"//
00450    skip
00500    position 1
00600    print expsal
00700    skip
00800    prefix "$"
00900    print salr
01100    print csal
01150    print lab
01200    line
01300    print /,prof
01400    line
01500    print /,inctax@3,/,profat@3,/
@
```

KEY WORDS

APL	Policy issues
BASIC	Procedural language
COBOL	PASCAL
Data-base management system	Personal computer
End-user computing	Prototype
Evolution of a system	Query language
FORTRAN	Spreadsheet system
Generators	SPSS
Graphic packages	Support center
Menu	Timesharing
Modeling language	Tools
Model	Word processing

RECOMMENDED READINGS

Canning, R.: "Query Systems for End Users," *EDP Analyzer,* vol. 20, no. 9, September 1982. (A good discussion of the use of query languages by end users.)

Hammond, L. W.: "Management Considerations for an Information Center," *IBM Systems Journal,* vol. 21, no. 2, 1982, pp. 131-161. (Discusses a center for providing user support and its requirements.)

Lucas, H. C., Jr.: *Implementation: The Key to Successful Information Systems,* New York, Columbia, 1981. (See Chapter 6 on two examples of systems development, including the example earlier in the chapter of a benefits system.)

Mason, R. E. A., and T. T. Carey: "Prototyping Interactive Information Systems, *Communications of the ACM,* vol. 26, no. 5, May 1983, pp. 347–354. (A helpful article with recommendations on prototyping.)

Naumann, J., and M. Jenkins: "Prototyping: The New Paradigm for Systems Development," *MIS Quarterly,* vol. 6, no. 3, September 1982, pp. 29–44. (A thorough discussion of prototyping.)

See also various business publications, for example, the information processing section of *Business Week.*

DISCUSSION QUESTIONS

1 What are the advantages of prototyping? The disadvantages?
2 How does a prototype for a computer system differ from an architect's model? How are they similar?
3 Why does a prototype need to be developed quickly?
4 What tools facilitate the development of prototypes?
5 How does a prototype secure more user input than conventional approaches?
6 How have microcomputers contributed to prototyping?
7 Do you think users should write programs in languages like BASIC or APL?
8 What are the disadvantages of not having complete specifications for a system, but instead letting it grow from a small prototype?
9 How does the role of the analyst differ, if at all, in prototyping versus traditional development for a custom system?

10 How does prototyping relate to things like higher-order languages and applications generators?

11 Define end user.

12 What are the key issues in the installation of a query language for users?

13 What are the advantages of problem-oriented languages in end-user computing?

14 What are the duties of a consultant trying to support end users?

15 Is word processing computing? How does it contribute to end-user computing?

16 Given the relative ease of using higher-order languages, why do users need support from a computer staff?

17 Why does the computer department have to worry about data integrity; the data actually belong to users, doesn't it?

18 Give several reasons for a policy that limits the firm to choosing microcomputers from only three different vendors.

19 If hardware vendors are developing standard hardware interfaces, is there any need to worry about connecting equipment from dissimilar vendors into a communications network?

20 What help does the end user need in trying to retrieve data from the files of applications that are already in operation?

21 What are the benefits of end-user computing? Does the computer staff receive any of them?

THREE

FOLLOWING THE LIFE CYCLE

14

PRELIMINARY SURVEY AND FEASIBILITY STUDY

INTRODUCTION

During inception the user develops an idea for a system. In the preliminary survey and feasibility study, the analyst is learning from the user what is expected of a new information system. The analyst uses technical skills and knowledge to delineate various alternatives to be considered for implementation. The preliminary survey and feasibility study inaugurate the relationship between the analyst and user and are extremely important to the ultimate success of a new system. This process can also be referred to as "needs assessment." The preliminary survey and feasibility study are generally described as the stages in which the computer application is either approved or disapproved. However, in reality, few applications suggested ever get to these stages without being subsequently implemented. Instead of forcing a "go–no go" decision, these studies should delineate different alternatives that meet some proportion of the objectives of a new system. Of course, we should also include the alternative of no system at all, that is, of continuing with existing processing procedures. The survey and feasibility study are designed to assist in choosing from among a range of alternatives rather than from two choices. That is, we should not be faced with the decision of undertaking the "ultimate" system of no system at all.

The major difference between the preliminary survey and the feasibility study is the amount of effort and level of detail involved. We conduct a survey to see what type of system is needed and to eliminate grossly inappropriate system alternatives. In a preliminary survey we suggest what types of systems might meet requirements. The feasibility study has to contain enough detail so that an alternative can be selected for development. Before any type of survey or feasibility study can be undertaken, we have to obtain a feeling for the existing system. Knowledge of the existing system will be developed in more detail at each succeeding stage in the systems analysis and design process.

THE EXISTING SYSTEM

In many instances it will be hard to identify any organized set of procedures that represent the existing information processing system. We need to enumerate problems and determine what motivated the suggestion that a computer system might help in processing information. Whether there is a well-defined system or not, we should develop the specific information listed in Table 14-1. First, we should identify crucial information flows, including the source, frequency, and volume of information. Information can be characterized according to the decision-making framework of Chapter 2. For example, we can look at the form in which data are gathered and processed, either written or verbal. If documents are involved, how many are there, and what is their information content? What types of decisions are supported?

We also need to identify what processing is done to information as it flows through a system; by whom is the information processed, and what are the peak and average loads? Finally, we should estimate the current cost of information processing.

For the preliminary survey we develop very rough estimates and collect

TABLE 14-1
ANALYZING THE
EXISTING SYSTEM

Decisions
  Decision maker
  Input
  Output
  Frequency of decision
  Level of costs
Information
  Flow
  Characteristics
  Form
  Source
  Retention
Processing
  Operations
  By whom performed
  Peak load
  Average load
Cost

---

samples of documents. We may interview only a few people and use approximations. After a list of objectives for the system is developed, we use the data gathered to make a rough sketch of several alternative new systems.

The feasibility study goes into much more detail, and instead of approximations, we actually sample the documents and develop more refined estimates. In the feasibility study, we trace the flow of information through the system and spend time with the various individuals who originate and process the data. Thus, the same framework used in the preliminary survey can be used for the feasibility study although our feasibility analysis will be much more detailed.

SURVEY AND FEASIBILITY STUDY CONTENTS

In this section we present recommendations for the contents of the preliminary survey and feasibility study. Basically, each of these documents consists of two parts: the present system and an alternative. The alternatives section actually presents several potential alternatives and evaluates them on technical, economic, and operational criteria. We must estimate technical and operational feasibility and compare costs with benefits.

New Systems

From a technical standpoint, what is the state of the art? This analysis is related to the discussion of risk, since few organizations should be pioneers in the development of all their new systems. Some pioneering may be desirable, but an attempt should be made to estimate exactly what is involved. Will existing technology as experienced by members of this organization be adequate for the application under consideration?

Operational feasibility addresses the question of whether or not we can run the system. Are schedules for processing realistic? Can input data actually be collected, errors corrected, and the system run on schedule? In one example an inventory system was planned in which files would be updated every 3 days. There were so many errors in the input that could not be corrected in time that the system had to move to a weekly updating schedule, reducing some of the benefits.

In examining costs versus benefits, there are a large number of factors to consider. System costs include:

Development
  Computer time
  Systems analyst time
  Programmer time
  User time
Operations
  Computer costs
  Communications costs

Operating staff costs
Incremental user costs
Maintenance costs

Development costs refer to the actual cost of analysis, design, and installation for the system. These costs are highly sensitive to the amount of time that must be spent to develop the system and are directly proportional to the number of analysts, programmers, and user staff involved and the length of their involvement. Computer time for testing tends to be far less expensive than the costs of staff time. Historically, the profession has done a poor job of estimating the time required to design and install a system.

We should not forget the cost of operating a new system when assessing total costs. A new system will require the use of part of the time available on an existing computer or may necessitate an upgrade on the present system or even a new computer(s). Many modern systems involve telecommunications, which can be very costly. Incremental staff in the computer center and for users may be required to operate the system. Finally, there are the costs of routine maintenance and enhancements. No system is ever finished; "bugs" will need repairs, and users will request periodic enhancements as they work with a system.

Traditionally, benefits have been analyzed from the point of view of tangible cost savings from a computer system. Often these savings have been measured by the reduction of employees currently employed or by an estimate of the number of future employees who would have been hired without the system. (Many times savings projected in personnel have proved illusory.) Tangible savings also come from more efficient processing. For example, an inventory control system may reduce inventory balances while maintaining service levels. The firm saves interest charges on the money previously required to finance the level of inventory needed before the computer system.

We should not only look at tangible cost savings, but we also must consider intangibles and unquantifiable savings. This is particularly true as we move from transactions-processing systems toward operational and managerial control systems where intangible benefits are more important.

The following list of benefits may prove helpful in this analysis (Kanter, 1972).

1 The ability to obtain information previously unavailable
2 The receipt of information on a more timely basis
3 Improvements in operations
4 The ability to perform calculations not possible before (for example, the simulation of production schedules)
5 Reduction in clerical activity
6 Maintenance of a competitive position
7 Improvements in decision making
8 Improvements in image, customer service, etc.

Thus, we shall want to consider both tangible and intangible benefits when comparing the advantages of a system with its costs.

System Alternatives

General   One of the major activities during the survey or feasibility study will be to sketch possible alternatives for a new information processing system. Each of these alternatives has to be evaluated on standard criteria selected in advance. The reports should show manual procedures, input and output, files, and processing schedules to characterize each alternative.

The technology has provided designers with a wide range of options for a new system. For example, we can develop a batch or an on-line system. It is also possible to design a system that features a combination of batch and on-line characteristics; for example, data entry might be on-line with major files updated in batch over night. Chapter 5 discusses various processing patterns as well; we can have varying degrees of distributed processing with local or central computers.

A number of alternatives built around minicomputers also exist. We can use a timesharing operating system as the supervisor for an application that is used by a number of people connected to the minicomputer with terminals.

Similarly, we may find that a particular software package like a spreadsheet program or simple file management program for a microcomputer offers an attractive alternative.

One important contribution of the analyst is to be familiar with the various possibilities and to conduct research on feasible alternatives for the system under consideration. The analyst needs to develop expertise in locating alternatives, matching them to the problem at hand, and explaining them to users.

It also will be necessary to estimate development time and effort. Unfortunately, making these time and effort estimates is a very difficult task. At least one author provides guidelines on programmer productivity to help in making estimates (Kelly, 1970). However, there is a wide variance in programmer and systems designer performance among organizations and individuals. In a later chapter we shall discuss project management and suggest some new approaches to programming. Our approach will be to record development data as projects are implemented so that each organization can make estimates based on its own past experience.

Finally, for evaluating the alternatives, the survey and feasibility studies should include estimates of the costs and effort involved in operating each alternative if implemented. Since we have far more experience and better data on operations than on systems design, this presents less of a problem than the estimates discussed above.

In summary, packages are a viable alternative, and they should be evaluated where they exist. After passing the screening requirements, packages should be considered in the same way as any other alternative and included in the survey and feasibility studies. It is still necessary to study the existing system and make estimates of technical, economic, and operational factors when an applications package is one alternative.

SYSTEMS PROBLEM 14-1

Harold Mathews is the vice president of planning for Chemway Products, a leading chemicals manufacturer. He recently attended a seminar on the use of computer-based planning techniques that convinced him that Chemway needed to carefully consider this approach. The instructor at the seminar began with the need to develop a sales forecast and discussed three or four forecasting techniques. Following this introduction, the leader discussed several ways to construct models of the business.

The model is an abstraction from the reality of the business; usually a series of equations is used in a computer to represent the firm. It is difficult to choose from among the many different types of models available. Most companies moving into this area for the first time turn to consulting firms that specialize in building models.

Harold Mathews has two major problems, and he has asked for your help. First, he would like to know what kind of firm he should contact to discuss modeling. He has two options: one is a firm founded by a prominent economist that offers a large econometric model of the United States economy. Consultants at the firm help a company build a similar model that takes output of the national econometric model as part of its input. Another firm he is considering offers a special high-level planning language on a timesharing computer system. The planning department uses this high-level language to construct a model of the firm with some guidance from the consultant. Which option sounds best for Chemway?

The second problem confronting Harold is how to cost-justify any type of modeling effort. Harold feels that, unlike many of the transactions-oriented computer systems at Chemway, it will be almost impossible to show a cost savings from the model. If it suggests a new course of action, how can Chemway demonstrate that it is better than continuing with old plans? Business and economic conditions change too rapidly for making an accurate estimate of the benefits of the model. How can Chemway justify the use of either of the planning model alternatives?

Organization Impact

An attempt also should be made to estimate the impact of each alternative system on the organization. What departments and individuals will be affected by the system, and what jobs will be changed? Will any existing work groups be reassigned, and what will happen to any employees who are replaced by a system?

Contents

The contents of one possible format for a survey or feasibility study are outlined in Table 14-2. The summary presents a brief overview of the reasons for the study and ranks each processing alternative (including the present system) on the criteria established by the steering committee. This summary is the primary input for decision making. Existing systems should be described according to the analysis above. Finally, each alternative is presented in detail. Here it is helpful to

TABLE 14-2
OUTLINE OF PRELIMINARY SURVEY AND
FEASIBILITY STUDY CONTENTS

 I   Summary
    A Goals
    B For each alternative evaluation on standard criteria
 II The existing system
    A Problems
    B Goals of new system
    C Decision considerations
    D Information flow
    E Processing
 III For each alternative proposed
    A Overview—percentage of goals achieved, benefits
    B Decisions
    C Information flows
    D Technical (files, I/O, processing)
    E Development effort, schedule, and cost
    F Operational aspects
    G Impact on the organization
    H Total costs and benefits

---

include a scenario; that is, a short story on how the system would actually be used, including management, user, and computer department activities under each alternative.

Approach

In Chapter 6 we advocated user-designed systems, although many organizations do not follow this approach. The outline presented above makes it appear as if the analyst does all the work. In the spirit of user-oriented design, the analyst should present the tasks involved to the design team and they should assign responsibilities to various members. The analyst needs to spend little time analyzing the existing system; users are familiar with it already. The analyst (1) serves as a resource in developing alternatives, given user goals; (2) assesses technical feasibility and suggests what processing alternatives are available; and (3) works on estimates for the time and cost for the development and operation of each alternative for a new system.

THE DECISION-MAKING BODY

Having discussed the purpose and content of the survey and feasibility studies, we can turn to their use as a decision-making document. The basic decision is what type of system to develop, if any, and our question is who should make this decision.

Alternatives

In the past, many times the computer department has made the decision whether or not to undertake a new system and what alternative to implement. The problem with this approach is that the computer department is not in a position to know the goals of the organization. It cannot answer questions on what areas in the organization management wants to emphasize. The computer department may make serious errors developing systems for areas that are not critical to management. The computer department lacks the information necessary to choose applications. Also, when the computer department does select applications, the decisions may appear arbitrary to users whose requests are denied.

Users are not really in a position to make the decision either. Clearly, users cannot be objective in trading off the needs of other areas versus their own. Can the decision be left to management alone? The answer to this question is also "no," as managers will want to hear the users' reasons for the system and obtain technical advice from the computer department.

All these considerations suggest that decisions on applications should be made by a joint group of users, management, and the computer department staff. In other words, a steering committee for the selection of computer applications should be formed. Management members of this committee furnish the overall goals of the organization and assure themselves that new systems being developed are consistent with the attainment of these goals. The computer department provides technical information, and users supply data specific to the problem area under consideration.

The decision is made jointly among the members of this committee. Users are able to understand why certain systems are chosen, and user participation in the decision should help obtain commitment to the alternative selected. The computer department serves a vital support role. Through the use of the committee, the department cannot be criticized for making arbitrary judgments. Management retains control over the development of new applications, which is an activity critical to the long-run success of the organization.

Steering Committees

Many organizations have formed steering committees for computer decisions, which have then disbanded after a short period of time. What are the reasons for this dissatisfaction? There are several possible explanations for the rise and fall of steering committees. The first problem is lack of commitment. Top management may not continue to participate after the first few meetings, and this action indicates to other members of the committee that committee activities are not important. Another reason for the failure of some steering committees may be a lack of purpose—no one seems to know why the meetings are held. If the committee is to decide on computer applications, then that must be the reason for the meeting. The steering committee should not allow its meetings to degenerate into design sessions; users not concerned with the area under discussion will not attend. Design should be confined to the design team, and the steering committee should select applications and decide on alternative computer systems for these applications.

Decision Criteria

Once a committee is formed it should choose a format for preliminary surveys and feasibility studies. Two questions arise at first: (1) what data should be included in a feasibility study? And (2) how many system alternatives should be presented? The committee and computer department staff should decide these questions before making any decisions on applications.

The committee also should select a set of decision criteria. A number of possible criteria a steering committee might use for selecting alternatives includes:

1 Time to implement the system. What is the estimated time required to implement this alternative?

2 Savings. What are the tangible and intangible savings?

3 Percentage of user needs met. What proportion of the needs expressed by the users for a system does this alternative meet? What are the benefits to users?

4 Total cost.

5 Impact on existing operations. What effect will this system have on existing computer operations, and will we need new hardware and software capacity?

6 Operating and maintenance costs.

7 Risk level. What is the chance of failure in developing the system? What is the level of technical uncertainty? What is the level of uncertainty in costs and benefits?

Not all the above decision criteria may be used for each committee; it is probably advisable to select five to seven criteria. Each survey and feasibility study should be evaluated on these criteria.

One of the most important considerations is the level of risk in the portfolio of applications undertaken. (For example, transactions-processing systems are usually better understood and less risky than strategic planning systems.) By undertaking a balanced portfolio of projects with a variety of risk levels, we should be assured of developing some successful applications. Undertaking too many high-risk systems may lead to a situation in which no new systems are developed that meet original specifications. On the other hand, by being extremely conservative and undertaking only simple processing systems, we ignore a great deal of potential return from more sophisticated applications.

The steering committee also has to decide on the weights to be assigned to each criterion; for example 10 percent to savings, 25 percent to the amount of user needs fulfilled, etc. An executive summary on the survey and feasibility studies should list the criteria and evaluate each alternative proposed on them. The committee uses the study document and the weights as a basis for discussion and as an aid in making their decisions on the proposed application.

SYSTEMS PROBLEM 14-2

Maxine Shapiro is a vice president of American National Bank and is a member of the executive committee. For the last 2 years the executive committee has been judging the feasibility of all computer applications estimated to cost over $50,000. Maxine and the committee have become extremely frustrated over the process through which decisions on applications are made.

Typically, the computer department is requested to perform a feasibility study. The study involves working with users to define several alternatives. The computer department with some consultation from users selects one option and prepares a report on its feasibility; an appendix usually contains a brief sketch of other alternatives considered and why they were rejected.

Next, the report is presented to the executive committee. Sometimes at a separate meeting, but most often as a part of its regular meetings on other bank business, the executive committee discusses the proposed project. In thinking back over the prior 2 years, Maxine could not recall a system that had not been approved for development.

"We always seem to be deciding between a very expensive system and maintaining the status quo," she said. "The last system we approved was done for marketing considerations, the one before that was required by a regulatory agency. Other times we approve systems because an area hadn't had one for a while. It is hard under these procedures to feel that we have done an adequate job in analyzing the situation and making a decision."

What advice could you give American National on how to alter its procedures for choosing computer applications?

THE HARDSERVE EXAMPLE

Progress to Date

Since we last visited Hardserve, much has happened. The president, Jim Green, agreed with Tom Roberts, the analyst from Manhold, that a design team was needed and decided to put Terry Carson in charge of it. Terry, as you may remember, was the order processing manager who had just completed a week's training session at a computer manufacturer's school. A third supervisor and one more part-time warehouse picker were added to Carson's staff to free some of his time for the project.

Art Hanley, Manhold computer department head, also visited Green and suggested the formation of a steering committee. Green agreed to establish the committee and serve as its chairman because he wanted to keep track of computer developments in the company. Green placed Steve Johnson, vice president of finance, Dick Hansen, vice president of purchasing, and Bob Moss, vice president of operations, on the committee. Art Hanley represents the computer department from headquarters and planned to attend all the meetings. Any time a decision on a particular application was being raised, the team leader, Terry Carson, and the chief analyst, Tom Roberts, from the computer department would be present at the steering committee meeting.

The steering committee met and decided jointly with Green that the first efforts at Hardserve should be devoted to inventory control. Many firms had experienced extensive savings applying the computer to managing inventories, and inventory is crucial to Hardserve's business.

Terry Carson was given complete freedom to choose other members of the team. He selected Nancy Collier, one of his supervisors, the warehouse manager Paul Jones, a purchasing agent named Harry Snyder, and an accountant, Stan Levine, to be members of the team. Of course Tom Roberts is on the team as chief analyst, and another analyst from the computer department, Mary Davis, was assigned to the project as well.

Steering Committee Action

The steering committee met several times and began to develop criteria for judging applications. At this stage the steering committee decided that no more than three alternatives for new systems needed to be presented in a survey or feasibility study. The group selected the following criteria and assigned weights to them for selecting alternatives.

1 Percentage of system goals met (30 percent)
2 Tangible savings—saving minus operational cost (20 percent)
3 Intangible benefits (25 percent)
4 Time to implement (10 percent)
5 Total cost (15 percent)

Before the design team actually undertook its activities, each member of the steering committee and the president met with the employees in each department and explained the reasons for developing a new system. They requested cooperation from users and stated emphatically that no one would be replaced by a computer system. In fact, it was their hope that working conditions would be upgraded and improved as a result of a computer system.

Work Plan

Tom Roberts, Terry Carson, and the rest of the design team began meeting for several hours each day. During the first week of activities, Tom described the purpose of the preliminary survey and feasibility study and showed examples from other projects.

The team readily accepted the idea of a user survey to pinpoint problems in advance and to inaugurate user participation in design. The team designed a simple questionnaire that asked the employees how they felt the computer could help them. The questionnaire was also intended to elicit information as to whether any employees had previous computer experience. Users were asked for their reactions to a computer system and for their expectations about how it might change what they did at work, how it would alter groups, and how knowledgeable they felt about computer systems.

The results of the survey were surprisingly favorable. It located two employees who had worked in a company where a computer system had been installed. These individuals helped other employees and prepared them for a new system.

The team divided the responsibilities for the preliminary survey. The Hardserve members planned to document the existing system and procedures with the help of Tom Roberts and other team members with a background in systems. The team developed a conceptualization of the inventory system shown in Figure 14-1. They saw the system as composed of five major components: inventory or the storage of goods; customers who ordered merchandise; purchasing, which ordered new merchandise; vendors who supplied the merchandise; and the warehouse, which was responsible for checking in new merchandise and processing customer orders.

There was some debate about whether or not warehousing should be separated from inventory since, after all, the warehouse contained the inventory. However, Tom Roberts prevailed on the group by saying, "Management really wants us to look at inventory control. Of course, we could consider it a part of warehousing, but let's separate it out at least in the beginning so that we can focus easily on it."

Bob Moss, vice president of operations, then said, "Why not consider receiving and order filling in the warehouse two separate functions? We have to look at each of those as well."

"That's a good point," Tom said. "It shows why this stage is so hard. There are a lot of different views of what constitutes a system. Here, I would say that we could at the next level of detail (or abstraction) break down the warehouse into two or more component boxes, one for receiving and one for order filling."

Terry Carson then asked, "If we do that, what about reordering? Where does that belong? It is a part of inventory control, but it is done by the warehouse staff."

"Given our current model of the system, we would put that with inventory control," said Tom. "It doesn't matter who performs the functions. At this point we're interested in the functions. If we were looking at a receiving system for the warehouse, then we might have a slightly different drawing of the system."

FIGURE 14-1
Hardserve overview.

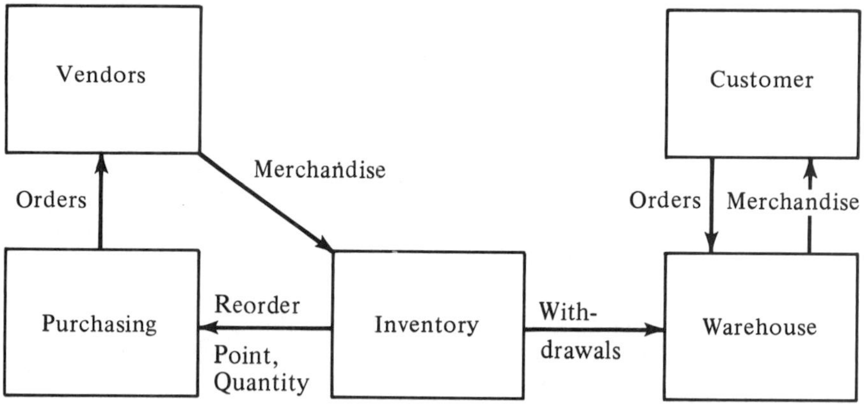

SYSTEMS PROBLEM 14-3

The computer department at Manhold and Hardserve has a real problem with users like Dick Hansen. Dick is very worried that a computer may replace some of the people who work for him. Such fears are not totally unfounded, at least at the clerical levels of the organization. Some organizations that are basically information processors like banks and insurance companies have been able to reduce clerical employment greatly through computer-based information systems. In some cases the existing level of the work force has not changed much, but the need to increase employment has been reduced.

Less evidence exists for the reduction of middle-level managers and other desicion makers. As systems move into managerial control and strategic planning areas, managers may fear that they will be replaced. Given your knowledge of computing, what do you think is the likelihood of such managerial replacement?

Specifically at Hardserve, if Terry Carson and Tom Roberts want to push the computer further into the purchasing department, they must find some way to reduce the resistance of Dick Hansen. The system would probably print reorder notices and some kind of buyer review notice. The purchasing agent would approve the review notice, and that would be used to trigger the automatic generation of a purchase order by a computer program. How could the design team at Hardserve obtain agreement and enthusiasm for such a subsystem?

At this point a lengthy argument ensued. Bob Moss from operations asked if they could computerize warehousing and other operations like purchasing in the system. He said, "Receiving is a real problem. How about a terminal so that we wouldn't have to look up copies of purchase orders? They always get misfiled and we waste a lot of expensive time."

Dick Hansen, vice president of purchasing, took the opposite point of view, "I don't want to computerize anything more than we have to until I'm convinced the thing will work. Some people have really gone too far. We can't replace our purchase agents; they know a lot more than any machine ever will about special demand and seasonal items."

Several meetings were held trying to resolve some of the philosophical disagreements about what should be included as a part of the system. Finally, Terry Carson and Tom Roberts met alone.

"I'm afraid," Terry said, "this argument about whether or not to include more than just inventory control in the system is splitting the design team and getting us no place. What do you think?"

"You're right," Tom replied, "Dick is afraid of the computer, and Bob thinks that they can do anything. He's too naive about the problems of developing a system."

The two men talked for a while and then sought advice from Nancy Collier, one of the supervisors working for Terry.

She said, "I've been thinking the same thing. What would you say to just sticking with inventory control as a test case? We could show purchasing that the system can work, and Bob will certainly get an idea of what is involved in building a system."

The three discussed this strategy further and decided to go to Jim Green, the president, for his advice. After a long discussion of the pros and cons of different alternatives. Green came to the same conclusion that Nancy Collier had: they should try for a modest success and then use it as a base for further achievements.

Over some opposition, the design team finally accepted this compromise and went to work on a preliminary survey. Tom Roberts investigated packaged inventory programs. Given the completed documentation of the existing system, he and Mary worked on developing two alternatives for new systems. Two weeks later a rough preliminary survey was ready for presentation to the steering committee. The survey is reproduced in the following appendix.

APPENDIX: Hardserve Preliminary Survey

EXECUTIVE SUMMARY

For several weeks we have been conducting a preliminary survey on the advisability of developing a computerized inventory control system. This document presents our findings for consideration by the steering committee.

Goals

We have identified the following goals for an inventory system:

1 Reduce inventory levels while maintaining a desired level of customer service
2 Improve reorder policies
3 Improve management for seasonal and slow-moving items
4 Capture sales data so purchasing can analyze trends and stock the proper merchandise

Alternatives

We identified one package program and developed two alternatives for new systems for consideration by the steering committee. The results of our analysis are summarized below:

1 Minor improvements in the present system
  a Percentage of goals met—5 percent
  b Tangible savings—$5000 per year
  c Intangible benefits*—10 percent
  d Time to implement—3 months
  e Total cost—$10,000
2 A batch computer system with a simple economic order-quantity model
  a Percentage of goals met—75 percent

    b Tangible saving—$20,000 per year
    c Intangible benefits*—30 percent
    d Time to implement—18 months
    e Total cost—$50,000
3 Computech inventory control package
    a Percentage of goals met—60 percent
    b Tangible savings—$15,000 per year
    c Intangible benefits*—25 percent
    d Time to implement—6 months
    e Total cost—$55,000 ($40,000 for package, $15,000 to install and modify)
4 An on-line inventory system
    a Percentage of goals met—95 percent
    b Tangible savings—$15,000 per year
    c Intangible benefits*—50 percent
    d Time to implement—24+ months
    e Total cost—$80,000

THE EXISTING SYSTEM

Problems

The existing system is illustrated in the flowchart of Exhibit 1. At the present time we have manual processing of papers and no real inventory control. For some items we tend to overstock from fear of running out, and in others we miss a reorder point and incur a stockout. Purchasing hears from the warehouse when a particular item has reached a reorder point marked on the bin. This reorder point is set by the warehouse manager, based on experience. We also have no real sales forecasting because we don't know what items are moving. Accounting analyzes the physical inventory, and at the end of the year purchasing looks at what items have sold. However, it's too late to do any good by that time.

Goals

The goals for improvement in the system are stated in the Executive Summary.

Decision Considerations

We have identified the following crucial decisions in processing inventory:

1 What should be ordered for each new season?
2 What should be reordered during the season and when?
3 How much should be reordered each time?
4 What items should be dropped from inventory?

    *Intangible benefits were rated on a scale 0 to 100 and include consideration of things like the user interface with the system, ease of use, improved decision making, etc.

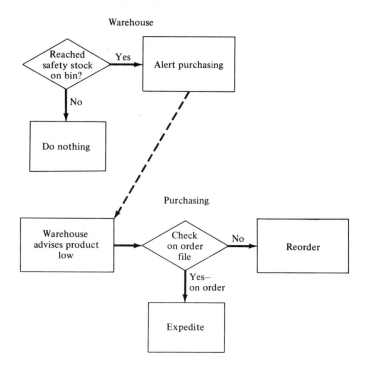

Exhibit 1 of survey.

Information Flows

The information in processing is shown in Exhibit 1. Basically, the warehouse supervisor notices when the physical stock has dropped below the reorder point and sends a report at the end of the day to purchasing. The purchasing agent either reorders the item, if it is not on order, or expedites it if an order has already been placed. At the end of the season, the purchasing department analyzes purchase orders and estimates what will be needed for the next season. Decisions on the reorder amount are based on the purchasing agent's negotiations with the supplier. Approximate volumes of orders and other related data are given in Table 14-3.

ANALYSIS OF EACH ALTERNATIVE

Improvements to the Present System

Overview   With minimal impact and cost we can make some improvements to the

TABLE 14-3
APPROXIMATE MONTHLY VALUES

	Average number of orders
January	4100
February	6700
March	7800
April	8400
May	5400
June	4600
July	5000
August	5100
September	6200
October	9500
November	10,100
December	8200
	81,100

Average orders/month: 6,758
Maximum orders in a day: 500
Average orders/day: 311
Average number of items/order: 5.1

present system. For example, we can set up tables for economic order-quantity amounts and put better reorder points on the bins.

Decisions and Information Flows These improvements would help us reorder a more economic quantity of goods each time and we would do so at a better reorder point. However, these improvements would do little for other decisions or information processing.

Technical There will be no computer processing involved in this alternative.

Development Schedule A few months would be required to implement these changes. We might use a computer program to set the economic order quantities and lot sizes, but this could be done very inexpensively on a timeshared system.

Impact on the Organization There should be minimal changes and a very small impact on organizations or on jobs. The purchasing agent would have to consult a table, which would make decisions on economic order quantities more routine. However, this lets the purchasing agent shop for a better deal, for example, by looking for a better discount or lower price. Warehouse managers should be happy to have a better system of reorder points, as the current haphazard way of establishing them is of concern to the manager.

Operational Aspects The only change this system would create is that purchasing would have a series of tables on the proper economic order quantities. Instead of the warehouse supervisor deciding on the reorder point, a more scientific calculation could be used.

Costs and Benefits   The costs in the Summary were estimated to include computer programs and printing the tables to choose the economic order quantity. We can use the computer for this task. The benefits from this system are estimates of savings through economic ordering and reductions in the number of stockouts.

A Batch System

Overview   This system would be updated once or twice a week with inputs from order processing providing data on usage. Information from the warehouse would show arrivals of merchandise. When a reorder point is nearing, the computer should notify the purchasing agent, who would place the order and notify the computer that goods were on order. Whenever desired, we could produce a usage report.

Decisions and Information Flows   This system would provide data for all decisions discussed under the Goals section. Information flows would be altered; the computer department would receive information from the warehouse on order processing and would send information to purchasing.

Technical   We would use key-to-disk input, and reports would be printed for purchasing. We would send copies of the inventory report to accounting as well. We would probably have one file on tape with all the data on inventory.

Development Schedule   Development should take about 12 months, but we have allowed 18 to be safe. The system would be run on the Manhold computer and we would have a remote batch terminal here for input and output. It should be easy to manage two or three updates a week, and we could vary the number of updates depending on the season.

Impact on the Organization   It would be necessary for us to add a data preparation and control department at Hardserve, and we would want to have a liaison here to interact with the Manhold computer department. We would remove the reorder notice burden from the warehouse supervisor. In interviews with the supervisors it was indicated that this removal would be a welcome change. The job is tedious and error-prone now, and they would just as soon spend time supervising their employees. Interviews with the purchasing agents indicated that the idea of better planning and sales data would be very appealing. They now are confronted with too many emergency orders and the necessity to expedite orders all too frequently.

Operational Aspects   The major changes in operations have been described. Almost all departments are affected, though the changes are relatively minor. A number of reports will be produced, and certain existing documents will have to be sent to keypunching for input into the computer system. However, there is very little additional work created for any individuals as far as manual processing is concerned.

Cost and Benefits   Benefit estimates were based on savings on inventory balance and a reduction in the number of stockouts. We did not really include a better service level for customers, although we think that this service will be provided. Cost estimates are based on a comparable system developed by Manhold's computer staff.

A Package Program

Overview   We also looked at several package programs and selected the best one for consideration by the steering committee. This package does much the same thing as our batch system, but has some functions we don't need and lacks certain features we would like to have.

Decisions and Information Flows   Basically, it would cover the same decisions as the batch system discussed above. In fact, all the items discussed above are similar for this package except for the development schedule, costs, and benefits. So we will omit discussing them again.

Development Effort   The development effort includes installing and modifying the program to produce the types of reports we would like to have. We estimate this effort will require less time than developing a system from scratch.

Costs and Benefits   The benefits of the new system would be much the same as the batch system described above. A large portion of the cost is the purchase price for the package. We would also have a small operating cost from subscribing to changes and improvements that are made in the package over time.

An On-Line System

Overview   This alternative is the most sophisticated one presented for consideration. It offers the advantage of not having to transcribe any data in batch mode. Instead, there would be terminals in the warehouse, receiving, and purchasing. Data would all be entered by the user.

Decisions and Information Flows   We will again cover the same decisions and have basically identical information flows except that now we would not use existing documents. Instead, information would be keyed into the system by various users.

Technical   The input and output are clearly different for this system. We would have to use direct-access files. Output would be selective, though we would probably still want to print some batch reports for a historical record.

Development Effort   This system will take more effort to develop, even though Manhold has several on-line systems running now. Moving to on-line requires a more sophisticated technology, which is reflected in the development effort.

Operational Aspects   Operationally, the system will be easier to use and there will be far fewer documents. However, we are somewhat concerned about whether people will be able to use the terminals in the various locations. In some respects, paper processing may almost be easier, since it is already familiar.

Impact on the Organization   This system would have the greatest impact on the organization, because we would have purchasing agents, warehouse personnel, etc., using terminals directly. There is also the possibility of problems with backup and computer downtime.

Costs and Benefits   Benefits are the highest here because of source-data capture and the fact that data are up to date when on-line. We would expect to have the same tangible savings as with the batch systems, but operating costs are somewhat higher, reducing total benefits.

KEY WORDS

Cost-benefit ratio	Packages
Criteria weight	Preliminary survey
Feasibility study	Steering committee
Information flows	System alternative

RECOMMENDED READINGS

Burch, J. G., F. R. Strater, and G. Grudnitski: *Information Systems Theory and Practice,* 3d ed., Wiley, New York, 1983. (A basic text on analysis.)

Mintzberg, H.: *The Nature of Managerial Work,* Harper & Row, New York, 1972. (How do managerial activities affect the preliminary survey and feasibility study?)

Semprivivo, P.: *Systems Analysis,* 2d ed., SRA, Palo Alto, Calif., 1982. (Another good text on design.)

Simon, H.: *The Shape of Automation for Men and Management,* Harper & Row, New York, 1965. (How do the predictions of the author on the automated factory affect current systems design activities?)

DISCUSSION QUESTIONS

1 What is the purpose of having multiple alternatives presented in the preliminary survey and feasibility study?
2 How should the steering committee choose among the alternatives presented?
3 How does the design team evaluate intangible savings; that is, how can intangibles be quantified and included in the decision?
4 What purpose does a preliminary survey have as far as users are concerned?
5 How do other projects that are underway affect the decisions that are made by the steering committee?
6 What is the impact of technological change (such as hardware and software) on the steering committee? (Hint: consider the impact of technological change in the cost-benefit ratio for an application.)

7 What is the danger encountered in undertaking a careful study of an existing processing system before designing a new one?

8 Who should initiate the preliminary survey and why?

9 How can a design team find out what applications packages are available that might provide an alternative for a system under consideration?

10 Evaluate the Hardserve preliminary survey. How would you respond to this survey as a member of the steering committee?

11 What different approaches can you suggest to estimating the value of information?

12 It has been suggested that an organization should consider risk in deciding which new computer applications to undertake and should strive for a balanced portfolio of projects. That is, some of the projects should not be risky, to compensate for other projects that may have high levels of risk. What are the risks in a systems analysis and design project? How should these risks be evaluated?

13 Why is it important to have the top management of Hardserve on the steering committee and involved in the selection of new computer applications?

14 Managers have complained about not really having a choice when it comes to approving a new system based on a feasibility study. Instead, the managers say that they are presented with one very encompassing system to approve; the only alternative is to do nothing. How does the approach to a feasibility study suggested in this chapter help solve this problem? What new problems does it introduce?

15 Why is it important to have heavy user input in the evaluation of an applications package after the package has passed the initial screening by the computer department?

16 Would Hardserve be well advised to undertake an on-line system as their first computer application? Is there a way they could have the benefits of on-line response with minimum risk? Is their position relative to Manhold an advantage or disadvantage in developing a computer capability in the firm?

17 Simulation involves building a model of some phenomenon and testing the model. For example, airplane models are first tested in a wind tunnel before the plane is built. Computers are often used to simulate various phenomena, such as an assembly line or the flow of jobs through a plant. How could computer simulation be used in the design of an information system? What are the drawbacks in using simulation here?

18 According to the information developed in the Hardserve feasibility study, how would you classify the different types of information provided by the alternative systems according to the Anthony decision framework?

19 In the Hardserve example, there appears to be a real need to improve information processing capabilities. What are other possible reasons for undertaking a system?

20 What are the possible disadvantages to Hardserve in using a computer system that is located physically at Manhold?

21 If the new information system being proposed for Hardserve were to fail completely, what impact would this have on the company? Develop a scenario for what you think might happen in the event that the system was implemented and failed completely.

CHAPTER 15

SYSTEMS DESIGN
SPECIFICATIONS

At the completion of the feasibility study, a system alternative is chosen for implementation. The design team must complete and document a number of tasks in creating the new system. The product of their efforts is a set of systems design specifications that are used as the basic blueprint for programming the system.

STUDY OUTPUT

Specifications

The results of this study should be complete specifications for the new system as shown in Table 15-1. Usually, we begin by specifying the desired output; that is, what does the user want from the system? Then is it necessary to determine what input is required to produce this desired output. A comparison of input and output identifies the data that must be maintained on files.

Next, we consider processing; that is, how are the input data transformed and used to modify the files? How often does a file have to be updated? How are the input and the contents of files processed to produce the desired output? Also, at this point the design team should specify manual procedures for other activities associated with the system.

For input and output files and processing, it is necessary to determine what kinds of errors are likely to occur and to design procedures to locate or prevent errors. The final output of the specifications for the system should be a work plan and schedule for implementation. However, we shall postpone discussion of these latter outputs until Chapter 19.

TABLE 15-1
DETAILED SYSTEMS DESIGN SPECIFICATIONS

Output	Errors
Destination and use	Design decisions
Medium	Modules
Reports (samples)	Processing
Frequency	Conversion programs
Input	Input
Source	Output
Medium	Errors
Document (sample)	Design decisions
Fields	Modules
Estimated volume	Processing
Files	Manual procedures
Medium	Error control
Contents	Input error conditions
Record format, field names	Processing errors
File structure (linkages, directories)	File integrity
Estimated file size	Output errors
Estimated activity	Backup
Updating frequency	Security
Processing	Work plan
System flow	Program schedule, milestones
Program specifications	Time estimates
Input	Personnel required, assignments
Output	

Work Responsibilities

At various times during the development of detailed specifications we will need to develop more data; there is no such thing as "a completed design." By this time, the design team should have developed many contacts with the rest of the organization, so returning to users for additional information should be easy.

During this stage users on the design team still have major tasks to perform, and computer department representatives continue to guide design activities. For example, user team members should develop the report contents with actual users of the report. The computer department staff can then design a format for the report and draw up pro forma examples. Alternatively, users can actually draw examples of the reports they would like. Pro forma examples are reviewed thoroughly by users before programming.

Given a brief tutorial, it should also be possible for users to design the input for the system and to specify most of the file contents. The computer department staff certainly has to specify the details of processing and file structures, but users can supply the overall logic. Users also specify manual procedures that accompany the system. Both users and the computer department staff should think independently of possible errors and of the necessary audit trails for the system. (An audit trail is a logical path by which a transaction can be traced through the computer system.)

Below we discuss specifications in batch or on-line systems. When we discussed patterns of processing in Chapter 5, we saw that many combinations of equipment and response are possible, from centralized through distributed to decentralized systems in some combination of batch or on-line processing. These alternatives will impart the options available to the analyst. However, the discussion below can be easily applied to designs for these various patterns of processing.

OUTPUT CONSIDERATIONS

The output of a computer system is the primary contact between the system and most users. The quality of this output and its usefulness determines whether the system will be used, so it is essential to have the best possible output.

Flexibility

In much of our research on the use of information systems, we have found that users have different requirements. Some users want exception reports; they wish to be notified only if sales fall, say, 10 percent from last year's levels. One user wants summary information; but another prefers to see complete details. To determine the different types of output desired, the design team should employ user surveys or have user members of the design team observe how other users work with information. Give the user sample reports for several weeks to think about their use.

How can we provide output flexibility? Clearly, data have to be maintained at the lowest level of detail desired for reporting purposes. However, there is no reason why everyone has to receive exactly the same output; summaries can be developed easily from detailed data for those who desire it. Designers should consider keeping a file of user preferences on report formats if there are substantial differences in user output desires. Then a report can be produced according to the preferred format of each user.

Another possibility to enhance output flexibility is to use file management packages or to develop a retrieval program that allows for easy custom-tailoring of reports. The use of such packages also makes it much easier to change reports as users develop experience with a system. In any case, report preparation should be done in a separate program or module that can be modified easily.

General Design Considerations

The design team should stress clarity in format and headings for output; one of the most frequent complaints we hear is that users cannot understand reports. Having users actually design a report increases their understanding, which is another good reason for this design approach. It is essential to use clear, descriptive titles for different fields on the report; avoid the use of obscure or little-known codes. If the data on a report are not obvious, use a footnote explaining how the numbers were derived or refer to the appropriate user documentation for an explanation.

Consider including a short description of how the computations were performed on the first page of the report.

When it is necessary to print exception or error messages, the system should provide as polite a response as possible. Here again, it is not desirable to use coded numbers such as error 13B. Instead, explain what is wrong and try to have the error message provide feedback so the user will learn from such mistakes.

Another chronic complaint we encounter is that too much data are produced by computer systems. Even if users do design the output, they still may be guilty of printing too much information. Assure users that information is available and can be printed when needed. Ask if an exception report will do. Are the data needed only infrequently? Can they be saved on a tape and printed only if necessary? If it is necessary to maintain large amounts of archival data for historical or legal purposes, it may be possible to use microfilm. The design team should also consider whether the addition of an on-line inquiry facility would eliminate the need for many printed reports.

The discussion above has referred primarily to batch processing output, and a few additional considerations should be included in the design of on-line output. First, there should be a key on the terminal the user can depress to obtain help. The "help" function provides an on-line set of instructions to show the user how to obtain information. In addition to a help key, there may be several levels of prompting in the system. For example, a more detailed mode of comments can be used for the novice and a terser mode for the frequent, experienced user.

Another important feature of an on-line system is adequate response time. Users who become dependent on on-line processing are very sensitive to degraded response times. Backup should also be provided because of this heavy user dependence on the system. Users have been known to become enraged when a crucial on-line system is not functioning. It is also helpful to use pleasing terminals: can a CRT be used if hard copy is not needed? Consider the use of silent printers where a permanent record is necessary.

INPUT

Source Data Collection

In the past years the trend in information systems has been toward collecting data as close to the source of the data as possible. The objective of this philosophy is to eliminate data transcription, both for the purposes of avoiding errors and to reduce the time required to get data into the computer. The ultimate in automatic data collection is sensors attached to the input of a realtime system, for example, a computer monitoring a space vehicle before launch. In most commercial computer systems the ultimate source data collection technique is to use an on-line terminal.

One method to avoid data transcription, which is gaining rapidly in popularity, is the use of optical character recognition (OCR) equipment. Consider a large sales force for which it would be too expensive to have computer terminals for each salesperson. Both equipment and communications costs would be too high, and it is not clear that it would be even desirable for sales personnel to use a typewriter to enter orders. Instead, if they print numbers carefully, the actual order form prepared by each person can be used as input to the computer system through the use of a scanner. In fact, the use of a scanner might actually be faster than an on-line terminal since, undoubtedly, the sales personnel would have to write their orders before they could key them into a terminal. Instead, the salesperson takes a few more minutes to write neatly and enters the order form itself directly into the computer system.

For input it is also possible to use mark sensing, in which the user darkens a box or circle corresponding to his or her choice. However, optical character recognition is easier for the user to understand than mark sensing and is generally preferred unless the input data are very simple. Unless there are very few alternatives, the mark-sense forms become clumsy, since a box or a circle must be provided for each possible answer.

General Design Considerations

Batch Input   Batch input suffers from its rigidity, since most batch input requires information in a strict format. There is also a lack of immediate feedback on errors with batch input. However, it is very economical, and batch systems have several advantages in backup and in processing error control. Wherever possible, the design team should consider the use of existing documents for input, since these will minimize user problems in understanding new and possibly more complicated forms. It is important to be sure that the data to be entered can be provided legibly on the form. If a document has to be transcribed by a keying operation, it is helpful to use boxes for each character; if this is not possible, a separate blank should be provided for each character, as this provision helps the keying operator justify the input (see Figure 15-1).

For input forms designed for optical character recognition or mark sensing, it is best to meet with the manufacturer's representative to determine the requirements for their particular machinery. OCR has very exacting requirements for the location of information and the quality of printing on forms.

On-Line Input   We have discussed the trend toward on-line systems in previous chapters. In particular, on-line input has a number of advantages, which

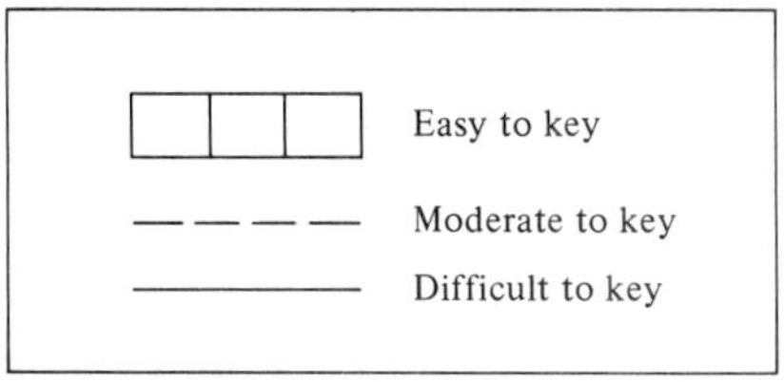

FIGURE 15-1
Three approaches to a three-column input field.

Martin (1973) has summarized as follows: First, the data-entry process is usually faster, owing to the dialogue with the computer; frequently fewer data have to be entered, since the computer can supply some of the data from its access to files—for example, name and address data from a given customer number.

Incorrect keying can be detected on-line and often corrected immediately; this on-line checking contributes greatly to improved accuracy and reliability of data. Operators may be saved, since input is speeded up. Martin describes one case in which throughput per operator was increased by 40 percent over card punching. Also, some organizations have found that existing clerical personnel can easily be trained to use a terminal; more expensive keypunch operators may not be needed with on-line input. Data enters the computer system more quickly with on-line input, since manual handling and verifying are avoided.

The design of input for on-line systems, particularly those featuring complex interactions between users and the system, is difficult. One helpful design tool for this type of system is a state-transition diagram, illustrated in Figure 15-2. Each possible user state (for example, logging on, using the command language, etc.) is represented by a circle; arrows between circles represent possible paths or transitions from one state to another. By following a series of arrows, the user can move between the states. Figure 15-2a shows possible states for a hypothetical time-sharing system.

The various input commands or options that result in the transition to a new state can be entered on the arrows if desired. Figure 15-2b is a state-transition diagram for a highly simplified hotel reservation system; this illustration shows single-letter user inputs for each transition. (The final system might employ function keys, that is, a key for the reservation function; or the user might enter a number to indicate the chosen option.)

These state-transition diagrams show clearly how the user interacts with the system, with each input and the resultant system response being evident. They indicate potentially clumsy design features and clarify design choices for input and interaction. The use of this type of tool should assist the designer in creating a pleasing and easy-to-use interface for on-line systems.

Dialogues　Martin (1973) has described 23 types of on-line computer interaction; the type of dialogue chosen depends on the application. The major design consideration is what format will be convenient for the user and will make it natural to enter data correctly. The advantages of different types of input must also be weighed against the cost and difficulty of programming them.

1 The first type of dialogue is a simple query; there is no elaborate conversation. The terminal operator keys in a number or symbol and retrieves the data; for example, an inventory part number produces a display showing quantity of that part on hand and on order along with the reorder point.

2 Mnemonics are memory aids; since most terminal users are unfamiliar with programming, we can construct abbreviations that have natural meaning to the user. The abbreviation requires less keying than full text. An example might be

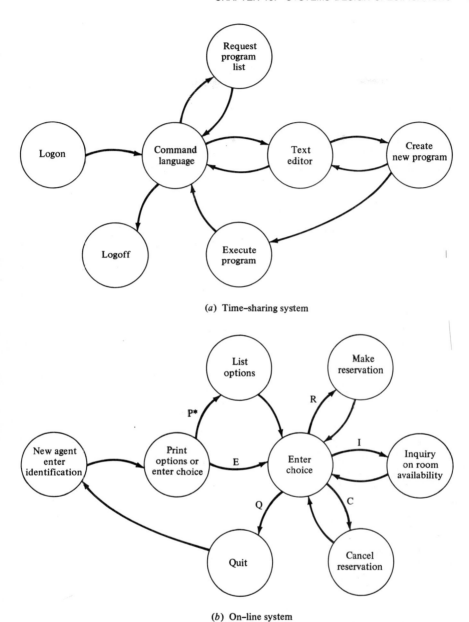

(a) Time–sharing system

(b) On–line system

*Each letter represents possible input such as "P" for print. In an actual system, each choice would probably be numbered and the user would only enter the number of choice.

FIGURE 15-2
State-transition diagrams for on-line systems.

SYSTEMS PROBLEM 15-1

Alan Shapiro has been asked to examine a new system being implemented by a small portfolio management company. The firm invests in a variety of securities for its customers, all of whom seem to have differing investment objectives. Some want maximum capital appreciation; others are interested in maximum current return on invested capital.

The system under examination is on-line and keeps careful track of all transactions affecting the client's portfolio. The portfolio manager enters all pending trades, and when confirmation of settlement is made by the broker, the pending trade is actually posted to the client's portfolio. All through this process, the transactions generated by the broker and the fund manager are carefully controlled and checked, both by the computer system and manually by clerks.

Alan has been asked to perform an overall evaluation of the system, since the president of the company is thinking of trying to market the system to other financial management companies. Alan has been impressed with the documentation of the system and its functional specifications.

The only point of criticism he has found is in the actual mechanics of interaction through the terminal. The major problem is the lack of consistency in expected user responses. Although there is some menu selection, the identification of alternatives in each instance is different; the user does not consistently enter a letter or a number to indicate the menu choice. Also, the screen is constructed in such a way that the top line is reserved for immediate interaction and the rest of the screen displays data. As the display changes, the data move around on the screen. What design considerations should Alan suggest to improve the interface of this system with the user?

RES to reserve a room. We must be careful with this technique, however, not to make the mnemonics too terse. One approach is to have two modes, one terse and the other verbose for the new user.

3 English-language entry can be helpful for the novice user but can lead to a great deal of typing. In a system for retrieving books and articles, we often find English-language input for the descriptors. For example, one might have an input command of the form: LOCATE EXPERIMENTS ON CATS OR DOGS SINCE 1979. In this sample, LOCATE and SINCE would be command verbs in the input language; the user would enter the other words for a retrieval request. This statement should retrieve articles with the keyword "Experiments" and the keywords "Cats" or "Dogs" written since 1979.

4 Sometimes the application justifies the use of a programming-like language. In certain instances a user will be accustomed to programming already, or the user will work so much with the system that it makes sense to learn a language. Various languages are offered on timesharing systems for performing special functions like financial analysis, corporate planning, etc.

5 Function keys are very popular and represent one example of what Martin calls action codes. Only a single key has to be depressed to indicate what the machine is supposed to do. One function might be to make a reservation and another one could be to cancel it.

6 The approach above can be extended to multiple-action codes, since in a complex system there might not be enough single-character codes or function keys. We might use different positions on the screen of a CRT and have a separate set of codes for each.

7 In some systems, it is helpful to build a record on a screen as the operator enters data. Consider adding a new customer to a file; here we might start with name and address. These data would stay on the screen as additional parts of the record were entered, such as type of customer, credit terms, etc.

8 Scrolling techniques are used to add information continuously to the bottom of the screen while the oldest information retrieved is larger than will fit on a single display screen. With such a display, it is helpful to have a move-up and move-down command so that the terminal operator uses the system like a scroll.

9 Some systems will feature simple instructions to the operator, such as to enter certain data elements. Often, the instruction contains the answers that are acceptable, such as ENTER Y FOR YES, N FOR NO.

10 The technique above can be extended to provide multiple instructions for the operator. One screen asks the user at the terminal to enter more than one piece of data. It is helpful to design this kind of dialogue so that the user does not have to follow a set order for entry. Most of the time, it will be easier to request the data one element at a time, however.

11 Menu selection is one of the most popular types of input for an on-line system. This approach works if there is only a limited set of valid operator answers to a question asked by the program. An example might be:

PLEASE INDICATE THE STUDENT'S DEGREE PROGRAM:
1. B.A.
2. B.S.
3. M.A.
4. M.S.
5. PH.D.

The user would only have to enter the number of the proper choice, such as a "3" for a student in the M.A. program.

12 If there are too many items on the menu for one screen, one can list all that will fit. The last entry is a continuation to the next screen, which has more choices for this question.

13 If there are many choices, say in the thousands, the menu selection becomes more like a telephone directory. The choices might be arranged alphabetically, and the user could direct the system to approximately the right location, for example, to the "L's."

14 The menu can also be expanded to provide for several questions and selections on the same screen, forming a multipart menu.

15 Menus can be arranged so that the user chooses more than one answer and completes a series of questions using the same display.

16 Some systems use a displayed-format approach to interaction. Here the system gives the format like ENTER DATE MM/DD/YY. The user types over the MM/DD/YY characters with the appropriate data. This operation is like a fill-in-the-blanks form, but one writes over the blanks and erases the format during data entry!

17 An alternative to the approach above is to have the program state the sequence in which data must be entered but not an exact format. The user who is quite familiar with the application then supplies the required data.

18 To provide flexibility, the program may give the user the choice of several formats or alternative forms for the data to be entered.

19 The techniques above lead naturally to the idea of form filling, in which the program presents the outline of the form to be completed by the user. The form has blanks on it, and the computer is programmed to tab to the beginning of each field after the completion of the prior field.

20 Sometimes entire lines are overwritten by a response to a question. Martin suggests that this technique is likely to be confusing and does not recommend its use.

21 Sometimes when the operator is making changes or there are many standard default options for the information entered, the user is presented with a display of completed data. The operator then uses the cursor (a point of light that indicates where the terminal is currently set to type) to move to fields of data and change them. If there are relatively few changes, the interaction can be very fast.

22 Text editing is a very specialized type of dialogue. Often the user is actually running a text-editing program with its own complex command language. Many on-line systems for timesharing come with text editors; the design of such a program is a complicated task. At a minimum the text editor usually allows the user to insert and delete characters, alter lines, move lines to other parts of the text, and search for combinations of characters in the text.

23 Martin's final type of dialogue is a hybrid technique: real interactive communication with the program. In this approach, the conversation is partly initiated by the user and partly by the program.

Personal computer software packages have established new standards for interaction. A good example of this type of interface may be found with the electronic spreadsheet systems like Lotus 1-2-3. When a user of this package depresses the / key, a one-line menu appears at the top of the screen. The menu has a series of words that are main commands. The cursor (bright light on the terminal marking one's place) can be moved across the line one command at a time. As the cursor stops on each command in the line, a line below displays the subcommands of that main command. One can think of the menu as a hierarchical data structure. The second command line then shows the next level in the hierarchy if the user selects the command on which the cursor is resting.

A command may be selected with the return key if the cursor is on that command, or by typing the first letter of a command regardless of the position of the cursor. An escape key lets the user back up to the previous level of command.

This approach is fast, uses a relatively small number of lines on the terminal screen, and yet provides the user with a great deal of information about the available commands.

Clearly there are many forms of interactive dialogue; the choice depends on the nature of the application, the volume of interaction, and the type of computer system being used. This list should provide some ideas for the analyst and user working to design a natural and pleasant computer dialogue.

The dialogues discussed above are all conversational. They do not deal with a specialized topic like graphics interaction. For many design and engineering tasks, such as the planning of a new automobile, graphics systems are helpful in saving time and labor. For typical business applications, an alphanumeric terminal can be used to draw bar charts and plot points that are often sufficient for the user. The same type of dialogue described above can easily be used in conjunction with a graphics terminal. Most frequently the interaction is more limited, and menu displays are often sufficient for graphics work.

In addition to general design considerations, for on-line data entry the user should be given courteous error messages (we shall discuss all types of errors in the system in a later section) and should have the opportunity to rekey data that

---

SYSTEMS PROBLEM 15-2

Margaret Fisher put down the 2-inch-thick set of specifications she was reading for the new on-line order-entry system for New England Mills, a major manufacturer of clothing. Margaret was manager of systems and programming for the firm, and this was the first system designed by the computer department since she had assumed this position.

Her major concern was with the coming user review and sign-off on the system. She convened a meeting of the design team to discuss the specifications.

Despite her requests, the designers and users felt that there was neither sufficient time nor staff resources for a user to play a major role in the design. Thus, the users were only slightly aware of what the system was supposed to accomplish.

"I don't see how you can expect a user to digest these specifications," Margaret said to the design team. "I have a hard time following them, and I've been in the field for 15 years!"

Her comments generated heated discussion and a lot of defensive comments from the design team. Finally, Margaret gave them the assignment to come up with a way to present the specifications to the users to ensure that they would understand them before signifying approval.

"I don't want them to sign off just to be rid of us and the specifications," was her parting comment.

What suggestions do you have for the design team in converting the specifications into something more easily understood by users? Develop a plan for the presentation and subsequent approval that describes both the content of the material and the process by which it will be approved.

---

are in error. Messages should be polite and explain the error to the user. It might be advisable to give no explanation unless the user types a question mark or presses some other key after receiving an error message. That way, the user familiar with the system can avoid tedious error messages really designed for someone with less experience.

FILES

The design of files for a system was described in considerable detail in Chapters 8 and 9. It is a good idea for the reader to review that discussion now, especially the section on file design considerations. We can add several additional comments here on file design.

First, plan for the future. Consider whether direct-access files will be required in a few years. If so, it is probably desirable to design them now in preparation for the time when they will be used. Second, be sure to plan for growth and leave some extra unused characters at the end of the record (particularly for disk files, where record and block sizes are constrained by physical track sizes) for changes that undoubtedly will occur during implementation and over the life of the system. Finally, in designing files, think not only of processing when the system is operating, but consider also conversion and the question of where the data will come from for the creation of the file.

PROCESSING

In this section we discuss processing from the standpoint of a custom-tailored system. If, for example, an application generator is used, the characteristics of that system will determine how processing steps must be defined.

System Flow

Usually, a computer system consists of a series of processing stages and separate programs. Systems level flow refers to the major programs, files, and their interaction. For example, in describing batch file updates, we saw that we needed one program to sort the input transactions into the same sequence as the file and another program actually to perform the update. It was also suggested that we might need another program to print output reports.

How do we decide what constitutes a separate processing stage? One good criterion is the separation of functions. Breaking tasks into their smallest components helps to make a large job smaller and easier to implement. For the system as a whole, we generally use file access needs as the basis for setting up processing stages. Any stage that has to access a file for updating processes it completely.

A criterion suggested by Parnas (1972) for breaking programs into smaller modules is also applicable at the systems level. The idea is that stages should be partitioned to "hide information" from other modules. That is, each individual piece of the system should isolate the activities of a program from all others to avoid problems if changes are necessary.

As an example, consider an on-line system; it is not desirable to have each applications program[1] access a file. Rather, each applications program should call a file-accessing module whenever it needs data from a file. Then, if it is necessary to change the file structure, we can do so by changing only the file format or processing logic in the module that accesses the file. If each individual program requests data from a file-accessing module, it should not be necessary to change each program. In a sense, this method of subdividing the tasks results in the underlying file structure being hidden from all the programs but the one that does file management. (This idea of the independence between data and the programs accessing them is one of the principles behind the data-base management systems discussed in Chapter 9.)

Program Specifications

After the broad stages or modules for the system have been defined, it is necessary to move to the preparation of detailed programming specifications. Again we apply our information-hiding modularization techniques. Modules are defined according to the functions they perform, not by the size of a program. Here, it is helpful to make a list of design decisions and to construct program modules around these decisions to hide them from other design decisions. (A program will usually consist of several modules.)

The decision on the format for input should be hidden from other parts of the system by having one module of the input program read the data. This module should pass the fields of data independently of the format or their layout to the other parts of the input program for further processing. Later, if it is decided to use a different input layout or input device, it would be necessary to change only the module that reads the input, not the entire input program.

This breakdown of programs into smaller modules makes it easier to debug the system and modify it. Of course, program specifications must be developed for each module. We should list all the data entering from another module, the number of characters and format of any source documents to be read, and, finally, any data to be read from a file. Output for reports or output that is to be passed to another module should also be specified.

Finally, we must specify any processing to be done by the module. How are the inputs and information derived from files processed? What should the program accomplish? The processing should be described in the form of an algorithm, that is, an effective procedure for accomplishing the goals of the module. The algorithm can be expressed in English, in symbols, or in some combination of the two. Some of the approaches in Chapter 7 are relevant here, especially the idea of using pseudocode to express some of the more complex

---

[1] In an on-line system, programs are generally divided into two types: applications and supervisory programs. Supervisory programs control system resources such as message queries and teleprocessing. They call applications programs that represent the logic of the application, such as making a reservation.

parts of the processing logic. It is often helpful if we include flowcharts or decision tables to clarify processing requirements.

In addition to specifying the programs that will constitute the system when it is in operation, we must also define any conversion programs needed to create files or manipulate data before the installation of the system. Since these programs will be run only once for the most part, efficiency is not as important as clarity and the speed of program development.

CODING

Often it is necessary in systems analysis and design to develop new codes to stand for some entity. The code can be used as a key to identify records or occasionally as an attribute of a record. Codes can carry much more information than an identification number. For example, consider a code that provides the designation for a tire and encodes information about the tire's size (Gore and Stubbe, 1979). This code might appear as XYYZZ, where X is a single character indicating the load-carrying capacity, YY is the ratio of tire height to width, and ZZ is the rim size in inches. A typical code, then, would be K8115, which is a carrying capacity of K, a tire 81 percent as high as it is wide, and a 15-inch rim.

There are a variety of ways to design codes using digits, alphabetic characters, and combinations of letters and digits. In some instances, it is easier to use mnemonics for the code, such as M for male and F for female. A fabric code might be COT for cotton, since this code is easier for someone to recognize than a numeric code. Later we shall discuss self-checking codes; these checking codes are important when input is on-line.

Frequently we are confronted with an existing coding scheme and are not free to develop a new one. The best action in those circumstances may be to use the code or to make only minor modifications to facilitate editing and error checking.

MANUAL PROCEDURES

The systems design is not complete until the manual processing surrounding the computer system has been specified. What volume of activity will there be? How much time is required to perform the manual tasks? We should specify what processing the user has to perform and indicate the flow of information and the time required to complete the processing. We may use simulation or some other means to test these estimates. (This point will be discussed more in Chapter 19.) We should point out here that manual input procedures have caused many otherwise well-designed systems to fail.

ERRORS

One of the major tasks of the systems designer and programmer is to determine error conditions and try to prevent them from causing the system to fail. A well-designed system will handle errors; that is, it will correct them or notify someone of the errors but will continue processing and will produce valid output. It is not unusual to find more than half the instructions in a program devoted to error detection and handling, especially in an on-line system.

Input

Batch Systems   Batch input means that the data are all entered together in batches. Whenever data are transcribed by some keying operation, they are usually key-verified to check for recording errors. One operator keys the data, and a separate operator verifies them on a machine that compares a rekeying of the original data with what the first operator entered. This verification process indicates discrepancies, which are then corrected. Of course, this kind of processing assumes that the data are recorded accurately to begin with; there is nothing that guarantees that the data provided for keying are correct.

Not all input fields need to be key-verified. For example, if a "check" digit (described below) is used, we may rely on the computer to catch any transcription errors. Some input fields such as a name or descriptive information are not crucial, and these data may also be transcribed without verification. When batch totals are used, the designer must decide whether or not to key-verify the amount field, since it will eventually be checked during input batch totaling on the computer.

After transcription, a set of checks is performed to see that the data were correctly entered into the computer. For crucial fields, such as those dealing with monetary amounts, a batch control total is often used. A batch total is computed by keeping track of the dollar amount of a field in one batch of input documents, usually around 50 documents. This total is put in a batch control record that comes at the end of the batch. When the computer reads the input, the program adds the data fields and compares them with the batch total. If the fields do not match, an error notice is provided. This procedure assures us that the data as prepared are entered into the computer and is also another check on the keying operation.

Having completed the checks on data transformation and input to the machines, we next check on the source of the information—was the correct data provided by the originator? For numbers that will be keys, such as an identification number, we use a check digit. Assume that the identification number for a part is four digits, for example, part number 4326. In processing, a fifth digit is added to this number as a check. We might compute the check digit by dividing the number by 11 and using the remainder as the check digit. The remainder of dividing 4326 by 11 is 2, so the number should appear in a parts catalog, in all input documents, and on file as 43262. The computer program that processes the identification part number performs the same calculations. That is, it divides 4326 by 11 and takes the remainder, checking to see that it is the same as the digit in the unit's position (2).

There are also a variety of more complex schemes for developing check digits, such as weighting each digit by a certain number. These calculations all have the same basic goal, which is to detect transposition and entry errors. Check digits are especially critical when optical character recognition or mark sensing is used, because of the possibility of reading errors on the part of the machine. These applications almost always employ check digits of some kind.

At the editing stage we also examine individual fields to be sure that no alphabetical characters have been placed in positions that should be all numeric. For example, if all inventory part numbers begin with the letters A, M, or R, we should check to see that the input field contains only these characters. If it is possible, we place boundaries on the input data to recognize invalid data. At this point we may be able to say that no transaction should be less than 50 cents or over $1,000,000. In a sequential update, it is likely that for many checks we shall have to wait until the file is actually updated. The data at the edit processing stage are likely to be unsorted, and the data affecting a single master file record will not be all together.

In later stages, when processing the sorted input, we can check the number of transactions affecting a single record to see if the amount of activity is reasonable. If there are too many transactions, this may signify a problem that should be checked. For example, if usage of a part exceeds 200 percent of the previous month's usage, human intervention may be necessary to find the reason for such high usage.

On-Line Input

A major problem with batch input is resolving the problems with rejected data. If data input are rejected, an individual must conduct research to determine the reason for the error; then he or she must prepare corrections. If many edits are very stringent, a large number of errors will be generated, and processing will be seriously affected. One reason for moving toward on-line input is to allow the terminal operator to correct as many errors as possible immediately when the relevant source document is easily available.

Most on-line applications will probably make use of check digits and will also require logical checks on the input. Often with on-line transactions we do have access to files, so more complete checks can be performed on the data as entered. It is certainly possible to do the same type of field checking as in batch, that is, upper and lower bounds on the value of input numbers. Also, input fields can be scanned to be sure that numeric fields do not contain alphabetic data. On-line processing will generally include consistency checks. For example, if an airline reservations agent books five seats, then five passenger names should be entered. In the case of extremely critical data that cannot be verified, the system may echo them back to the user and ask for confirmation. In certain applications a number of input forms are keyed on-line in a group so that batch totals can be used.

If we are updating a system on-line, we have to use special backup procedures to be certain that we can recover from a file-updating error. We usually record all the transactions on magnetic tape and we may even record a "before" update version of the records. Periodically the entire set of files altered by the transactions is copied as a backup to magnetic tape.

Processing Errors

In addition to safeguarding against input error, we need to protect the system against program bugs or operator errors while running. The first and simplest check is on file labels to be sure that correct files are being accessed. Many errors are made by mounting the wrong file; for example, using an old master file for an output tape. Most operating systems provide for file labeling. A label is a special record read by the operating system that contains the name of the file, the date of creation, and other data unique to that file.

For the program to check that the right files are mounted, there should be an input that gives the current date and the proper date for the old master file. The program then checks to be sure that the various dates are correct, and a date should be included on any new files created by this run.

We also have to guard against errors in running the various stages of the program. We can use intermediate files to be sure that prior stages have completed processing successfully. For example, an intermediate file might show that the edit run was completed before the update. The update program would then access this intermediate file to be sure that processing had been completed for this processing cycle before it tries to update the file. This safety feature guards against the omission of a processing stage.

Programs should also check the processing of any prior processing stage where feasible. We should never assume that the input has been sorted; instead, the program that expects to find sorted input should perform a sequence check to be sure that the sort operated as specified.

Control totals should also be used in processing to keep track of the number of records in the file and changes made in the file. We mentioned previously comparing such a total to total from the last update kept on the last record in the file. As an example, suppose the total physical inventory is accumulated during processing along with any changes. Say that the balance at the end of the current run is 17,512 items; 6113 items were used, and 5312 replacements arrived. At the end of the old file there should be a control total from the last update of $17,512 + 5312 - 6113 = 16,711$. If the two numbers match, the program should write the new balance of 17,512 on the control record at the end of the new master file. The same type of logic can be used for debits and credits in accounting transactions. Simpler checks can be done on intermediate files to be sure that the number of records written matches the number of records read.

Output Errors

If there has been correct input and processing up to the stage where output is produced, we expect correct output to result. However, it is still necessary to take

SYSTEMS PROBLEM 15-3

Marvin Kelly was angry as he returned to his office at Consolidated Insurance. As president, Marvin had become increasingly concerned over the inability of the insurance company to process information. "We seem to have the slowest response time to a claim in the industry," he complained to the head of the data center, Bob Jackson.

"Our systems are old," Jackson tried to explain. "I've done the best I could under the circumstances. We inherited a bunch of 10-year-old batch processing systems that just take a long time to process. There are no master files; all we have are groups of transactions files with hundreds of thousands of records on them. A management report takes forever because we have to summarize the transactions for each report request."

Kelly had just heard from the manager of accounting that the processing for the current month would be late again because of the large number of error rejects on data entry. Of 325,000 input transactions, over 100,000 were rejected, and the dollar amount placed in a suspense account because of this action was over $75 million. The accounting manager indicated that they could not close for this month, the last one in the quarter, until some of those errors were researched and corrected; the dollar amount of imbalance was too great.

Kelly called Jackson in a rage and demanded an explanation. "If you can't fix the computer, then get your staff to fix the errors or look for a new job." Jackson sighed as he put down the phone. "Now what can we do?"

Can you suggest a short-range action plan and a longer-range strategy for Jackson and Consolidated Insurance to correct their input problems?

certain precautions. It is likely that the report program will read data from the output of some other program. We may want to have control totals on the different amount fields when the report contents are written to some intermediate file. The report writing program computes the same totals and checks them against the intermediate file. When the reports are actually printed, the report printing program checks different calculations, for example, by crossfooting various output totals. We should also be alert to rounding problems, though most computer languages for information-systems development now feature decimal arithmetic capabilities. Some older machines that only had binary arithmetic created errors when financial statements were off by several pennies due to rounding. In one particular company these inaccuracies were not appreciated by the accounting department, which lost all faith in the computer because of this easily correctable error.

Error Action

Many of the above input and processing checks are designed to ensure file integrity, that is, to avoid the introduction of erroneous data or the destruction of portions of the file. This goal must be balanced against having a system that is overcontrolled, that is, a system with too many error checks so the system is never able to run to completion.

For input errors we can try to reject only bad items and continue processing. In some instances it will be necessary to provide the opportunity for manual intervention if too many errors are encountered. However, the goal should be to try to reject individual transactions or, if necessary, the entire batch in error and continue processing.

For gross processing errors such as an incorrect file, it is necessary to abort processing until the operator corrects problems. Where a series of transactions appears to be incorrect in updating the file, the particular record in question can be skipped and an error notification printed. Alternatively, that record can be updated, but a field on the record should be used to indicate that some type of authorization for the change must be received on the next updating cycle. If control totals do not match at the end of a run, then appropriate notices have to be issued and the operations staff will have to decide whether a rerun is necessary.

Backup

In addition to error controls during processing, we have to consider the availability of backup. An audit trail is necessary; that is, some way to trace transactions through the system from input to output. In an on-line system one reason for keeping a tape of transactions is to have an audit trail. Special audit transactions may be created as a legitimate type of input for use by auditors in checking the system. An even simpler method for verification is to have an auditor create legitimate but fictitious records and process transactions against them. These records are deleted on the next processing cycle.

Batch updating provides automatic backup and security in the form of the old master file plus a record of transactions. We can re-create the new master file easily if anything happens to it. Usually, two versions of the master file are kept, giving rise to what is called the grandfather-father-son backup strategy. For on-line systems the contents of the files are dumped to tape, possibly several times a day. If a catastrophic failure occurs, the dumped files are reloaded and the transaction log tape is used to restore the file contents.

Because batch computer systems also occasionally fail for hardware and software reasons, batch file updates may make use of checkpointing procedures so that a complete rerun is not necessary if an error is encountered. Some computer languages feature automatic checkpointing facilities. During a sequential update, a request for checkpoint results in all data areas and the program status being recorded on file. In addition, information on the records that have finished processing is recorded. Then, if the system fails for some reason, the program can be restarted at the last checkpoint without returning to the beginning of processing.

The major problem with restarting on-line systems is that we do not know how many transactions were in process at the time of a failure. Because of the time involved, we may not want to reload the dump tape but would like to recover from a minor failure as quickly as possible. It may be feasible to ask terminal users to verify that their last transactions actually updated a file. Alternatively, the time of update may be a field on the file, and a recovery program could identify suspected transactions that were entered but not completely processed at the time of the failure. On-line error control is a very specialized topic; for further discussion of these points, see Yourdon (1972).

TABLE 15-2
SUMMARY OF BASIC CONTROL TECHNIQUES

Input

Log of source documents   When source documents are transmitted from one area to another, they should be logged.

Transactions logs   In an on-line system all input transactions should be logged on tape for control and backup purposes.

Check digits   For some fields it may be possible to use check digits, a particularly useful technique for on-line data input.

Verification   When check digits are not used or batch controls are not adequate, data should be verified some way independently by being keyed twice by different individuals.

Edit checks   There should be checks on input; typical programs edit for incorrect characters in fields, illegal codes, incomplete data (items missing).

Reasonableness tests   Often called limit tests, these checks seek to determine if input values are within reasonable ranges.

Control totals   On input there should be control totals where appropriate, both for batch and on-line data entry; there should also be totals for rejected transactions so that runs can be balanced.

Duplicate data entry   Programs should check to be sure that the same data are not entered twice.

Processing

Labels   Internal and external labels should be used on files; internal labels should be checked by programs to be sure that the right file of the right date is being accessed.

Run totals   Where there is a sequence of runs, run-to-run totals should be produced and checked.

Sequence checks   Where a sequence is required for processing, programs should perform sequence checks to be certain the sequence has been maintained in prior processing steps.

Audit trail   It should be possible to reconstruct a transaction from input through processing and final output.

Date checks   Programs should check to be sure all dates are reasonable.

Passwords   On-line systems should use some type of password to be certain the operator is authorized to use the system.

Limited access   On-line systems should recognize terminals and operators; certain terminals and/or operators may be limited to certain functions on the system.

Encryption   It may be necessary to encrypt (code) critical information, especially where there is any form of data transmission.

Output

Totals   Batch systems often provide control totals to check output fields.

Extra output   In an on-line system extra identification data may be provided to verify that an inquiry response is correct.

General

Documentation   One extremely good control is adequate documentation.

Backup   Control is enhanced with adequate backup including offsite file storage, arrangements for alternative processing sites, or duplexed computers for on-line systems.

Security and Fraud

There has been a great deal of publicity generated by the problems of fraud and security with computer systems. In designing a system, we have to take reasonable precautions to avoid the possibility of fraud. Independent programmers should be used for critical parts of the system, and multiple users should be involved. Procedurally, we should avoid giving authorization for sensitive changes to only one individual. One of the easiest ways to develop reasonable precautions is to include an internal auditor on the design team. Security is enhanced not only by having backup files, but by storing them in separate locations. We shall talk more about physical security in a later chapter on computer operations. See Table 15-2 for a summary of error controls.

WORK PLAN

The work plan should show programming schedules, time estimates, and personnel needed for the various work assignments. We shall postpone discussion of the work plan until Chapter 17. In Chapter 16 we present an example of a detailed systems design for Hardserve, Inc.

KEY WORDS

Audit trail	Information hiding
Backup	Manual procedures
Batch controls	Modularization
Check digit	Processing stages
Checkpoint	Reasonableness checks
Control totals	Response time
Conversion programs	Restart
Data transcription	Security
Error control	Source data collection
Exception reporting	System flow
File labels	System specifications
Flexibility	Verification

RECOMMENDED READINGS

Christie, B.: *Face to File Communication,* Wiley, Chichester, England, 1981. (A psychological approach to information systems.)

Couger, J. D.: "Evaluation of Business Systems Analysis Techniques," *Computing Surveys,* vol. 5, no. 3, September 1973, pp. 167–198. (A historical survey of business analysis approaches.)

Gilb, T., and G. Weinberg: *Humanized Input,* Winthrop, Cambridge, Mass., 1977. (Some guidelines for design.)

Martin, J.: *Design of Man-Computer Dialogues,* Prentice-Hall, Englewood Cliffs, N.J., 1973. (A comprehensive view of the user interface.)

DISCUSSION QUESTIONS

1 What is an audit trail? Explain the importance of an audit trail. How would you include an audit trail in a batch file-updating system?

2 How would you design a computer system to produce exception reports for a variety of different users, each with different exception ranges in mind?

3 Consider a system to prepare a telephone book from punched cards and describe the processing stages.

4 Take a program that you have written and describe the important design decisions included in planning the program. Then use the information-hiding criteria discussed in this chapter to design a series of modules for a new program to accomplish the same processing.

5 How could you checkpoint an on-line system and then restart it?

6 What approaches can you recommend for improving the security of a system? How should management decide how many resources should be devoted to security?

7 What are the advantages and disadvantages of using an on-line terminal for input data collection?

8 What action should a system and its operators take if the totals at the end of a master file do not match new totals developed during the update?

9 What factors influence the response time seen by a user of an on-line system?

10 Are there manual procedures associated with on-line systems? If so, what types of manual procedures are involved?

11 How would you audit a computer system? That is, how would you verify that processing was correct and the data on the files were not erroneous?

12 Why do you suppose some managers are uncomfortable with exception reports? How can an exception-reporting scheme be made more attractive?

13 What are the major advantages of modularization in the design of a system?

14 Do conversion programs need to be highly efficient? Under what circumstances is a conversion program likely to be run on a regular basis? (Hint: consider the discussion of direct-access files.)

15 How does the philosophy of data-base management systems compare with the modular approach to design discussed in this chapter?

16 It has been suggested that the United States needs a universal identifier, that is, some number that would be issued to each individual for use in all record keeping about that person. The social security number has evolved into such a number, at least for many applications. What are the disadvantages of the social security number as a universal identifier?

17 Can a computer system be overcontrolled? That is, can there be too many error checks?

18 Are error checks more demanding for a batch or an on-line system? Why? What types of error checks differ for the two kinds of systems?

19 In a batch system, programs are often run in a set sequence. How can one program be sure that prior processing was completed by other programs?

20 What are the major approaches to verifying that a program processes data accurately?

21 Compare and contrast the menu selection approach to on-line input with one other of Martin's techniques.

22 Why should internal and external file labels be used? What can happen if labels are not checked?

23 What kind of audit trail can be developed for an on-line system?

24 Some on-line systems log all input transactions for backup, and others log the original file record and file changes during on-line update. Under both approaches, the entire file system is copied to a backup medium at regular intervals. What are the advantages and disadvantages of the two approaches to logging?

25 What checks can be performed on the output of a system to ensure its accuracy?

26 Explain the concept of modularization. What is "information hiding" in the context of modularization?

27 What is the advantage of isolating, to the greatest extent possible, programs from the data files they access?

28 What kind of controls are needed to prevent unauthorized program changes by applications programmers? By systems programmers?

29 What are the advantages of fill-in-the-blank input screen techniques?

30 What batch totals can be implemented for typical on-line systems? What batch totals are not possible?

31 Is error control easier or more difficult with an on-line system when compared with batch processing?

32 Why is there a trend toward more on-line input of data?

33 What ways to train input operators in the use of a system can you suggest? Is there any way to have the system teach its operators?

34 Some terminals have identification codes that can be read by the computer. What uses would this code have?

35 For what applications do you think a printing on-line terminal is best, and for what systems would a CRT be best?

SYSTEMS DESIGN PROBLEMS

1 One of the most common computer applications is payroll. Many organizations have custom-designed payroll systems, and a large number of service bureaus offer packages to compute an organization's payroll. The logic of the payroll process is fairly simple and is common across many organizations.

Usually a payroll master file contains data about each individual who is on the payroll. Examples of the data to be included in setting up this file for employees would be:

NAME
NUMBER OF DEPENDENTS
MARITAL STATUS
DEDUCTIONS
UNION DUES
HOSPITAL PLAN
MEDICAL PLAN
PENSION
EMPLOYEE NUMBER
WAGE RATE
SOCIAL SECURITY NUMBER

On a periodic basis, such as weekly or monthly, input must orginate to trigger the computation of the payroll and the production of a check for each employee. This weekly input would have to include at a minimum:

> Employee number
> Regular hours worked
> Overtime hours worked
> Sick leave
> Special deductions

Once the system is run on a periodic basis, checks should be produced along with various accumulations for different year-to-date categories. The computer program would subtract all deductions and withhold funds for tax purposes. Also included in the output would normally be a payroll register. On an annual basis, the computer system would produce W2 forms, which are summaries of earnings and taxes withheld from wages, for the IRS.

a Design the input forms to be used to place a new employee on the payroll file, and the forms to be completed weekly for each employee to be paid.

b List the file contents and approximate field sizes for the payroll master file. Do not forget to include year-to-date totals.

c Draw a system flowchart for this payroll application.

d Describe the modifications necessary for the system to mail a check automatically to the bank, if the employee so elects, and to include a notice to the employee.

e Design the file maintenance and change cards necessary to alter information about employees.

2 Most organizations have some kind of accounts receivable, whether they are in manufacturing or a service company. Accounts receivable was one of the first applications undertaken by many firms when computer systems were acquired. Service bureaus also offer accounts-receivable packages for sale or rent. In the early days of computers, most accounts-receivable packages were typically batch applications; today, however, there is growing interest in on-line and payment processing.

Consider an on-line accounts-receivable system. An accounts-receivable transaction is generated by a shipment of a product to a customer. An operator at a terminal enters the following information:

> Order number
> Shipment number
> For each shipment:
> > Product code
> > Quantity
> > Date
> > Shipping costs
> > Special shipping mode
> > Special discounts
> > Comments

The program accepting this input responds with the customer name and address once the order number is entered; it also prints the product descriptions, the price extension, and the total invoice cost.

The customer receives the statement and sends in payment for one or more invoices. The next task is for an operator to enter the payments and to match them against invoices. The operator enters the invoice number, the total payment, and exceptions to indicate partial payments for items on an invoice that have not been paid.

In addition to the printed invoices, invoice register, and monthly statements, the system would provide an accounts-receivable listing, a daily cash balance, and exception reports for invoices that were partially paid or have not been paid at all. There would also be a function to allow on-line inquiry concerning payment history.

Of course, as with any system it is necessary to establish a new customer. The new customer information would have to include:

The account number
Name and address
Credit
Payment terms
Normal shipping mode

a Design the customer master file and the shipment and invoice files, and show any directories necessary to access these files.
b Describe the overall logic of file access.
c Design the screens for data input and inquiry using a CRT.
d List the edits and controls that would be necessary on this system.
3 Accounts Payable

Accounts payable has also traditionally been a batch processing application; however, on-line input improves the editing and the user interface with this system. To add a new vendor with whom a firm does business, it is necessary to assign a vendor number and include a name, address, and list any terms and discount that apply.

The first activity that generates an accounts payable is the issuance of a purchase order. The purchase order must contain:

Vendor number
For each item:
  Item number
  Item description
  Quantity
  Cost
Cost for the whole order, shipping costs, and special discounts

For on-line accounts payable, the system would respond with the vendor, name, and address as soon as the vendor number was entered, and would perform all the extensions of price times quantity. The output from this part of the system would be a printed purchase order. It would be also desirable to allow the purchasing department to make inquiries on a purchase order number.

The purchase order would be used as a document for receiving. The receiving department enters a purchase order number when merchandise arrives and notes any exceptions on the items, such as a particular item that was not received, or a quantity that is not what was indicated on the purchase order.

Next, the organization receives a bill from the vendor. This bill should contain the company's purchase order number and the amount owed. An individual in the accounts-payable section accesses a terminal, enters the purchase order number, and compares the bill with the original purchase order and the quantities received. On authorization for payment, the system prints a check ready for mailing to the vendor and a check register.

a Design the system flow for this system.
b Design the vendor and the open purchase order files.
c Design the input edits and controls for the system and the displays for a CRT screen.

4 Sales reporting can be a very important computer application. Often, data for sales reports come directly from shipping and/or invoicing systems in the organization. At a minimum, this application requires a customer file including a customer number, geographic code, shipment date, order number, item number, quantity shipped, and price.

From the data, it is possible to generate an output sales report. This report might be summarized by product, product type, region, or salesperson.

a Would you recommend that this system operate in batch or on-line mode?

b Design an inquiry system that would answer questions interactively concerning customers or products. Would these answers be computed on-line, or would a summary file be developed?

c Assume that historical data are available on sales for the last 10 years. What kind of forecasting system would you design for this organization? What would be your considerations in choosing a forecasting system?

5 The manufacturing or production function in an organization includes many activities, such as materials acquisition, production scheduling and control, work-in-process inventory control, and finished goods inventory control.

One way to start the manufacturing process is with the preparation of a bill of materials. A bill of materials lists all the components necessary to manufacture a product. Usually the input that is provided is the number of new products identified by product number and quantity. The output from this system is a lists of subassemblies and the quantity required; that list contains all the parts needed to manufacture the particular product. (This is called an explosion program.)

a Design the file structures for a bill-of-materials processor.

b Describe the logic of the explosion program.

c Assume the input to the bill-of-materials processor contains the product and the date it is to be shipped to the customer. Design a system to produce a report on products that must be manufactured by a given due date.

6 A budget is a fundamental managerial control tool in an organization. In setting up budgets, minimal input includes an account number, the type of account, a description, and where a control break is to be taken to add up the totals for a subaccount. Then for each budget cycle, input is provided on the account number, the budgeted amount of money, and the actual money spent.

The output from such a system is the budget report. It shows the account, the description, the budgeted amount, the actual amount, variance amounts, and usually percentage totals as well.

Design a master file for a budget application and describe the format of a budget report.

7 One unusual application was suggested for a retail grocery chain. This particular organization computes what is called a markup and markdown plan each week. The markup is the general gross profit the store wishes to obtain on groceries; this markup might be 20 percent. The markdown is the amount of margin acceptable when the regular and special discount items are sold; so, for example, if a special is to be held on frozen peas, the sale on frozen peas might be 10 percent off, which is estimated to reduce the total gross profit to a level of 18 percent, which is the markdown.

In this grocery chain, pricing specialists make estimates of the sales of discount special items and the sales of all items sold at regular price. The markup goal is then compared with the estimates for the actual markup to determine if the markdown resulting from sales plan specials is acceptable.

A consultant has recommended this activity as a possible computer application. What kind of computer application does this suggest? What would be the interface between the pricing specialist and the computer? What mode of operation do you recommend?

a Design the files for this system.

b Describe the interaction between the system and the pricing specialist.

c Design an output report that shows the prices to be charged for items on special.

8 General ledger is an accounting application to produce a final consolidation of all financial transactions in a company. A file must be created showing the chart of accounts for the firm. Many subsystems automatically produce entries for the general ledger, and other input comes from journal entries. Examples of input from different subsystems include payroll, vendor invoices, accounts payable, cash receipts, check writing, work in process, fixed assets, and shipments.

General ledger programs traditionally include a trial balance that is run before the final general ledger for the month. The output of the system is a detailed general ledger showing transactions against individual accounts and a consolidated ledger at the account level.

a Design the files necessary to produce a consolidated and a detailed general ledger.

b Draw a flowchart of the general ledger system showing the inputs from other systems.

c Design the logic for the production of financial statements (an income statement and balance sheet) from the general ledger. What alterations have to be made in the file design in **a** above to produce the financial reports?

9 Computer technology is being applied to the retail industry, particularly to supermarket checkout operations. In these systems, some type of optical character recognition scanner reads the universal product code on items sold in the store. A minicomputer in the store contains a file with the universal product code numbers and the current price. As the items are scanned, their price is read from the file and the entire cost of the grocery order is computed.

All during the day the computer in the store maintains a record of items sold. In the evening, the data can be transferred to a central host computer to update master records, which represent sales and, more important, inventory balances. These inventory data can then be used to restock the supermarket, so that it is not necessary for store personnel to place formal orders with the warehouse.

Such systems were designed to speed the checkout process and to ensure more rapid response for the resupply of grocery products.

a Design the files for the local grocery store and the files for the central host computer.

b Develop a backup plan that will become operative if the minicomputer in the supermarket fails.

c What reports could be generated from the system for the use of store management?

16

SYSTEMS DESIGN FOR HARDSERVE

PRELIMINARY SURVEY

After the Hardserve preliminary survey was completed, it was submitted to the steering committee. Members of the steering committee read the report and discussed it at length. They decided that a new system would make a positive contribution to the company and that it should be implemented. The steering committee rejected the package system for a number of reasons[1] and asked the design team to pursue two alternatives in the feasibility study: the batch and the on-line systems.

The design team spent 2 weeks refining the estimates in the preliminary survey. Further study convinced them that the cost and time estimates had been too conservative. The estimates for the batch system were revised to 12 months and $40,000, while the new estimates for the on-line system were 18 months' development time and a cost of $65,000.

The steering committee examined the feasibility study and focused primarily on the percentage of the original goals met and the impact of the system on the organization. They felt that given Hardserve's limited experience, the best approach would be to develop a batch system and implement it successfully before moving on to a more sophisticated system. However, the committee did ask the design team to develop a system that could be converted easily to on-line inquiry in the future.

---

[1]In a real situation the committee would have seriously considered the adoption of the package since it is a good way to implement a system quickly and gain experience. However, for the purpose of the example we shall eliminate the package so we can illustrate systems design techniques.

DESIGN TEAM MEETINGS

Shortly after the steering committee met on the feasibility study and made their request, Terry Carson (the user in charge of the new system) convened the design team to discuss the committee's decision. He presented the results of the feasibility study review, and the members of the design team agreed that a good decision had been made. They turned to Tom Roberts, the lead systems analyst from Manhold, on the question of what to do next.

Tom's talk covered the material of Chapter 15, and he put together a list of tasks similar to Table 15-1. Paul Jones, the warehouse manager, asked, "How do we undertake these different tasks? I really don't know anything about designing forms or files."

"That's all right," said Tom. "We'll work together on it. Mary and I will furnish technical support. We'd like to have you meet alone with users or with us and users to define the data requirement. For example, take a report we plan to include in the system. First, we might meet with the users and observe what they do for several hours. Then we could come back a second time and interview them and ask for the data they would like to see on the report. Mary and I will design a sample report layout and will leave it with the users for a week and let them think about it as they work. Then the users can suggest revisions."

Nancy Collier, from order processing, spoke up. "That should be easy; I work with the data a lot and can probably come up with what we need."

"That's good," Mary Davis said. "Would anyone else use the data in your report?"

"Yes," said Nancy. "Several of the people working with me use it."

Mary said, "In that case you could make a first pass at the report and then try the ideas out with other potential users."

Tom added, "Better still, you could convene the group and ask them to submit what they would like to you."

Nancy said, "I see what you mean. If I do it all, they may feel they have to take it because I'm a supervisor. I like the group idea best. Let me take the responsibility for the output for order processing."

Paul Jones, the warehouse manager, then volunteered, "I'll see what I can do for the warehouse group."

Harry Snyder, one of the purchasing agents, suggested that it would be easy for him to get the purchasing agents together and work on their needs. Stan Levine also volunteered to check with accounting to see what types of output they might want.

"What about the vice presidents and presidents, what will our system do for them?" asked Terry Carson.

"I was hoping you'd ask!" Tom Roberts said. "Perhaps you could meet with them. I'd be happy to come with you; we should begin by seeing what kind of decisions they make on inventory matters. For a while we might just want to be silent observers and then try to interview them."

"That sounds like fun," said Terry. "I've always wondered what a vice president does!"

SYSTEMS PROBLEM 16-1

Tom Roberts and Terry Carson encountered a potentially serious problem during the design of the Hardserve system. Paul Jones, the manager of the warehouse, asked them for a speical report that would show productivity by picker for each shift. On the one hand, Tom was concerned about the usefulness of the report and wondered if Paul had really thought through the request. On the other hand, Tom did not want to seem arbitrary and reject a report that might be useful. He spoke with Terry and described his concerns.

"I'm afraid this report will be viewed as a policeman by the crew in the warehouse. How much variance is there in picking productivity? How much can the individual control the rate? I suspect a lot of it has to do with the assignments the picker receives. What do you think?"

"From my observations in the warehouse," Terry responded, "you're right. Sometimes a picker will actually help to load the merchandise, which clearly detracts from the picking total for that person."

The two discussed the problem further and wondered what Paul could do with the report. "Is he really free to fire someone?" asked Tom. Terry thought that because of union rules and other procedures, the answer was no. The basis for firing can hardly be productivity unless it is about 50 percent of the warehouse average. In that event, Paul doesn't really need a computerized report; he can look at the actual lists turned in by the pickers.

Terry and Tom have asked your help to determine how to approach Paul with their concerns about the usefulness of the report. They want to encourage his participation and support in the system but feel the report he has requested is not a good idea.

Design Progress

After a few more exchanges the meeting was adjourned. A number of subsequent meetings were held between users and various design team members and among the design team members themselves. The users proved cooperative and interested in designing their own reports and input forms. Mary and Tom took the various inputs and went through several rounds of design for different reports. Attention then turned to what type of input would be needed to generate the desired output. After input had been specified, Tom and Mary made a first pass at designing the file contents; the rest of the team critiqued the file design, and modifications were made. Tom and Mary then roughed out processing steps and with the user team members estimated the manual processing requirements.

Review Meeting

After having specified the system to this level of detail, Tom Roberts suggested the idea of a large review meeting. His reasoning was as follows:

"I know we've spent a lot of time with users, but we've met in small groups or with one department. Before we commit ourselves to developing the program specifications, I'd like to have one final check."

Terry asked, "Does this mean the system is frozen, no more changes after our review meeting?"

"I wish it did," Tom answered. "No, I'm afraid we've found that no system is ever frozen. We shall defer changes around the time of implementation for several months and then make them when everything is running all right."

Mary said, "What we want to accomplish with this meeting is for every person to see what is happening with each part of the system. Sometimes a group like this will come up with some spontaneous ideas that really improve on the design."

"We have to be very careful of the way we present the system. We want to appear flexible and we don't want to use elaborate charts, just rough sketches so the users will be encouraged to suggest changes. We'll make as many changes as possible in front of the audience to reinforce their input," said Tom.

"We've really come a long way," Terry said. "We have draft reports, input documents, files, and a rough system flowchart. I can see that it would be good to get input from the group of potential users before Tom and Mary begin to develop program specifications. However, when can we ever get a group like that together?"

Tom suggested that they either hold the meeting on a Saturday with time-and-a-half pay for the people who attended, or on a slow day, since this was a slack time of the year. Terry agreed to take the idea to the steering committee with Tom.

The steering committee listened to the reasoning behind the meeting request and felt it was worth the expense to have it. The meeting was held by closing down the next Thursday after lunch and having all employees assemble in the cafeteria for the session. The president, Jim Green, chaired the meeting, and various members of the design team presented different parts of the system. The audience, because of its prior involvement, grasped the system quickly, and a number of changes and additions were made to the system.

As a result of this meeting, the design team began to work on two different areas. First, the user members worked on more rigorous specifications of the manual procedures, training, and user documentation. Second, Tom and Mary began to work on program specifications, error control, and a work plan. The rest of this chapter presents the results of these efforts, with the exception of a work schedule that will be discussed further in Chapter 17.

SYSTEM SPECIFICATIONS

The specifications presented here[2] follow the general guidelines described in Chapter 15. In many organizations, different practices will be found, such as variations in how much detail is presented in the specifications.

We have also presented a simple system to illustrate concepts; we could easily develop more reports and include some of the purchasing, receiving, and

---

[2]It should be pointed out that the specifications presented here are for a very simple system compared to the complexity of most information systems. However, this illustration does serve to communicate the basic contents of system specifications.

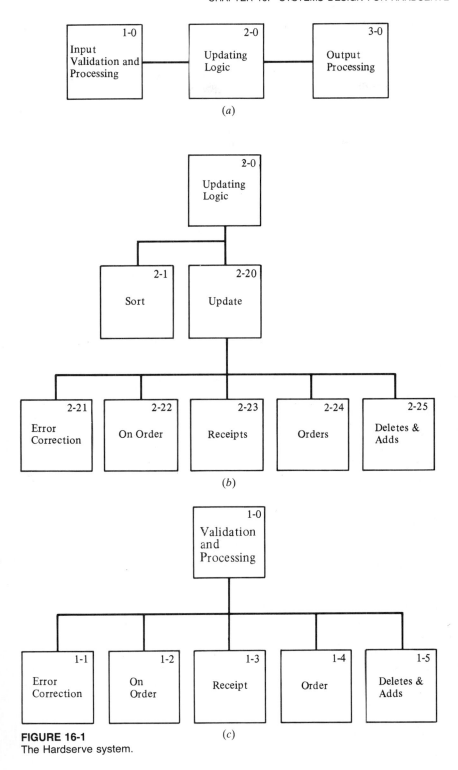

FIGURE 16-1
The Hardserve system.

accounting operations in our system. However, we shall leave this for future systems work. In all probability we would use a package for much of the inventory processing. We would probably not write our own retrieval program but would purchase a commercial file management package. Again, for illustrative purposes, we include this program in our design.

In the specifications that follow, the reader should note that all parts in inventory are currently identified with a seven-digit number. The first two digits of the number are the class code for the type of item (such as lawn care), and the remaining five digits are the item number within the class. For the purposes of the computer system, a check digit will be added to this number.

Figure 16-1 provides an overview of the modules in the system.

Output

The major reports from the system are shown in Table 16-1. (Normally, rough samples of report formats would be developed by the users and systems design team for inclusion in the specifications.) All users agreed that they needed an inventory balance report to check inquiries and for historical records. However, several users confirmed that this report would be referenced infrequently. The systems design team suggested the use of microfilm with one reader each in order processing, accounting, warehouse, and purchasing.

One major goal of the system was to speed reorder information to purchasing on a regular basis, and a reorder report will be prepared each updating cycle to accomplish this. The recommended order quantities and the reorder points are computed in a program using a simple formula (see Buffa, 1961):

$$Q = \sqrt{\frac{2\,RS}{Ci}}$$

where Q = order quantity
R = requirement or usage rate
S = the ordering cost
i = the carrying cost as a percentage of inventory
C = the cost of an item

All the data needed to compute Q are readily available from purchasing records.

The economic order quantity is first computed when a new item is added to the inventory or when costs change. When the balance on hand reaches the reorder point, a reorder notice is included on the order report for the item. The reorder point is computed based on estimated usage during the leadtime. To compute this point the usage for the last month is divided by the number of days in the month and this figure is multiplied by the leadtime in days to obtain the expected usage during the leadtime as the reorder point. The percentage is included in the

TABLE 16-1
REPORTS

---

1 Inventory balance report

Distribution:	Order processing
	Warehouse
	Purchasing
	Accounting
Form:	Microfilm
Sequence:	(1) Inventory class (first 2 digits of item number)
	(2) Item number (next 5 digits of item number)
Frequency:	Each update
Contents:	Item number
	Description
	Units
	Previous month's balance
	Current month's balance
	Current month's usage
	Current month's receipts
	12 months' usage
	Reorder quantity
	Reorder point
	Cost
	Physical location in warehouse
	On order quantity
	Average balance
	Leadtime

2 Reorder report

Distribution:	Purchasing
Form:	Printed
Sequence:	(1) Inventory class
	(2) Item number
Frequency:	Each update
Contents:	Item number
	Description
	Units
	Previous month's balance
	Current month's balance
	Current month's usage
	12 months' usage
	Reorder quantity
	Reorder point
	Cost
	On order quantity
	Number of stockouts
	Average balance
	Expedite (if already on order)
	Leadtime

3 Order analysis report

Distribution:	Purchasing
Form:	Printed

TABLE 16-1
REPORTS (*Continued*)

Sequence:	(1) Inventory class
	(2) Item number
	or
	(1) By number of units ordered
	or
	(1) by number of units ordered by class
Frequency:	As requested
Contents:	Item number
	Description
	Units
	Yearly orders
	Reorder quantity
	Reorder point
	Number of stockouts

4 Inventory turnover report

Distribution:	Purchasing
	Accounting
Form:	Printed (summary or detailed)
Frequency:	As requested
Sequence:	(1) Class
	(2) Item number

Contents:	Item number	(or class)
	Description	Description
	Units	—
	Balance	Balance
	12 months' usage	12 months' usage
	Reorder quantity	—
	Reorder point	—
	Cost	Cost
	Average balance	Average balance
	Total usage	Total usage
	Average usage	Average usage
	Turnover	Turnover

5 Physical inventory adjustment report

Distribution:	Accounting
Form:	Printed
Sequence:	(1) Inventory class
	(2) Item number
Contents:	Item number
	Description
	Units
	Previous 12 months' balances
	Current balance (book)
	Previous 12 months' usage
	Current month (usage)
	Date of physical inventory
	Physical quantity
	Adjustment quantity

Note: For size and type of fields, see file specifications.

calculation to let us increase the safety stock if we experience too many stockouts.[3]

The order analysis report was developed by the purchasing agents to assist them in planning. The agents hope it will allow them to see trends and decide what to order during each season. Purchasing agents will also override the reorder point on seasonal items; for example, they do not need to stock too many lawn care items during November. When desired, the purchasing department can request the order analysis report, and it will be prepared as a part of the update. The report will be produced by item number in detail or will be sorted and presented by decreasing usage.

The vice presidents and Jim Green suggested the inventory turnover report during the half-day system review meeting. The purpose of this report is to allow analysis of items that are selling well. The report can be obtained by inventory class-summarized for all the items in the class or by individual item.

The inventory adjustment report was requested by accounting. Periodically, accounting takes physical inventory and adjusts the book inventory to reflect the amount actually in storage (discrepancies come from loss, damage, etc.).

Not shown in Table 16-1 is a generalized retrieval report for management. In observing top management, the design team found the requests for inventory information were erratic; it would be very difficult to satisfy management with a formal, prescribed report. Instead, managers wanted an inquiry capability to support their decision making. (As mentioned earlier, in a real situation we should probably use a standard retrieval package, but here we will develop a program for illustrative purposes.) At first, computer department staff members will be used to formulate inquiries for the program; later, managers should learn how to prepare the program input themselves.

Input

Four basic types of inputs in the system are shown in Table 16-2. First, customer orders come into order processing, which represents the demand for goods. Receipt of merchandise reflects items that have been ordered by purchasing to replenish inventory. These items arrive at the warehouse, are uncrated, and are put on the shelves.

On-order data come from purchasing so the reorder program will know whether something has actually been placed on order or not. Error corrections come from a number of places; these corrections include file maintenance for correcting errors and for physical inventory adjustment.

---

[3]There are more sophisticated approaches to setting the reorder point and safety stock (see Buffa, 1961). However, Hardserve felt that this rule of thumb would be adequate.

TABLE 16-2
INPUTS*

---

1   Orders

Source:	Current purchase order		
Media:	Keyed input		

Fields:

	Position	**Type**
Customer number	1-8	Numeric
Item number	9-17	Numeric
Quantity	18-23	Numeric
Vendor number	24-29	Numeric
Price	30-37	Numeric (2 decimal positions)

Estimated record volume:
Average 1600 per day
Maximum 2500 per day

2   Receipt of merchandise

Source:	Warehouse copy of Hardserve purchase order
Media:	Keyed input

Fields:

	Position	**Type**
Item number	1-8	Numeric
Quantity	9-15	Numeric
Vendor number	16-21	Numeric
Purchase order date	22-27	Numeric

Estimated record volume:
Average 800 per day
Peak 1500 per day

3   On order

Source:	Purchasing department
Media:	Keyed input

Fields:

	Position	**Type**
Item number	1-8	Numeric
Quantity	9-15	Numeric
Vendor number	16-21	Numeric

4   Error correction

Source:	All users
Media:	Keyed input
Fields:	To be designed by update programmer

---

*The programmer should number transaction type and assign the numbers to positions, e.g., 79-80.

Files

Table 16-3 lists the three major files in the system. First, there is a file created from editing the input transactions (file a in Figure 16-2). This file is the input to a sort routine that places transactions on input file b in Figure 16-2 in the same order as the master file for updating purposes. Finally, there is the master file itself (file c in Figure 16-2).

The master file for this application has been placed on disk for two reasons. First, there is the plan to move toward on-line inquiry in the future. Second, the

TABLE 16-3
FILES

---

1 Master file

    Medium: disk

Fields:	Size	Type
Item number (key)	8	Numeric
Description	50	Alphanumeric
Units	5	Alphanumeric
Previous month's balance	8	Numeric
Current month's balance	8	Numeric
Past 12 months' balance	8@ = 96	Numeric
Current month's usage	6	Numeric
Past 12 months' usage	6@ = 72	Numeric
Reorder quantity	8	Numeric
Usage during leadtime	6	Numeric
Most recent cost	9	Numeric (2 decimal places)
On order quantity	8	Numeric
On order date	6	Numeric
Number of stockouts	3	Numeric
Three most recent vendors	6@ = 18	Numeric
Number of orders this year	3@ = 9	Numeric
Dollar value of orders this year	7@ = 21	Numeric
Vendor address pointers	6@ = 18	Numeric
Leadtime (days)	3	Numeric
Delete indicator	1	Numeric
Expansion space	20	Numeric

2 Transactions file

    Medium: tape

    Fields: see forms

3 Directories Item number and vendor number

    Medium: disk

    Fields: to be designed by programmer

---

president has an unusual request for information on very short notice. He spends much of his time meeting with customers and vendors. With vendors the president tries to obtain the best price possible and, in times of short supply, to get what Hardserve orders. It helps him to see what types of items are purchased from a particular vendor before meeting with that vendor. The president is curious about both the amount and the dollar volume of business that is done with his firm so that he can negotiate better service. To answer his inquiries on short notice, the designers included a directory and a linked list of pointers on vendor number for up to three vendors for each item. A study showed that, in general, no more than two vendors were ever used for a single product.[4]

---

[4]This is a fairly unusual request and is included to illustrate the use of directories and a threaded list.

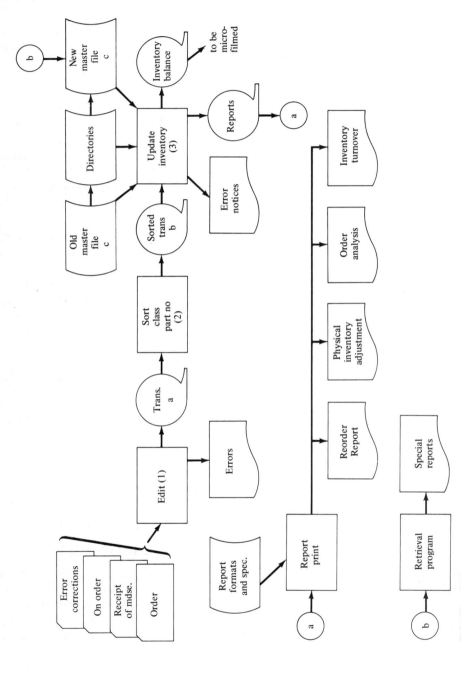

FIGURE 16-2
System flowchart.

TABLE 16-4
SYSTEM FLOW DESIGN DECISIONS

Input all types of transactions together
Edit batches before sorting
Update file and produce reports sequentially
Develop retrieval program
Place master file on disk, directory on item number, directory and threaded list on vendor number

---

Processing

Table 16-4 highlights the design decisions at the system level, and Figure 16-2 presents the overall system flowchart. All input enters the editing program and is edited at one time. Then the input transactions are sorted to update the file. During the file update various reports are spooled to an intermediate file, and error notices are printed. The report print program uses the report file to output each report. A special retrieval program uses the master file to produce custom-tailored output reports.

Program Specifications

Table 16-5 contains program specifications; again, we should point out that organizations differ in the amount of detail provided to programmers. Note particularly the modularization of the programs in the specifications. Some organizations might leave the modularizations up to the programmer. In any case, the programmers certainly have the latitude to change some of these modules after checking with the analyst.

Manual Processing

Basic manual processing operations are shown in Figure 16-3. Order entry in Figure 16-3a begins with the receipt of a customer order and the production of copies. The order is divided into warehouse locations where the different items can be found. That is, orders are divided into the regions of the warehouse where the merchandise is shelved to make picking easier. Four copies of the order are filed for the day on which they are to be filled (picked) in the warehouse.

Before that date, the orders are removed from the file and sent to the warehouse. As the order is filled, the picker marks whether the full order requested is shipped or not and turns in the forms with the shipment. One copy of this form now goes to the computer department, which is the only change in procedures for order processing.

The activities in placing an order are shown in Figure 16-3b. The purchasing agent makes out an order but now works from a computer report instead of a

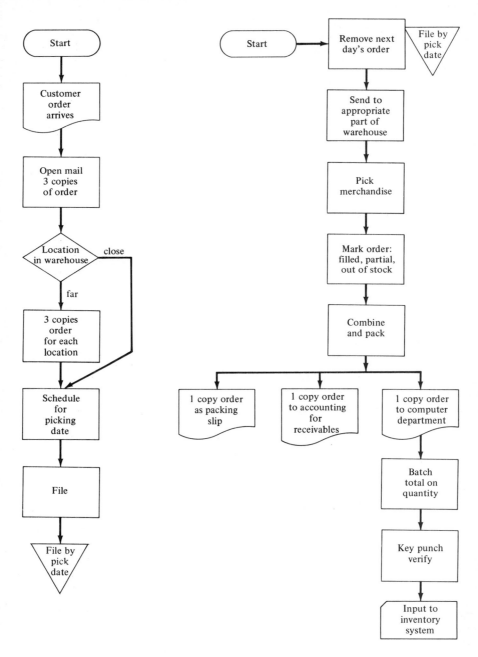

(*a*) Order processing

FIGURE 16-3
Manual processing.

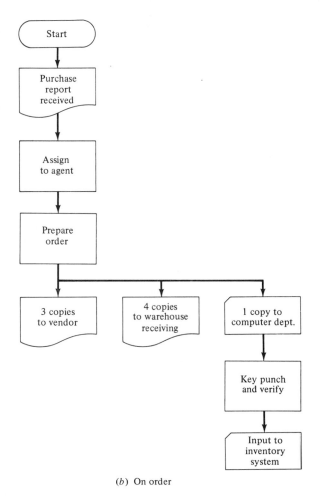

(b) On order

FIGURE 16-3 (Continued)

notice from the warehouse. Four copies of the purchase order go to the warehouse to be filed by purchase order number for receipt of the item. One copy goes to the computer department, which is the only other change in purchasing procedures.

Receipt of the merchandise in the warehouse is shown in Figure 16-3c. When the item is ordered, four copies of the purchase order were put on file in the warehouse by purchase order number. When a shipment arrives, these purchase orders are pulled to check whether or not it is a complete or partial shipment. If it is a partial shipment, two copies are filed to be used when the back order arrives. The extra copy of the marked purchase order, indicating arrival, is sent to the computer department to indicate receipt, which is the only change in receiving procedures.

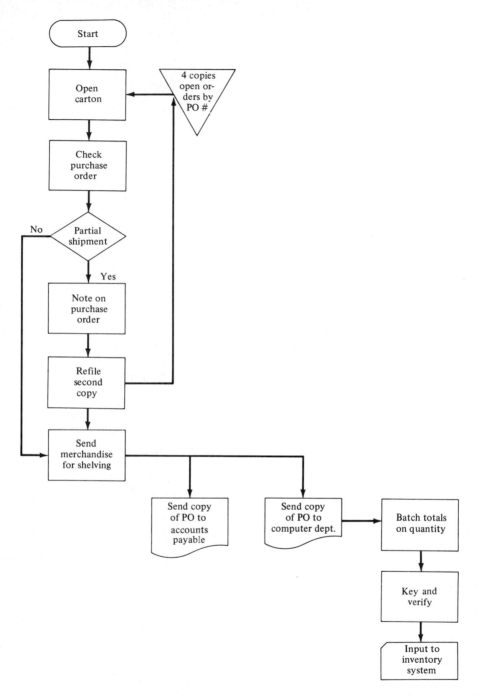

(c) Receipt of merchandise

FIGURE 16-3 (Continued)

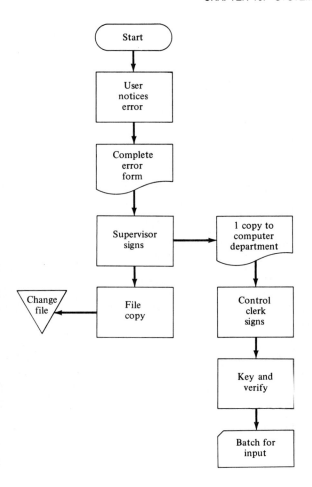

(*d*) Error corrections

FIGURE 16-3 (*Continued*)

Error-correction procedures are shown in Figure 16-3*d*. The supervisor in each user area must authorize a change in the file by signing a form. An individual in the data control section of the computer department also examines and authorizes each change.

Errors

Various error checks are listed in Table 16-6. The goal is to anticipate as many errors as possible and account for them. Each programmer is asked to think of more error checks as programs are planned and written.

TABLE 16-5
PROGRAM SPECIFICATIONS

---

1 Edit program

Input:	All input transactions
	Input with date and number of errors allowed before aborting program
Output:	Error notices
	Tape of approved transactions
Errors:	See input error documentation
Design decisions:	All input to the same program
	Edit individual transactions and batches
Functions:	Batch total check
	Input transaction check for each transaction type
	Output error messages
	Output of accepted transactions to tape
Processing:	For specific details, see input error documentation. Input the parameters for error control; that is, the number of bad transactions before aborting the program and the number of bad batches before aborting the program. Design a header input with a date and put the date on the output tape. Keep all transaction types and ranges in the table for easy modification. In general, the program should invoke the batch checking module whenever a batch is encountered. (The transaction type indicates whether a batch check is in effect or not.) Check each transaction to be sure it is of the current batch type and call the edit routine for each transaction type. Output good transactions to tape and bad to the error report. When completed with processing, write a notice to an intermediate file with the date so that the update program will know that the input tape has been properly edited. Also indicate on this file the number of good records that were written to the file so the update program can be sure it reads all transactions.

Note: Be sure to design a manual procedure for controlling erroneous transactions. Errors should be logged in and retained until corrected in a revolving file. (Each erroneous transaction remains in the file until the corrected transaction has been processed.)

2 Sort program

Using computer manufacturer's utility program, sort by class, part number, and transaction type

3 Update program

Input:	Sorted transaction tape
	Intermediate file indicating completion of editing
	Input with date
	Inventory holding costs
	Percentage factor for setting safety stock
Output:	Error notices
	Five reports (see system flowchart and report formats for details)
	New master file
Errors:	See processing errors for documentation
Design decisions:	Update and prepare reports on one pass through the file
	Use direct access storage updated sequentially (except for vendor number)

TABLE 16-5 PROGRAM SPECIFICATIONS (*Continued*)

	Include pointers and directory on vendor number
	Use delete indicator to keep chains intact; do not update in place except for additions to vendor linked list
Functions:	Get input transactions and check sequence
	Check number of transactions processed against intermediate file
	Get old master record
	Move records between buffers
	Write new master record
	Modify given field of master record
	Error-check module for each field and record
	Modules for each output report
	Output error message
	Module to write record to new master file
	Modules to modify directories to item number and vendor numbers*
	Economic order-quantity calculation
	Reorder point calculation
Processing:	Standard sequential file updating procedures should be used. To reorder, check the current balance against the reorder point. Before reordering, see if an item is on order; of so, print an expedite notice. For a deletion, use a delete indicator pointer to keep chains intact. For the addition of a new record, modify the directory for vendor and the ponter field on the record to which the directory ponts. Also calculate a new reorder quantity for each addition or each time a data item changes. For each item placed on order, enter the date. Use the order date on the purchase order as the date on which the order was placed. Keep all input and output in separate modules to facilitate changes. Be sure that control totals for report program error checking are included. Keep the error ranges in tables for each master file modification. Place the directory for item number and vendors on a disk file at the end of processing. Include a module with an economic-order-quantity calculation to set the reorder quantity when a new item is added to inventory. Compute the EOQ as $\sqrt{2RS/Ci}$, where R is the usage, S is the cost of an order, C is the cost of an item, and i is the inventory holding cost. Whenever an item is received, calculate a new leadtime for setting safety stocks using a separate module. This leadtime is today's date minus the order date. Take last month's usage divided by the number of days in the month times the leadtime. When calculating reorder points, take the current factor to avoid excessive stockouts in force (for example, 110 percent) times this anticipated usage during leadtime.
	Note: Because of the simple economic-order-quantity model, set limits on the reorder quantity. No order should be for more than n months' supply or for less than m weeks' supply regardless of what is calculated. (The n and m parameters will be supplied by the purchasing department.)

4 Retrieval program:

Input:	Special requests on a form designed by the programmer. The user should only have to specify the field by easy-to-remember names such as "Balance" and should be able to use logical relationships such as less

---

*Item number directory is included for later on-line inquiry versions of the system.

TABLE 16-5
PROGRAM SPECIFICATIONS (*Continued*)

	than, greater than, plus or minus, times, divide. The user also describes (very simply) the type of report format wanted.
Output:	Report of selected output items according to user-desired format
Errors:	Defined by programmer; check all input for legitimate names and operations
Design decisions:	Process all requests together
	Free format input
Functions:	Analyze input
	Check variable names
	Check operators
	Analyze format
	Check format
	Build retrieval string (field and conditions)
	Get record from file
	Match against retrieval string and conditions
	Output report record to intermediate storage
	Read report from intermediate storage
	Format report
	Print report
Processing:	The program must first analyze input and the requested report format. Then is should process the file once, retrieving all requests and putting selected records for each user on intermediate disk storage. Then retrieve the report records for each user, develop the appropriate format, and print the report. Also, provide summary totals and allow the user to specify where the totals are to be printed. As a special option include a vendor retrieval request. Use the directory of vendor names (on disk) and follow the chain through the file to list all recent activity for the vendor, including number of orders, dollar value by item, class, and in total. A single, simple request with vendor name would trigger this option.

5 File creation/conversion program

Input:	Old inventory file or keyed input for conversion (programmer designs input format and documentation for conversion)
Output:	Master file, error list
Errors:	Use input errors for checking
Design decisions:	Use disk file
	Build directory for item number and vendors
Functions:	Input (keyed or disk file)
	Check errors for each field
	Build directory for item number
	Build directory for vendor number
	Write output record
	Write directory
Processing:	Read the input and build a record address directory in order for item numbers. Check each field for errors and reject all errors; they can be included in a later update. Build reverse directory for vendors; that is, have the directory point to the most recent occurrence of the vendor number and chain backwards through the file. When the record is completed, write it to the file. At the end put both directories (item number, vendor) on a disk file.

TABLE 16-6
ERRORS

Input errors
1   Input item with date and error conditions (number of bad batches or number of bad transactions before aborting the run).
2   Label transaction tape with date.
3   Check each batch for batch total and for incorrect transaction type in the batch. Reject bad batches.
4   Inventory units and item number check digit; divide item number by 11, take remainder and compare with units digit. Reject input if check digit wrong.
5   Range checks based on units, e.g.:

Unit	Quantity	Cost
EACH	1-1000	0.01-1000
GROSS	1- 500	1.00-1500
BOX	1- 200	0.50-2000
DOZ	1- 750	0.10- 500

6   Produce an error notice to be sent to user for correction and return.

Processing errors
1   Read header input with date and error conditions (e.g., a, b, c, d).
2   Check sequence of incoming transactions to be sure they are in order.
3   If receipt greater than a × average use or greater than b × reorder quantity, print exception report.
4   Count the number of transactions for a record. If greater than b receipts or c usages, print exceptions report.
5   Continue update for all exception conditions.
6   Check sequence of master file; if error, abort processing after printing out-of-sequence records.
7   Compute total of inventory balance, usage, and receipts, compare with summary record at the end of the file; update summary record and, if incorrect, print message.
8   Print an asterisk beside any record on inventory status report when error correction needs to be made.
9   Print total number of errors to be checked manually on each error-notice page.

Output errors
1   Read header input with date.
2   Check label of report file.
3   Check records for each report for completeness.
4   Recompute any summary levels and compare with report data as read from file.
5   If errors encountered, abort report-writing program and print message.

Backup
1   Retain the transaction tapes for 6 months.
2   Retain the old master file for two updates.
3   Permanently file old microfilm copy of inventory balance report.

Security
1   Store old version of master file at separate location.
2   Store old transactions tapes at separate location.
3   Have all file changes authorized by user and by control group in the computer department.

SYSTEMS PROBLEM 16-2

Partway through the design process for Hardserve, the president asked for a meeting with Tom Roberts and Terry Carson. He did not understand why it was taking so long to develop the specifications. "When we built the warehouse, the planning staff took less time than what you are spending to design this system."

Tom and Terry replied that design, like architecture, is a creative undertaking. However, interacting with a systems design project is much more personal than with a building. One can learn to live with a building, because interaction with it is more functional and less personal than with a system that supports an individual's task in the organization.

They also explained that we know less about building systems than warehouses; there is so much more standardization in architecture. Once the aesthetics have been settled, the engineering work is well understood. Unfortunately, with a computer-based information system, there are myriad ways to realize the design. There are many choices for input, for the way the data are processed, and for output. Given the specifications, one has a number of ways to design program modules and to test the system. It is all these choices that make systems analysis and design a time-consuming activity.

Terry and Tom are concerned about the future, because they know the project is just beginning. What will the president's reaction be as the project continues to require time and resources? What help can you offer in dealing with this problem?

Work Plan

Discussion of a work plan will be deferred until Chapter 17.

KEY WORDS AND RECOMMENDED READINGS

Please see Chapter 15.

DISCUSSION QUESTIONS

1 How would you classify the Hardserve system; what decisions are supported in each department?
2 Where should the greatest savings come from through use of the new system at Hardserve?
3 Design the report format for the inventory balance report.
4 Develop a procedure for taking physical inventory. How do you enter physical inventory information into the system accurately, given the leadtime between counting the items in the bin and updating the computer system?
5 Design the retrieval program, including both the input language and the retrieval processing.
6 How would you identify each of the different cards and number the transactions?
7 How would you answer the president's request for vendor information without using a chained direct-access file?
8 Why are so many existing forms continued in the new computer system?

9 What extensions of the system would you recommend for accounting, warehouse, and purchasing areas in the future?

10 Is there any way to eliminate the manual files of purchase orders in the warehouse and at the receiving station?

11 If the system is placed on-line at some time, what kind of inquiries would you expect from each department? How would you design the files and directories to answer these inquiries?

12 Besides the files and directories, what other major changes would be needed to develop an on-line version of the system presented in this chapter?

13 How do you think the design team should function during the programming and conversion of the new system? Is it necessary to continue to work as a team? Would you recommend leaving extra, unused room in each file record? Why?

14 How do you think the computer department estimates the programming time required to implement a system such as the one presented in this chapter for Hardserve?

15 Where do you anticipate the greatest behavioral problems will occur in implementing the new system at Hardserve?

16 What conversion steps will be necessary before the new system can begin operating?

17 Design a training program for users of the new system.

18 What role should the members of the steering committee play during implementation?

19 Does it make sense for Hardserve to begin planning other applications now? Why?

20 How does the extensive user involvement in design prepare Hardserve for implementation and operation of the system?

21 How would you design programs for Hardserve to hide as much as possible of the data files from the programs that must access the data?

22 What do you think the biggest weakness is in the Hardserve design? What would you recommend to overcome it?

23 What would be the advantage of on-line input in the Hardserve example?

24 Would on-line input be desirable in some future version of Hardserve?

25 What other way could the linked-list file be designed for Hardserve?

26 Why do you think such a simple economic-order-quantity model was included in the system? Would you recommend a more sophisticated version now or later on?

27 Is the Hardserve inventory control system well-suited for a package application? Why or why not?

28 Would you follow a similar team design approach to develop a decision-support system for Hardserve?

29 What is the future of batch systems? Will they all eventually be replaced by on-line processing? Why or why not?

CHAPTER 17

MANAGING COMPUTER SYSTEMS DESIGN PROJECTS

One area where there has been a notable lack of success is in managing system design projects. We may have a conceptually good system, but if the development of the system is not managed properly, it will not be successfully implemented. A number of problems have been reported in the development of information systems: Schedules are not met on time, systems do not meet their original specifications, and there are often high cost overruns.

Early in the history of information systems, there was much debate over whether or not computer-systems development projects are sufficiently different from other types of projects to demand special management practices. Can similar management techniques be used for all types of development projects regardless of whether a computer is involved? Developing a computer system has many of the characteristics of any research and development project. Although there are some project management tools and guidelines common to systems analysis and design and other types of research and development projects, certain characteristics of the systems design task also require special consideration.

UNCERTAINTIES

One of the major problems in systems analysis and design is the high level of uncertainty associated with these activities. Users are often unaware of the problem creating the need for an information system. In fact, users are probably unaware of their own information and decision-making activities. The design team has to work with the user to elicit the data for designing the system. The activities of the design team also create uncertainty: Are the decisions made and the information used adequately understood by users and designers?

Lack of certainty is also reflected in the development of the system itself: Is the model developed by the design team close to reality? Once given the system design, programmers have to interpret the specifications and write programs. It is difficult to forecast in advance what is involved in writing, testing, and debugging a program. We are usually uncertain about the time required, whether or not the program works, and whether or not it meets specifications.

If the program and system meet specifications, then user acceptance tests can be undertaken to see if the design as represented by system specifications fits user needs. The task of project management is to attempt to reduce all these uncertainties, coordinate the activities of diverse parties working on the project, and be certain that the project is completed within cost estimates and on time.

MANAGEMENT TASKS

Early Stages

Referring again to Table 5-1, we have advocated the use of a small design team and a relatively unstructured approach through the stages of systems design up to and including the feasibility study. In these stages we define the system and complete a rough design. Careful consideration of user needs and their involvement was suggested; we advocate that users control the project while the computer department staff members act as technical liaison, furnishing guidance and direction. After detailed specifications have been developed, the nature of the project management task changes dramatically.

Implementation

There are several major components of the development effort:

Develop programs
Refine the design
Test programs
Train users
Test the system
Conversion
Final installation
Cutover

How should these tasks be managed, and who on the design team should assume responsibility for them?

Program development clearly should be assigned to the computer department staff. After the completion of specifications, programmers should be added to the design team. Refining the design involves several activities. Usually, further systems analysis is necessary, and some of the specifications will probably have to be altered; these activities involve the analyst and programmer. There also may be questions that require returning to users, so the analyst or programmer must meet with user representatives. If there are major changes or additions to design, the team can revert to the original systems analysis mode discussed in earlier chapters.

The unit tests of individual programs are the responsibility of the computer department staff. However, to test programs with realistic data, assistance will be needed from users to generate the data. The same is true for testing the system; we want users to generate data to check processing and error handling.

Often, special conversion programs are required to cut over from an old system to a new one. Here the user and the computer department staff must work collaboratively. During the actual conversion, users must verify that the results are valid; for example, by checking the contents of a newly created computer file. The final implementation and cutover require extensive effort on the part of both users and the computer design team.

In this chapter we focus on the technological parts of the project—that is, the activities concerned with the development and testing of programs as opposed to the testing of the overall system. In the past, we have not been able to predict accurately how long programs will take to develop or what they will cost. We have trouble coordinating projects as well. In this chapter we suggest some new approaches that have the promise to reduce drastically the uncertainty associated with the technical components of systems analysis and design.

PROJECT SCHEDULING

At a seminar on the management of large-scale software development projects, the consensus among many of the participants was that most formal scheduling techniques did not help much in managing computer-related projects. These techniques, such as the critical path method (CPM), had been successful in the development of military hardware but did not seem to apply to programming projects, where the prototype is the final product.

The reasons these approaches have not been successful is due to bad estimates of completion times for project activities and the need to refine data as expected completion times change. The use of any scheduling technique requires constant updating. It appears in the computer profession that many projects have begun with a schedule but have failed to devote resources to continually updating it.

Critical Path Method

The critical path method was developed from a military system for project evaluation and review called PERT. PERT involves the use of probability distributions to compute the most likely completion time for the major events in a project. CPM is conceptually simpler than PERT and is better suited to the development of computer systems. The basic idea of CPM is to break a project down into a series of subtasks and to arrange the activities in a "network" according to precedence relationships. We indicate if one task must precede other tasks, e.g., the survey precedes a feasibility study. The length of time required

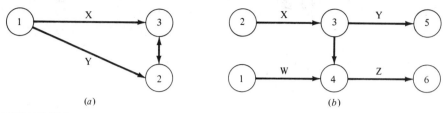

FIGURE 17-1
Dummy events.

for each task is estimated, and the various tasks are arranged in the network to reflect precedence relationships. Then the critical path—that is, the path through the network requiring the greatest amount of time—is identified. As tasks are completed and estimates for completion times for remaining tasks are changed, the critical path also changes. Project management can add extra resources to critical activities on the path.

The basic components of CPM are events and activities. An event is a meaningful milestone accomplished at the end of some activity. Preceding events must be completed before following events can occur; that is, a succeeding event cannot occur until a preceding activity has been completed. There are several rules for CPM diagram construction (Olsen, 1968). All CPM networks can have only one beginning event, and all CPM networks can have only one ending event, to which all activities must lead. Concurrent activities cannot be represented by the same arrow. Event numbers must reflect the presence of an activity; that is, preceding event numbers must be less than succeeding ones. There must be a critical path through the network; that is, all events must be connected. There must be only one occurrence of any individual event.

Dummy events are introduced to handle several problems in constructing a network. First, a dummy event can be used to show the relationship between two activities performed concurrently. In Figure 17-1, dummy event 3 shows that X

TABLE 17-1
MAJOR ACTIVITIES IN A SYSTEMS DESIGN PROJECT

Activity	Immediate predecessor	Completion time (days)
A Survey	—	4
B Feasibility study	A	20
C Analyze existing system	A	10
D Develop and revise system	B,C	5
E Prepare detailed file specs	D	10
F Prepare I/O requirements	D	7
G Specify programs	E,F	12
H Develop manual procedures	F	10
I Ready to program	G,H	—

SYSTEMS PROBLEM 17-1

Harold Gray is the systems analyst in charge of the design of a new computer-based information system for Rogers Metals, a producer of aluminum products. The new system is an important one for Rogers, as it will help control and schedule production at two major factories.

The system has been designed, and programming is underway. Gray is now concerned with managing the programming project. One of the programmers, Sam Nixon, is proving very difficult; Sam resists providing any estimates or progress reports. "Why does anyone need to know what I'm doing? I'll get the job done; all this reporting takes away time I could be using to write programs. The same goes for documentation; that will follow when I get the coding done, and not before!"

Harold is concerned with his problems as a manager; he must control the project and see that it is completed on schedule and that the system does what was specified. To accomplish this goal, he has broken all the programming tasks into modules. Rather than request reports on what percent complete each module is, he wants to hear only when the module has been successfully tested with real data. "The 95 percent complete program is a legend; it takes three weeks to get 95 percent done and a year to finish the last 5 percent."

However, Harold depends on reports from the staff on progress, such as notification that testing is complete. He also asks for reports on the number of test runs so that he can tell if one particular part of the project is requiring a great deal of extra work. Such extra work could be indicative of a problem in that module or with that specification. Harold's management system will not work without cooperation from the programming staff. What can he do to overcome Sam's reluctance to report progress?

---

and Y are performed concurrently. We also use dummy events when two sets of concurrent activities are involved and only one of the second set of activities depends on the first. In Figure 17-1b, X and W are concurrent, as are Y and Z. Activity Z depends on both activities X and W, while activity Y depends only on X. The dummy arrow in Figure 17-1b connects events 3 and 4.

In developing a CPM diagram, each activity and its precedence relationship with other activities must be specified along with time estimates. The best way to obtain time estimates is to interview individuals involved in the project. As more knowledge is gained, time estimates should be revised and the chart updated. As an example, Table 17-1 contains the major activities and a hypothetical systems design project up to the point of beginning programming. We have to specify activities, completion times, and the immediately preceding events in order to construct the network.

Figure 17-2a shows the network that reflects the precedence relationship among the activities, and Figure 17-2b shows the network with the nodes numbered so that every node has a higher number than any preceding node. The duration of activities has been included (note that dummy activities have a completion time of zero).

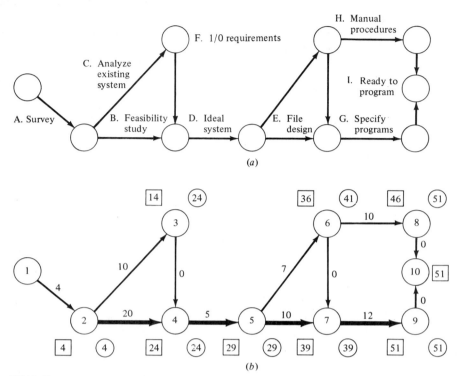

FIGURE 17-2
CPM network for example in Table 17-1.

There are two steps involved in finding the critical path through the network. First, we must determine the earliest possible start date (shown by the number in the square at each node). This number is the longest time interval along any one path from the beginning of the network to that point. For example, to get to event 4 we can go through nodes 1-2-3, which takes 4 + 10 + 0 = 14 days, or we can go through events 1-2-4, which takes 24 days. In this case we take the longest path, 24 days, and put that in the square by activity 4. This process is completed for each of the events in the network. The earliest start time for the last event is the minimum time to complete the project: in this example, 51 days.

Next, we must find the latest start date to finish on time (that is, within 51 days). Here, start at the last event (number 10) and work backward. Record the smallest rather than the longest number of days to reach each node, as shown in the circles in Figure 17-2b. For example, for node 5 we can go through nodes 10-9-7-5, which has a start date of 51 − (0 + 12 + 10) = 29, or nodes 10-9-7-6-5, which has a start date of 51 − (0 + 12 + 0 + 7) = 32. Finally, nodes 10-8-6-5 are possible, which give a start date of 51 − (0 + 10 + 7) = 34. Thus, for node 5 the number in the circle is 29.

The critical path through the network is the path for which the earliest start date in the squares and the latest start date in the circles are the same; no slippage in these activities is possible if we are to finish the project on time. In the simple example of Figure 17-2b, the critical path is shown by heavy lines. In a more complex example, we would find many more activities, and, as the network is updated, the critical path would probably change radically.

The use of critical path networks requires a great deal of effort, because time estimates will change. It is vital to keep updating the networks and to take management action to ensure that the tasks on the critical path are completed on schedule. Management can allocate additional resources and transfer effort from noncritical activities to critical ones by slowing a noncritical activity or scheduling its start date to occur at a later time. It should also be noted that we can develop CPM charts at different levels of detail. The example in Table 17-1 might be appropriate for the survey stage; a more detailed list of activities would be developed for the feasibility study. As work on actually specifying the system begins, the list of activities becomes even more detailed. For a programming critical path chart, each module would be considered a task. As some of the earlier modules are completed, time estimates should be revised for succeeding ones. One can envision a hierarchy of critical path charts, with a master chart referencing more detailed ones.

Fortunately, a number of computer packages are available to compute the critical path through a network. We can enter the data in Table 17-1 on activities, precedence relations, and durations, and a computer program will automatically develop and update the critical path network for us. Some of these programs are offered on interactive timesharing systems, which make them extremely useful to project management.

There are also a number of project management packages available for personal computers. Given the low cost of these devices, it is reasonable for a computer department to purchase a package and a microcomputer to devote to project management activities.

One of the greatest objections to formal project management is the time it takes. However, a great deal of time can be taken by projects that incur overruns because they are not managed! The other objection to formal project management is the volume of input necessary and the need to constantly update the critical path chart.

One company developed its own project management system to overcome some of these objections. Each analyst or programmer makes an estimate of the amount of time required for the activities assigned to him or her.

The idea is that the individual doing the work is in the best position to estimate how long it will take, as opposed to a manager who would estimate how long he or she thinks it should take for a task to be completed. Letting the individual doing the work make the estimate also creates some commitment to achieving the target implied by the estimate.

The company developed a computer program to accept initial estimates and the hours worked on each task provided by the programmers and analysts each week. (A project manager and analysts first break the project into tasks.) For example, suppose a task was estimated to take 15 hours. If a programmer had worked 10 hours on the task and made such a report, then the manager's report would show 5 hours left. If the programmer reported 20 hours, the manager would know there is a problem; the task proved harder than expected.

The key is to keep the tasks short, so that one cannot get too far behind, and to provide help to those who have overruns, rather than punishment. It is easier to estimate short tasks, and we find out quickly when the project is falling behind.

Each organization must determine what is the best style of management. However, formal project management can make a major contribution to the successful completion of information systems development projects.

TECHNICAL MANAGEMENT

As we discussed earlier, the most technical parts of computer project management and the greatest amount of uncertainty are associated with the task of writing and testing programs. In the past we have not been able to estimate completion times effectively or to coordinate people working on different parts of a program. In this section we present some new ideas and approaches to these tasks that should help to simplify and improve project management.

The techniques described below, combined with the structured approach to systems analysis and design presented earlier, provide a method of building systems that is sometimes called "software engineering." Software can be constructed according to plans, and the development can be disciplined. Although the development process is not as well developed as, say, civil or electrical engineering, we can still improve it for software by applying the techniques presented in this and other texts.

Programming Goals

In many development projects, management has not considered that there are different objectives in writing a program and has not informed programmers what they should adopt as a design goal. An experiment conducted by Weinberg (1972b) found that by giving groups of programmers explicit objectives, each group ranked first on the achievement of its objectives. The objectives in this experiment were minimum core usage, output clarity, program clarity, minimum number of statements, or minimum hours of development time. The study also found that some of the goals were incompatible, for example, the goal of output clarity and the use a of minimum number of statements.

The implications of this experiment for management are quite significant. Managers should make programming goals clear and explicit. Lacking goals, the programming staff may make different assumptions; one programmer may stress minimum completion time, while another tries for the minimum number of statements in the program. For most organizations developing information systems, the overriding goal probably will be clarity of program coding and output. In developing information systems we usually do not want elegant and sophisticated programs. Clarity of output is important to the users, and clarity of coding is important to programming management so that program changes can be made easily.

Egoless Programming

For the most part, we have always thought of programming as an individual task. Programmers are often detached from their coworkers but highly attached to the programs they write. Errors in programs are taken personally, and programmers tend to be highly defensive about their programs. Weinberg (1972a) has also suggested a new approach to programming that he calls "egoless programming." His basic idea is to treat programming as a group activity rather than as an individual effort. Management must create an environment in which the program- mer expects errors in the code and recognizes that help is needed to find them. Programmers in a group trade programs and look at each other's code. Many examples are cited by Weinberg that show the advantages of this approach in increased efficiency. There are also other advantages, aside from easier debug- ging and faster completion time. First, each programmer becomes better aware of the entire system and develops an understanding of how different modules fit together because of this involvement in the construction of other parts of the system. Also, more backup is provided, since several people are familiar with each module.

Programmer Teams

A structure for egoless programming teams having the potential for greatly improving project management activities, has been suggested by Baker (1972). This concept involves a chief programmer team consisting of a senior chief programmer, one or more backup programmers, one to five more junior programmers, and a programming librarian (Mills, 1971). The chief programmer directs the activities of the group, holding a position similar to that of a senior engineer. Instead of viewing programming as a profession leading to a systems analyst or management position, one looks at the highly paid chief programmer position as a senior staff position in an organization. This approach presents a better career path for programmers and recognizes that skilled programming is a worthy profession in itself.

All other programmers report to the chief programmer, whose job is to design and code programs, and who will program the most critical segments of the system. This person also works with other programmers to define modules for them. The chief programmer is responsible for the management of the team as a whole, having the opportunity to be a high-level creative programmer and, at the same time, a professional manager.

The backup programmer is equivalent in talent to the chief programmer, becomes totally familiar with the activities of the chief programmer, and furnishes backup. As long as the chief programmer is able to continue to manage the project, the backup programmer serves as a research associate to help develop new ideas and program test data.

The programming librarian maintains records of the project, including a complete file of programs, flowcharts, and program specifications. An index or directory to each part of the library is also maintained. The librarian is responsible for keeping a list of all the data elements so that all data are called by the same program identifier in each program. Old versions of programs are maintained in the archives so that useful information is not thrown out. For the same reason, copies of test data and test runs are filed in archive. The idea is to maintain the status of the programs and the projects so programmers can work more easily with them. For this reason, a complete and accurate directory or index to the items in the file is required.

The entire programming team functions as a group. Various programmers follow the guidance of the chief programmer; they work on different modules and read each other's programs. Heavy use is made of the library to build, store, and retrieve information for the team. For large projects it may be necessary to have several levels of teams, with the highest level reporting to the project manager. To implement this approach requires an extensive effort by management to provide an environment for and to encourage group-related activities.

Top-Down Programming

Most systems are designed from the top level down; that is, a general plan is developed and refined to greater levels of detail. Then systems tend to be implemented from the bottom up; that is, basic modules are written first and then integrated into subsystems. Some evidence suggests that it may be better to alter this development process (Baker, 1972; Mills, 1971). Under this approach, we write the highest-level programs and test them while the next lowest level is being written. Dummy subroutine and procedure calls are used for lower-level modules that have not been written yet.

Gane and Sarson (1979) offer some cogent reasons for top-down design and implementation. The conventional approach to development creates an interface problem. The conventional approach is to divide the system into programs, write and test each program separately, assemble the programs into subsystems, and form the subsystems into a working system. Lower-level modules are combined to form larger groups. Because of problems of communications and changes, the different subsystems may not fit together. If one major subsystem does not fit because it fails to pass data properly to another one, then a great deal of modification has to be done. These interface bugs are not found until near the end of the project during final assembly of the system. We can also avoid the need to redesign lower-level modules because of some oversight discovered when lower-level modules are combined to form a higher-level routine.

In top-down development, all the high-level logic and important system interfaces are developed before a great deal of detailed code has been written.

Also, tangible evidence of progress is more readily available; the top-down design serves as a high-level abstract model of the system. Further details are filled in during the design and coding process.

Documentation

During the development of a system, all the structured methodologies produce documentation as a by-product of the design process. At this stage, we must communicate among the design team members; communication with users is also important. Techniques that move from a conceptual level to more detailed levels should facilitate this kind of communications. We need to be able to return to a higher level of detail if the current level becomes too confusing. It is important to begin with an overview and then to explore various components of the overview in depth. Documentation that reflects this design philosophy becomes the key coordinating document that all individuals associated with the system can rely on for an accurate representation of the current version of the system.

Reviews

We have advocated review sessions with users, and now we stress the importance of design reviews for the technical project team. Design reviews in which processing is described in detail should be scheduled for different parts of the system. For example, the logic of an input error check could be presented by the programmer in charge of the module. The audience consists of other programming team members and perhaps a user representative from the design team. The audience notes errors and inconsistencies and makes suggestions for improvements in the module. Someone in the meeting records these comments for whoever is making the presentation. The purpose of these reviews is constructive; we are trying to find what has been omitted or what errors in logic are included in the design. The review is not held for employee evaluation; the goal is to improve the product, not to be critical of the speaker. Clearly, this approach requires an open and nondefensive attitude that is consistent with the environment required for egoless programming.

Modularity Revisited

We first discussed modularity in Chapter 15 in connection with the development of programming specifications.[1] Some additional considerations in defining

---

[1] Organizations differ in assigning the responsibility for detailed programming design. In some, the analyst produces quite detailed program specifications; in others, the task is left entirely to the programmer. In this text, we are assuming that the broad outlines of the modules were developed with the specifications. During programming, it is necessary for the programming staff to specify the details for each module.

modules will greatly contribute to the project management process. By establishing the following design criteria with programmers, the programming effort
should be reduced and systems should be more flexible. (For more details on
module design, see Gane and Sarson, 1979.)

First, a module should be manageably small so that an individual can read a
listing of the module and keep a picture of its functions in mind. The modules
should be developed and interconnected so that there is no ripple effect; that is,
there are no obscure connections or couplings among modules. (A coupling exists
when modules pass data values to each other, access the same data, or share
some resource.) Because of an unobvious coupling, a change in module A causes
a change in module K, though it was not clear that the modules were at all
related. A might have changed a switch used by K in some shared storage area.

Gane and Sarson have used the analogy of a superior-subordinate relationship
to illustrate how modules are best coupled. The worker or subordinate modules
are not in communication with each other. See Figure 17-3. By constructing the
modules in this fashion, one produces a structure chart. The chart shows the
function of the modules, and arrows show the data passed between the modules.
See Figure 17-4. Note that a structure does not show the sequence of module
execution over time; a flowchart or some other graphic aid is necessary to
demonstrate when modules are executed.

How are various modules coupled to achieve our objective of a changeable

FIGURE 17-3
Coupling of modules.

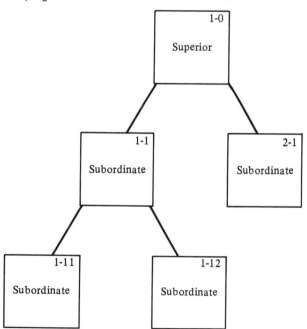

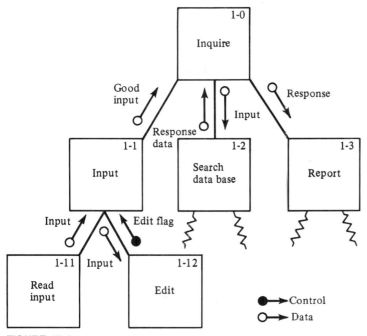

FIGURE 17-4
A structure chart.

system? The most desirable form of coupling is one in which only data are passed between modules and in which the amount of data is small. It is also better if the data are passed as parameters of call statements in the language rather than as part of a large pool of common data accessible by all modules.

It is usually not possible to design a system with only data coupling, since various subordinates must report back to their superiors that a task has been completed successfully. This type of coupling is usually accomplished by passing some type of control variable or status flag between modules. The more switches and flags, the more complex the task of module modification. It is best if the control flag is simple and the subordinate performs only one function.

The worst type of coupling occurs when one module refers to data that is inside another module, for example by requiring data defined within the second module, branching into the second module, or modifying the execution of a second module. Gane and Sarson recommend that any form of coupling except data and control coupling be avoided.

Modules can also be characterized by their cohesiveness. To what extent do all parts of a module belong together? A highly cohesive module does not need much coupling. There are a number of ways to characterize the cohesiveness of modules. The best cohesion occurs when modules are functionally cohesive; that is, each module carries out one and only one identifiable function. Functional

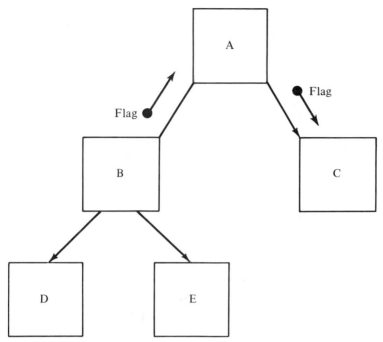

FIGURE 17-5
Scope of effect exceeds scope of control.

cohesion is better than temporal cohesion—in which module design is based on events that occur sequentially in time—or procedural cohesion, in which a module represents procedure boxes on a flowchart.

The last consideration in module design is the scope of effect and scope of control of a module. Modules often make decisions and then invoke another module as a result of the decision. The scope of control of a module is all the modules that it calls, the modules they call, and so on. If a module is considered a grandparent, then all its offspring through various generations are within its scope of control. The scope of effect is the result of a decision that determines which other modules are invoked. The scope of effect should be within the scope of control.

Gane and Sarson offer an example in which there is a scope of effect beyond the scope of control. Module B passes a status flag to module C, so that the scope of effect of B now lies beyond its scope of control. In Figure 17-5, B affects C, a module not in B's scope of control. The solution here is to redesign the modules so that the scope of effect is encompassed within the scope of control.

Stepwise Refinement and Structured Programming

In addition to modularization, we also suggest the use of structured programming (Baker, 1972; Mills, 1971). Structured programming is a methodical approach to developing programs. The term "stepwise refinement" is usually associated with structured programming. In fact, we have borrowed this terminology in our discussions of the task of systems analysis and design.

The idea behind stepwise refinement is that we move to successively lower levels of detail. At the highest level, the plans for a program are abstract and global. In successive stages, we break the program down into more detail; the last of these successive refinements is the coded program. Just as with systems analysis and design, stepwise refinement lets us cope better with the complexity of the programming task. The highest level of abstraction gives us an overview; then we can concentrate on details of what are usually smaller pieces at lower levels of abstraction.

Mills (1975) offers a concrete example of stepwise refinement in programming. Assume that we wish to write a module to perform key-to-address transformation for a file. To simplify the problem assume that requests are never for keys not in the table of addresses; i.e., there will be a match for each input key when the table is scanned. Figure 17-6 illustrates the process of writing specifications for these modules or functions in a graphic format.

At the highest level in part *a* of the figure, we express the problem to be solved as transforming a key to an address. The *b* part of the figure shows an example of not using stepwise refinement. A mental discontinuity here depends on some unrecorded insight. Somehow in Figure 17-6*b*, part of the processing is defined as an iteration through the table, stopping when the input key equals the lookup value in the table. Figure 17-6*c* shows the same end result from stepwise refinement. Here the program is first refined into two parts, input and table search; then the table search is broken into two parts. The table is searched for an entry that matches the key, and then the search is terminated.

This is, of course, a simple example, and the benefits of stepwise refinement are not as obvious as they would be in other circumstances. However, perhaps it is evident that the sequence of refinements from Figure 17-6*a* to *c* to *d* is more logical and less subject to error than the path through Figure 17-6*b*. By recording the intermediate steps like *c* on the road to *d*, we document mental processes and design decisions. Many days later, when questions arise, there are no unrecorded insights to recall to understand part of a system. Stepwise refinement aids in making logical design decisions and in reviewing them at a later date.

Structured programming follows from stepwise refinement. It is based on the fact that any program can be constructed using the following statement types:

Sequential operations (including procedures calls)

IF THEN ELSE
DO WHILE

The most conspicuously absent type of statement is the GO TO; by eliminating GO TO statements a much more readable program results. It is not possible to find a transfer of control within a program segment. In a well-structured program there is only one entry point and one exit per module. Therefore, a programmer can read a program segment from top to bottom without worrying about

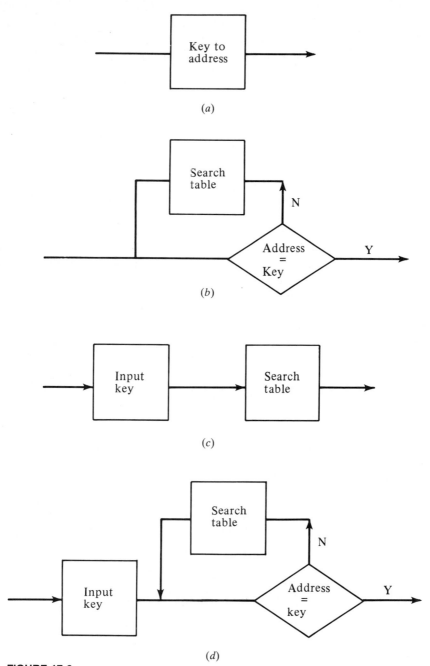

(a)

(b)

(c)

FIGURE 17-6
Stepwise refinement.

(d)

TABLE 17-2
INDENTATION OF CODE

```
DO WHILE A>B;
   IF K<2 THEN:
      DO I = 1 TO 5;
         X(I) = Y(I);
ELSE;
   Q = '1'B;
END;
```

---

intervening jumps. This technique makes it much easier to modify existing programs.

Clearly, it takes more skill and planning to write such a code, but it is much easier to understand and change. This approach to structured programming should be combined with modularization, the use of program comments that describe what each segment of code is meant to accomplish, and code indentation to make the structure of the program clear. For example, statements in the range of DO loop are indented (see Table 17-2). This practice also enhances the readability of code by grouping related portions of logic together. The programmer should also attempt to have one comment for each related block of code or at least one comment every four or five statements.

Data Dictionaries

It is very important to define and describe adequately the elements of data in a system. Gane and Sarson have suggested documentation that includes the name of the data element, its description, and the data structure in which it may be found (for example, a record of a particular file). To assist in this task, commercial data dictionary packages are available to facilitate entry, editing, and the use of data elements. These systems use indexes and pointers so that users can trace relationships through the dictionary, often on-line (see Chapter 9).

An automated system like this can provide a great deal of assistance, for example, by producing a report of where a data element is used in all programs that mention it. It is also possible to search for a data name, given keywords that describe the name. For example, one might want to determine the name of the variable that stands for net pay; entering keywords would produce a list of possible identifiers and their definitions. Using keywords one would search the dictionary to locate the proper identifier to use in a program. Some automated dictionary packages can generate the proper data structures for input to a data-base system or a programming language.

Support

Is there any evidence to support the use of the techniques discussed in this selection? There have been a few attempts to collect data, but it is hard to design an experiment. Very few systems are programmed twice just so that two techniques can be compared! What data exist, then, are drawn from projects that are potentially incomparable, since each project used different programming techniques.

Walston and Felix (1977) developed a data base of 60 completed software projects and analyzed the data to evaluate factors associated with programming productivity. Their data indicates that greater use of structured programming, top-down development, chief programmer teams, and design and code inspections are associated with greater productivity as defined by the delivered lines of source code per person-month of effort. These data combined with the intuitive appeal of the programming techniques described in this section suggest that some combination of them should be considered when managing the development of a software project.

Estimates

For all stages of project management, we need estimates of the time required for various tasks. Historically, these estimates have been difficult to develop and have been inaccurate because of the uncertainty involved. Because of the way in which programming has been viewed, the time required for a program to be written is highly dependent on the talent of a single programmer. There are various rules of thumb for estimating analyst and programmer time, such as the number of lines of debugged code expected per programmer per month. However, these old ideas are not too helpful if we plan to follow the new approaches suggested in this chapter. In fact, it is not clear that such generalizations across all organizations and projects will always be possible.

Instead of these rules, we need to develop data within each organization. The systems librarian already maintains some of the data needed to develop estimates. The librarian should also keep track of original estimates and the actual results. These results are used, not to embarrass programmers, but to adjust future estimates to make them more accurate. Gradually, we can build a set of data to determine if estimates are unique to the staff, the design team, the project, or the organization. We do not have enough information at the present time to develop valid guidelines for the number of lines of debugged code per programmer or to know if such guidelines will ever be meaningful.

As an example, the Walston and Felix data base discussed above showed that for the projects included

Total effort in person-months
$$= 5.2 \times (\text{thousands of lines of source code delivered})^{.91}$$

For these projects, the amount of programming effort was almost linearly related to the number of lines of source code. This finding is not surprising, since one would expect total effort to be proportional to the size of the project. This example illustrates the importance of gathering data for each organization on what it can expect to accomplish.

SYSTEMS PROBLEM 17-2

Ruth Leavitt is manager of systems and programming for Financial Services, Inc. This firm, founded only 5 years ago, has grown rapidly and now has over 100 employees and its own timesharing computer system. The firm offers financial data bases to subscribers and sophisticated computer models to manipulate the data. Also, a special higher-level language is available that was designed by the computer staff at Financial. This language features the kind of vocabulary that a financial analyst might use and eliminates the need for a professional programmer for about 75 percent of those wishing to write special programs for financial analysis.

Ruth's assignment is to manage the systems design and programming effort for internal systems developed by Financial. There also is a staff of consultants who help clients use the Financial computer and programs. In addition to direct project management, Ruth has been thinking of approaches that would facilitate programming productivity for all projects at Financial in general. She has recently read some of the references cited in this chapter, and they have provided the impetus to develop a research program at Financial.

Ruth's ideas, though quite preliminary at the present time, are to develop a computer-based project-management system that can be used for day-to-day management and to collect data for making estimates of the time and effort required for future systems. She realizes that it will be necessary to categorize projects, because different types of development efforts will require different resources and estimates. Ruth would like to design a system where all the needed information is captured as a by-product of program development and testing so that the programming staff has to provide as little data as possible. Prepare a design for such a system and describe how it would work.

Conclusion

The techniques of earlier chapters, especially applications generators, offer exciting possibilities for systems design, particularly since we are currently limited by available personnel in developing new systems. Systems design is a very labor-intensive task, and these approaches, far from replacing the computer professional, will allow more time for the development of information systems of higher quality. Any resources freed from technical tasks can be applied to developing a better understanding of user and organizational needs.

THE HARDSERVE EXAMPLE

In Chapter 16 we developed detailed design specifications for the batch inventory control system for Hardserve. From the current chapter we can see how Tom Roberts, the analyst from Manhold, and Terry Carson, the user in charge of the new system, might staff and organize the technical implementation effort. Three programmers were assigned to the project: a senior programmer, Carl Norris; a backup programmer, Barb McNeal; and a team member, Joe Torres. Because of the small scope of the system, Joe Torres also serves as systems librarian for the team. The team had worked together before and had practiced egoless programming. They also believed in structured coding, top-down implementation, and frequent informal review sessions to go over logic and processing routines. Mary Davis, the other analyst, continued working half time with users and half time on implementation issues and with the programming team. Tom was also beginning work on another project and planned to spend only half time on Hardserve's inventory system.

Scheduling

The design team decided to aim for an 18-month target for the system's installation. To arrive at this schedule, Tom Roberts met with each of the team members to get their estimate for how long each task assigned to them would take. He and Terry then developed the Gantt scheduling chart in Figure 17-7. This high-level chart forms the basis for more detailed breakdowns for individual tasks.

　　The Gantt chart is helpful for reviewing overall progress, but it does not show the dependencies among design tasks well. Therefore, the design team agreed to develop a detailed CPM chart and to keep it up to date. Each of the major groups

FIGURE 17-7
Hardserve high-level Gantt schedule.

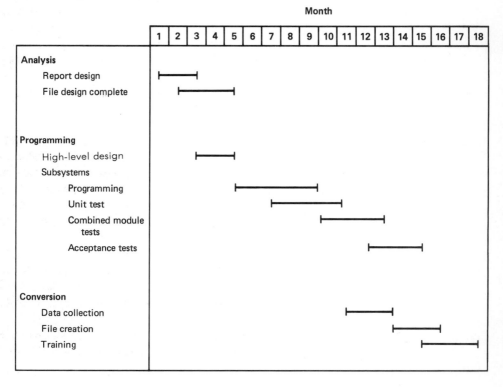

TABLE 17-3
THE PROJECT MANAGEMENT
ASSIGNMENTS AT
HARDSERVE

Terry Carson (user)
  Overall project responsibility
  Implementation
Tom Roberts (analyst)
  Programming management
  Implementation
Carl Norris (programmer)
  Senior programmer
Barb McNeal (programmer)
  Backup programmer
  Maintain CPM charts
Joe Torres (programmer)
  Team programmer
  System librarian

involved was asked to identify tasks in their area of responsibility and to develop time estimates for these tasks. For example, Carl and his team used the detailed systems specifications to identify each activity to the level of program modules. The program modules were defined using the criteria described earlier in the chapter, and the precedence relationship for the CPM chart followed a top-down approach to programming. Mary and Terry worked on the tasks for implementation and obtained time estimates from the users involved in the design effort (see Table 17-3).

Recognizing that the CPM approach would be beneficial only if continually updated, Barb McNeal as the backup programmer took the responsibility for maintaining the system and reporting the output to different levels of management. A timesharing terminal was installed at Hardserve and connected to Manhold's computer system, which has an interactive CPM program. After initially entering the data each week, Barb updated time estimates and prepared a new critical path chart. Tom and Carl studied the events on the critical path chart carefully while Terry kept abreast of the overall project schedule. Minor changes in work assignments and activities planned for each week were made in response to the revised critical path.

KEY WORDS

Backup programmer	Coupling	Egoless programming
Chief programmer team	CPM	Events
Code indentation	Data dictionary	Modularization
Cohesion	Documentation	Network
Comments	Dummy events	Nodes

Precedence relation   Software engineering   Systems librarian
Programming goals   Stepwise refinement   Top-down programming
Review sessions   Structured.programming   Uncertainty
Scope

RECOMMENDED READINGS

Baker, F. T.: "Chief Programmer Team Management of Production Programming," *IBM Systems Journal*, vol. 11, no. 1, 1972, pp. 66–73. (An article describing the use of a chief programmer team and many of the techniques discussed in this chapter to develop a retrieval system for the *New York Times*.)

Byte and other microcomputer magazines for project management packages.

Jensen, R. W., and C. C. Tories: *Software Engineering*, Prentice-Hall, Englewood Cliffs, N.J., 1979. (Chapters by different authors on design, programming, testing, and security.)

Mills, H. D.: "Chief Programmer Team's Principles and Procedures," IBM Federal Systems Division, Gaithersburg, Md., 1971. (A thorough discussion of the organization and principles behind chief programmer teams.)

Weinberg, G. M.: *The Psychology of Computer Programming*, Van Nostrand, New York, 1972a. (A revolutionary book suggesting the concept of egoless programming.)

————: "The Psychology of Improved Programming Performance," *Datamation*, vol. 18, no. 11, November 1972b, pp. 82–85. (An experiment is described in which different programming teams are given different goals in writing a program.)

Zelkowitz, M. V., A. C. Shaw, and J. O. Gannon: *Principles of Software Engineering and Design*, Prentice-Hall, Englewood Cliffs, N.J., 1979. (Contains material on program design and examples for systems software.)

DISCUSSION QUESTIONS

1 What do you think motivated the development of chief programmer teams?

2 What factors contribute to developing readable code? Why is the development of readable code important in a commercial as opposed to an educational environment?

3 Take an old program that you wrote at least 6 months ago. Can you read it now? How would you change it to be more readable? What chance do you think there is of someone being able to understand your logic?

4 What type of documentation should accompany a program?

5 Develop a list of goals for a program. Rank-order the importance of these goals and explain your reasoning for the following programs: (1) a program for class, (2) a program for a commercial batch processing system, and (3) a timesharing program for a manager to use.

6 What programming aspects become more difficult if one is restricted from using a GO TO statement? Why does not having a GO TO statement impose a structure on a program?

7 Is the absence of a GO TO alone enough to result in "structured programming"?

8 Compare and contrast a computer systems development project with a project to design a new commercial airplane.

9 What are the major advantages of top-down programming?

10 How does the presence of a systems librarian facilitate work on a computer project?

11 It has been said that structured programming is more than the absence of GO TO

statements. It is also an approach to programming that stresses modularity and a structured method of problem solving. What are the major reasons why such an approach is advantageous in programming?

12 Many information systems projects have been completed well beyond their original schedule and with high cost overruns. Looking at the entire cycle of information systems design from the initial survey through conversion and implementation, where are the most likely places where delays can occur?

13 What are the major risks involved in the development cycle described in problem 12? What can be done to minimize the probability of not completing successfully a systems design project?

14 What would the development of a professional position for "chief programmers" do to change the career path for computer department staff members?

15 Some experts have argued that programming is such a craftlike trade that it defies management. Does this view agree with or contradict the suggestions made in this chapter? Why do you disagree or agree with this observation?

16 Is it possible to write structured programs in a language like BASIC or FORTRAN that do not offer nested and compound conditionals?

17 From a management standpoint, what are the disadvantages of using assembly language for developing information systems?

18 What are the arguments in favor of using assembly language in a commercial environment? Under what conditions would you recommend the use of assembly language?

19 How does code indentation contribute to the readability of a program and to subsequent programming changes?

20 Why do programmers resist making changes in working programs after a system has been implemented? How would the use of the techniques recommended in this chapter affect this resistance?

21 How can a review session for a program or some aspect of a systems design be conducted in a nonthreatening manner for the individual making the presentation? How would the presence of a programming team facilitate this structured review?

22 Design a project-reporting system to aid the manager of a systems development project.

23 What output from a programming team is needed by the manager of a programming project? How can accurate output be obtained without disrupting the progress of the project?

24 Is the management of a programming project to install a packaged program any different than for a project where a system is being developed from the beginning?

25 After reading this chapter, what conclusions do you have about the advantages of package applications programs? What are their disadvantages?

26 What implications do continuing reductions in hardware costs have for systems? Will systems be designed differently? What kind of concerns that sometimes delay projects will be reduced?

27 Describe the concept of stepwise refinement for both systems analysis and design and program design.

28 What kind of tools help in systems development? What kind of automation is likely in the development process?

29 How can a data-base management system contribute to improved development schedules?

30 Why does it take so long to program and install a computer-based system?

DESIGN DOCUMENTATION
  Purpose
  Contents
USER DOCUMENTATION FOR TRAINING
  Purpose
  Contents
  Training
OPERATIONS DOCUMENTATION
  Purpose
  Contents
USER REFERENCE DOCUMENTATION
  Purpose
  Contents
  Help
  Learning from Packages
KEY WORDS
RECOMMENDED READINGS
DISCUSSION QUESTIONS

CHAPTER 18

DOCUMENTATION

Documentation is a term used to describe all the instructions, programs, narratives—that is, virtually anything written about an information system. Documentation serves several purposes; first, during systems design it is the evolving product developed by the design team and users. After installation it is the basis for making changes to the system. The quality of documentation determines how much flexibility the computer department has in being responsive to user requests. Finally, good documentation serves to reduce the conflict between users and the computer department, since a well-documented system is easier for users to understand. Good documentation means that an adequate reference is available when problems arise, and this information helps users learn how to solve their problems with the system.

DESIGN DOCUMENTATION

Purpose

In Chapter 17 we discussed some of the documentation needed during systems design and saw that documentation is a joint effort of all members of the design team.

Many structured approaches to design include the production of documentation as a part of the design process itself. This documentation aids communications among those on a design team; it represents the current conceptualization of a new system or the understanding of an existing system. The librarian is the member of the design team who is responsible for maintaining documentation.

During design, another purpose of documentation is one of control: providing a record of what has been developed and of changes. It is vitally important to be sure that all parts of a system affected by a change are considered and that those responsible for the components of the system affected by the change are notified. If a file format or the contents of a file are altered, what program modules and what programmers are affected?

Control is also the ability to retrieve past test runs and old versions of programs or files. As we have discussed before, this type of documentation builds an excellent data base for making future estimates of how long it will take to develop a similar system. The librarian should maintain a copy of all runs and progress reports so that a complete description of project activities can be found easily.

Contents

Some of the most essential elements of the design documentation are described in Table 18-1. Many of these documents will be used for other purposes in a slightly

TABLE 18-1
COMPONENTS OF DESIGN
DOCUMENTATION*

Table of contents (hierarchical)
Survey
Feasibility study
Existing systems documentation
Specifications for new system
  Output
  Input
  File versions
  Logic specification
  Hierarchical program modules
  Actual programs (all versions)
    Flowchart/decision tables/pseudo code
    Cross-references for variables
    Modules (hierarchy)
    Module interface cross-reference
    Variable identifier library
  Tests
    Design
    Data
    Runs and results
Manual procedures
  Hierarchical flowcharts
  Narratives
  Error controls
Work plans
Progress reports

---

*For more details on some of these categories, see Table 15-1.

modified form. Probably the most important document is the table of contents, which serves as a directory to the manual files containing all the other information describing the system. The table of contents should be hierarchical, and parts of it may be distributed to another location. For example, the main table of contents points to the location of output specifications. At the beginning of the file of output specifications, another directory points to each output.

The library should contain the survey and feasibility studies and documents relating to the analysis of the existing system. It is also a natural place for detailed specifications for the new system. As items such as system flowcharts are changed, the originals are filed as backup copies in archival storage. Keep the most recent document in the working library with each sheet dated and with a pointer to the location of past versions in the archives.

Another major portion of the library is the actual programs as they are developed. It is particularly important to keep copies of input, output, file record formats, and lists of modules. The various modules and files should be cross-referenced according to what other modules interface with them. There should be a cross-reference list of module calls and of modules using different data elements. Then, when it is necessary to change a calling sequence or a record format, the various programmers affected can be notified by using the cross-reference list.

It is also desirable to keep a central program identifier library; this is particularly crucial in data-base management applications. The same piece of data should be known by the same identifier or variable name in all programs. This practice makes it much easier to debug and make modifications, especially if group programming is used, since programmers become familiar with the same variable name in all programs. It is very confusing having inventory balance called ONHAND in one program and CURRENTBALANCE in another. Standardizing on one name throughout the system makes things much simpler.

The systems librarian should distribute lists of identifiers to programmers. Identifiers should be highly descriptive of the entity they represent, because good identifiers make program logic much easier to follow. When a programmer needs to add identifiers to the library, he or she should make out a list and check with the librarian before writing the program. The identifier library should be cross-referenced by subject area and maintained alphabetically by identifiers. When the system is completed, this library of variable names provides complete documentation on what each variable means in the programs. Note that most data dictionaries provide this feature.

There is also a need for documentation within the program itself. If code indentation, comments, and structured programs are used, then the blocks of logic in the program are a form of documentation. This is the reason we advocated including many comments, particularly at the beginning of a module, showing how it is used, the calling sequence, and exit and error conditions.

In addition to various program versions, the systems librarian should file all test runs. This filing provides a record of runs that can be used for later analysis and makes it possible to refer to a test to avoid duplicating effort. Error conditions also should be included in the system library; there are many different modules, and various team members may want to refer to these error checks and controls. Centralization of the record of error messages and controls promotes coordination.

As we have previously discussed, the work plan, the progress records, and versions of the critical path chart are maintained in the library. These items provide valuable data for postimplementation audits and for developing benchmarks for systems design activities in the organization. The final version of the design documentation library is the basic document used in making program changes after implementation.

USER DOCUMENTATION FOR TRAINING

Purpose

Training documentation prepares the user for implementation and the eventual use of the system. Most of the information needed for training can be developed from the systems documentation discussed above. User-training documentation is used to bridge the gap between old, existing procedures and those required for the new system. This documentation should be developed by user members of the design team in conjunction with other users in the organization.

Contents

Table 18-2 contains the minimal components of user-training documentation. We have found it best to begin training by first looking at the output of a system; this is the desired end product that motivated the development of the system. Output documentation should focus on key decisions and reports.

Having briefed users on the output, we can discuss the input and the files necessary to produce the desired output. Finally, the computer processing logic and other procedures involved are discussed. It is important to include error conditions and the remedial actions taken by users in training documentation.

TABLE 18-2
COMPONENTS OF USER
DOCUMENTATION

Output
Input
Files
Processing procedures
Errors
Transitional considerations
   Testing
   Conversion

TABLE 18-3
TRAINING NARRATIVE FOR FLOWCHART OF FIGURE 16-3*b*

ORDERING PROCEDURE
Areas Affected
  Warehouse
  Purchasing
  Computer department

Procedures
The computer department sends the purchase order report to purchasing, indicating that the items on the report are below the reorder point. (A sample of the report is attached with an explanation of each piece of data to show how it is derived or calculated.) The chief purchasing agent assigns items to agents for a review.
    The purchasing agent uses this report to place an order if necessary. The agent will consider the usage pattern and any on-order quantities plus the most recent leadtime in placing the order. If the item should be ordered, the purchasing agent follows present procedures to place the order.
    Under the new system one extra copy of the purchase order, which goes to the computer department for keying, is prepared. The keyed document is entered into the system as the source of order information that appears on various inventory reports.

Transition
Because much of the data on the inventory master file will be developed over time, the system will not have sufficient data to begin recommending orders at first. Recommended purchase orders will be phased in gradually as the data become available. In the interim, purchasing agents will receive the customary notices from the warehouse based on a physical examination of the bin.
    As the computer file data develop, the system will begin to issue reorder reports. The warehouse will mark the bins of items now on computer order. Warning: During the transition be sure to check warehouse orders against reorder reports from the computer system in case the warehouse did not catch an item that is now on computer ordering. If such a situation is found, notify the warehouse to mark the bin to show that it is now the computer system that is reordering the item.

User training should also include consideration of the transitional effects, especially testing and conversion. These problems can be presented to the user group for help in developing a solution. In fact, it is best at first not to have a completely detailed plan formulated. After plans have been jointly developed for these stages, they can be documented as conversion procedures.

An example of a training document is shown in Table 18-3; this illustration applies to purchase order preparation as flowcharted in Figure 16-3*b*. The narrative of the procedure describes what is depicted in the flowchart. The documentation should also contain a copy of the proposed report and an explanation of what each field means and how it is derived, that is, what calculations are involved. For example, leadtime is the most recent time required for purchase in days. It is computed by subtracting the date on the purchase order copy that indicates an order has been placed from the date received stamped on

---

SYSTEMS PROBLEM 18-1

Betty Nash is a consultant with Markins, Haskhouse, and Roberts, a large firm of certified public accountants. She has been assigned to conduct an audit of the computer department at Monroe National Bank. One of the first tasks in the audit is to examine the documentation of the bank's computer systems.

The auditor is interested in documentation for a number of reasons. First, documentation makes it possible to provide backup for personnel. If a programmer or analyst leaves the bank, adequate documentation makes it much easier for a new employee to learn about the system and to operate or maintain it.

Documentation also makes it easier for the audit staff. The auditor will want to run some special programs to help in conducting the certified audit. If the system is well documented, the auditor can independently replicate the logic from the documentation and write a program to simulate the bank's program. If there is no documentation, the auditor must obtain the information from the programmer at the bank, removing some of the auditor's independence.

Betty is concerned by what documentation she has found at the bank. The only way to describe documentation on the questionnaire she is completing for the audit is "minimal." Basically the bank has program listings. There are no file record layouts, program descriptions, or logic specifications. Betty has found that bank turnover for the programming staff is running something like 35 percent a year and that maintenance of existing systems requires 80 percent of the systems programming effort.

What should Betty do? How can she convince the bank to remedy the situation? Is it serious enough to qualify the auditors' opinion on the financial statements—a very serious action?

---

another purchase order copy by the warehouse. A similar explanation should be given for each output field. The other major portion of the procedure in Table 13-2 deals with transition. During gradual implementation of the system, the reorder process will slowly evolve from the current manual procedures to a fully computerized approach. This section of the procedure deals with the change-over.

For input documents or reports on which there could be an error, we also include an example of what conditions cause the error, what actions are taken by the system, and what the user should do in response. The example of Table 18-3 is continued in Table 18-4, where we show the input procedures and errors from the edit along with what actions the user takes to correct the input on the next processing cycle. For input with batch totals we also have directions for the computer department control group on how to handle the error.

Training

If the procedures for systems design advocated in the previous chapters are used, training should be relatively easy. If the users designed the system and had a significant say in its development, they have reviewed all relevant parts of the

TABLE 18-4
AN INPUT EXAMPLE

ON-ORDER INPUT
Areas Affected
  Purchasing
  Computer department

Procedure
The on-order input is used to notify the system that an order has been placed. The input form is an extra copy (the eighth copy) of the purchase order which is sent to the computer department for keying. The input is verified, though no batch totals are run.

Errors
  Editing:
  1 Condition:
    (1) any alphabetic character (all fields are numeric)
    (2) item number-check digit error
  2 System action: input rejected by edit program
  3 User action: correct input and submit on next processing cycle
  Updating:
  1 Condition: on-order quantity deviates plus or minus 50 percent from economic order quantity
  2 System action: update master file and print warning message
  3 User action: check accuracy or desirability of quantity ordered; if wrong, correct through file maintenance procedure on the next updating cycle

system during development and should be well prepared for training. Following our approach, if there are new problems raised in training, the user group should solve them. Training should be coordinated by the user member of the design team or by knowledgeable users who are not on the team. Certainly, the computer department members of the design team should be available for reference, but it is probably best for users to work together and train each other.

OPERATIONS DOCUMENTATION

Purpose

The operations section of a computer department has to operate the system after it has been implemented. This group needs information on normal operating procedures and on how to respond to errors. This information is best prepared by the systems analyst and programmers, and much of it can be derived from the design documentation described earlier in this chapter.

Contents

The minimal contents of this documentation are shown in Table 18-5. First, we need a complete systems flowchart that shows the input required for each program, the files necessary, and the output that should be produced similar to

TABLE 18-5
COMPONENTS OF OPERATIONS DOCUMENTATION

Systems flowchart (identity of programs and their execution sequence)
List of programs to be run in order
For each program:
  Input required and format (e.g., header cards)
  Files required
  Processing narrative
  Output produced
  Error conditions, messages, and operator responses
  Machine components used
  Set-up requirements
Distribution and processing of output
Maintenance programmer responsible for system
User responsible for input
Normal cutoff date for input
Normal run cycle (e.g., Friday night)

Figure 16-2. This documentation should also include a list of programs to be run, including the input files, the output files, and the order in which programs should be run. Also, be sure to include scratch files, such as a tape or a disk used for temporary storage by the program (the data are not saved, but are "scratched" after use).

Detailed descriptions of each program should also be provided showing the input, its format, the medium (for example, card or tape), the files required, and the output to be expected. Where should the output go, and should the computer department do any manual processing, such as bursting the paper or removing the carbons from between copies? It is also very important to describe error conditions and operator procedures; for example, is a program checkpointed at some place? The name of the user representative and the normal cutoff time for processing should be included. It is mandatory to list the name of the programmer responsible for the system so that the operator can get in touch with him or her if a major problem develops that the operator cannot solve.

USER REFERENCE DOCUMENTATION

Purpose

The last type of documentation that should be developed is for user reference after the system has become operational. This information should be referred to by the user who has a question or a problem before contacting the computer department. If this documentation is of sufficient quality, the question can be answered without having to contact the computer department, which will serve to reduce conflict between users and the computer staff. There is a tremendous amount of frustration when something goes wrong with an information system and the user does not understand why it has problems or how to fix it.

Contents

Fortunately, most of this material can be taken directly from other documentation, for example, from the procedures parts of the training documents in Table
18-3. This documentation should be assembled into a reference manual like a
loose-leaf binder that can be updated easily as the system evolves and changes
over time. Table 18-6 shows the minimal contents of such a manual. A detailed
table of contents is necessary to make this documentation easy to use as a
reference. Detailed discussions of the input, output, and processing logic should
be available. One of the most important components in this documentation is a
list of error conditions and fix-ups (how to correct the error) such as that in Table
18-4. Also, it is helpful to include the names of the most knowledgeable user and
the maintenence programmer who is now in charge of the system.

A more detailed version of the training manual concerning processing logic is
shown in Table 18-7. The idea of this user documentation is to anticipate and
answer all user questions on input, processing errors, and output. For example,
where do output fields originate? Certainly, sample versions of input and output
documents should be included with the contents of the files. This information
should describe also how the systems design team envisions the data being used.
What types of decisions are supported by the information? (For an extremely good
example of the user reference manual, see Nie et al.,1975.)

Help

Many on-line systems are designed with "help" functions. When the user does
not understand what to do, he or she types "help" or "?" and the program
branches to a help routine. These routines can be thought of as a tree; the user
sees one level and then asks for further details, and more explanation is
presented. After the user has solved the problem, the system returns to where help
was requested and resumes processing.

In addition to freeing the user from the need to access bulky documents, an
interactive help facility serves as a training device; the user is learning more about

TABLE 18-6
COMPONENTS OF USER REFERENCE
DOCUMENTATION

Table of contents
Input documents
Output reports
Processing logic
Error condition
Manual procedures
Program and maintenance staff
User representative

TABLE 18-7
EXAMPLE OF PROCESSING LOGIC SECTION OF USER REFERENCE DOCUMENTATION

ECONOMIC ORDER QUANTITY AND REORDER CALCULATION

Economic Order Quantity

On the reorder report a recommended order quantity and reorder point are printed.. If the current balance drops below the reorder point and nothing is on order, the item is printed on the reorder report.

When a new item is first added to the file or when enough are available, the economic order quantity and reorder point are calculated. Alternatively, if there are no data (for example, on usage), a manual file change may be made to input a reorder point.

In the case where data are present, how is the calculation made? The economic order calculation is based on a simple formula that balances the cost of holding an item against the cost of holding an item against the cost of ordering. The economic order quantity is given by $\sqrt{2RS/Ci}$

where R = the demand during the year (in our system it is the past year's usage)
S = the cost of ordering
i = the inventory-carrying cost, for example, 10 percent cost of capital, space, and insurance
C = the cost of the item

What does this formula mean? It says that if the demand is high and/or the cost or ordering is high, we should order more at a time, reducing the total number of orders placed (this is indicated by the 2RS term in the numerator). On the other hand, if the item is costly and we spend a lot to keep it in inventory, we should order fewer at a time even if it means placing more orders (Ci term in the denominator).

Reorder Point

The economic order quantity tells us how much to order, but we also need to know when to order it. The basic inventory graph is shown in Figure 18-1. Here we do not allow for safety stock; we plan to have an ending inventory of exactly 0 just as the new shipment arrives.

Because of uneven usage, we do not know exactly how much will be used before our reorder arrives. The reorder point is based on the cost of a stockout and on how much we expect to use of the item during the leadtime from placing an order to receipt of the merchandise.

The computation for the reorder point proceeds as follows: first, to get expected usage, we take last month's usage per day and multiply it times the leadtime. (The time the order was placed to the time received for the most recent order.) This calculation gives an expected usage during the leadtime. Then we multiply that by a safety factor (say 110 percent) to get the reorder point. We can change the safety percentage figure as we gain experience to adjust the stockout level.

FIGURE 18-1
Inventory cycle.

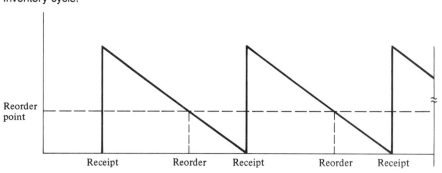

This approach to setting the reorder point is not mathematically optimal, but given our data, it should work well. Since we can change the safety factor if we have too many stockouts, we feel this rule of thumb is adequate.

Numerical Example
Consider the following example:
Usage during the year equals 300 units
Cost of ordering equals $75
Inventory cost equals 10 percent
Cost of item, $400
Usage per day last month equals 2
Leadtime for last order, 5 days
The economic order quantity equals: $\sqrt{[2(300)(75)]/[.10(400)]}$ — 34 units
We plan on ordering about 300/34 — 9 times a year.

We can obtain the item in about 5 days. Last month we used 2 per day on the average, so we expect to use 5 × 2 or 10 during the leadtime. Our reorder point would be 1.10 × 10 or 11 units.

SYSTEMS PROBLEM 18-2

Peter Columbo put down the phone after listening to a complaint by a user of the new order entry system at True Lock Company. True Lock is one of the largest manufacturers of locks for doors, windows, and other fasteners in the United States, and Peter is the vice president of administration. The user did not understand how to use the system, and apparently there was no documentation to help.

Peter was impressed with the quality of the new system and how easy it was to use. He noted that there is a "help" command that the user can enter to obtain documentation on-line. However, the user on the phone did not know enough even to ask for help. He felt that some kind of manual should be furnished with each terminal so that the novice user could work with the system.

Peter admitted that the user had a good point; a system, no matter how well designed, could be formidable, particularly for the inexperienced user. Peter also wondered how to arrange for the documentation. He knew that the systems and programming staff was spread very thin. The new system had taken almost all their resources, and now as a high priority they were extending on-line input to the warehouse so that accurate inventory records could be maintained. Not only was the staff busy, but Peter wondered if they really were the best people to prepare user documenta-tion. The typical programmer and analyst at True Lock liked to do computer work, but Peter had often heard disparaging comments about documentation and the need to prepare it.

One of Peter's friends at another company related an experiment they were trying. Instead of using the computer staff for user documentation, this firm had hired a group of English majors and given them the responsibility for preparing user documentation. Since they know little about computers, the English majors insisted that they understand the system and be able to explain it clearly.

What are the pros and cons of such a strategy? Would you recommend it to True Lock?

---

the system while actually using it. As an example, it is possible to learn how to use some of the electronic spreadsheet programs for personal computers through the help feature and a summary card that lists each command.

We expect to see much greater use of help facilities in future software. This approach offers many advantages and is far more appealing than large manuals. The manuals are necessary for very detailed problems, but the vast majority of questions can be answered on-line.

Learning from Packages

Some of the best documentation of any type available today comes with packages, especially for personal computers. Because the market is so large and since users are not expected to necessarily be computer experts, firms developing personal computer packages must provide an easy user interface and a package that can be used without training.

For good ideas on how one might create user documentation for both training and reference, consult the popular software manuals for personal computer packages. Some of the simple word-processing systems can almost be used without a manual; the command menu is simple enough that most questions can be answered by experimentation rather than reference to the manual. The electronic spreadsheet packages also have good on-line interaction and reference documentation.

Packages such as these can provide ideas on how to document and on the possible format for documentation. As we expect users to take more responsibility for the design and use of information systems, it is important to provide them with as much help as possible. Although not terribly exciting, documentation does make a substantial difference in ease of use and in reducing frustration for users.

KEY WORDS

Archival documentation	Identifier names
Comments	Operations documentation
Cross-reference lists	Reference documentation
Design documentation	Systems library
Flowcharts	Training documentation
Hierarchical documentation	

RECOMMENDED READINGS

Lotus 1-2-3 instruction manual and computer-based tutorial.
Nie, N. D. Bent, and H. Hull: *Statistical Package for the Social Sciences*, 2d ed., McGraw-Hill, New York, 1975. (This book is an outstanding example of user documentation for a statistical applications package.)

DISCUSSION QUESTIONS

1 What are the advantages of using common identifier names for variables throughout a computer system? Why should descriptive names be used?
2 Design the format for operator documentation for an organization.
3 Design the user documentation for the purchasing agent at Hardserve.
4 How does good documentation serve to reduce user conflict with the computer department staff?
5 Why is documentation generally the weakest part of a systems design?
6 How does the presence of a systems librarian aid documentation?
7 What can be done to facilitate and encourage documentation besides employing a systems librarian? Are there any mechanical tools that will encourage documentation?
8 Design a set of standards for documenting programs within the code itself. That is, consider where comments should appear, what program statements should be indented, etc.
9 Who should write the documentation for each different part of the Hardserve system?
10 What is the role of documentation after a system has been implemented successfully?
11 If the design team at Hardserve is worried that a single safety factor (the 110 percent) cannot be applied to all items, how would they have to change the files and input to remedy this problem? How can they tell if there is a problem?
12 What role does documentation play in subsequent changes to a program or system?
13 How should program changes be controlled? Is it necessary to have more than one person agree on the change? Why or why not?
14 The documentation outlines suggested in this chapter will result in a large amount of information on the system. How can this material be made easily accessible? Where should the systems library for this application be stored? Are backup copies necessary, and if so, where should they be kept?
15 Would the presence of industrywide standards for documentation facilitate or hinder the development of information systems? What factors mitigate against the development of industry standards?
16 What is the purpose of a cross-reference list for program variables (cross-referencing variable names to program lines)? How is this list used in writing and modifying a program?
17 Why should test results be kept as a part of the documentation of an information system?
18 Why do users need to have documentation on the data files?
19 How can the computer operator use documentation to determine if an error has occurred because of a programming problem, a data problem, or a malfunction of the computer itself?
20 How do the structured design approaches discussed in Chapter 7 contribute to the documentation effort?
21 Design a system for providing user documentation at a terminal as a part of an on-line system.
22 Is there less or more need for documentation for users with an on-line system compared with batch processing?
23 What kind of documentation would you expect for a package program?
24 Why should management be willing to devote resources to documentation?
25 What documentation problems does a multinational company face?

CHAPTER 19

TESTING AND INSTALLATION

The final stages in the development of a computer system include testing and installation. Heavy user involvement is mandatory to facilitate cooperation in the operation of a new system. The entire design team continues to work together to ensure a successful implementation.

TESTING

Testing includes verification of the basic logic of each program and verification that the entire system works properly. In all program testing, we cannot be exhaustive, because there are a combinatorial number of paths in a program. Testing individual programs involves an attempt to be sure that the most likely paths work properly. As mentioned in Chapter 18, the systems librarian should keep test results for reference purposes. Programmers facilitate testing by coding as clearly as possible. With the old tests available and with clear coding, we are prepared for debugging and the changes that will be requested by users. However, we should remember the saying that "no program is ever fully debugged" and plan our systems so that errors are easy to find and correct.

An experiment by Myers (1978) provided some rather discouraging statistics on our ability to debug programs. Myers found a PL/1 program for text formatting and intentionally introduced errors. The program consisted of 3 procedures and 63 statements; 15 known errors were included. The subjects in the experiment were experienced programmers with 7 to 20 years in the computing field (though some of the individuals were currently not practicing programmers). They used three methods to debug the program.

The results showed tremendous amounts of variability in individual results and in the actual errors detected. Some individuals detected only a single error, and a number of the 15 errors were hardly ever detected. Myers felt that the inability to detect some of the most obvious errors was alarming. None of the three methods used alone was very satisfactory, since each detected only about a third of the errors in the simple PL/1 program.

Myers then used the experimental results to simulate other possible experimental treatments involving independent program testing. The conclusion from this analysis was that the most cost-effective way to test a program is to employ two independent program testers. The evidence also suggested that working through a terminal with a copy of the program would be the favored approach for each of the independent testers.

A walkthrough inspection technique, where programmers review a program as a group, was costly and seemed to be no more effective than independent testers working together. One observation made during the experiment suggested that the inspections focused too much attention on the logic of the program at the expense of the input and output of data. (It should also be noted that the experiment included only walkthroughs concerned with programs, not the logic of a system.)

This discouraging experiment on the ability of professional programmers to find program errors is consistent with many of the reports in the field of poor systems and instances of program failure. Although the systems analyst is not usually responsible for programming, the fate of the system depends on accurate and reliable coding. Therefore, the analyst must work with programming management to be certain that adequate testing is done and that the software will be reliable. What is the best way to develop reliable software? There is no single answer, but experiments such as those above offer some guidelines.

A number of researchers in the computer science field are working to develop techniques for proving programs. However, at this time the proofs are extremely tedious and time-consuming to construct, even for a simple program. Also, it is very easy to have errors in the proofs! It will be a long time, if ever, before applications programs are proved to be mathematically correct.

Myers' results support a recommendation by Thayer and Hinton (1975) of independent test and analysis. Thayer and Hinton are in the military environment and advocate the use of a separate contractor from the group responsible for constructing the software for validation purposes. Myers' results argue for the use of independent programmers for testing. In each case, we recommend that at least one person beyond the programmer constructing the program be involved in testing it.

If the project team is following a team approach to programming, input from other programmers will naturally help identify missing logic. The backup programmer can also generate test data for other programmers. An independent tester should attempt to find pathological cases that cause different modules to fail.

Programming management can help by providing automated tools for debugging. A number of proprietary systems are available to generate test data

SYSTEMS PROBLEM 19-1

Steve Williamson has been in the computer field for 20 years; he began writing assembly language programs and then learned COBOL. He is now a manager of programming for his employer. Recently he attended a conference on the problems of testing and debugging programs.

Speakers at the conference discussed structured programming, top-down design, structured walkthroughs, and other approaches that have been developed in the emerging field of software engineering. Steven, although skeptical at first, began to feel that some of these approaches might have merit when he thought about his own experiences programming.

He was particularly impressed with the idea of putting more emphasis on the design effort and less into programming. Also, he felt that developing smaller modules would have to make programming easier and reduce testing. (Why should this be so?) Since the group of programmers reporting to him had a good collegial relationship, Steve felt that the idea of a structured walkthrough would work well. His main concern, however, is how to implement these changes.

He asked several of the speakers how to get programmers who were used to working in different ways to accept these new approaches. None of the speakers was very helpful, so Steve felt he had to solve the problem for himself. One thought that occurred to him was to use a phased implementation. He would introduce one technique and see that it was working well before trying something else.

Steve's main worry was how to motivate the programming staff to change their behavior. What approaches can you recommend to help implement these techniques? How do they contribute to testing?

---

automatically. Often, debugging versions of compilers are also available, which facilitate traces of program logic and the inclusion of special debugging information. The objective of testing is to see that every part of the program is executed at least once, including paths that emanate from conditional branches. It is often a path from such a conditional branch, never tested during debugging, that causes an error when the production program follows the path.

Finally, as discussed in Chapter 11 we can substitute applications generators and nonprocedural languages for languages like COBOL. By working at a higher level, errors should be easier to find and the time spent debugging should be reduced. These higher-level languages are also easier to change so that we do not run the same kind of risks as with languages like COBOL when it is necessary to make revisions. Often, in conventional languages an error that is fixed in one part of a program causes an unintentional error to be introduced into another part of the program.

We also can use applications packages to reduce testing and debugging time. The parts of the package that have been programmed by the vendor and used in other installations should be reasonably well debugged, at least better than new code that we are writing and using for the first time ourselves. Of course, modifications that we or the vendor make for us are likely to be like other new code. Also, because our staff has not written the package in the first place, modifications to it can introduce errors. For these reasons, we want to find packages that require minimal revision. When it is necessary to make changes, we or the vendor should try to keep the modifications to clearly marked modules. It is vitally important to document changes so that when the vendor develops new, improved versions of the package we can install them with our unique changes in place.

Unit Testing

All during the system design activity, basic program modules are tested by the individual programmers who wrote them. At this stage, programmers usually make up their own test data or use a program that generates test data. When one follows top-down programming approaches, it is not necessary to build "driver programs" to test lower-level modules. With top-down programming, use dummy module calls for uncoded lower-level programs.

Unit testing with programmer data is necessary, of course, but it is not sufficient. Although it is important to know if the logic included in a program works properly, we are also concerned about conditions that the programmer did not include in the program. The egoless programmer and team approach help here, since there will be input from other programmers who might think of missing logic. The structured review sessions also point out omissions.

Combined Module Testing

As modules pass unit tests, they are combined for testing. Here, top-down programming helps, since errors frequently occur in calling sequences (for example, the order and values for dummy arguments in a subroutine). Program-ming lower-level modules first creates major changes when the higher-level routines are developed and an omission in a lower-level module is recognized. Careful specification of the interface avoids problems.

At this point of combined module testing, we again stress independent test-data generation. It is important to include users in developing test data, because the data will be less contrived and more realistic. In one instance, management offered a prize to the user who designed the best error-detection scheme and the best processing logic for his or her department's processing. The idea was to create input data that would cause another department's processing logic to fail (Lucas, 1974). This game resulted in the development of realistic test data to run against programs developed in each user area.

Prototyping and Simulation

In addition to a parallel test of the entire system discussed later in the chapter, various aspects of the design can be tested through prototyping. A prototype is a model of the logic being proposed. A good example would be the testing conducted on a forecasting routine. We would run the forecast with past data and compare it with what actually occurred. If the results of the prototype are acceptable, the prototype's logic is incorporated into the final system.

Since information systems often feature subsystems or modules using logic never applied in the organization through a computer before, small-scale prototypes and simulations can be extremely important. They help prove that a design concept can work, and they ease the anxieties of users (and the design team) over whether a feature of the system is likely to work properly.

Testing Manual Procedures

The testing described above is concerned with programs themselves. Another major activity that occurs simultaneously with the development of programs is the design and testing of manual procedures. Manual procedures are sometimes overlooked, but they can determine the success of a system.

In one case, an airline developed an automatic seat assignment option as a part of its on-line computer reservations system. This on-line, CRT-based system replaced the old approach of using cardboard cutouts of the seats placed on an outline of the plane's body. The new system was implemented at a peak holiday travel season; at one San Francisco gate, it featured a spotlight on the CRT screen at the check-in counter. This lighting effect made it difficult to read the CRT. In addition, the device was positioned so that the agent operating the console could not stand straight; he had to bend over slightly. Long lines formed while a nontypist agent tried to assign seats and enter passenger names using the terminal. The old approach of tearing off the seat stub from the cutout and handing it to the passenger was several times faster.

What happened in this example? The airline spent millions of dollars on a computer system and obviously spent no time testing manual procedures. A very simple queuing model could have been employed or even a small timesharing computer simulation used to test the manual operations. In fact, the airline might even have programmed a simple version of the system on a timesharing computer and had airline employees or passengers simulate the boarding process.

Where there are major changes in existing manual procedures, pilot testing is essential, especially when a terminal is used or the system interfaces directly with a customer. It is relatively easy to simulate parts of a system by developing a few input forms and having users work with these forms. It is also important to design pilot tests so that they are real experiments. One company conducted a pilot test but had the entire computer department present in the small user department to answer questions and help with the test. Because of all the attention and extra help, the experiment succeeded; it really could not have failed! However, when the system was introduced into the whole manufacturing plant, it was a total disaster. The experiment was not a fair test and was not representative of what would occur during actual operations.

After the computer department is satisfied that the system is working well, there need to be user acceptance tests. It is very important for users to specify the data for such tests; it is also critical to use data that are out of the ordinary to test the editing and error-checking features of the system. Finally, one should test for sensitivity to volume. Can an on-line system handle all the transactions expected during peak processing?

In one insurance company, a new on-line input system was installed to provide data for the rating bureau. This bureau accepts data from a group of companies and then computes risk factors based on their claims histories. The firm in question was behind and installed the system after checking to see that the edits worked, but without checking to see what the impact of a high volume of transactions would be on the system. Because the new edits were so stringent, most of the transactions were rejected, and hundreds of thousands were placed in a suspense category.

As a result, there were no financial statements, and a team of auditors had to be formed. Their job was to investigate why all the poor input was being prepared in the first place and then to suggest improvements. The systems study should have determined that input was not adequate; failing here, the acceptance tests at a high volume using old transactions should have demonstrated that the firm was not ready for such careful editing yet.

Cutover and Parallel Testing

In many cases, it is possible to run parallel tests during conversion, that is, to convert to the new system but continue the old method of processing in parallel. The results from the two systems are compared as a further check on the new system before the old approach is discontinued. Parallel tests offer many advantages, but they place a heavy burden on the user to keep two systems operating. A parallel test is realistic only for a short period of time.

In any conversion, we should attempt a gradual transition to the new system. For example, it may be possible to phase a system in by department, geographic region, or on some other basis. A great deal is learned from the first unit implemented that can be used to prepare for the next portion of the cutover. Full-scale cutover of an entire system at one time runs a high risk of disaster.

USER CONSIDERATIONS

In the above sections we have covered some of the technical aspects of installation. What is the impact of the system on users? The ultimate success of a system depends on whether or not it is used.

Impact

Chapters 1 and 4 discussed some of the impacts of computer systems, both those expected and recorded. We focused on three levels of change. The first was changes to organizational structure primarily through transfers of power among departments. The second change we considered was to work groups; information systems may affect long-standing social relationships. Finally, we examined the impact on individuals; each person may have a different reaction to a computer system depending on personal and situational factors.

A Change Program

We can take several actions to channel the personal energy of users toward constructive use of the system and successful implementation. First, it is important to plan carefully for training. Manual procedures should be defined and pilot-tested as described above. The more users involved in the design and testing of the system the better, because this involvement serves as a training investment. Very exacting documentation is also needed (we described user documentation in detail in Chapter 18).

Before completing a detailed design of the system, consider the type of impact the system may have and include it as a design variable. First, predict the impact of a system on the organization. What dependencies are created between the user department and the computer department by this new system? Will power be redistributed drastically among departments? Can simple changes be made in processing to reduce the impact of the system on departments?

SYSTEMS PROBLEM 19-2

Mason, Bosworth, and Clancy, a major advertising firm, is in the process of developing a new computer-based system to help account managers select advertising media. As a part of the computer system, elaborate models have been developed by the management sciences department at the advertising agency.

The president of the firm, Ted Mason, was disturbed by something he heard from a competitor at a recent meeting. The other firm had attempted to develop a similar system, which had been very costly, only to find that no one in the company would use it when the system was finally installed. Ted tried to find out more, but all his friend could say was that evidently people just didn't like to change their ways.

Ted felt that there had to be something more to the problem than that, but he was not sure what it could be. He called together the staff working on the project to find out how they planned to install the system. He was worried when he found that little thought had been given to the implementation process itself in the pressure to get this rather advanced system up and running.

Ted immediately announced a slowdown in the installation schedule and asked the project leader, Mary Rinehardt, either to take someone from the team or hire a new person to think about the question of implementation. He suggested that this person should have some background in the social sciences.

What advice would you give the individual assigned to prepare for implementation? Develop an action plan to be used to help ensure that this system is installed and used at Mason, Bosworth, and Clancy. What are the most serious likely problems? What can be done to prepare for them?

The same concern should be given to the impact of the system on work groups and individuals. Are work groups being altered needlessly by the system? Is there some way that procedures can be modified without affecting the social system? We should also predict how individual workers will react and what their motivation will be to use the system (Mumford and Ward, 1968). Consider our earlier model of complex man and plan implementation accordingly.

Participation

All our previous comments on participation apply doubly when it comes to the final installation of the system. A major goal of our careful, time-consuming involvement of users has been to ease the way for this final stage. Let us review once again the reasons for participation.

First, participation helps the user retain some control over processing; it means less power is transferred to the computer department. If the user has helped design the procedures for a system, he or she should understand them better and be prepared to use the system. Participation can create commitment to change. If an individual or work group has invested some of itself in a new system, the system's success provides ego rewards. If individuals and work groups participate, they make changes consistent with their own social systems. Participation also creates familiarity with the system and contributes to training. Users are better prepared for the actual implementation. Because of participation, more salient features are included in a new system, and it should provide more benefits for users.

Our conception of the role of the systems analyst described in Chapter 6 applies to all aspects of the systems development process. Users can and should be the designers of their systems. The systems analyst and the computer department act as a resource to guide the design team and manage the more technical parts of the design effort.

THE AFTERMATH

Changes

At some point nearing the cutover, it is necessary to freeze the system temporarily as far as changes are concerned. During this critical period all resources have to be devoted to implementation. However, the freeze in changes should be clearly specified as temporary in nature. Changes that are suggested are held in abeyance until implementation has been completed.

If the systems are to serve users, we must expect continuing requests for changes. In fact, a responsive computer department will look for useful changes and suggest them to the users. The fact that users are heavily involved with the design should reduce the number of modifications, but important requests for alteration will be made as users gain experience with the system. Another reason for structured programming and good documentation is to facilitate these changes. A system is literally never completed if it is successful and is being used.

Postimplementation Audits

After the system appears to be working smoothly, it is time to examine what was accomplished and the resources that were required. Now is the time to talk with users and see how they have reacted to the system. What could be done better next time? Were the tangible savings that were forecasted achieved? How do users evaluate the intangible benefits? Do users see this as an effective system? Did it achieve its goals?

We should also look at the original estimates and determine if they were achieved. The accuracy of forecasts and the experience for this system provide the data from which to make future estimates. These data reflect what can be done with this design team and this organization. They are the best source of information available for estimating the requirements for the next system for this team and this organization.

REVIEW OF THE ANALYST'S ROLE

A short review of the role of the systems analyst seems appropriate now that we are at the end of the portion of the text devoted to systems analysis and design. Listed below are some of the basic activities undertaken by the analyst:

1 Work with users to identify the basic needs for a new information processing system and prepare a preliminary survey. Consider both the task of systems analysis and design and the relationship between designers and users.

2 Develop a thorough understanding of present information processing procedures through a study of decisions and information flows; data collection techniques include the study of documents, interviews, and questionnaires.

3 Prepare a feasibility study in conjunction with users, delineating different alternatives for a new information system.

4 During the above stages, teach users about information systems.

5 Help users design a system for the chosen alternative.

6 Convert file contents and systems logic into detailed file structures and programming specifications.

7 Work with users to develop the types of documentation described in Chapter 18.

8 Participate in the technical management of the project, especially program and system testing.

9 With users, prepare an installation plan for the new system.

10 Guide and participate in the actual conversion to the new system.

11 Conduct a postimplementation audit with users.

Even a casual perusal of this list suggests that a systems analyst faces a creative, varied, and demanding set of tasks.

THE HARDSERVE EXAMPLE

Hardserve design and programming teams have been hard at work. The backup programmer helped generate data for unit tests. Users and user members of the design team have been organized to work on testing the manual procedures. Dummy forms have been developed and used to test the input. Users also volunteered to develop test data to validate the input processing routines.

Programmers have held sessions to review their program modules and have participated in reviews of manual procedures. The user design team members also met with user department members to present problems. Each user department was asked to develop an implementation plan. The steering committee went over each department's plan with the design team, and members of the committee met with their departments to review the plan.

The major conversion effort necessary was to generate a master file for the first time. Raw inventory data will be prepared by purchasing, the warehouse, and order processing, with help from the accounting department. Much of the data will be omitted from the file at first. These data can be developed as the system operates. For example, different vendor numbers will be added over a period of time. The conversion effort will concentrate on getting item identification numbers, units, description, and the physical balance on hand into the file. Data on the economic order quantity, the reorder point, and cost will appear on the file gradually. At first, the warehouse will continue to send manual reorder notices to purchasing. On-order information will be sent for computer processing, and this function will gradually add the cost information and vendor data to the file. Usage and arrivals also will be entered to develop a usage history. With time, different balance data will be developed in this fashion. As the master file becomes complete, the computer system will begin printing reorder notices. A notice—that is, an extra report copy—will be sent to the warehouse so that the bin can be marked as now being on the computer system. No more warehouse reorder notices for this item will be sent to purchasing.

The preparation of the special report retrieval program has been deferred until after file conversion. There will be no relevant data for reporting for at least 6 months to a year when the file is complete. As a result of careful planning, the system implementation effort is already ahead of schedule. Users appear enthusiastic about the new system, and there is a high level of understanding of its capabilities and limitations.

KEY WORDS

Changes	Parallel testing
Combined module testing	Participation
Cutover	Postimplementation audit
Independent test data	Unit testing

RECOMMENDED READINGS

Mumford, E., and D. Henshall: *A Participative Approach to Computer Systems Design,* Associated Business Press, London, 1979. (An excellent case study of user design.)

Myers, G.: "A Controlled Experiment in Program Testing and Code Walkthroughs/ Inspections," *Communications of The ACM,* vol. 21, no. 9, September 1978, pp. 760–768. (This paper describes an experiment to evaluate testing.)

DISCUSSION QUESTIONS

1. What are the reasons for user participation in testing a system and planning implementation?
2. What issues should be examined in the postimplementation audit?
3. Who should conduct the postimplementation audit, and what should be done with the results?
4. Are there any aspects of the Hardserve system needing experimentation to test planned processing procedures before implementation? What kind of experiment would you conduct?
5. If the design team at Hardserve is worried about excessive stockouts, what could they do to test the economic order quantity and reorder logic in the system?
6. What kinds of test data will Hardserve need to check out the system?
7. Can Hardserve run a parallel test before implementing the system? Why or why not is such a test necessary?
8. Who should accept a system, that is, who is responsible for indicating the system is working properly and can be considered implemented?
9. Describe different approaches to the gradual implementation of (1) a batch computer system, and (2) an on-line system.
10. What are the problems and disadvantages of parallel testing?
11. How does the approach to systems design presented in this book facilitate training and conversion activities?
12. After conversion, are the responsibilities of the design team ended? If not, what other tasks should they attempt to accomplish?
13. At some stage, a newly implemented system is defined as "operational" and responsibility for it usually shifts to a maintenance programming group. How can we determine at what point the system is operational?
14. Why is it unwise for programmers to design all their own test data?
15. Do conversion programs need to be documented carefully? Why or why not?
16. What action should a design team take if it suspects sabotage or user resistance for some aspect of a new system? Of what is such resistance a sign?
17. Why is it unwise to make a major change in the organization (such as a departmental restructuring) concomitantly with the implementation of a new information system?
18. How does the design approach we have advocated prepare for installation?
19. Is user participation in design sufficient to guarantee successful implementation?
20. How can training be approached for a system that will affect hundreds of individuals?
21. Are there any mechanical or automated approaches to training that can ease the problems of preparing a large number of people to use a system?
22. What can be done to identify the people most likely to resist a new system?
23. What approaches are there to overcoming the resistance to change?
24. What are the benefits of having users design test data from an implementation standpoint?
25. Why is it difficult to test every path in a program module?

CHAPTER 20

HARDSERVE ON-LINE

A NEW VERSION

A little more than a year after the Hardserve system was installed, the system was working smoothly except in one or two areas. We join Terry Carson as he is chatting with several other employees at lunch.

"They did it again! How can we operate a business when we aren't able to check in goods? We can buy the merchandise, but if it never hits the warehouse, what good is it?" fumed Dick Hansen, vice president of purchasing for Hardserve.

"Hold on, Dick," said Paul Jones, warehouse supervisor. "We occasionally make mistakes, but we move a lot of goods through that warehouse every day. What happened now?"

"I'll tell you what," said Bob Moss, vice president of operations. "We failed to fill customer orders for 500 snow shovels because they sat on the receiving dock for 2 days while people looked off and on for the receiving copies of the purchase order so they could be checked in. I suppose we're lucky no one refused the shipment because they couldn't find the paperwork. Terry, I thought this new inventory control system would solve our problems. Instead we seem to be having more and more trouble checking in receivings."

"Wait a minute, Bob," responded Terry. "We never claimed this system would solve all our problems. Given what it was supposed to do, it's working pretty well. Remember, we made almost no changes in the warehouse."

"We certainly didn't," complained Bob Moss, "and now we are drowning in paper. Our volume has almost doubled and we have a horrible time checking in shipments. My staff always finds a way to misfile the purchase orders, so that we waste a lot of time when the truck arrives with the merchandise. The shovels are only one example. I know we didn't want to do anything to change the procedures, but we need help now."

A few days later, Terry Carson sought out Tom Roberts for a meeting. "Tom," Terry began, "I think we may have blown it with this inventory system. We were too conservative in our estimates of volumes and our fears of change."

"How can you say that, Terry? The system was installed easily, and it's working, isn't it?"

"Yes, it is, but I guess we should have included some more features." Terry related his luncheon conversation and his own fears about the ability of Hardserve to keep up.

"Is there a solution to the warehouse problem?" Terry asked.

"Yes, there is, an on-line system. Remember, we decided not to go that route because of the costs and the inexperience here with computers. I'm not sure we would make that same decision today if we were starting again."

"Why not?" asked Terry.

"The computer industry has changed in the last few years. On-line systems used to be considered only when there was a real need for coordinated access to a set of files, like the reservations systems. Now, we can easily justify an on-line system for ease of input and response to queries. In addition, the cost of on-line systems has dropped dramatically as the hardware and software have advanced."

Terry asked, "Why don't we modify our current system and go on-line? Then we could solve all these problems. Maybe we could even include some of purchasing, which we had to leave out of the current version of the system."

"It sounds good, Terry, but there's a lot to it, even though I said it was simpler now than a few years ago."

"What's more complicated?"

"Well, we could simply put a few inquiry terminals around. We have direct-access files, so it would be easy to have inquiry on inventory contents. But, we have no file of purchase orders and that's what they need to access in the Warehouse when receivings arrive."

"Is that the only problem?" asked Terry. "If so, we can just add to the system."

"We could," said Tom, "but let me work out a little presentation for you on what might be possible and the various alternatives. A little bit of a preliminary survey, if you will."

ALTERNATIVES

A few weeks later, Terry convened a small group of interested staff members to hear some of Tom Robert's ideas on a possible on-line system. Tom distributed copies of a document that he used as a basis for the discussion (see Table 20-1). "As you can see," he said, "we have a few choices as to how we can go on this one. We have learned a lot with the batch system, and it is working pretty well, given the large increase in volumes. Let's look at the first alternative. Here we would just put a terminal in the warehouse for receivings."

"How fast could we do that?" asked Paul Jones.

TABLE 20-1
LOGICAL ON-LINE SYSTEMS ALTERNATIVES

Features	Changes	Advantages	Disadvantages
Inquiry from warehouse	Add purchase order file keyed on vendor number, PO number, item number. Add terminals in warehouse and purchasing (?)	Simplest alternative and least cost	Does not help input of data; only solves warehouse receiving problem
Warehouse inquiry and on-line data collection	Same as above plus edit data on input and put on batch file for overnight update	Extend on-line system to input; ensure more accurate data entry	Files are not up-to-date on receivings or orders
Fully on-line; terminals for inputting purchase order, customer orders, receipts of merchandise	Same as above plus restructuring of all programs to operate on-line	Complete up-to-the-minute information; fewer incorrect stockouts, better control and service	Cost, need for major systems redesign

Terry responded, "I asked the same thing. It wouldn't take more than a few months if we were willing to use the computer at Manhold."

"From a simple inquiry," Tom continued, "we could go to on-line data collection. This means that we could do a lot of the data editing as the data are entered. We would probably not key the data twice the way we verify now but instead would enter it once with a lot of error checking going on. The data would be placed on a file, and the master files would be updated overnight.

"Our last possibility is to go completely on-line. Now all the files would be up to date all the time. Purchase orders would be noted, the book inventory updated with withdrawals as soon as an order was prepared for picking, and receivings updated as soon as the goods enter the warehouse."

"Wow!" exclaimed Bob Moss. "That would be terrific! Why didn't we do that in the first place?"

"A few years ago when we started," Tom explained, "it might have been too costly for such a system. In addition, you didn't really have any computer experience, and we were afraid to try too much. Today we might start differently because it is a lot easier to develop an on-line system."

"I really like this idea," Moss went on. "Where do we go from here?"

"Well," Terry replied, we should probably do a study of the costs of doing each of these systems and then bring together the steering committee to make a decision."

Several people began to talk at once. Paul Jones tried to summarize.

TABLE 20-2
PHYSICAL ON-LINE SYSTEMS ALTERNATIVES

Alternative	Headquarters	Programming	Discussion
Current central computer	Print reports for headquarters	Use software package for on-line systems	Least reprogramming; most expensive communications costs
Distributed processing (computer at Hardserve)	Transmit reports to headquarters	Redo most of applications programs	Reduce communications costs; only terminals are local
Decentralized local computer at Hardserve	Mail reports to headquarters	Redo most of applications programs	Can reporting needs be met this way?

"Look, I think everyone here agrees that we ought to go for the on-line system. Can't we just study it and then see if there is some way to justify it? Why do we have to spend time and money studying alternatives that we consider inferior?"

Terry and Tom agreed to sound out the members of the steering committee, and especially Jim Green, the president of Hardserve, to see if he would agree.

Physical Alternatives

With substantial agreement within the firm, Tom Roberts and Terry Carson began to look at processing alternatives. They developed the chart shown in Table 20-2 to present to the steering committee. Even without doing detailed estimates of communications costs, they saw that it would be too expensive to use the central Manhold computer, since no one in Manhold needed access on-line to the Hardserve files, and only batch reports were to be supplied to headquarters.

The steering committee quickly chose the second alternative of a local computer at Hardserve. They thought it would be desirable for design, and they liked its capability to transmit data to headquarters.

Terry Carson asked Tom Roberts what programming would be needed.

"We must look at different physical computer systems for Hardserve while we are in the process of the logical redesign of the system," Tom said.

"What do you mean, 'the logical redesign of the system'? Can't the programming staff just convert?"

"We can do some things, but there is a big difference between an on-line application and the equivalent batch processing version. Now, we must design input screens for all input data and all the inquiries. There are a large number of alternatives here and users will have to help. We don't want to do the entire design of something as personal as input screens for the users."

"Can't we use many of the same programs?" asked Terry.

"We can use some of the logic," Tom said, "But there's a lot of reprogramming. Let me try to explain. In a batch system we have programs that run

---

SYSTEMS PROBLEM 20-1

Eatout is a chain of fast-food restaurants in the South. The firm has grown rapidly in popularity owing to a combination of low prices, high-quality food, and pleasant, convenient outlets. The director of systems has just been given the responsibility for planning the type of information processing the firm should have in the next 5 years.

The company is organized into five regions, with an approximately equal number of restaurants in each region, though the sales revenues differ markedly among the regions. Currently all transactions processing systems are manual. The stores account for their own income and expenditures and send standardized reports to the regional headquarters. These reports are studied and summary statements are prepared for headquarters in Atlanta.

The director of systems has formed a planning team of two other individuals on the staff. Their major problem is to determine what kind of applications should be developed for the restaurants, the regions, and for headquarters. Next, they must address the problem of developing this system.

Whereas no decisions have been made, given current technology and trends in the computing field, the staff is leaning towards on-line systems. "In today's environment," one member said, "there is almost no reason to go with a batch system when we have this much data collection." Most of the team agrees with this philosophy. Can you help the planning group delineate the alternatives for applications and the location of hardware for the chain?

---

sequentially. First we sort, then we update, then reports are printed. In an on-line environment, the arrival of different transactions to be processed against the files follows a random pattern. The first transaction might be an order for one item, followed by an inquiry from purchasing, followed by the processing of a purchase order, and so forth. Multiple types of transactions are all being processed at one time."

"What does this do to the design?"

"Well, of course we have to design interactive input and output as described above. We must reexamine output reports that are now printed to see what ones are needed and whether new reports are needed. A new file for purchase orders must be added, and we'll have to establish linkages among the files for inquiry purposes. Users must specify the types of inquiries that are possible before design, because it can be hard to add them later."

"That does sound like a major change in philosophy, all right," said Terry. "What about programming?"

"The programs for the most part will be rewritten, but they will follow the same logic as present for the transactions currently in the system. Now, however, we shall try to have each program module responsible for some part of the transaction. For example, one module may be called by the supervisor to process an item ordered by a customer. This module in turn would call a file management module to actually retrieve the record desired and another module to rewrite it after updating.

TABLE 20-3
SAMPLE MENU SELECTION

Hardserve on-line system

DO YOU WISH TO:
    1   ENTER ORDERS FROM CUSTOMERS
    2   ENTER MERCHANDISE RECEIPTS
    3   INDICATE AN ORDER HAS BEEN PLACED
    4   INQUIRE
    5   PRODUCE PICKING SLIPS
    6   RECONCILE INVENTORY
    7   CORRECT ERRORS, MODIFICATIONS
ENTER NUMBER OF FUNCTION DESIRED 4

(a)

INQUIRY
    1   INVENTORY ITEM
    2   CUSTOMER ORDER (BY ORDER NUMBER, SHIP DATE DESIRED, CUSTOMER
        NUMBER, SEARCH-BY-DATE ORDER)
    3   CUSTOMER
    4   PURCHASE ORDER NUMBER
    5   SHIPMENTS DUE IN
    6   CUSTOMER NAME/NUMBER
    7   VENDOR NAME/NUMBER
ENTER NUMBER ___

(b)

"This gives rise to what we call multithreading, where each transaction may be in a different stage in processing. With two people entering orders, one item could be in the process of being fetched from the file while another is being updated, and so on."

"It sounds complicated!"

"It isn't as bad as it seems because of the operating system on the computer. This supervisor handles a lot of the messy problems of developing an on-line system today; we weren't so fortunate when on-line systems were new. We do have to think carefully about the applications programs modules and construct them."

"What do we have to do from a systems design standpoint?" asked Terry.

"Just about what we discussed a few minutes ago. As in a batch system, we need input from users on input and output and the kinds of data that must be in the files. The actual way we choose to write the programs and design modules will depend on what computer and language we choose."

AN ON-LINE SYSTEM

The following pages contain some of the features developed by users and the designers for an on-line version of Hardserve encompassing the receivings area in the warehouse. Table 20-3 is a sample of the type of input menu selected by users for communicating with the system.

TABLE 20-4
PROCESSING LOGIC FOR MAJOR TRANSACTIONS

---

1 Order entry from customer
  a Key in customer number, and ship date using fill-in-blanks on formatted screen. System responds with name, address
  b For each item ordered, enter item number, vendor desired, price, and quantity. System responds with item description. See sample screen format

2 Receipt of merchandise
  a Display purchase order
  b Enter quantity received if different from purchase order in additional column next to ordered quantities

3 Order placed
  a Enter purchase order number and vendor number using fill-in-blanks on formatted screen. System responds with vendor name and address
  b Enter date due, route code, carrier, terms
  c For each item ordered, enter item number, quantity, description, price. System responds with item description
  d Key in total price of purchase order for check against system computed total

4 Inquiry: retrieve requested data from appropriate file
  a Inventory item: display inventory record
  b Customer order: display customer order status including customer's name, address from customer file. Option to retrieve by order number, ship date (all orders), customer number following order date
  c Customer: Display customer file record
  d Purchase order number: Display purchase order including vendor name, address from vendor file
  e Shipments due in: for date entered, display one screen at a time the purchase orders to be received on that date
  f Customer name: use first six consonants to retrieve Hardserve customer number
  g Vendor name: use first six consonants of vendor name to search directory for vendor name and display name, address, and Hardserve vendor number

5 Produce picking slips
  a Enter date due or customer order number for slips
  b Compare order to inventory, update inventory, modify order to show actual amount shipped

6 Reconcile inventory
  a Display requested customer orders
  b Enter deviations in shipping
  c Adjust inventory file, order file

Users are currently working on developing edit checks for the on-line input. Simultaneously, Tom Roberts and his staff are investigating various physical computer options. It is hoped that within another year, the on-line system can be up and running.

Certainly these preliminary specifications for the on-line system will be changed as the system is refined and users begin to contribute more to the design.

The remainder of the chapter illustrates how the on-line system might look and how radically it differs from the original batch processing version.

Table 20-4 presents the major types of transactions that will be processed by

FIGURE 20-1
On-line system overview.

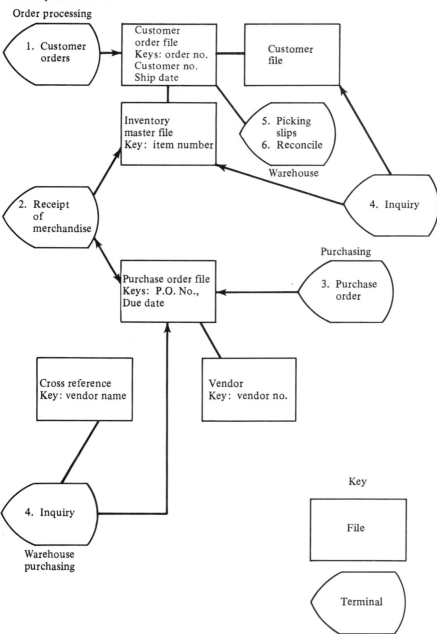

the system and provides an overview of its capabilities. In the batch system, we spoke of output, input, files, and processing. In the on-line example, it is clearer to present a discussion based on major transactions that are processed by the system. Figure 20-1 shows the overall structure of the system.

Order Entry

A major activity in the new system is order entry. To provide the input for processing and inventory control, we include an on-line order-entry capability. Table 20-5 contains the expanded data that must be keyed at the CRT as an order is being entered. To begin operations, the order-entry clerk would log on to the terminal. After entering his or her identification and password, the display shown in Table 20-3 would appear, asking for a selection of function from the menu. The clerk enters a 1, producing the screen shown in Figure 20-2. Table 20-5 shows the data that have to be entered, and Figure 20-2 is one possible screen layout for the CRT. Note that the system responds with the capital letters in the figure, and the operator fills in the blanks that are shown in italics.

The order-entry program leads the operator through each order. For example, the operator enters only the customer number. The system retrieves the data on the name and address of the customer from the customer file and displays it. At this point, the operator should check that the address on the screen corresponds to the name and address on the order. If not, some type of escape facility would permit hitting a special key to renew the screen or backspacing over the customer number to erase it and retype the correct number. (The specific form of error recovery depends on the computer system and terminals being used. For all subsequent discussions, assume that it is possible to make these typing corrections when they are noticed by the operator.)

The operator continues to enter the items indicated. The computer program

TABLE 20-5
ON-ORDER INPUT

Expanded On-Order Input	Characters	Type
Purchase order number	10	Alphanumeric
Vendor number	6	Numeric
For each item ordered		
Item number	8	Numeric
Quantity	7	Numeric
Description	40	Alphabetic
Price	8	Numeric
Date ordered	6	Numeric
Date due in	6	Numeric
Route code	8	Alphanumeric
Carrier for delivery	15	Alphanumeric
Terms	10	Alphanumeric

HARDSERVE ORDER ENTRY 4/15/81

CUSTOMER NUMBER *12345*   JONES HARDWARE
                                            75 MAIN STREET
                                            BOSTON, MASS. 02139

ORDER NUMBER *89654321*   SHIP DATE 5/12/81 ACTUAL

ITEM	DESCRIPTION	VENDOR	QUANTITY	PRICE	EXTENSION
7777777	SHOVEL	*672931*	*12*	12.00	144.00
8888888	HAMMER	*473612*	*24*	5.00	120.00
					264.00

(Computer-generated messages in capital letters, user entry in italics.)

FIGURE 20-2
Draft customer order-entry screen.

automatically performs the extensions and adds the total for the purchase order. The operator enters the total amount of the order, and the computer checks this total against its own total. If there is a discrepancy, the operator is asked to correct the order. If the order is acceptable, the operator so indicates, and a new screen is started for the next order. Another key is depressed to stop order entry.

Depending on the type of application, it might be desirable to compute a running total of all the orders entered and compare them with the total on a batch of orders obtained from an adding machine. In a very high-volume operation, such an additional check might be in order to be certain that all orders are entered each day.

Receipt of Merchandise

The warehouse uses the system to check in merchandise that has been ordered. The Hardserve purchase order number should be included on the packing slip with the merchandise. From this number, the warehouse staff displays the purchase order. A clerk enters any discrepancies between what was ordered and what was received. These data update the inventory files at the same time that they update the file of purchase orders.[1]

If the purchase order number is missing, the clerk can enter the due date and browse through the file until the right purchase order is located. It might be necessary to enter several dates because the shipment might not be exactly on

---

[1]The possibility of including a back-order capability is being evaluated. The design team is collecting data to determine how many back orders occur when Hardserve is out of stock, and whether goods would be received in sufficient time to fill the back order.

SYSTEMS PROBLEM 20-2

Kitchen Servant is a manufacturer of small home appliances, particularly for the kitchen. The company buys some components but manufactures more from raw materials. There are three plants, the newest of which is the largest and most efficient.

Kitchen Servant is considering the development of an on-line, factory-floor data-collection system. The manager of production control and scheduling has complained often that he has no good information with which to control production. Because the appliances are small and there are many steps in production, there are places where work is hidden away waiting further processing. It is very difficult to get an accurate count of work-in-process inventories.

The manufacturing vice president and the systems department manager have agreed that a feasibility study should be done for this system. However, the director of labor relations is concerned. "We just had a long strike over wages and working conditions," he said. "It is clear that a number of our workers are concerned about working conditions here. How will workers react to working with a machine? They now feel they have too little opportunity for social contact on the job. A computer will make it worse; they will view the system as a mechanized policeman."

The other individuals thinking about the system recognize this as a valid concern but are unsure of how to deal with it. The director of labor relations also pointed out that some firms have had trouble when union workers began using terminals; the union tried to use this as an argument for unionizing the entire computer staff as well.

What approach can you recommend to Kitchen Servant to successfully install an on-line, factory-floor data-collection system?

---

schedule. Before the system is programmed, the systems staff should ask the warehouse to research the number of shipments that do not contain a purchase order number. If there are too many, it may be necessary to establish an inquiry based on vendor or some other piece of data included on the packing slip or bill of lading that accompanies a shipment.

Ordering for Inventory

A major addition to the new on-line system will be the installation of terminals in the purchasing department. This department will now have the responsibility for entering the data on purchase orders as they are prepared for vendors. The operators should key the data using a CRT: the data can be used to produce a printed copy for mailing to the vendor. This screen follows the same general pattern as the order-entry example; it will be a fill-in-the-blanks format, and the program will lead the clerk through each of the pieces of data to be entered.

Inquiries

One of the major advantages of an on-line system is the powerful inquiry facility it can provide. For Hardserve there will be a number of inquiries for different groups in the firm.

1 The warehouse and order-entry and purchasing functions will be interested in inventory balances; they need to be able to inquire on inventory-item number and obtain display of the pertinent data about the item.

2 The system will be able to display a customer order; retrieval will be possible by order number, customer name with a link to each successive date (in case the customer phones and does not know the order number), and by shipping date (primarily for the warehouse).

3 The contents of the customer file record can be displayed.

4 By entering the purchase order number, an operator obtains a display of the order.

5 By entering a date, warehouse personnel can display (one at a time) the purchase orders with merchandise due on that certain date.

6 By entering the customer's name, the system will retrieve customer names and numbers that match, based on the first six consonants of the name. The purpose of this facility is to locate a customer's number given only the customer's name.

7 Vendor name: using the same approach as (6) above, an operator can obtain a vendor's number.

Packing Slips

The warehouse can now call for picking slips as they are needed. The operator enters a due date or specific customer order numbers to obtain the picking slips. The system checks available inventory, produces the slip, decreases the quantity in inventory, and sorts and prints the list.

Reconcilement

After the order has been picked, it is necessary to reconcile the picking slip with the order. Frequently, there is a discrepancy between physical inventory and book inventory. The system may suggest that something can be picked when, in fact, the item is out of stock. While filling the order, the picker crosses out the quantity ordered and writes in the quantity actually selected if there is a difference. These differences must be input to the system to maintain an accurate record of what has been shipped to the customer. At the same time, depending on company policy and control questions, the book inventory may be adjusted to reflect the stockout.

Extensions

As with the batch example, we have tried to keep the on-line system relatively simple. A number of possible extensions would be fairly easy to implement; for example, we could provide for backordering when an item is out of stock. It would also be very easy to produce statements for customers based on the order file. However, the system sketched here provides a good basis for an on-line system for Hardserve.

TABLE 20-6
HARDSERVE CUSTOMER ORDER FILE

Customer order file (medium: disk)		
Fields	**Size**	**Type**
Order number	8	Numeric
Customer number	8	Numeric
Order date	6	Numeric
Order date pointer	6	Numeric
Ship date desired	6	Numeric
Ship date pointer	6	Numeric
Ship date actual	6	Numeric
For each item ordered		
Item number	8	Numeric
Vendor desired	6	Numeric
Quantity	7	Numeric
Price	8	Numeric (2 decimal)

Directory: Order number
Customer number (note order date pointers within customer number)
Ship date

File Structure

Tables 20-6 and 20-7 contain the new and revised files for the on-line system. (In an actual system, we would consider very carefully using a data-base management system to build the new on-line version of Hardserve's application.) The first major addition is a customer order file that is also one of the most complex. There are trailer records for the actual items ordered, since there will be a different number for each order. Trailers may be created through the provision of extra records between orders with a chain to an overflow area or through a separate file of trailers that are chained to the order record and chained to each other.

This file has a directory on the Hardserve order number and another one on customer number. Since there may be several orders for the same customer, a date chain of pointers in the file connects each order for a given customer to the next most recent order. There is also a directory and pointers on ship date for the warehouse. Figure 20-3 shows the file.

Another new file contains data on the customer. Since each order for a customer refers to the same basic information, it would be wasteful of input time and file space to key name, address, credit, terms, etc. for each order. Therefore we create one file, keyed on customer number, to contain all the constant information about the customer.

The next major file is the one containing purchase orders prepared by Hardserve. Like the order file, it uses trailer records to contain the data on each

TABLE 20-7
OTHER NEW AND MODIFIED FILES

Customer file (medium: disk)

Fields	Size	Type
Customer number	6	Numeric
Customer name	30	Alphabetic
Customer address—line 1	25	Alphabetic
Customer address—line 2	25	Alphabetic
Customer address—line 3	25	Alphanumeric
Customer address—line 4	25	Alphanumeric
Credit rating	4	Alphabetic
Volume year-to-date	6	Numeric

Directories: Customer number
First six consonants of customer name

Purchase order file (medium: disk)

Fields	Size	Type
Purchase order number (key)	10	Alphanumeric
Vendor number	6	Numeric
Date due in	6	Numeric
Due date pointer	6	Numeric
Date ordered	6	Numeric
Route code	8	Alphanumeric
Carrier for delivery	15	Alphanumeric
Terms	10	Alphanumeric

For each item ordered (trailer records)

Item number	8	Numeric
Quantity	7	Numeric
Price	8	Numeric (2 decimal places)
Description	40	Alphabetic

Directories: Purchase order number
Due date

Vendor file (medium: disk)

Fields	Size	Type
Vendor number	6	Numeric
Vendor name	30	Alphabetic
Vendor address line 1	25	Alphabetic
Vendor address line 2	25	Alphabetic
Vendor address line 3	25	Alphanumeric
Vendor address line 4	25	Alphanumeric

Directory: Index sequential on vendor number

Cross-reference file created by sort of vendor file when new vendors added (medium: disk)

Fields	Size	Type
Vendor name	30	Alphabetic
Vendor number	6	Numeric

Directory: First six consonants of vendor name

Order no.	Customer no.	Order date	Ship date	Actual	Item Trailer Section
12345678	8765432	04 22 81	05 13 81		
12345679	8888888	04 24 81	05 15 81		
12345680	8765432	04 25 81	05 15 81		
12345681	9999999	04 25 81	05 13 81		

Notes: Directory points to Customer number, then customer orders are linked by order date for customer (a link) above, ship date directory points to beginning of chain for each ship date (b links above)

FIGURE 20-3
Customer order file linkages (examples).

item included on the purchase order. The key for the file is purchase order number; there is also a directory and a linked list on the date the shipment is due to help the warehouse receiving area.

There is a need for a vendor file—similar to the customer file—to contain fixed information about the vendor. Because frequently there will be a need to locate a vendor's number assigned by Hardserve (the vendor is unlikely to keep track of a number assigned to it by each of its customers), the system has a cross-reference file. Each time a vendor is added, this file is recreated by sorting the vendor name and number into alphabetical order, based on the name. A simple directory is constructed, based on the first six consonants of the vendor name, to support inquiries to determine vendor number.

Errors and Modifications

We have not talked about errors or modifications yet. From the discussion on the files, it should be clear that there will be a need to make changes as customer orders change, as delivery dates are altered on merchandise due in, and for a number of other reasons. These changes must be defined, along with the impact on each file. A major effort will have to be devoted to this exercise, because the system must be able to alter data that will change during the course of business.

Summary

In this section we have presented a sketch of a possible on-line system for Hardserve. Comparing this system with the batch system should demonstrate the more pleasant user interface and higher levels of responsiveness of the on-line system. Now, users have instantaneous response to inquiries; much paperwork is eliminated. Errors in data entry are corrected as they are made, for the most part. The warehouse problem with merchandise due in from customers should be alleviated, and the work of the purchasing department should be simplified.

At the same time, the on-line system is more complicated; complex, additional files are required for this application. However, as we have discussed earlier in the chapter, the hardware and software technology is becoming less expensive and more capable of supporting on-line systems. We expect to see increasing movement toward on-line systems.

KEY WORDS AND RECOMMENDED READINGS

Please see Chapter 15.

DISCUSSION QUESTIONS

1 How could the designers have forseen the problems in the warehouse with the batch system?
2 What changes in cost trends make the development of an on-line system more attractive?
3 What are the major differences in the program structure for batch versus on-line systems?
4 Is a different supervisory program required for on-line systems?
5 What are the changes needed to convert the logic of a batch application to on-line? Use some of the modules for Hardserve from Chapter 15 to illustrate your answer.
6 Design a screen format for one of the on-line functions in the Hardserve system.
7 What edits would be required for on-line entry?
8 Compare and contrast menu selection and fill-in-the-blank techniques for on-line input.
9 What batch tests can be duplicated in an on-line system?
10 What are the differences in backup requirements for an on-line system compared to a batch system?
11 Design a backup system for the Hardserve on-line system.
12 What guidelines can you suggest as to when a printing terminal is appropriate for an on-line application and when a CRT should be used?
13 Design a back-ordering capability for the Hardserve on-line system.
14 Compare and contrast the file structures of the batch and on-line versions of Hardserve.
15 Make a list of the file fields that can be changed by the transactions processed by the on-line Hardserve system.
16 What reasonableness checks can you recommend on order entry?
17 What have computer manufacturers done to make it easier to develop on-line applications?
18 How does a data-base management system contribute to the development of an on-line system?
19 What physical on-line systems alternative do you recommend for Hardserve and why?
20 What logical on-line systems alternative do you recommend for Hardserve and why?
21 What data model does this application fit: hierarchical, network, or relational?

EXAMPLES OF
INFORMATION SYSTEMS

EXAMPLES OF
INFORMATION SYSTEMS

We have seen the Hardserve system illustrated in detail. In this chapter, we present an overview of five other information systems. The purpose of this description is to provide an idea of how computers have been applied to real organizational information processing problems.

The first system we discuss is an advanced administrative application; the system is on-line and performs a number of functions related to transactions processing, operational control, and managerial control. The second application describes a system applied to fiscal policy determination for state and local government. The third application is a decision-support system developed to help trust investment officers better manage their portfolios in commercial banks. The fourth system is a complex decision-support system for planning purposes. The final system is an office automation application: electronic mail.

All these systems are considerably more complex than Hardserve, but they were developed utilizing some of the same techniques we have presented in the text. The applications in this chapter illustrate well the power and effectiveness of computer-based information systems. These applications show the results of the creative process of systems analysis and design.

AN ON-LINE ADMINISTRATIVE SYSTEM

International Business Machines Corporation (IBM) operates an on-line system that performs many of the administrative functions of branch and regional offices and features CRT terminals. Because of the immense size and complexity of this system we cannot present it in the same detail as the Hardserve example;

however, we shall try to describe the system's functions and enough of its underlying technology to provide a feeling for its capabilities. Much of the discussion comes from Wimbrow (1971), although this source has been updated through demonstrations and company material on the system.

IBM is a large manufacturer of business and computer equipment. Branch offices sell computer equipment and maintain contact with customers. Before the development of the Advanced Administrative System (AAS), IBM's order-entry system[1] was being strained by increasing sales volume and the increasing complexity of computer equipment that could be ordered by a customer.

For these reasons, AAS was developed to perform order entry and some 450 other logical transactions interactively. The order-entry process at IBM consists of the following steps:

1 An order is sent to the processing center.
2 The order is checked for validity.
3 The order is exploded into components for manufacturing.
4 A delivery date is assigned and the order is sent to the branch office.
5 Inventory records are updated.
6 The order is summarized for manufacturing and sales control.

There are many opportunities for delay in this process. In the original system, acknowledgments and delivery dates were transmitted through the mail. The validity check for an order was very time-consuming when performed manually. A validity check is necessary because of the complexity of computer systems; each system usually involves a number of systems components that are interdependent. For example, certain peripherals and controllers can be used only on certain central processing units. A validity check is performed to ensure that all prerequisite devices are present on the original order and to be certain that all configurations ordered can be manufactured and operated. In the original manual system, errors in orders resulted in a cyclical revision that delayed order processing further. These revisions also created inventory control and management difficulties in reconciling on-order backlogs and order totals at manufacturing plants.

Management and inventory control in the original system consisted of three files: (1) open orders, (2) installed inventory, and (3) uninstalled inventory (manufactured but not yet installed). The installed inventory file is the source of rental invoices sent to customers. The original system had difficulty coping with geographic mismatches between receiving centers and customer-paying centers, which complicated the billing process.

All these problems were compounded in the mid-1960s when IBM planned the introduction of the 360 computer system, which dramatically increased the number of possible configurations for systems. Projections indicated that the

---

[1] The reader should not be confused because the company in this example is a manufacturer of computer equipment. The system under discussion is an application of computers within the company.

complexity of the order-entry process and a growing volume of orders would seriously overload existing information processing procedures for order entry.

Objective

By 1965, a study group recommended a new order system that would (1) operate interactively, that is, on-line; (2) connect branch, regional offices, plants, and headquarters—some 320 geographical locations requiring about 1500 terminals; and (3) operate in a conversational mode.

One important feature of the new system would be conversational, on-line interaction. A user provides one item of information at one time and in several minutes enters more data. The underlying computer system associates the information with each operator without exclusively dedicating itself to any one terminal. The approach is the same we observed with timesharing and on-line systems in general. The on-line computer appears to the user as if it is maintaining a continuous and exclusive conversation with that user, although actually several hundred users are having "exclusive" conversations at the same time.

SYSTEMS PROBLEM 21-1

Midwest Airlines is a regional carrier serving a number of states in the Midwest. The company was founded shortly after World War II and has been growing steadily. Five years ago, the airline no longer needed federal subsidies, and it has been profitable since that time. In addition to scheduled passenger service, the company offers charter trips to Las Vegas and the West Coast. In addition, the air freight part of the business has been increasing.

The marketing department at Midwest is considering the introduction of a special overnight express air-freight service. A package would be delivered to the airport 45 minutes before a departing flight, and Midwest would arrange delivery to the door at the destination. Some regulatory problems need to be overcome, but the new service looks promising.

The marketing area would then like to extend to all its air-freight customers the right to make reservations for packages on certain flights. This way a shipper could be certain of the time the package would arrive at its destination, since the customer, not the airline, would choose the flight. The problem here is figuring capacity, since the amount of freight that can be carried varies according to the number of passengers on a flight. Also, shipments come in many different sizes and weights, unlike a customer, who occupies a single seat.

The marketing department and the air-freight department have requested information from the computer department on what modifications to the company's passenger-name reservation service would be required to accommodate reservations for freight. The problem is further complicated by the fact that Midwest does not have its own reservations system but is served by a system at one of the trunk carriers. How would the reservations application differ between passengers and freight?

The system was originally designed to handle order-entry processing, inventory control, and accounts receivable. However, the design expanded to approximately 850 applications, including order entry, delivery scheduling, territory assignment, payroll, commission accounting, validation of computer group configurations, accounts receivable, customer master record, inventory of installed machines, billing, customer-student enrollment in IBM courses, and user training through computer-aided instruction (CAI).

The system has dramatically reduced the prior 2 to 4 week order-confirmation cycle. Four years after installation, IBM was processing 30 percent more transactions with 18 percent fewer people, a productivity gain of greater than 12 percent a year! The flexibility of the system is illustrated by the ability of the company to completely reorganize the assignment of clients to branch offices over a weekend.

Special Features

One problem with a large-scale system is ensuring that only those with authorization are permitted to use it. Managers are authorized to have access, but they usually delegate this authority to operators. The manager registers employees, who then receive security cards generated by the system. The manager and operator must be recognized by the system, and neither can perform functions for which they are not authorized.

The system gives the operator two attempts to enter a security code. An attempt to execute actions for which the operator is not authorized or for which the operator is untrained brings a reminder on the first attempt from the system. If the operator makes a second attempt to enter an unauthorized action, or to log on with an error, or makes any other security error, the system locks the terminal. The terminal remains locked until an authorized security individual unlocks it.

The need to train over 5000 operators in branches throughout the country led to the inclusion of computer-aided instruction in the system. Classroom training would have been too expensive and time-consuming. Training courses are designed in a modular fashion for the overall system and for each different application. The system keeps track of operator progress and training, and an operator is not allowed to execute transactions for which he or she has not completed the appropriate CAI course. Some 5 percent of machine cycles are used for training the clerical staff, demonstrating the importance of training and the effort devoted to it.

The System

The closest analogy to the type of system envisioned by the designers was SABRE, the first on-line airline reservation system. This second-generation system was developed on a dedicated computer using a specially coded supervisor in assembly language. Because of the progress between the second and third generations of computers in the development of operating systems, IBM utilized a

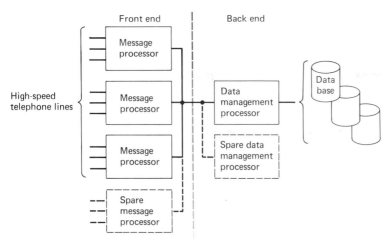

FIGURE 21-1
Original AAS computer configuration. (*From Wimbrow, J. H.: "A Large-Scale Interactive Administrative System," 1971, courtesy* IBM Systems Journal.)

more general-purpose operating system for the on-line AAS system. The AAS system was first developed under an operating system developed for real-time operations for NASA. When the version of a standard IBM operating system became available, the designers converted AAS to it.

Input-output devices for the system include over 2400 CRT terminals and low-speed printers in over 200 branch offices, plants, and corporate headquarters. There are some 12,000 users of the system. The data are sent over low-speed lines and concentrated by nine geographically distributed computers for transmission to the central computer site over high-speed lines. System design parameters include a 5-second response to 95 percent of the input. Originally designers estimated it would be necessary to process 1½ million inputs per 12-hour day or an average of 50 inputs per second. By 1977 the system was processing 750,000 transactions per day with an average response time of 5 seconds.

Because processing loads on the system are so great, multiple computers are involved. The workload is divided into two logical components: message processing and data management. The "front end" consists of multiple message processing computers that handle all terminal input and output. Message processors develop all file requests and pass them to the data management computer as shown in Figure 21-1. Formatted data retrievals from files become responses to message processor requests (much of this information is transmitted to terminals by the message processors). There is a spare message processing computer and spare machines for data management. Normally the spare machines do off-line work unless one of the on-line computers malfunctions.

The basic programming structure of this system is illustrated in Figure 21-2. There is an expanding number of applications, each having a group of transactions. For example, order entry consists of a number of transactions, such as

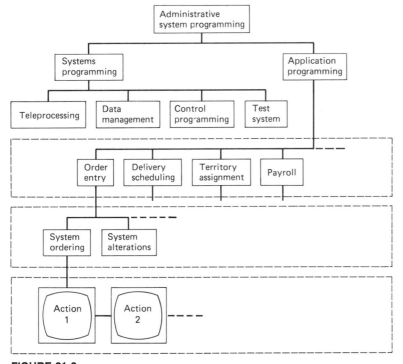

FIGURE 21-2
Organization of administrative system programming. (*From Wimbrow, J. H.: "A Large-Scale Interactive Administrative System," 1971, courtesy* IBM Systems Journal.)

locating a customer record and entering a new equipment order. The lowest level consists of action programs that interact with the operator at the terminal. An example of an action program is one that lists available colors for a computer system. By 1977 there were about 10,000 applications programs in total.

The message-processing computer's memory is allocated to the teleprocessing module, operating system action programs, data management for message processing, and program buffers for communications with the data management computer. The operating system controls all the operations of the message processor, and the teleprocessing monitor controls communications with terminals. The system maintains working-area storage on a secondary storage device for each terminal. The message-processing data management routines control the movement of working storage data between primary and secondary memory.

The system stores action programs on secondary storage and fetches them into primary memory as needed. Action programs are the applications programs; they provide all logical operations necessary to service the user at the terminal. Each message processor has a series of entry blocks that are used for entering messages from terminals, processing information, and transmitting responses back to terminals. There are fewer message and data blocks than terminals, so the system must process messages rapidly enough to prevent delays. The system assigns messages awaiting service to a queue in the teleprocessing monitor. (If the input queue becomes full, the teleprocessing monitor stops polling terminals, so the system runs out of time, but not space.) Enough capacity is provided for most transactions to be processed in 5 seconds. Message processors transmit data management requests to the "backend" data management computer, and this computer returns the desired record from the data base to the message processor.

The data management processor receives inputs (data management requests) from the message processor and responds with an output. The data management programs are all reentrant and reside in primary memory of the data management computer at all times.

The data base is structured hierarchically with individual records, strings, groups, and files. A record is a series of logically related fields (see Table 21-1). One record, for example, is for a 2401 tape unit installed at a particular customer location. This record contains complete information about the unit, including description, manufacturing date, system number, serial number, color, and so forth. All fields in the record are stored contiguously in the data base.

All records related to installed machines are stored in the same file, and the records in Table 21-1 constitute the installed machine file. The format and the length of the records vary widely. However, all records of the same type adhere to the same format and length. Each record has a unique key such as the serial number in Table 21-1.

Logically associated records in a file are called strings. The tape unit in Table 21-1 is associated with its control unit CPU, and so forth, to make up a configured computer system. This system is identified by the system number (the string key in the table).

TABLE 21-1
INSTALLED MACHINE FILE

Record key (serial number)	String key (system number)	Group key (customer number)	Description	Date of manufacture	Color
1234	A9421	27123.00	2401 tape unit	xx/xx/xx	Blue
2345	A9421	27123.00	CPU		
			card reader		
3456	A9421	27123.00			
0112	B0942	27123.00			
0479	B0942	27123.00			
4823	B0942	27123.00			
7894	B0942	27123.00			
3168	A9111	87941.00			
.	.	.			
.	.	.			
.	.	.			

Source: IBM Systems Journal

We also have associations among strings called groups. A group could be used to relate all systems (string keys) belonging to a specific customer (group key). In Table 21-1, a customer with group number 27123.00 has more than one system, each of which in turn consists of several machines. The file logic is illustrated in Figure 21-3.

Collections of identical types of records, which are possibly associated by strings and groups, form files. The complete data base has about 200 such files. A file may have up to three keys (record, string, and group), although it does not have to; for example, only two levels of association are found in the accounts-receivable file. Naturally, directories connect keys to logical record numbers in the file. Each key field has its own directory or index file. For record keys there must be one entry in a directory for each record. String keys, however, take advantage of physical contiguity in the file, and pointers in the directory reference only the first record in a string. The system retrieves subsequent records in the string by reading sequentially.

The system places new records in an overflow record it creates and modifies directory records to reflect the addition. Periodically, files are reorganized as retrieval time degrades because of the necessity to refer to overflow areas. As discussed in Chapter 8, reorganization consists of reading the old file, writing data in proper sequence in another location, and eliminating the original file. The system recreates directories to point to the new locations. The size of the data base in the early 1970s was over 20 million data records and about 27 million directory records; over 2.5 billion characters of data are in the system and over 0.5 billion characters of directories.

It is also necessary to provide for reconstructuring the data base in an on-line system in case of failure. The designers of the AAS system chose to minimize day-to-day backup costs and incur higher emergency reconstruction costs. The system also includes a trail to allow determination of what data were changed, by

FIGURE 21-3
AAS file logic.

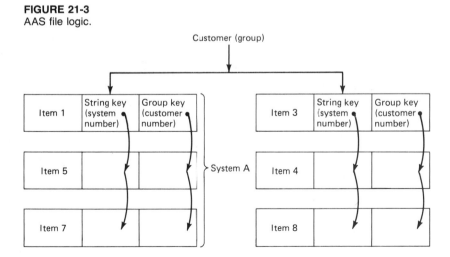

SYSTEMS PROBLEM 21-2

Astro Electronics is a major producer and retailer of electronic equipment, specializing in audio and television products. The firm sells to department and hi-fi stores throughout the United States. There are regional offices and warehouses in almost all major U.S. cities. Business has been expanding rapidly because of the increased level of affluence in general and the increasing consumption of audio and TV equipment by young adults.

The firm is designing a new sales information system to keep track of sales to retailers and to maintain information on the status of inventories. Because of the large amount of input and output and the need for recently updated information, the company decided to develop an on-line system.

Currently, Astro is organized on a regional basis for sales. However, management feels that, at some time in the future, it may be necessary to organize both by region and by product line. For example, TV equipment might be handled separately from audio products.

Top management of Astro wants the design team for the new system to be sure that they do not constrain the firm's prerogatives by creating an inflexible system. The computer department feels the most likely problem area will be in the file structures of the new system. How can they design the files so that the company can easily reorganize its sales activities?

---

whom, and when. All changes to the data base are journalized in the data-file journal and appropriate cross-references are noted. Changes include additions, modifications, and deletions of records. The system creates journal records and logs them onto tape. This record consists of the new version of the record after a change, and the signature of the "requester" (program, terminal, and user ID).

Each record of the data base has a control field to record a folio number for the last update. When a record is created, modified, or deleted, the system posts the number of the data-file journal tape currently being used by the system to the folio field in the record (each journal tape is sequentially numbered from the time the system became operational). The previous contents of the folio field associated with the record are also recorded on the journal to show where the previous journal entry for this record is located.

The journal fields forming the audit trails can also be used to recreate the files, although because of the volume of activity it would be impractical to begin from where the system first started. Therefore, periodically the system copies the data files to tape. Whenever a file is reorganized, the system creates an image containing an exact copy of the new file. The time of reorganization and the first folio number reflecting the reorganization are recorded. If files are damaged, the system processes journal tapes since the last reorganization to remove and compact records affected by the damaged file (compaction is used to eliminate duplicate updates, since only the most recent version of the record is needed). The system reloads the latest image tape and uses the transactions affecting the file to update it.

AAS is an extremely good example of a system that has grown over time; the application is almost 20 years old. Each year it is extended to include more features and AAS becomes more vital to the operation of a firm. Given the cost of developing a system and the fact that users become dependent on vital transactions-processing applications, we can expect to conduct systems analysis and design both to create new systems and to extend (without necessarily replacing) existing applications.

RAFT

Rapid Analysis Fiscal Tool (RAFT) is an information system designed to provide Minnesota government with a tool for evaluating fiscal policy (see Johnson, Kozar, and Ruch, 1977). Fiscal policy here is applied to the processes of taxation and distribution of funds affecting state and local governments; taxation involves property, income, and sales taxes. Distribution includes state aid to local governments, schools, and federal revenue sharing.

The purpose of the RAFT system was to improve information use in fiscal analysis. The system is to serve as a repository of data that are accurate and timely. For studies of property taxes, all data on tax rates, property values, and levies for all local governments must be comparable and accurate. The system is to include analytic techniques that allow for the simulation and comparison of various alternatives.

The system designed for this purpose was intended to serve a variety of potential users, including legislators and their staff, administrative officials, planners, citizens, etc.

The Data Base

The designers developed a data dictionary containing the definitions of all the data items included in the data base; in this process they defined 16 categories of data such as business activity, debt and interest of local government, employment, land values, expenditures, income, land use, tax levels, population, etc.

Conceptually the data base can be viewed as a three-dimensional matrix. One axis is the data elements, another the year, and the third the units of governments. Because there is an overlap in local governments, the designers defined a new unit of government called the location. A location represents the intersection of six level boundaries in the state, including a planning region, county, municipality, school district, and location.

Data collection proved to be a major problem in the system; there are about 5000 different government units in the state, and each has unique record-keeping and reporting approaches. The data base requires 200 million characters of storage for each year. The designers reported three major problems in data collection:

1 Data was currently reported in categories defined by statute; no new data were available to evaluate new policies.

2 Changes in the laws altered the categories for reporting data, making comparisons over time difficult.

3 Different reports at the state level used different methods for defining and identifying local government units.

The analysts developed new forms and standard categories that will not change for future data collection.

A further problem that had to be solved was that of indicating when units of government are comparable so that policies could be examined from year to year. (Redistricting would change school district boundaries and make the districts incomparable from one year to the next.) The designers assigned unique identification codes to each unit of government; when a unit changes, new codes are assigned. Year-to-year comparisons focus only on units of government whose codes match for the years in the analysis. The need to simulate fiscal policies over time led to the development of a different simulation model for each year for each tax or distribution process. The data, governmental units, and tax laws are accurate for a given year, and each year must be viewed separately.

Simulation Models

The simulation models in the system are deterministic; they apply formulas that determine particular tax or aid. The tax impact is calculated on the level of an individual, and aid is simulated at the governmental unit level. By changing parameters, the user evaluates programs with "what if" questions. The models include for taxation:

Individual income tax
Federal income tax
Tax on real property of local units of government

For distribution of funds:

Aids to education
Aids to local government

The system computes the taxes and aid exactly as they would be computed to administer the tax laws. The models use hypothetical or actual data for input and allow the user to simulate different alternatives by changing the parameter values in the formulas.

Output

The first output from the system was reports containing tables of numbers. Later additions included arithmetic manipulations, sorting, graphing, ranking, and the application of simple statistics. The system also makes it possible to create a file from the data base that can be input to statistical packages for further analysis.

Use

The RAFT system has been used on some 13 projects, 7 of which have required special programs beyond those contained in the base system. One study analyzed a plan to increase the state credit given homeowners on their property tax. The study simulated several alternatives and compared the results; the analysis was performed quickly in 1 week; a manual analysis would have required many weeks. Another project involved the analysis of a plan to provide property tax relief to homeowners by providing a property tax credit on a sliding scale based on income and house value. A special-purpose program was used to calculate property tax as a percentage of income with and without the plan for 4 geographical areas and 3 age groups in 20 income categories, 12 house value classes, and 20 rent categories.

An original goal of this system was availability for any user. The complexity of the analysis requested and its unique characteristics made it impossible to achieve this goal. Complexities exist because of changes in the data elements from changes in new laws and the changing boundaries of governmental units. Also, tax and distribution formulas change as new laws are passed. The RAFT staff has found it necessary to work with users to help them obtain benefits from the system. The system does require a technical specialist to act as a liaison with the user.

This specialist helps resolve data-definition problems, identify government unit changes, and determine the data needed for various analyses. The specialist also provides general technical assistance while maintaining and developing models.

A PORTFOLIO SYSTEM

Background

The system described in this section was developed as a research project and is documented in a paper by Gerrity (1971). The system has been expanded and converted into a commercial product, and more recent information for our description was developed from a study of the system. The prototype version of this portfolio management system was developed for a pension-fund management section of a major bank. The trust officer manages assets for a trust, buying and selling securities to maximize the objectives of the trust, such as growth in capital and maximum return. The bank receives a management fee for its efforts.

Under the conditions existing before the system was developed, managers of the portfolio had three main sources of information: (1) portfolio-related information showing the holding structure of each portfolio, (2) security-related information of historical and predictive variables for alternative investments, and (3) security prices.

The accounting group provided the portfolio information, and security data came from investment research groups. Newspapers furnished security prices. Managers received only fully priced portfolio status reports monthly from the accounting group.

The available information was fragmented and focused on individual security holdings rather than total portfolio status. Management tended to define problems in terms of single security holdings, although from a normative view, overall portfolio structure is what determines performance.

The manager's activities were carefully analyzed through observation and the administration of psychological tests. A number of problems with the current system were discovered in addition to those above.

1 The prices on status reports were often out of date and had to be updated manually.

2 Data were fragmented into two files, one on portfolio holdings and the other on stock history and performance data. The managers needed to see the research information juxtaposed with the account information.

3 There was a lack of an aggregate measure of portfolio status and structure that would enable a manager to look at the distribution of the portfolio on a single dimension or to compare two variables.

4 There was a lack of formal mechanism to compare portfolio status with goals.

5 There were rigid report formats; for example, the holdings were listed only by industry groups. It was not possible to obtain a listing of portfolio contents, say, in order by earnings per share.

6 Managers tended to search locally for stock buy-and-sell candidates. They rarely considered the entire list of 350 approved stocks for investment because of the effort involved in searching the list for stocks with certain criteria, for example, a price/earnings ratio less than 20.

7 There was no method to consider alternatives, that is, to develop and monitor a hypothetical portfolio.

8 In general, information sources exhibited a slow response.

A New System

The designers tried to solve some of the problems above by providing an interactive decision system with a graphics CRT. The original system operated on an existing timesharing computer, although present versions run as a part of a standard operating system capable of supporting mixed batch and on-line systems. Most potential users can operate this system on their own internal computer.

One version of the system currently in use has the following functions:

1 Directory This function provides a tabular overview of all accounts under the manager's jurisdiction. The table generated can be sorted on a number of fields, such as account identifier, market value, or fixed income performance. The manager can compare whole portfolios in a number of different ways in addition to simply listing the ones under the manager's jurisdiction.

2 Scan This operator allows the user to view the holdings of a particular security across a group of accounts. The manager selects the security, a sort key, and other information; a report is produced that includes the units of the security held for each account and certain data on that security, such as the percentage of the account devoted to the security.

3 Groups This operator produces a picture of the distribution of the holdings of an account by broad industry groups, such as consumer, petrochemical, and so forth. The display is a graphic histogram.

4 Table This function provides a way for the managers to design their own reports for reviewing the holdings of an account. The user types the account name and a list of the data items desired for each holding, and a report containing this information appears on the screen.

5 Histogram The histogram operator allows the manager to view the distribution of any available data item for all the holdings of an account; for example, the user might want a histogram of the total market value of accounts.

6 Scatter The scatter operator provides the manager with the capability of viewing the relationship between two data items associated with the securities in an account. An example of such a plot is the relationship of current price/earnings ratio against 10-year average price/earnings ratios for the holdings in the account.

7 Summary The summary function displays various account summary data such as holdings, type of account, and account description.

8 Issue The issue operator displays all the information pertaining to a specified issue on the list of issues approved by the bank for investment. Examples of such information include price/earnings ratio, historical price/earnings ratio, and dividends.

It is interesting to note that the designers did not take a fully normative approach. The theories of normative portfolio construction and the "efficient market hypothesis" are not included in the system. Instead, a true decision-support system was developed so that the managers could use information in a manner consistent with their own decision styles.

Results

A monitor in the experimental version of the system showed that managers made heavy use of the graphics commands and switched back and forth among portfolios. Sessions tended to be lengthy and to generate a number of reports. Almost all the functions were used; there was no concentration on one function, for example, obtaining the status of the portfolio. Later studies of the system in full-scale operation found that the number of sessions dropped, as did the number of reports produced per session.[2] There tended to be much more of a focus on a single function by each user.

The designers of the original system felt it would provide the tools necessary for managers to change their approach to decision making. They could not focus on a

---

[2]Charlés Stabell, discussion at MIT Conference on Implementation, April 1975.

single portfolio; they were not forced to look only at a single stock. The follow-up research indicated that this type of change did not occur. However, from our discussion of change, these results are not too surprising. The system could be used to support existing security-by-security approaches to decision making. There is no reason why a normative portfolio-centered approach should necessarily be adopted unless the individual decision maker feels that it is best. Did the managers all desire to adopt a more portfolio-centered view, or were they basically content with their current decision process?

We have said that organizational change should not be implemented through information systems. Organization and behavioral changes should be made, and then a system to support the new style can be developed. It appears in this case that the new system could be used to improve existing decision approaches or to change one's approach to decision making. Apparently the decision makers felt no pressing need to change their approach, so they used the system to support existing patterns of decision making.

A STRATEGIC PLANNING SYSTEM

Few examples of computer-based information systems support decision making at the strategic level; the system described in this section is a notable exception. This planning system features a number of advanced operations research techniques integrated through a user-oriented interactive computer system. We hope to illustrate some of the exciting possibilities of how information systems can be used to support management decision making with this example.

Background

Strategic financial planning is an important activity for an organization, especially large multidivisional firms. The decision maker is confronted with many competing alternatives for investment and numerous sources of funds. Government regulations and other conditions place restrictions on these decision makers. One of the most important goals of a system for planning is to increase the effective use of executive time by:

1 Focusing attention on key variables
2 Providing rapid feedback
3 Evaluating alternative allocations of resources
4 Providing computer capacity to analyze a large number of alternatives

For planning purposes, alternatives can be classified into the following categories:

1 Momentum strategies representing continuation of the present lines of business
2 Development strategies representing incremental effects of proposed changes in momentum

3 Financing strategies, including alternatives on how to fund existing and proposed activities for the corporation and divisions

4 Divestment strategies, including the sale of a unit in an effort to discontinue a policy

5 Acquisition strategies for different ways to enter a new activity or expand

An Example

Before discussing the structure of the planning system, we shall present a scenario to demonstrate how the system can be used. Assume that a user has created the necessary data bases and wishes to run an operations-research optimization model contained in the system.

First, the user logs on to the system; the system responds with guided instruction after the user types the key words OPT. PHASE to select the part of the system to be used. The instructions ask the user to specify the different files for this run of the model (to provide flexibility, designers separated models from data so that the models can be used on many sets of data contained in different files). File specifications are required for a permanent file and a temporary file and to guide preparation of the output reports.

Next the user has the option to print or modify the data base. In this case the user does not wish to make changes; however, if changes were desired, an edit program would be called automatically.

The system asks for specifications of different data and options; for example, what predefined strategies are to be included? Is group-level financing to be in the form of a long-term debt or common or preferred stock? The user proceeds interactively by answering questions. If the answer is long-term debt, the user responds to questions about the year of debt issue, interest, principal, compensating balances, and so forth. When all parameters have been specified, the system saves the data as an input file for an optimization run.

The user types the key word OPT. PHASE and the system requests file names and performance options. The user again is given the opportunity to change input parameters. The system asks the user to choose between two objective functions, maximizing either earnings per share or return on equity. After answering several more questions, the system begins its optimization calculations. The user can wait for the results or come back later to display the output. The user can run several analyses, changing parameters to reflect different strategies.

When finished with the runs, the user can undertake postoptimality analysis. This analysis might include changing the "right-hand side" constraints of a model by providing a range of parameters to test. The system responds with results for each parameterization step. In the reporting stage, the user can graph various results using bars, lines, or special characters. The user can also generate standard or custom-tailored printed reports to display results. Finally, at the completion of the run, the user logs off.

The System: An Overview

One of the major advances represented by this system is its large number of integrated components. It is not just a single model, but instead the planning system represents a collection of models coordinated by a computer system. The corporate-level focus, financial orientation, and long-range planning horizon clearly make this a model to support strategic planning (see Figure 21-4). The central analytical component is a large mixed-integer mathematical programming model that maximizes corporate performance over a multiperiod planning horizon. The model selects appropriate operations, acquisitions, and financing strategies. A corporate simulation model computes the detailed implications of alternatives and projected financial statements for each set of inputs. A third econometric model supplies external data and projections for the national economy, specific industries, or subsidiaries. The user can employ risk-analysis models to evaluate the business mix and the implications of various strategic alternatives.

To use the model, corporate management communicates its assumptions on planning to the group management and subsidiary management that control strategic planning units. This communication process ensures uniform global assumptions. The strategic planning units submit as a minimum (1) a profit-and-loss statement, balance sheet, and sources and applications of funds for the case where all proposed marketing, development, acquisition, and financing strategies were accepted; (2) an abbreviated profit-and-loss statement showing the source and application of funds for each development and acquisition strategy; (3) financial data for each existing or proposed financial investment showing principal amount, payment schedule, compensating balance, category type, and restrictions on funds.

These data are assembled at corporate headquarters and used as input to economic models that generate alternative data bases. The risk-analysis system prepares other data bases to determine confidence levels for the performance of selected strategic planning units. Information from these activities is transferred to the optimization subsystem to formulate a goal-constrained plan for each alternative data base. The simulation subsystem determines the financial impact of the plans in the form of profit-and-loss statements and various other financial output. Nonfeasible alternatives will arise, and an iterative process is required to develop a plan acceptable to management.

Subsystems

There are several discrete subsystems in Figure 21-4. The information subsystem controls all information flows in the planning system. It contains an executive program, input editors, output generator, data-editing routines, and the system data base. The executive program organizes the flow of information and controls the conversational timesharing mode of operation. The input editors organize raw inputs in card-image form on strategic planning units and place them in the data

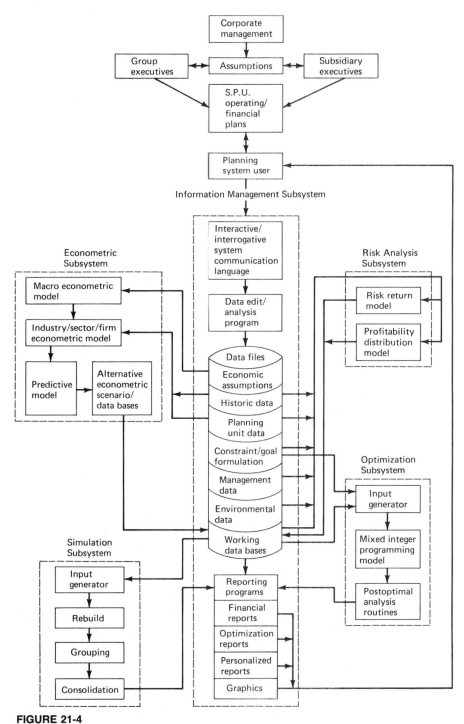

FIGURE 21-4
The strategic planning system. (*From Hamilton, W. F., and M. A. Moses: "A Computer-Based Corporate Planning System," 1974, courtesy* The Institute of Management Sciences.)

base. These data are edited for reasonableness and compared with historical data and economic projections. The input editor organizes data in the strategic planning unit files, strategic files, and financial files. (There are also files for historical data at the corporate level and for strategic planning unit management and environmental data such as tax rates, prime interest rates, and so forth.) The output generator is responsible for all output report preparation and includes a graphics option for producing graphs and charts.

The consolidated simulation subsystem conducts deterministic, as opposed to stochastic, financial simulations for predetermined sets of strategies. This model is based largely on accepted financial accounting variables and relationships. A rebuilding facility allows the consolidation and definition of new strategic planning units. These units can be configured into a group, and then the model is used to generate group financial projections. A consolidation model is used to eliminate interest flows, to finance deficits from a corporate pool, and to produce annual consolidated statements of corporate financial conditions.

The corporate optimization subsystem maximizes corporate performance over the multiperiod planning horizon. It selects an optimal set of strategic funds sources while considering a complex set of financial, legal, and operational

---

SYSTEMS PROBLEM 21-3

Judy Carver is a systems analyst for Beauty Aids, a cosmetics manufacturer. The manager of the planning department just made a request for the computer department to investigate the development of a planning model for Beauty Aids. The firm has in the past relied on intuitive forecasts or simple extrapolations of past sales history for making future plans.

The manager of the planning department now feels that some type of modeling might improve the accuracy of forecasts. He does not want to eliminate the intuitive part but instead wishes to have several possible forecasts from which to choose.

After a reliable forecast has been developed, the manager would like to experiment with the development of a model of Beauty Aids. "If we could succeed in building a model of the firm coupled to a forecast, we could really improve the planning effort. Right now, we spend too much time guessing and reacting. The financial officer is always under pressure as we change our demands and create new capital requirements," said the manager.

Judy has had some experience with modeling, and she knows a variety of planning models is available. Some firms specialize in the development of these models; some are tied to national econometric forecasts of the entire United States economy. Others offer special timesharing languages to assist the model builder. Judy is unsure of what to recommend to Beauty Aids. Should she and the computer department actually develop the model, or should they serve as an interface between the user and an outside vendor? What course of action would you recommend? How should the decision be made? What roles does the planning manager have in the decision on how to proceed?

---

limitations at the corporate and strategic planning unit levels. A mixed-integer mathematical programming model is the most important component of this subsystem; several performance measures may be maximized by the model. Planning variables include all available momentum, development, acquisition, divestment, and financing strategies. Restrictions on the pattern of growth in earnings per share, return on assets and equity, corporate cash flow, and various ratios consistent with management desires are considered by the model. The data necessary for the model are drawn from the data base and placed in a matrix for analysis. The data in the matrix are frequently a function of basic input parameters, so there is a matrix modification module to perform computations and create new variables.

The economic subsystem provides projections for the economy and industry where the company is planning to operate or is currently operating. This subsystem contains national- and industry-level models. The economic models were not built especially for the planning model but are among many commercially available economic forecasting models. Another part of the model uses computerized financial information available from proprietary sources to generate financial planning data for companies being considered for acquisition.

The risk-analysis subsystem generates alternative data bases to show the effect of the variability present in the point estimates provided by planners. For example, one model in conjunction with forecasting models determines the probability distribution of performance for strategic planning units based on historical data and subjective input from management. These data are used to generate confidence intervals for different levels of profits.

New profit estimates are used by the simulation subsystem to create the required financial data. A worst-case minimum profit is derived for every strategy and becomes a constraint in the optimization analysis. All strategies selected during the optimization phase must exceed this minimum level by an amount specified by management. A separate model computes the proportion of corporate assets in businesses of different characteristics. A business-mix evaluation uses portfolio-type analysis to recommend the allocation of corporate assets to different lines of business to maximize expected return on equity for different variances. The optimization subsystem is used again to search for an optimal solution within the bounds of the new allocation of assets.

Summary

The computer-based planning system described here is a sophisticated approach to top-management decision making. It can be used for periodic studies or as a part of the annual planning process. The system can also be used for special planning activities that arise on an ad hoc basis. The objective is to assist in developing strategies, and exact solutions with detailed accuracy are not as important as rank-order consistency. Although such a system is expensive to develop—in the neighborhood of one-quarter to one million dollars—it can provide significant benefits to management.

ELECTRONIC MAIL

Digital Equipment Corporation (DEC) is a multinational manufacturer of computers and electronic equipment. Today the company has over 6000 active subscribers to an electronic mail system (EMS), which is used internally, not by customers.

Frequently telephone calls are not completed because the person being called
either is not at his or her phone or is using it at that moment. Telephone calls also
interrupt the individual receiving the call, when often an immediate response is
not needed.

The electronic mail system at DEC uses a series of computers to store and
forward messages. Each subscriber has a computer account and an electronic
mailbox, a file to which the mail program can write messages. Individuals are
addressed by name. Users work with terminals to enter and read messages (see
the discussion of electronic mail in Chapter 3).

The mail file is more than a repository of messages, however; it also serves as
an electronic filing cabinet. The user can write and edit a message, read and
answer mail, forward it, file mail, and create distribution lists so that the user can
send a message to several individuals by typing the name of the group. This
addressing feature is useful for project teams or for managers who wish to
communicate with the staff reporting to them on a regular basis. There are also
reminder or tickler files, and a user can keep a calendar on the system.

DEC has found that 63 percent of the users are managers, 23 percent individual
contributors, and 14 percent secretaries. Some 62 percent of the users interact
with the terminal, and the remainder rely on a secretary or administrative aide to
provide their messages in hard copy and enter input messages to the system.

DEC developed the system with a great deal of care. First, an experiment was
conducted as a pilot project. About 40 subscribers began to use the system on a
single computer node; additional users were brought into the system from various
international locations to test the capacity and performance of the system. The
pilot lasted almost 18 months and involved users from a broad range of positions
and functions within the firm.

In general, the users were happy with the speed and effectiveness of
nonsimultaneous communications. The system was rated as highly effective for
broadcasting information, assigning and following up on task assignments, and
answering short questions. Information exchange was more timely, and the
distribution of information was simplified. A majority of the users felt that their
personal productivity had been increased by 5 to 15 percent. The only cautionary
finding was that the system appeared to reduce the amount of face-to-face contact
among users.

An electronic mail system is generally not advocated for cost-saving reasons;
proponents claim that the benefits described above should justify the system. At
DEC, the economic analysis showed that the breakeven on electronic mail versus
traditional methods was one additional phone call or one additional copy of a
message. "For any additional copies or addressees beyond the second, EMS is
significantly less costly than either the interoffice memo or the telephone call even
if the manager relied on an administrative support person to do EMS work"

(Crawford, 1982). The costs savings do not totally pay for the system; the major justifications for it are the features of the system and improvements in productivity.

The best evaluation came from the president of DEC: "We are so used to electronic mail, and we have become so dependent upon it, that I have forgotten what life was like without it. Being able to immediately send and receive messages to approximately 6000 stations around the world is so efficient that we now can't conceive of life without electronic mail" (Crawford, 1982).

IMPLICATIONS

The five systems described in this chapter differ considerably from each other. The differences are not really pronounced in terms of computer technology; rather, the major contrast is the type of decision supported. The immediate requirements for information in systems such as AAS necessitate instantaneous updating. In decision-support systems like the portfolio application, most of the updating does not have to be done in real time. In these systems, it is the decision maker's need for on-line interaction that necessitates an on-line system; instant conversational response means that the decision process does not have to be interrupted to wait for the computer.

The electronic mail system at Digital is the most unusual of the systems in this chapter. Immediate updating is important because the system is interactive. Since messages are personal and are used for a variety of purposes, it is not really possible to characterize the kinds of decisions, if any, supported by the electronic mail system. We can say that this is a communications system that offers a great deal of potential benefits to the organization. Many firms are organized by grouping together individuals who depend on each other to facilitate communications. Electronic mail makes it easy to communicate across organizational boundaries and offers a great deal of flexibility in creating new organizational structures, temporary task forces, and other organizational mechanisms.

Systems dealing with transactions processing and operational control like Hardserve and AAS become a part of the control process in the organization. They tend to embody a few decisions that are actually programmed in the procedures of the system; a certain minimal level of use is mandatory, since the systems are installed. Certainly the systems are capable of providing management with information for making decisions, but this is not the major reason the systems were developed.

On the other hand, the portfolio and planning systems provide very little routine information processing; their use is almost exclusively voluntary. These systems provide information to support decisions; they do not actually make the decisions. A number of decisions are programmed into the systems, but they are required to evaluate different alternatives and process information that is presented to and acted on by the decision maker. This type of system is risky to develop, potentially expensive, and almost impossible to justify on a cost-benefit basis. What is the value of better planning? How do we know the decision makers using these systems perform better than under previous manual systems?

Will decision-support systems be limited to research projects or to organizations with large amounts of capital to invest? Ten years ago the answer to this question would probably have been "yes." However, recent advances in technology make decision-support systems easier to develop for one-shot or novel decisions. Now there are economical timesharing systems available based on minicomputers that can be acquired for internal use in the company. If more computer power is required, a number of external timesharing service bureaus offer services, and the user pays only for what is consumed. Low-cost graphics terminals are also available to provide a variety of output alternatives. Finally much of the use of personal computers is for individual decision support.

More suitable hardware for developing decision-support systems has also been accompanied by better software. Simple timesharing languages are available so that even a novice can program a small decision-support application. Many service bureaus have packaged programs that can be used alone or in combination (for example, by interfacing them through a file) to solve management decision problems. For some applications, special-purpose, higher-level languages can be utilized; these languages are designed for the nonprofessional programmer who wants to develop a system in a language more natural than most general-purpose computer languages. As the complexity of the application increases, more elaborate packages and more computer processing power are available. Also, many organizations now have implemented data-base management systems, so much of the internal data for use in management decision making already exists. Only the analysis routines and external data need to be added. On the personal computer side, electronic spreadsheets provide the most frequently used software for decision support.

As more transactions systems are completed and we look to support decision making, the technology is present to facilitate the development of advanced applications. These systems, it is hoped, will become regarded as a standard tool for management in the coming years. The analyst who is aware of the potential of such decision aids and knowledgeable about computers and information systems should be at a distinct advantage.

KEY WORDS

Alternatives	Mathematical programming
Bottlenecks	Normative models
Conflict	On-line updating
Consolidation	Optimization
CRT	Parameters
Decision support	Portfolio
Editor	Postoptimality analysis
External data	Report generator
Graphics	Risk analysis
Hypothetical portfolio	Simulation
Integer programming	Strategic planning
Interactive response	

RECOMMENDED READINGS

Crawford, A. B.: "Corporate Electronic Mail—A Communication-Intensive Application of Information Technology," *MIS Quarterly,* vol. 6, no. 3, September 1982, pp. 1–13. (A good discussion of implementing electronic mail.)

Gerrity, T. P.: "Design of Man-Machine Decision Systems and Application to Portfolio Management," *Sloan Management Review,* vol. 12, no. 2, Winter 1971, pp. 59–75. (An article describing the portfolio management system of this chapter in more detail.)

Hamilton, W. F., and M. A. Moses: "A Computer Based Corporate System," *Management Science,* vol. 21, no. 2, October 1974, pp. 148–159. (An article presenting useful insights on the planning system discussed in this chapter.)

Johnson, J. C., et al.: "RAFT: An Information System for Fiscal Analysis," *MIS Quarterly,* vol. 1, December 1977, pp. 29–39.

Wimbrow, J. H.: "A Large-Scale Interactive Administrative System," *IBM Systems Journal,* vol. 10, no. 4, 1971, pp. 260–282. (An article containing details and a description of the IBM AAS system in its early stages.)

DISCUSSION QUESTIONS

1 What types of decisions are supported by each of the systems in this chapter?

2 Describe the underlying technology, for example, batch and timesharing, for each of the systems in this chapter. How does the technology compare with the types of decision support in the systems?

3 How could managers have been prepared to take a normative approach to portfolio selection before the introduction of the portfolio system described in this chapter?

4 When they are not working, the interactive applications create problems for users because of computer or systems problems. Why do users become so dependent on these systems? How does the batch system provide a buffer between the user, on the one hand, and the information services department and the computer on the other?

5 What decisions have you encountered where one of these systems would have been useful?

6 How does an information system serve to integrate the components of the planning system in this chapter?

7 Is an operations research model a form of information system?

8 How can management justify the expense of a strategic planning model that costs over a quarter of a million dollars?

9 One author has claimed that strategic planning information can come from a company's transactions-oriented data base. Does the example of a planning system in this chapter agree with this observation? What else is needed?

10 How has technology changed the cost-benefit ratio for these decision-support systems since the early ones were developed in the late 1960s?

11 How might decision or cognitive style affect a manager's reactions to graphic output?

12 Why are such stringent authorization procedures necessary in a system like AAS?

13 Is a backup processor often required in on-line systems?

14 What is the purpose of a concentrator in the AAS system?

15 Why is a printer also used at branch offices in the AAS system along with CRTs?

16 Would transferring accounts among branch offices be difficult or easy in the AAS system? How would such a change be accomplished?

17 Compare and contrast AAS with an on-line airline reservation system.

18 Could a system like AAS be developed using packaged programs, for example, for telecommunications and data-base management? If so, why were such packages not used?

19 Why is CAI successful in training people for the use of AAS? How does this training differ, say, from training students in high school or college?

20 What kinds of inquiries do you think customers would make of AAS? Are the record keys and directories sufficient to answer these requests?

21 Why do you suppose one computer is dedicated to data management and a series of machines is devoted to message processing in AAS? Why are there not multiple computers, each processing messages and accessing files?

22 Are there manual procedures in the AAS system? What controls do you recommend over orders and order-entry processing?

23 How could AAS backup procedures be modified to reduce the cost of recovering from damaged files? What added costs would your solution incur?

24 Why is an audit trail needed in an on-line system? What is its equivalent in a batch system, specifically in the Hardserve example?

25 How would you estimate requirements for on-line systems equipment? What data would you collect?

26 How is conversion to an on-line system different than that for a batch system?

27 What is the purpose of the preliminary survey and feasibility studies?

28 What are the advantages from the user's standpoint of on-line systems for data entry and retrieval, and what are the drawbacks?

29 Would you predict that the systems described in this chapter would upgrade or downgrade the skills required of clerical users?

30 What management information could be developed from each of the systems discussed in this chapter?

31 In what other areas could RAFT be applied?

32 Why have information services departments generally not developed decision-support systems? Why do they seem to concern themselves more with transactions-processing applications?

33 Why is on-line updating not always a requirement with decision-support systems, while most of the time interactive response is necessary?

34 What software advances are needed to facilitate the development of decision-support systems?

35 How can we evaluate the effectiveness of the systems in this chapter after they are installed?

36 Make a list of the types of computer systems we have discussed, from transactions through strategic planning, and describe the benefits you would expect from each. What does your list suggest about problems with feasibility studies?

37 What would be the capabilities of a general-purpose decision-support system that could be used across a number of applications by different decision makers? Do you think such a system could be developed and would be advisable? What might the implementation problems be?

THE MANAGEMENT OF INFORMATION SYSTEMS

CHAPTER 22

THE COMPUTER DEPARTMENT

The computer department is relatively new within organizations; its historical roots date back to tabulating card operations. In the 1950s or early 1960s the tabulating department acquired electronic computing equipment. These early computers were used to replace old EAM (electronic accounting machines) or card-processing equipment. After focusing on transactional systems, the computer has moved into budgeting, inventory, and all types of operational control applications. Now we are seeing attempts to develop more management-oriented systems.

We should point out that an organization may have several computer departments. A large corporation typically has some central computer group reporting to a high level in the organization. This central group may have direct or consulting responsibilities for numerous smaller computer departments, say, one in each plant location. These plant computer departments may in fact be as large or larger than the entire computer department of a smaller firm. In this chapter we shall discuss the computer department as a single entity, recognizing that it may take many different forms depending on the organization.

STATUS OF THE DEPARTMENT

Historical Background

In the vast majority of organizations, the computer department was first organized under accounting. This location for the department seemed logical, given the bookkeeping nature of many early computer systems that performed billing operations, receivables accounting, general ledger, etc. The computer department has often stayed within the accounting or financial wing of the organization. Many problems are created by this reporting position for the department. Users in other areas, sometimes with good justification, feel that accounting applications receive first priority and their own interests suffer in comparison. If we remember our discussion in the first part of the book on the transfer of power, the user is giving up power to the accounting department, which may be unpalatable.

Independence

In most organizations today, computer activities require sufficient resources that it is reasonable to establish the department as a separate, service-oriented entity. Where the organization is small or the computer effort is very new, the computer department and other staff-related activities can report on an equal footing to a vice president of administration. The idea is to create a separately identifiable computer department in the organization so that users can view the computer as an organizational resource. The computer should not be seen as a part of some foreign department that might help the user's department if there is nothing else to do.

DEPARTMENT ORGANIZATION

Activities

Until now we have paid most attention to system design activities within the computer department. This is only one portion of the range of activities undertaken by this department, although they are probably the most creative and interesting parts of the computer department's function. Because the second part of the text is devoted to systems analysis and design, we shall pay less attention to it in this chapter. Once a system is installed, the computer department is responsible for operating it on a routine basis. Some computer applications may run for 5 to 10 or more years with only minor changes over their lifetime. After the systems design is completed, the day-to-day contact between the computer department and users is through the operations staff. We will explore operations activities and problems more in the next section.

Operations versus Systems Design

The tasks of the operations component of the computer department are very different in nature from those of the systems design staff. The personnel involved in operations and design activities have different time orientations and approaches, and these differences can create many management problems.

The computer department is almost like two departments in one. (You may want to review our discussion of Mintzberg's organizational model in Chapter 1.) The systems design group has a long time horizon and expects a project to take many months to complete. This group spends much of its time thinking and planning or in group meetings and activities. Much of the pressure to do a good job is internally generated, and they consider themselves professionals. Generally, these individuals have a high level of education, including at least some college or training beyond secondary school.

The operations side of the computer department, on the other hand, is characterized by a short time horizon; operations run by the clock, and an hour's delay can make a difference in doing a good or a bad job. Almost no group activities are involved in operations, nor are there long, reflective periods. The rule in operations is continual action. The pressure on the operations staff is incessant and comes from computer users, the computer itself, and the schedule that must be maintained. Operations jobs are often considered of low status in the organization. There is a high degree of immediacy to the work flows and there is reciprocal interdependence between the computer department operations staff and users.

SYSTEMS PROBLEM 22-1

International Associates is a worldwide insurance firm specializing in casualty insurance. The company has subsidiaries throughout the free world including the Far East, Europe, and South America. All these local companies have demands for information processing. The firm has grown rapidly, with little coordination of local sites or company policy on information systems. Thus, a situation exists in which a regional center may serve two or three countries, and small subsidiaries in other countries have their own small computer systems.

Because information processing service has been unacceptable, the company is trying to reorganize. Reports are late, input data are incorrect, and systems do not seem to work. The users are blaming the computer department, while the computer staff complains that users do not provide accurate data on time and do not understand systems.

Recently, Steve Nussbaum was hired as vice president of information systems at International Associates and given the task of straightening out the information processing systems in 18 months. Steve's first problem is to decide how to reorganize the company's information processing department. Now there are regional data centers, and data centers in individual companies with no clear pattern. Some users have a data center right in their firm; others must find someone in a regional center when they have a problem.

One possibility Steve is considering is to establish regional representatives to whom users could turn with any problem. These representatives would handle all problems, from operational difficulties to requests for enhancements and the design of new systems. What are the advantages and disadvantages of such an approach? What problems will the regional representatives encounter in performing their roles if this course is taken?

Several types of conflict occur between the operations and design groups within the department. Consider the following examples. Programmers want test time and may try to interrupt operations to obtain the needed time. Testing leads to the development of a new system, which means more work for the operations staff. (One solution is to set aside specific amounts of test time and have adequate capacity so that operations are not adversely affected by tests.)

More conflict within the computer department develops when errors occur; who is responsible, the systems design and programming staff or operations? In a later section we discuss maintenance programming (the responsibility of a group to keep an implemented system operating successfully). To avoid problems when errors occur, a formal turnover procedure can be used in which the maintenance group reviews documentation and tests and signs off that it feels ready to maintain the system on an operational basis.

Probably the easiest way to handle the differences between the systems design and the operations staff is to organize the department in two subgroups. Certainly, the presence of an operations division and a system design division is the most frequent solution to this management problem. Department management must then work to integrate the two groups. For example, management can require that new systems development efforts show an estimated time for operating the system. System designers can be required to work with the operations manager to be sure that when implemented, there will be enough capacity to handle a new application.

Subgroup Organization

For the operations subgroup, the most natural organization is a functional hierarchy. That is, each function, such as machine operations, tape and disk library, etc., has employees who report to a single supervisor. Although employees may rotate among functions, a single manager has the responsibility for each function. We should keep in mind that modern organization theory generally recommends a relatively flat organizational structure: that is, having few levels of subordinates and superiors when we design the operations organization.

Defining an organization for the systems design group presents a problem. The staff is assigned to different projects and design teams, but it is also comforting to have one manager who is responsible for evaluation, raises, promotions, etc. One commonly adopted solution to this problem is to use a matrix form of organization. A matrix organization looks like a table in which the rows of the table represent system analysts, programmers, and users. The columns represent the various projects as shown in Table 22-1. Usually a systems design and/or programming manager works with the analysts and programmers to determine their interest and to make assignments for different projects. This individual is also responsible for staff reviews and evaluation. On specific projects, systems designers and programmers work with the project leader, as we saw in the Hardserve example.

Many organizational forms for systems design other than the matrix organiza-

TABLE 22-1
MATRIX SYSTEMS DESIGN SUBGROUP
ORGANIZATION

Systems design manager*
Programming manager*

	Project				
Staff members**	1	2	3	4	. . . n
Systems analysts					
Programmers					
Users					

---

*Responsible in general for analysts and programmers.
**Assigned to temporary project groups under the supervision of a project manager.

tion have been used. In some large installations, it may be possible to have a group of analysts and programmers assigned to each functional area in the organization such as marketing, accounting, production, and finance. These individuals develop a good knowledge of the requirements in their functional area, and this approach can be very user-oriented. Whatever final organizational structure is chosen for systems analysis and design, we should remember that research results support the use of a participatory, employee-centered leadership style for managing these individuals (Mumford, 1972).

MANAGING COMPUTER OPERATIONS

Surprisingly little has been written about the operations subgroup in a computer department. Possibly, the operation of a computer department is considered mundane compared with the creative nature of systems design. However, well-designed systems will work successfully only if they are operated competently by the computer department.

One of the most difficult tasks in the computer department is to develop a service orientation on the part of employees. The only purpose of the computer department is to provide a service. As we have seen in past chapters, information processing is of vital importance to the organization. However, it is easy for the computer department staff to develop the idea that its end product is more important than the output of the organization. A service orientation on the part of the computer department reduces conflict with users; it also means that the user has more control over processing, as requests receive a prompt response.

How do we create a service orientation in the department? The best approach to developing proper attitudes is through management leadership and rewards. First, the management of the computer department serves as a model for others in the department. Rewards for computer department staff members should be under the control of the department manager, who can give promotions, raises, and bonuses to employees who work well with users and who are responsive in providing service.

In most organizations the operations component of the computer department is structured on the basis of function. Figure 22-1 provides an overview of the major functions of the operations subgroup.

The Computer Room

Computer room activities include the responsibilities of loading jobs, running the machine, and mounting various files. The major problems in the computer room revolve around scheduling and work flows. The operator needs a schedule to know what jobs to run and when to run them. There should be a fixed schedule for repetitive jobs and a detailed schedule for each day. Each job should have a routing sheet that indicates the operations to be performed in processing it. The operator also needs documentation on how to process the job; we discussed some of this operator documentation in Chapter 18.

Programs are usually stored in a compiled (object) form on disk and initiated by the operator when that application is ready to be run. In the case of on-line systems, the operator needs procedures that clearly are specified for restarting the machine or cutting over to a backup machine when the primary machine fails.

Installations always maintain a log at the computer console that shows what has been run and operator messages. One copy is held for machine repair purposes, and the other is filed with the control group to answer questions about jobs.

The operations staff is also responsible for the file library, which is a nontrivial management task in a large organization, which may have 10,000 reels of tape. As with any library it is necessary to keep a record of where any file is located and a description of what version this file represents. Most computer tape and disk libraries are maintained manually, though there are several mechanical systems that operate the library completely, even to the extent of selecting and loading a tape on a tape drive automatically.

FIGURE 22-1
Functions of the operations subgroup of the computer department.

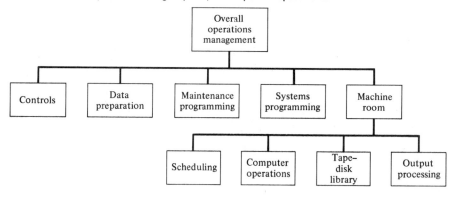

Managing the Network

Most organizations with more than one location also have multiple computers. Even one large physical site may have a number of microcomputers scattered throughout the operation. How does the computer department manage under these conditions?

A highly distributed or decentralized environment introduces many new complications, at least for hardware and software. Users expect support, but it may not always be easy to provide. As the firm acquires computers from different vendors, connects them with a network, and purchases a large amount of software from various vendors, support becomes more difficult. First, the entire configuration of computers is just more complex, and second, there are more kinds of devices and programs to support.

For these reasons, many firms try to develop some guidelines or operational policies for managing a network. They may standardize on one to three different brands of microcomputer and require certain communications capabilities for each machine. Similarly, the firm may choose only a few software packages and offer to support them only.

In such an environment, the computer department must worry about the management of the communications network and distributed equipment. Usually there will be some kind of a "help desk" where users can call to report problems. The staff in the help area then tries to use the computer itself and various monitoring software to determine where the problem lies.

Software consulting can also be provided through the help desk, as many problems can be solved with a phone conversation. However, it is still not clear how to help remote users of systems when the application is entirely local, such as a complicated spreadsheet analysis on a personal computer. It is hard for the expert consultant to understand the problem without access to it. In the future, however, this situation should change, as the user will be able to send the problem over the network to be studied by the consultant.

Controls

Most computer departments have some type of control area, and some even have separate control departments. The basic responsibility of this group is to log input data and record the progress of the work through the department. Users should be able to contact one person at any time and learn the status of their jobs. This group keeps statistics of the jobs completed on schedule so that computer department management knows what type of service is being provided; for example, management should know that 90 percent of all jobs are returned within 1 hour of the scheduled delivery time.

When errors occur, this group checks to see if the user data are in error or if some processing mistake was made in the computer department. The control group is also responsible for proofing batch totals where this type of control mechanism is used. Since the quality of input is one of the major keys to successful processing, the activities of the control group are vital.

Data Conversion

The computer department is also responsible for some types of data conversion, particularly for keying operations. This activity has to be supervised and the work assigned and scheduled to complete processing on time. The movement to on-line systems means that there will be much less data conversion in the computer department. Users with terminals will enter data and become responsible for control and error correction.

Output Processing

Just as errors occur in input, mistakes are possible on the output. A well-run computer department checks the output to see if it is reasonable. Do the report totals add up? Are crossfootings correct? Are there processing-error messages that affect the reports, and do the data themselves look reasonable?

Another type of output processing is more physical in nature; often the documents from the computer require manual operations, especially for transactions-oriented computer systems. For example, a bank may have to put charge slips with a credit card bill, place the entire package in an envelope, and mail it. A report may have been printed in multiple copies with carbon paper interleaved between them. Decollating uses a special machine to separate the copies and remove the corbon paper. Also, it may be necessary to burst the output, that is, to split apart continuous forms at their perforations.

Maintenance Programming

Earlier we described the duties of a group of maintenance programmers. The motivation for maintenance programming is that no program is ever fully debugged; we can expect to find errors in operational systems over time. Also, a responsive computer department can expect to make changes in systems as users become familiar with them.

The maintenance programming group has to locate errors and correct them. This is the reason for much of the documentation described in Chapter 18. We also usually make this group responsible for routine changes requested by users, such as the modification of a report.

Because this group has significant amounts of user contact, it must be very responsive to user needs. There should be a formal procedure that users can follow to request a change. The formal request should be processed and placed in the library of documentation for the system. The maintenance staff should strive to return written responses to requests to the user within 48 hours. The response should explain to the user what will be done, how long it will take, and what the cost will be. Also, the staff should be sure that the request is clearly understood. By the same token, if the request cannot be granted, the computer department should explain why. For example, if the change is too expensive or too costly a change for maintenance programming, the user may want to request a more major revision, such as a new systems design project. In a responsive computer department, the maintenance group also works with users to suggest changes in systems to make them more useful.

Systems Programming

It is useful to distinguish between maintenance programming, which is oriented toward applications, and systems programming, which is focused on systems software such as operating systems, compilers, and communications programs. Many installations do not have system programmers and rely solely on the computer vendor's representatives to generate an operating system or make modifications to it. In a large-scale installation, however, there probably will be more than one of these specialists. These individuals have almost no user contact and are responsible for keeping systems software working or developing new systems software, such as the implementation of a data-base management system.

Data Administrator

As organizations move towards large data bases and the use of data-base management systems, a new computer department position has been suggested, that of data administrator. The data administrator is responsible for the creation and maintenance of the data base. What data are to be contained in the data base in the file system? What files are available for what types of processing? This individual is also responsible for maintaining the security and privacy of the file. The data administrator must set authorization levels to determine who is allowed to access what types of data; for example, access to payroll information may be restricted in some companies.

Operations Flow

The flow of jobs and the activity in computer department operations is very much like a job shop, at least for batch processing computer applications. There are a variety of processing steps, and not all are performed on each job. On the other hand, the computer room for an on-line system appears as if almost nothing is happening. However, when the system experiences a failure, there will be a frantic level of activity. Modern hardware and software make possible on-line and batch operations on a single machine, so there are many mixed installations.

There is a need to consider scheduling for almost any computer installation. Usually, there will be a number of jobs that are run on a fixed processing schedule, for example, payroll every Thursday night. Also, a number of short requests will occur regularly, such as the execution of a batch information retrieval package.

One of the major tasks of the machine room supervisor is to establish a schedule and modify it if reruns are needed or if higher-priority jobs appear.

Because of the variety of jobs, formal scheduling networks have not been too helpful, since changes almost always have to be made. Just as with the job-shop scheduling problem, there are a combinatorial number of paths through processing, and the problem is too complex to solve analytically. The computer department has fewer processing stages than the typical job shop, but it has to be very flexible in scheduling. Problems are also created because the completion time for a job in a multiprogramming system may depend on what other jobs are operating concurrently with it.

It may be helpful to use some of the commercially available scheduling devices such as magnetic scheduling boards or Gantt charts (Olsen, 1968). In principle, a Gantt chart is nothing more than a bar chart of several concurrent activities with time as the horizontal axis. In a computer context one might assign a horizontal line to a single computer in a multicomputer shop or even to a particular partition in a multiprogrammed computer. Schedulers may also need lines for other required resources such as tape or a disk drive. Then, using the approximate time and sequence of operations, the scheduler works with the chart to schedule all the jobs to be run.

Security

The security of computer systems and operations has become a major concern (see Hoffman, 1977). There are two different types of security, logical and environmental. Logical security is directed to maintaining the privacy and security of information that is proprietary. Is it possible for someone to use a system or access data fraudulently or for purposes for which the system was not designed? Environmental security refers to protection and backup in case of some disaster. Various threats to security are shown in Table 22-2.

Logical Security   Logical security is provided through systems design and by operating controls. We have discussed program error checks extensively in previous chapters. By having a large design team and a group of programmers, the entire group has to conspire to include a capability for fraud in the application. Of

TABLE 22-2
SECURITY HAZARDS

Logical hazards
  Operator error
  Program error
  Theft and fraud
  Penetration
Environmental hazards
  Environment (fire, flood)
  Mechanical failure
  Sabotage

course, this hindrance does not stop an individual-user employee from using a system fraudulently, and systems designers have to build checks and safeguards into a system. For example, the system might notify operators of strange transactions or too much activity on one account, etc. It is also important to use identification procedures and passwords for terminals that can access a system. It should also be possible to audit the computer system; that is, to check all stages of processing.

In the machine room it is recommended that several employees be involved in operations. Operator errors are reduced through good design and documentation procedures. Most installations also avoid having nonessential people in the computer department operational areas. Also, it is a good idea to require cross-checks and authorizations for program changes.

The constant probing of sensitive systems may be necessary (Allen, 1968). A special team can be given a mission to penetrate security precautions to check on their effectiveness.

Environmental Security   We have only a limited ability to prevent disasters, and the best strategy is to be prepared in case one does occur. Certainly, a secure building should be used for the computer center, and various fire detectors and fire-extinguishing devices should be considered, However, the only way to safeguard absolutely against catastrophe is to be prepared for it. In our discussion of files we mentioned the importance of backup; past copies or duplicated copies of active files should be kept in a separate physical location that is secure. Many cities have firms that rent space for important documents in special, secure vaults, sometimes located well outside the city. Extra copies of programs and essential documentation (for example, a microfilm copy of the system library made once per year) should also be stored in a safe location away from the processing site.

Companies frequently arrange backup agreements with other organizations that have the same type of equipment. After reaching this mutual help agreement, each side should attempt to run programs on the other's systems. Too often, similar equipment is different enough (for example, on the amount of memory or number of disks or tape drives) so that applications for a slightly different system will not run on it. The computer vendor can be of assistance here. As with any other critical resource, information processing capabilities have to be ensured by taking reasonable precautions against disaster.

CONTROL OF PROCESSING

With a wide variety of hardware and software available today, the problem of the control over computer-based processing becomes quite complex. We should emphasize that the physical location of equipment does not necessarily correlate with the managerial control of computer processing. By managerial control, we refer to by whom and where basic decisions are made about computer process-ing, such as decisions on what equipment to obtain and where to locate it, what new applications to undertake, the standardization of software and procedures, personnel management, and the authority to commit organizational resources in general to information processing.

Table 22-3 shows a range of processing possibilities in the physical sense compared with possible patterns of managerial control. The rows and columns in the table represent continua; there are many possible patterns between the ones depicted here. On the equipment side, we can have highly centralized computers, distributed processing in which various computers form a network of some type and communicate among each other, and totally decentralized processing in which computers are placed in different physical locations with no interconnections among them. From a management control standpoint, it is simplest to consider either fully centralized or fully decentralized control.

Centralized Processing

With centralized computer equipment, we can have all systems analysis and operations at the centralized site. All new systems are developed here, and clearly they must be operated from the central location. The major management issue under this approach is to see that the central site is responsive to users, especially those at remote locations. It is also possible to have centralized equipment and decentralized control. For example, programmers and analysts work for various user areas, making use of central computer resources through a terminal. The

TABLE 22-3
CONTROL OF INFORMATION PROCESSING

	Management control	
Equipment configuration	Centralized	Decentralized
Centralized	All analysts, programs, operations staff at central site	Analysts, programmers work for various area divisions, make use of central resource through terminals
Distributed	All analysts and programmers controlled by central site—assigned to different projects; programs downloaded to distributed processors	All programs development done locally—control through standards and procedures; central coordinating group optional
Decentralized	Analysts and programmers assigned to project, local operations staff	Complete local control over systems and operations staff

control problem here is one of coordination of the decentralized analysts; for example, to see that common software is used in all applicable locations to prevent duplication.

Distributed Processing

Even with a distributed network that places computers at local sites, it is possible to maintain central control over all important information processing decisions. All analysts and programmers can be controlled by the central site and assigned to different projects, even though the staff may have to spend considerable time at the local sites. From an operations standpoint, all software can be provided by the central site to be certain that compatibility exists among the various nodes in the network. The local site then only follows very specific operating instructions and has no real decision-making capabilities in the control of information processing.

Conversely, all programming and development can be done locally in the distributed network. However, if this is the choice, there usually must be some type of central coordination, since it is desirable for the various nodes in the network to communicate. The coordination can be provided by standards and some type of a central control group to develop and enforce the standards. A good example is in data-base construction and updating policies that have distributed data bases. Queries from one location may have to be answered with data from another node; if the local nodes have complete control with no coordination, this communication may prove impossible. Thus, for control purposes there has to be some staff group that can coordinate the activities of autonomous local staff members.

Decentralized Processing

Even with a totally decentralized physical configuration for equipment, it is possible to maintain central control over systems analysis and design and programming, though operations must be managed locally. Here again, the challenge of central control is to be responsive to users in return for the easier coordination provided by centralization. With decentralized equipment, complete local control over systems analysis and design, programming, and operations is possible. Unless opportunities exist for common applications that can be shared across two or more local sites, there may be little demand for central control and coordination. However, it is desirable to have a central staff group for coordination purposes even though the need for such a group may not be obvious. Even with total decentralization, it may be desirable to maintain compatibility among different computers in the organization and to have some central planning for equipment systems. The purpose of such planning is to prevent suboptimal decision making by local sites, which may not be aware of corporate needs or the needs of other subunits of the organization.

A major impetus for decentralized systems came from the development of minicomputers. These computers were inexpensive enough that they could often be justified for a single, dedicated application. A second impetus for decentralization, probably stronger than the first, has come from the microcomputer. These computers are very inexpensive, and users are acquiring them at a furious pace.

Although there may be a number of valid, decentralized applications for microcomputers, we should keep in mind that processing trends strongly suggest that systems of the future will all be interconnected, at least for some portion of the day. In presenting alternatives that include microcomputers, we should pay special attention to the ability of the hardware and, more important, the software to function in an interconnected network of computers.

Design Considerations

The availability of different types of processing becomes an issue in systems, especially those that will have interactive components. The analyst has to be aware of the issues of control, cost, and processing patterns. For on-line systems, the key factor in most decisions will be the location, ownership, and updating

---

SYSTEMS PROBLEM 22-2

Susan Miller is responsible for information systems planning at Chem Fibers, a large chemicals firm. Chem has been considering the possibility of moving toward distributed processing. A large number of plants and administrative departments are scattered throughout the United States. There really seems to be no need to have data from all these locations processed centrally, as is now done.

The computer department has developed a plan for equipment location that places a great deal of processing with distributed computers at different manufacturing and sales offices. Susan and her superiors are concerned that users will get the wrong impression about distributed processing and be disappointed with the results. "Certainly there will be local processors, but there is no guarantee that these systems will be any more responsive than the central systems. It all depends on how they are managed," remarked the head of the computer services department.

Susan has been given the responsibility of determining what centralized controls must be placed on applications development and operations at the distributed sites. In addition, she is supposed to assess the impact of any standard policies on the user and the flexibility of local sites.

Susan is trying to delineate the areas in which policy needs to be developed. Her first list includes the acquisition of software, the acquisition of computer hardware, the selection of new applications alternatives, the authorization to proceed with a new application, the acquisition of systems software, the charging mechanism for computer services, reporting within the computer department from remote locations, and relations with users. She is also concerned with the task of coordinating the far-flung computer staff under distributed processing. Susan fears that if she develops a set of bureaucratic procedures for central approval, users at various sites will take shortcuts or service will become totally unresponsive. What policies do you suggest for Chem Fibers?

---

demands of the data base. If data are to be owned, updated, and accessed primarily from one location, then it makes sense to place the data base at the local site to reduce communications costs.

As the need to access data from a variety of different locations grows, the task of choosing between a centralized or distributed processing configuration becomes more difficult. A careful cost analysis that considers the volume of communications, reliability considerations (distributed processing can offer greater reliability than centralized processing), and managerial philosophy will be necessary. In some cases it may be desirable to simulate the proposed design to estimate costs. In any case, the variety of physical alternatives for computer processing and the different approaches to managerial control of processing create a wide variety of choices for systems analysis and design. This abundance of alternatives provides a great deal of power and flexibility, at the same time greatly complicating the design task.

RELATIONSHIP WITH USERS

One of our major themes throughout the text has been that the computer department exists to provide a service; the department is only successful if its customers (users) gain some benefit from its activities. Our approach to systems design is a radical one; we suggest that users should design their own systems. In this section we explore other approaches to a productive relationship between users and the computer department. Remember that at the organizational level we have been concerned about information systems creating changes in power relationships among departments, and at the individual level we have worried about the high potential for conflict created by information systems activities.

The Computer Department Manager

We discussed the activities of the computer department manager inside the department earlier in this chapter. Now we explore this role in the rest of the organization and in working with users. One organizational theorist has proposed that one role of managers is to serve as a linking pin (Likert, 1961). The manager links groups of subordinates with groups of superiors; this conceptualization of the manager's role is very similar to integration as defined by Lawrence and Lorsch (1967). Because of this position, the manager of the computer department serves to integrate the department with users and with top management.

What are the activities of computer department managers in this role? First, they have to provide rewards to the computer department staff for developing user-oriented systems. It is necessary for computer department managers to meet with user managers and explain the role of the design team. They must encourage users to choose the design team leaders and ask them to add employees to free resources so that knowledgeable users can participate in the design of a system.

The computer department manager may also have to suggest the formation of a steering committee and guide the committee in its role in making decisions.

Informal contacts with heads of user departments should be maintained to determine if they are having particular problems with new systems or with the operation of existing ones. The computer department manager must determine if there are any ways a new system could be helpful in the information processing activities of these departments.

Steering Committee

A steering committee played a central part in our systems design example in the Hardserve Company. That committee was composed of several functional managers and met with one specific purpose in mind. It did not try to act as a design group. The steering committee met to consider several alternatives and select one for implementation. The use of such a committee is an important part of the management of computer activities. First, the committee makes decisions consistent with the goals of the organization. The user department and the computer department do not have the information to know the direction in which the organization is moving. Through participation each user knows the reasons why a particular alternative was selected. In separate meetings, the committee can also approve the plans and budget for the computer department and is in an excellent position to make a trade-off in resources between investing in new services or enhancements to existing applications.

Design Teams

The systems design team is essential in out approach to systems design, and we recommend that a user should be the leader of the team. The team consists of users and computer department staff members. Let us review again the reasons for these suggestions. First, by having users participate in the design team we obtain better information about present information processing procedures and decision-making activities. Participation also prepares the users for the system. Users make a psychological commitment to the system and better their understanding of it by working on the design. Finally, a heavy role for users in systems design is another illustration of the computer department's service orientation.

Other Integrators

The suggestions made above for various managerial activities, steering committees, and design teams are aimed at further integrating the diverse and technological computer department with users. There are some additional mechanisms that can help to accomplish this goal (McFarlan, 1973).

The User Interface   Much of the frustration and conflict from computer systems develops over the user interface with systems. In our approach, with the user designing the input and output, some of the potential for conflict should be reduced. The design team should also consider the possibility of using technology in reducing interface problems. For example, OCR equipment, on-line terminals, and similar devices can be used to ease data entry and/or retrieval. For batch systems, it is important to use control logs so that users are aware of the status of processing for each job. Also, the documentation procedures described in Chapter 18 should help to reduce user problems with the computer interface.

User Representatives   A number of organizations have developed special user liaisons for each system that is in operation. When users have a problem or a question about the system they contact the user representative in the computer department. Users do not have to figure out to whom they should turn in the computer department; instead they have one consistent contact. The user representative finds the answer to the question and responds to the user. In some organizations the user liaison actually has a desk in the user area. In the Hardserve example, a liaison was placed on location at Hardserve, since the computer actually doing the processing would be at headquarters.

Formal Procedures for Changes   There are both advantages and disadvantages to the use of formal procedures for change requests. The major advantage is that there is a record of the request, and the computer department will be reminded to respond quickly. We have suggested this approach for maintenance changes or enhancements and recommended that the computer department respond in writing within 48 hours to such a request. The user request will not be forgotten or delayed if a formal change document and procedures are used.

The disadvantage to the use of formal procedures is that the computer department can use the process to create bureaucratic red tape and delays. If the procedures involved are complicated or the response is late and the user becomes discouraged from suggesting worthwhile changes, then clearly the procedures are not serving a useful purpose. Thus, the change form should be simple, and the response should be guaranteed within a short time period.

Decentralized Analysts   One organization with a very large computer department encourages analysts to accept jobs with other user departments when they are offered. These analysts work for the user, but they have good contacts among their former coworkers in the computer department. This approach is only applicable in a fairly large organization, but it does help to link the computer department and user departments together.

Summary

The goal of these and other integrators is to reduce problems created when specialized computer department staff members interact with individuals in user departments. These devices serve to reduce the transfer of power to the computer department from users when systems are designed and operated to reduce the potential for conflict between individual users and the computer department. The key to success is to have users control as much of the design and operations process as possible. Where the computer department must have control, for example, in running a job, the department should be responsive to the user. It is most important for the users and the computer department to develop empathy for each other. Computer department staff members should be able to place themselves in the user's position and understand user reactions to information processing problems.

CHARGING FOR SERVICES

One of the major points of contact between the computer department and users is the charge made to the user for computer services. The method of charging can create conflict and dysfunctional behavior on the part of users and/or the computer department.

Two basic types of cost are associated with computer activities: development and operations. Development costs are incurred during the design of a new system. They can be estimated in advance, but the record has not been one of conspicuous success in staying within the estimated cost. Investment cost can be highly variable, especially if a project is not completed on time.

Components of Cost

Based on our experience in the Hardserve example, we can see that the major costs of systems development are personnel expenses. For most systems, the cost of computer time for testing and debugging is small compared with the labor cost. Our philosophy of having users design systems also makes it difficult to estimate costs in advance. The systems analyst has to estimate the number of days and average costs for computer department employees to design the system. Management may also want to allocate the salary expenses of users to the project when they are heavily involved in systems design activities.

Once the design has progressed to the point of knowing the type of response desired and having some idea of files and programs, the analyst can estimate programming requirements and costs. The best guide for these estimates is the experience of the organization on similar projects.

In contrast to development costs, operations costs are usually more predictable, at least by the time program testing has begun. These costs include charges for computer time, supplies, and labor. Sometimes all the various components of

TABLE 22-4
COMPARISON OF CHARGING MECHANISM FOR OVERHEAD VERSUS CHARGE-OUT

Overhead advantages
  Cheaper
  Responsibility for control remains with computer department
  Makes all computer costs visible
  Computer expenses reviewed by top management
  Creates stability for computer department

Charge-out advantages
  Users have to allocate resources to computer services and consider tradeoffs for other uses of funds
  Shows how computer department is interacting with user departments
  Provides data for comparison of external services with internal computer service
  Provides information on relative costs of applications
  User does not see computer as a free good

---

computer cost are combined into one hourly charge keyed to computer resource utilization, for example, X dollars per CPU minute, Y dollars per 1000 lines printed, etc. Other charging algorithms are based on the units of work processed by the department, such as the number of checks processed, bills printed, etc.

Charge-Out Mechanisms

There have been two polar approaches to accounting for computer expense: overhead charge-out and full charge-out to users. Table 22-4 describes the advantages of each approach (McFarlan, 1973; Dearden and Nolan, 1973).

Overhead Charges In one approach all expenses for computers are treated as company overhead. Accounting is cheaper, and it is not necessary to keep track of many individual charges or go to the expense of developing and executing a charge-out procedure. Some advocates of this approach argue that it leaves decision making in the computer department, where technical competence exists to make decisions. However, we have suggested that decisions should be made jointly with users.

Because of the large expenditure charged against overhead for computer expenses, it is possible that top management will review computer expenses more under this charging system. However, there are other mechanisms to gain the attention of top management, such as budgets, plans, and steering committees. Overhead charging does create stability for the computer department, since it can count on the same processing load. For example, under a full charge-out scheme, if user departments change their processing activities, there can be wide fluctuations in the computer department budget.

Full Charge-Out   In a full charge-out scheme all computer expenses are charged to users. Users have to make resource allocation decisions; this approach leads to the complete decentralization of computer decisions. By examining the accounting system and comparing charges, management can see where the computer department is providing the most service and has developed the most applications. The charges make it possible to compare an internal department with an outside computer service organization, which is always an alternative to internal processing. Charging also provides data on the relative cost of each application. Since the computer is not a free good, users may exercise more restraint in requesting systems.

Partial Charge-out   The partial charge-out approach offers a flexible alternative to full overhead or full charge-out accounting. The exact nature of the partial charge-out scheme depends on the individual organization. One approach that has been used is to charge users for operations, since a more certain amount is involved. New applications are treated as a research and development effort and are charged to overhead. This partial charge-out approach recognizes that a new computer application is a capital investment, just as is adding a new piece of machinery.

Choosing a Charging Method

An approach to selecting a charging mechanism based primarily on user and organizational considerations has been suggested by Dearden and Nolan (1973). If the user population is not too knowledgeable about computer systems, the opportunity for applications in the organization, and the cost and limitations of systems, then overhead accounting is favored. On the other hand, if users have widely diverse needs and are sophisticated and knowledgeable about computers, then full charge-out schemes are more appropriate.

For most organizations today, our research indicates that users are not sufficiently knowledgeable to make decisions without help from the computer department; that is why we have advocated joint teams, liaison agents, etc. This evidence argues for charging costs to overhead. On the other hand, there are advantages to charge-out schemes in allocating resources and maintaining the possibility of competition for the computer department to encourage a service orientation.

For these reasons we recommend a partial charge-out approach. For new systems development, at least a portion of the cost should be charged to overhead. Depending on organizational practices, management may insist on some matching investment funds from the user department or division. However, the user should not have to bear the full cost, especially given the uncertainty in cost and payoff in developing a new computer application.

For operations, develop a charge-out scheme for users. It may be desirable to set up some type of a flexible rate to help in allocating resources (Nielsen, 1970);

for example, charge less for jobs that can be run on the third shift and charge more for daytime use of the computer. The cost allocation method should assure users of roughly the same charges for the same job; otherwise it is very difficult for them to budget. A rate can be established for each application based on its average computer run time for the past 12 months. Some charge for volume of transactions can be added if appropriate.

The problem with any full charge-out approach is that at the end of the year, the computer department may not be a zero profit or zero cost center; that is, it may not have charged out enough cost to equal its actual expenses. To handle this problem, a reserve account can be established and the rates set so that a profit is expected. Then either the profit can be distributed to users at year's end or it can be used to reduce next year's rates.

With this type of partial charge-out method combined with the steering committee and our approach to user participation in system design, an organization should be able to obtain a rational allocation of resources for both the design and operation of information systems.

PERSONNEL
Hiring

One of the most difficult and time-consuming activities in an organization is hiring. There are a variety of approaches to hiring that generally include interviews, reference checks, and possibly an aptitude test of some type. How can we select the best computer department personnel?

The traditional approaches to hiring have been criticized by Haire. Assume that we are trying to select a group of employees for the computer department that will perform better than the rest of the population. If we use a test such as those for programming aptitude, our success in hiring a superior performing group depends on (1) the validity of the test, (2) the number of applicants we can afford to reject, and (3) the range of performance in the rejected group. In administering a test, we must ask if the test discriminates adequately among the population. In a tight labor market (the case for computer professionals) we may not be able to reject many applicants at all. Also, if the range of potential performance is fairly uniform across the population, almost anyone selected will do the job well.

Haire gives the following example to demonstrate how difficult it is to achieve marked improvements in performance through hiring and selection. Suppose that we have the luxury of being able to reject 40 percent of all applicants. Assume that we have an aptitude test that is as good as the very best around (a reliability of around .45), and also consider that the differences between the best and the worst people on the job are in a ratio of about 3 to 2. Using these data, Haire calculates that the improvement brought about by using a selection test will be a group of new hires about 4 percent better than the rejected group!

Are there marked performance differences in computer jobs? Several old

---

SYSTEMS PROBLEM 22-3

Ted Carbone has been given the assignment of coming up with a charging mechanism for Stirling and Livingston, a large manufacturer of prescription drugs. Currently there are two major branches of the computer services division, business and research. Under a new plan the two areas are to be consolidated.

Currently the business group charges users based on elapsed machine time. The machine time (plus other items like printing, storage, etc.) are estimated for the year and the computer department budget is divided by that sum. This calculation provides the amount to be charged to users in the form of a rate. The rate is set so that the computer department is a zero cost center.

Because the demands for scientific data processing are so hard to estimate, the scientific center has been run as a straight overhead charge. Users are not charged for their computations or systems development. Much of the work in this division is timesharing. There are major batch systems in addition, however, such as an application that tracks the development of a drug and its path through testing and regulatory agencies. Another application is the analysis of the results from experiments with drugs on animals and on humans.

Ted is concerned about his assignment because he fears that the wrong type of charging scheme could create a lot of problems for the organization and users. A major difficulty will develop if there is contention for services during times of peak demand. If the charging scheme favors the administrative user, then the researchers will not receive adequate time. On the other hand, if he provides a flexible charging scheme, the scientific users who are not accustomed to considering computer charges may exhaust all their funds quickly by running at high priorities. What charging policy do you recommend to Ted?

---

experiments on programmer productivity show a high variance in programmer performance. However, the material discussed in Chapter 19 suggests that these results could be due to a wrong assessment of the programming task. First, we should make goals explicit. In these old programming experiments, the various programmers may have had different goals that were unknown to the experimenter. If we look at programming as a group activity, then we want to compare the performance of groups, not individuals within a group. At this time, certainly it is not obvious that there is a wide variation in the performance of programmer groups. Yet programmers are the computer department personnel for whom aptitude tests are most often used.

The most important factor to keep in mind, at least for systems design activities, is whether potential employees will be congenial colleagues for existing members of the design team and whether they will add needed skills. Does the systems analyst believe in the same approach to design as the rest of the organization? Do programmers feel that egoless programming is important, and are they willing to work in a group? How do operations candidates view the computer department? Do they see their role as providing a service to users?

Training

In place of the use of elaborate recruiting procedures, many organizational theorists like Haire advocate training. We should be able to improve performance by at least 10 percent and possibly up to 40 percent by on-the-job training.

There are several types of training that can be undertaken; in one sense all managers or project leaders should work to train the staffs working with them. Our use of programming groups means that a peer group will help train individual programmers. A programmer can begin as a junior member of a group, rotate through the system's librarian position, work to sharpen programming skills, and become a backup programmer. Finally, this career path will lead to a chief programmer if the individual wishes to continue programming activities.

On the operations side of the computer department, on-the-job training is more difficult; however, we certainly can try to rotate operations staff members among different jobs. Also, it is helpful to rotate programmers between maintenance and new systems development on 6-month to 1-year intervals. Few programmers like maintenance work, and at least the option to change jobs should be open for maintenance programmers.

In addition to these types of informal on-the-job training, more structured training should be available for computer department personnel. Many of the skills, including those of the computer operator, programmer, or systems analyst, and even the manager can be improved through classroom experience. Universities, computer vendors, and consulting organizations all offer a variety of courses ranging from highly technical to managerial for computer department personnel. Many of these courses can be taught within the organization. These courses improve existing skills and teach new approaches; they help to keep the staff aware of changing technology and approaches to problems.

OUTSIDE PERSPECTIVE

A major problem with computer departments is that they become isolated and encapsulated within the organization. As a result, computer department staff members become inbred and remain unaware of new approaches and ideas. In a setting as creative as systems design, it is helpful to observe what others have done and to see trends in new types of applications. How can a computer department obtain this outside exposure?

First, management and staff members should join and attend professional society meetings. Every year there is a National Computer Conference, with exhibits by different manufacturers and papers by leading figures in the computer field. Local groups of computer departments can provide perspective by arranging exchange programs and meetings. It is helpful to get together with individuals performing similar tasks in other organizations to discuss common problems. Outside speakers also contribute by presenting stimulating or controversial new ideas. Professional groups also can arrange visits to each other's installations or reports on new applications.

The computer department staff should also make an attempt to follow trade and technical publications in the computer and management field to keep aware of new ideas. Finally, outside consultants can be used to audit computer operations or to present a series of talks in the organization on new approaches/to computer activities.

PLANNING

Because of the pressure of new project schedules and the deadlines of computer operations, it is often hard for management to take the time to plan for computer activities. However, planning is an important part of good management, as it sets the overall goals and directions for the organization. A plan should be developed at least each year and approved by the steering committee in a special session.

What should be included in a plan for the computer department? Some ideas for planning are presented in Table 22-5. First, there should be a short management summary indicating where the department is headed. The summary stresses the goals of the plan and the resources required to attain the goals. Then the specific goals should be discussed in detail; how were they established?

One section of the plan should deal with fixed-base activities. These are activities to which the department is committed because of systems that have already been implemented or new ones that are now close to implementation. Variable-base activities represent new projects that were planned for the future or that are barely under development at the present time. It may even be desirable to divide different projects into classes and have plans for each type. For example, a major project may be considered one that costs over X dollars and requires more than Y years to develop.

Both the fixed- and the variable-base activities are combined to compute the resources required to achieve the plan's goals. The plan should also show scheduled accomplishments and requirements over time, including technical

TABLE 22-5
COMPUTER DEPARTMENT IDEAS
FOR A PLAN

Management summary
Goals for plan
Fixed-base activities
   Operations and systems maintenance
   Projects underway
Variable-base activities
   New projects
Resource requirements
   Schedule
   Hardware and software
   Operations staff
   Systems design staff

considerations and staffing levels. In addition to short-run plans, which probably have a 1- to 2-year horizon, the computer department may want to develop a broad 5-year plan. This plan of course will be in less detail because of rapid technological changes and uncertainty. However, it gives the steering committee an opportunity to set directions for computer activities.

Because of the relatively long development times and life spans for systems, the planning activities of the information systems area may force new efforts at organizational planning. The typical information system takes 1 to 2 years to design and install; it may have a lifetime of 5 to 7 years. This means that the organization may be deciding today on systems that limit its flexibility or allow it certain options 7 to 9 years in the future. Most organizations do not plan that far ahead!

The information systems area may also pose very difficult decisions for the management of the organization. Consider the major undertaking of acquiring and installing a data-base management system. Such a decision may require several years of preparation before the first application makes use of the data system. The decision to adopt data-base technology will require the commitment of a substantial investment in software, hardware, training, and systems development time. The payoff for this investment will not come from the first application using the data base; instead it will take several applications until some return is obtained from the investment. The first system will be the hardest; subsequent systems will be able to take advantage of the investment to develop the data-base system and the knowledge gained from the first development effort using the data-base system.

It may be very difficult for management in the organization to cope with demands such as a request for a major investment like the acquisition of a data-base system, the move toward distributed processing, or other technological decisions that involve a long payback period and a substantial investment. The information services department will have to work closely with user management to help make the best decisions for the organization.

In addition to a plan, it is also helpful to prepare a short annual report of the computer department's activities; this report should be tied to the previous year's plan. What was scheduled to be accomplished and what actually was achieved? In what areas should the computer department concentrate in the next year to achieve its objectives?

THE COMPUTER DEPARTMENT MANAGER

In an insightful paper, Nolan (1973) has described the plight of the manager of the computer department. The computer professional can work better in a computer department if the problems of the manager are understood. Nolan's observations are also helpful for the individual who is interested in a career path leading to the management of a computer department.

What are the problems of computer department managers? First, they have a wide variety of subordinates reporting to them, ranging from highly technical computer professionals to clerical personnel. Second, the department is responsible for a broad range of activities from creative systems design work to routine clerical chores. Third, the department impacts many, if not all other, areas of the organization. The manager controls a large budget and is responsible for a major investment in equipment. As the department becomes larger, needs become less technical and the emphasis shifts more toward managerial problems. Unfortunately, we often find managers of computer departments with no management background because they came through the technical side of computing.

Management of the organization has tended to treat the computer department manager as a scapegoat. More seriously, top-level management often views a computer department manager only as a technical person; they assume that the manager has no desire or ability to progress further in the organization. Given this set of attitudes, the only option open to the computer manager is to become manager of a larger or better computer department in another organization.

How should top management of the organization respond to the computer department manager? First, they should see computer department managers as change agents and give managerial support to their change activities within the organization. Management must provide extra resources and encourage users to join in design teams; we shall discuss this point further in Chapter 24. Management should also consider the broad exposure to all other areas of the organization that the computer department manager obtains. Is this person not a good candidate for other managerial positions if so desired? Top management should not view computer department management as necessarily a terminal position within the organization.

SUMMARY

In this chapter we discussed the overall management and organization of the computer department. We saw that most computer departments are split into two components: one that handles systems design, and the other, operations. Much of the discussion focused on computer operations, a frequently overlooked element of the management of the information systems effort. We also discussed some common problems of computer departments, especially those related to personnel and relationships with users. Charging for services, the importance of outside perspective, and the plight of the computer department manager were discussed. In Chapter 23, we examine the evaluation and acquisition of computer hardware and software, a frequent activity for the personnel of the computer department.

KEY WORDS

Centralization	Data preparation	Full charge-out
Change procedures	Decentralization	Hiring
Controls	Design teams	Investment cost
Cost center	Distributed processing	Job rotation
Data administrator	Fixed-base activities	Linking pin

Logical security
Maintenance programming
Matrix organizations
Network
Operating costs
Operations

Outside evaluation
Overhead charges
Partial charge-out
Physical security
Plan
Profit center

Scheduling
Service orientation
Steering committee
Systems design

RECOMMENDED READINGS

McFarlan, W. F.: "Management Audit of the EDP Department," *Harvard Business Review,* vol. 51, no. 3, May-June 1973, pp. 131–142. (This article describes some of the points management should examine in evaluating its data processing department.)

McFarlan, F. W., and J. L. McKenney: *Corporate Information Systems Management,* Irwin, Homewood, Ill., 1983. (An excellent book presenting issues for managing information processing.)

———, R. L. Nolan, and D. P. Norton: *Information Systems Administration,* Holt, New York, 1973. (An excellent discussion of the management of computer departments including numerous cases.)

Nolan, R. L.: "Plight of the EDP Manager," *Harvard Business Review,* vol. 51, no. 3, May-June 1973, pp. 143–152. (It is helpful to review this article on the role of the computer manager when examining steps to improve relations with users.)

Nolan, R. L.: "Managing Information Systems by Committee," *Harvard Business Review,* vol. 60, no. 4, July-August 1982, pp. 72–79. (An important article on how to establish and run an executive steering committee.)

DISCUSSION QUESTIONS

1 How should general management in the organization regard the position of the computer department manager?

2 What technical and managerial skills are needed by the computer department manager? Is business training enough? How much technical knowledge does the computer department manager have to possess?

3 Why has the computer department tended to be regarded as a low-status group in the organization?

4 To what level in the organization should the computer department report? On what factors is the decision on a reporting level for the computer department dependent?

5 What factors inhibit the operations subgroup in the computer from being service-oriented?

6 What are the major differences in designing new programs and maintenance programming? Would you expect these two types of programming to appeal to different individuals? Discuss the general problem of managing these two types of programmers.

7 What percentage of the computer budget should be used for enhancements to existing systems? Take a position and defend it as to whether or not enhancements are important.

8 What is the role of a user representative, and what type of individual should be placed in such a position?

9 How does a steering committee serve to reduce user conflict with the computer department?

10 What technical integrating devices exist or what approaches to systems design have we advocated that help to reduce conflict and differences between the computer department and the rest of the organization?

11 Why would an organization with sophisticated users think seriously about using a full charge-out method for allocating computer costs? Why would an organization with naive users employ overhead charging for allocating computer costs?

12 Why use formal change procedures for existing computer systems? Why have formal change procedures not always been successful?

13 What is it about computer activities that makes integration of the computer department with the rest of the organization necessary?

14 What mechanical devices and what type of systems design philosophy can be used to reduce the number of manual operations, such as output processing, in the computer department?

15 Describe the role of the data administrator. Why is this individual important to the successful functioning of a computer department?

16 A matrix organization was discussed in this chapter for a computer department. What alternatives are there to this type of organization for the systems design and programming activities of the department? What are the advantages and disadvantages of your alternatives?

17 What is the purpose of a plan for information systems development in the organization?

18 How can the computer department plan for new information systems if the demand for these systems has not manifested itself yet?

19 What is the role of the steering committee and top management in the development and review of a computer department plan?

20 What will the impact of the increased use of programming packages such as data-base management systems and telecommunications control systems be on the systems programming function?

21 What are the major constraints on the manager of a computer department? What happens if this individual becomes too heavily involved in technical problems? What are the likely results if the manager concentrates too much on the organization and too little on his or her own technical capabilities?

22 What is the easiest way to bypass security precautions in the computer facility? How can this breach of security be discouraged?

23 Where does the responsibility lie for preventing the misuse of a computer system, with the design of the system or the operations group?

24 What is the role of an outside auditor in the management of the computer department?

25 If there are continuing schedules for computer resources and users are complaining, what is the most likely problem? What solutions are possible?

26 How can a manager of a computer department determine user reactions to systems? Why is this just as important a part of an annual report as financial data?

THE EVALUATION AND ACQUISITION OF HARDWARE AND SOFTWARE

THE EVALUATION AND ACQUISITION OF HARDWARE AND SOFTWARE

The computer department is frequently involved in the evaluation of hardware and software. The motivation for evaluation is to achieve higher performance levels from existing hardware and software or to acquire new equipment or programs. This chapter explores some of the methods for evaluating computer systems' performance and various selection criteria.

BACKGROUND

The Computer Industry

In the early days of computers, manufacturers offered all the software and hardware together in one rental or purchase price. This practice was known as "bundling"; the user had no choice of what to acquire. It was very difficult for independent companies to write software and compete with manufacturers who appeared to be giving away programs free.

In response to customer pressures and possible government antitrust actions, most major computer manufacturers have "unbundled" and now have separate pricing for hardware and software. Usually, the manufacturers include the operating system and some language compilers in the basic rental for the equipment on the grounds that the equipment cannot really be operated without them. Other types of software, especially applications programs, have to be rented or purchased. Separate pricing has created a larger marketplace but has increased the complexity of the decision process; now the user has to select among competing alternatives.

In addition to the trend toward separate pricing for software, a number of independent manufacturers (independent from the large mainframe vendors) are competing for the lucrative market for computer hardware components other than the central processing unit and the minimal primary memory that accompanies the CPU. These independent companies began by offering peripherals such as tape drives, disks, and control units for these devices. Now a number of firms offer these devices plus items such as additional primary memory for computer systems.

There are very few problems with "plug-to-plug compatible" devices; these products match the hardware and software interface of the computer manufacturer and can be substituted for the manufacturer's product directly. The manufacturer, of course, may change this interface, which makes things difficult for the independents. Independent components such as main memory may require modifications to the computer. In the past some computer vendors refused to service their machines once they had been modified. However, these cases are rare, and pressure on the manufacturer has generally been effective in changing this policy.

The fastest-growing market today is for personal computers and software packages. Personal computers are manufactured by a number of different vendors. In addition, one can purchase one vendor's processing unit and various other components from different suppliers, components like diskette and disk drives, expanded memory, printers, and other peripherals.

Likewise, the market for packages for all types of computers—mainframes, minis, and micros—is exploding as individuals and firms try to avoid the high cost and long time required to write programs.

TO BUY OR NOT

Throughout the text, we have emphasized the process and task of systems analysis and design. Previous chapters have illustrated how one can design a custom information system, while emphasizing that we need to find ways to try and reduce the time required by following the traditional steps in the systems life cycle.

The Application

Let us examine the problem of what and when to buy from the standpoint of the systems analyst. A request is made for a computer-based system; assume the analyst responds with a preliminary survey that is positive. Should one stop at this point and look for a package? Some in the field, particularly package vendors, would say "yes"; further analysis is a waste of time.

There are, however, several compelling reasons why there should be further work before examining packages. First, a preliminary analysis of the present system should be undertaken, followed by a high-level logical design. This design includes output requirements, file contents, and input needed. Detailed file design is not required, nor do the exact formats of input and output transactions need to be specified. However, we should have a good idea of the functions of the system and some of the features that users must have to work with it.

Now the design team has a plan, a benchmark specification against which to judge the various offerings from different vendors of packages and services. It is far too easy to be swayed by a convincing sales presentation; with a benchmark, the design team can determine exactly what is present and what has been omitted from various systems that are already available. Now different packages can be arrayed against a custom system model and estimates made of the extent to which each alternative meets user needs and desires.

Figure 23-1 shows how we might proceed. First, the problem is identified and a preliminary design document prepared for a new system. Note that at this point one is not concerned with the acquisition of hardware unless corporate policy requires that a certain in-house computer be used for a new application.

Although it is premature to think about acquiring computer hardware, it is important to determine roughly what scale of hardware will be needed for the

FIGURE 23-1
Selection alternatives.

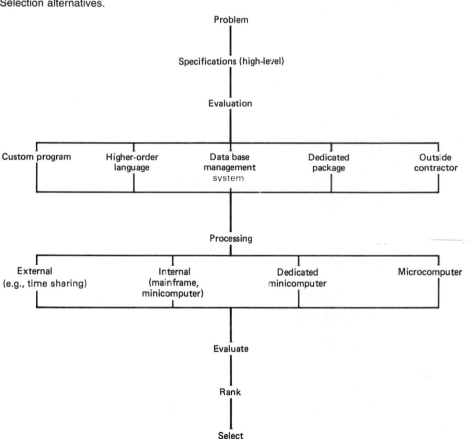

system that is being planned. Is the system capable of being run on microcomputers? Will it require a minicomputer or a mainframe?

These questions can be answered by estimating the size of the system: How many transactions have to be processed? What are the file sizes involved? What is the volume of file activity? If the system is on-line, how many terminals are required? What is the peak volume versus the average? The answers to these questions will help narrow down the hardware alternatives and, in turn, will allow us to think more about the kind of package we need, since packages are often written for certain sizes of operations.

Given a rough design and a feeling for the overall size of a system, alternatives such as those shown in Figure 23-1 can be explored. A common alternative is a custom system programmed to do exactly what is requested in the specifications. Of course, the specifications will have to be developed in much greater detail for programming, but this is the traditional way of developing a system.

We have also discussed the possibility of using a higher-order language for development; if the firm already uses such a language, it would be a good candidate. If not, the design team might want to investigate whether such a language would be a good investment for this and subsequent systems.

Similarly, we could consider a data-base management system if one is not already in use. This package and the associated software for querying the data and possibly generating the actual application can speed development while still providing many of the features of a custom system.

There is also the option of a dedicated package: software written by an external vendor particularly for the application under consideration. One difficulty is finding out whether such a package exists. Several trade journals publish annual surveys of packages; there are also proprietary services that purport to list all major software packages. If your organization already has a computer, someone should contact representatives of the vendor to determine if they are aware of any packages for their computers. Another good source of information is trade journals in the industry, for example, banking journals for a bank application. Finally, the analyst can attend industry trade meetings to learn from other firms in the industry if they have used or considered packages in the applications area under consideration.

Finally, we can locate an outside contractor to undertake all or part of the development process. A variety of software consultants provide services in all phases of the life cycle. For example, we could hire a firm to actually design the system with and for us. Another possibility is to hire programmers and staff from an external firm to carry out all the steps following detailed design. Thus, a variety of external services is available, either as a separate alternative or as assistance with one of the other alternatives shown in Figure 23-1.

Processing

In many instances, the decisions made in the top half of Figure 23-1 will determine the hardware that must be used for processing. For example, if we have chosen a package that runs only on an IBM computer, then we shall have to find IBM compatible equipment for processing.

If we are not constrained by the decisions made at first about how the problem will be solved, what are some of the processing alternatives? First, one can use an external service bureau; these organizations provide timesharing and/or batch processing. They may have special packages or data available that contribute to solving our problem. More typically, we shall use some type of internal processing. For internal computing, we will usually find the options of the mainframe computer and possibly a minicomputer. Personal computers may also be an acceptable alternative for our application.

After the options have been explored, the various possibilities can be compared. Each alternative should be examined on a number of criteria; then a decision can be made on the best way to proceed, considering both software and hardware processing.

THE SERVICES INDUSTRY

We have stressed that custom development is no longer the automatic choice when a new application is being planned. There are a number of ways to obtain computer support, both in the development and operation of computing applications. In this section we discuss some of these possibilities.

Computing Power   Service bureau–type organizations have offered computing time and power for a number of years. Although some organizations have the need for extra computing power, the low cost of hardware and the steady decrease in hardware costs suggest that the market for raw computing power in general will shrink. Service bureaus already offer a number of custom programs and proprietary data bases so that the customer can obtain a service that is not available in-house.

Proprietary Applications   Software houses, service bureaus as discussed above, computer vendors, and others all offer dedicated applications. Many of these systems have been through several major revisions based on feedback from users. The discussion of packages in Chapter 12 points out some crucial considerations in evaluating this type of software. What is the quality of the package? How well does it suit our needs? How much are we willing to change procedures, given the cost of modifications?

Proprietary Data Bases   There is a large body of data that can be used for making various analyses and decisions; by making the data machine-readable and easily available, vendors of information have created new businesses. One can purchase information on the expected trends in the economy, various statistics about companies, stock prices, and the text of legal cases, to name a few. These services can be used as an adjunct to an application or may furnish some of the needed input directly.

Communications   A number of vendors offer communications services and equipment; see Chapter 10. Some of these services act like common carriers and provide communications networks. Other vendors offer services like electronic mail, in which individuals communicate by sending messages to each other's electronic "mailboxes" in a computer file.

Software consultants or vendors (software houses) offer programming and systems design services for both batch and on-line systems, and some offer special packages as well. The software vendor may contract to manage an entire systems development effort or furnish programmers to perform work assigned by the client. The staff of a software house writes and tests batch and/or on-line programs. However, it is unusual for the average organization to have such a firm develop a timesharing application; most organizations adopt an existing timesharing package or write their own programs.

A "turnkey system" is a new variation on contract services made possible by the development of minicomputers. The turnkey vendor is a private contractor who provides not only the computer, but also programming, training, and installation support. The user contracts with the vendor for a complete system, and most frequently these systems involve a minicomputer. The customer owns the computer but does not have to manage a computer department or staff. Most systems are designed so that someone already employed by the customer can operate the system; computer professionals are not needed. Turnkey systems have proved very popular for small organizations that would like to take advantage of computer processing without establishing a computer department. Large organizations also use turnkey services to supplement the efforts of their own computer staff.

COMPARISON OF SOURCES

What are the advantages and disadvantages of different sources for hardware and software? We can look at the two extremes for discussion purposes: All activities are undertaken either internally or externally through an outside organization (see Table 23-1).

Hardware

With an internal computer department, an organization has to deal with the problem of managing the computer; overhead is introduced into the organization. For this price, management gains control over its own computer operations. Data remain exclusively within organizational confines and are accessible only to employees. Processing priorities are established internally, and no other organization can preempt time from an organization with its own system. Management must provide sufficient resources to accommodate peak loads, so there can be high fixed costs for computer equipment that may not be fully utilized under this alternative. Usually, extra capacity is not provided because of the cost. Backup may be limited by the resources management is able to provide.

TABLE 23-1
COMPARISON OF INTERNAL VERSUS EXTERNAL SERVICES

	Internal	External
Hardware		
Management	Must manage computer department	Contractual arrangement; no line management responsible except for data preparation
Control	Control potential high	Only through contract, influence, withholding payment
Security	Under own responsibility; data remains at internal location	Data in hands of external organization; other customers a threat
Priorities	Assigned by own employees	Determined by external management
Resources	Must accommodate peak loads; high fixed cost	Variable cost, pay only for what is used (beyond possible minimum charge)
Capacity	Limited to what is needed	Frequently more powerful equipment than could be justified by clients
Backup	Limited by internal resources	Usually available because of higher capacity
Software		
Management	Must manage program development	Contractual arrangements, specifications on cost, time, performance
Staff	May have to hire experts	Expect vendors to have expertise
Implementation	Probably easier in terms of user reaction to internal staff	May be more difficult for "outsiders"

Organizations choosing to rely on external services have a contractual agreement with the servicing firm. There are few management responsibilities of a supervisory nature because these tasks have been delegated to an outside company. Control may be less than under the internal alternative, because litigation over contracts is costly and time-consuming. Instead, the customer seeks to influence the service organization. Many firms worry about having sensitive data in the hands of another organization, particularly when other companies have access to the same computer resources. The priority for applications is also in the hands of the organization providing services; management influences, but does not control, processing priorities. With an outside organization, the customer incurs a variable cost and pays only for the resources consumed. Frequently, the client has access to more powerful equipment than would be installed internally, since it is being shared among a number of users. Availability is less of a problem, because the service bureau has high capacity to serve all the customers.

Software

With internal software development, we must manage the development process. Internal program development often results in duplication: There may be a tendency to start from the beginning with each new system. Because there are "not-invented-here" complexes, packages are not adequately investigated. Implementation problems, however, should be minimized, because internal employees deal directly with the users in the firm.

External software services are handled on a contractual basis. However, a customer may still need some individual who is familiar with computer technology to work with the contractor and monitor progress, although, for the most part, clients will rely on the vendor's expertise. Implementation can be difficult for "outsiders"; however, the client may be able to take advantage of an existing package or set of routines whose cost has been amortized over a large group of users.

ACQUISITION STRATEGY

No matter what alternative is selected, the customer has to acquire computer equipment and/or services. How do we approach this problem? There are several considerations a potential customer should have in mind. First, check a vendor's financial condition; a number of small companies have gone bankrupt in the computer industry. Even major firms have sold or discontinued their computer manufacturing activities. How likely is a vendor to be around in the future to service the product and improve it?

What kind of documentation is available, particularly for software, since modifications may be necessary? Documentation describes how the system works and how it can be used, and without it, a customer has little information on the product purchased. What kind of vendor support is available? Does the price include installation and training by the vendor?

An extremely important research activity for a customer is to contact present users of a product to determine their level of satisfaction. How well does the product or service meet vendor claims? What problems did users have? If possible, visit users without a vendor representative to ask these questions. If it is not possible to see a product demonstrated, do not buy it. Too often, announced products are delivered years late; insist on a demonstration and attempt to evaluate the performance of the product.

Before we discuss some of the factors to be considered in the acquisition of computer systems and software, we examine techniques for evaluating computer system performance. Performance evaluation is important for a number of reasons, and it should be a component of most acquisition decisions.

PERFORMANCE EVALUATION

One of the major activities in acquiring new equipment and software is an evaluation of the performance of the product. We also use performance evaluation techniques with an existing system to improve its performance, either through the acquisition of additional equipment or the reduction in the amount of equipment in use. There are many approaches to performance evaluation; the following suggestions are taken from Lucas (1972).

Analytic Modeling

Analytic modeling involves a mathematical approach to performance evaluation and is best suited for design calculations such as the queuing analysis of an on-line system. For the average computer department, consulting help would be needed to develop such a model. Usually, analytical approaches do not model software and, therefore, do not have wide applicability to the average computer installation.

Simulation

Simulation has been used extensively to evaluate the performance of computer systems. Simulation is not suitable for the selection of a specific piece of software such as an applications program, but simulation can include software considerations in evaluating the performance of a total computer system. Various types of simulators are available, or users can write their own using a special-purpose simulation language. (In general, this evaluation method is not advised for the typical computer department, since it is a research project.)

A computer department can also use computer simulation packages offered by various independent vendors. For several of these packages the user describes the job load, files, input-output volumes, and equipment in detail, and the package constructs and executes a simulation model. These complicated packages can be expensive to run and difficult to calibrate. Because they are proprietary, the user does not always know the logic of the model, which makes it difficult to obtain a feeling for model validity. When using these packages, it is best to first construct a model of the existing system. If this model is not accurate when compared with the performance of the existing system, then the approach should be rejected for evaluating a new system.

Benchmarks

Benchmarks represent a sample of an existing workload, and they include software considerations. Any aspect of the system can be evaluated, from an entire computer system to a file management package. Strictly speaking, a benchmark is an existing job that has been recoded if necessary for the system being evaluated. The benchmark job (or jobs) is simply run on the new equipment. The use of the benchmark assumes that the existing job mix or this particular sample is representative of how the product under evaluation will be used. For a thorough evaluation job with benchmarks, many different benchmarks must be developed and executed. However, benchmarks offer a high degree of flexibility, and the evaluation effort can be tailored to the importance of the decision.

Synthetic Modules

A synthetic job is coded to represent a typical function and is not restricted to being an existing job. Like a benchmark, a synthetic program is actually executed. This approach offers a great deal of flexibility; it is possible to include estimates of how the job load will change in the future. For example, certain activities such as file processing can be more highly weighted if a new data-base application is being planned.

It is possible to use a small group of synthetic modules to model a much larger workload by combining and weighting the different modules. As with benchmarks, the evaluator can perform a number of experiments consistent with the importance of the decision. An extensive group of synthetic modules can be developed and scientific experiments planned for evaluation. On the other hand, a few modules and limited runs can be used to get a rough idea of performance comparisons.

Monitoring

Monitoring is a type of performance evaluation technique different from those described above; it is primarily oriented toward evaluating existing forms of hardware and software. The techniques described earlier are most useful in deciding whether to acquire something new; monitors are often used to tune or improve the performance of an existing system. Two types of monitors are in use, but the distinction between them is blurring because they have been combined to produce a hybrid or integrated monitors.

A hardware monitor contains a set of probes that are attached to the component being monitored at critical points. The device collects data on elapsed time or counts of some value, for example, the number of disk accesses. The recorded data become input to a separate batch data-reduction program. The major disadvantage of the hardware monitor is limitations on what can be measured and the fact that it is often difficult to relate the data collected to software performance.

A software monitor is a program that is embedded within or interfaced in some way with the operating system. It is called as a high-priority task every so often to collect statistics on machine status. These statistics are also generally analyzed after the end of the monitoring period. Since the software monitor has access to all operating system tables and data, it can keep track of more items than a hardware monitor. The problem with software monitors is that the measurement tool interacts with what is being measured; that is, a software monitor is a program, and its execution affects the system.

Hybrid or integrated monitors use software and hardware to collect data. Often the hardware monitor is a minicomputer operating under program control. Hybrid monitors will undoubtedly become more common in the future because of their flexibility and measurement capabilities.

Monitoring can be very useful, and many installations have found impressive savings by tuning a system. However, there are a few drawbacks. First, it is usually necessary to sample the system for a very short period of time, which may be unrepresentative. Too much happens quickly when machines operate in the 100 nanosecond (100×10^{-9} seconds) range. Even with the restricted sampling period, a mass of data may still have to be analyzed. The user must study the data and determine what to modify to improve performance. A monitor also only shows the existence of a bottleneck; it does not indicate whether performance will improve by $\frac{1}{10}$ of a percent or 25 percent if the bottleneck is removed. Finally, if the system is tuned for one particular job load or some portion of it, what happens when other jobs are added or the workload changes?

Recommendations

The role of performance evaluation has changed with declining hardware costs and increasing power. We are using very fast computers to run relatively inefficient software like dedicated packages and higher-order languages; it is important to save systems development time. Where does performance evaluation fit in?

First, in acquiring a package, especially one that will operate on-line, we need to be sure that the package can support the size of our application with acceptable response time. As an example, one package for use by the registrar of a university can handle only 128 terminals. If this limit cannot be changed through an upgrade to a different computer or easy changes in the software, it may be an inappropriate system for a large university. If a large installation is not available for a demonstration, then one might develop a simulated or synthetic load to test the limits of what can be demonstrated to a potential buyer.

On the hardware side, if a computer is considerably faster than another for a particular task, then that speed is a factor in its favor. (See the following discussion on hardware acquisition.) Given the amount of processing power available today and the importance of packages, it is unlikely that hardware evaluation will be as important as in the past.

Monitoring, however, may become even more important as software increases in complexity and the range of design alternatives increases. For example, a monitor may show us how to better allocate or even design the files in an on-line system to improve response time. A software monitor can help us understand the behavior of a system during its development, something very helpful in looking for errors and tuning performance. We can also use monitors to improve the performance of programs rather than having a programmer try to figure out what code is least efficient.

Thus performance, not raw speed, of a computer is the issue. Rather, we must be concerned with how software and hardware work together. If there is not

TABLE 23-2
ITEMS INCLUDED IN REQUEST FOR
PROPOSAL

1 Present applications
File characteristics
Input-output
Volume
Frequency
Batch or on-line
2 Same as (1) for proposed systems
3 Vendor service
4 Reliability data
5 Backup
6 Demonstration
7 Evaluation arrangements
8 Conversion and transition
9 Descriptive material (hardware and software)
10 Price

enough processing power, what are the alternatives? Can we improve perform-ance through small increments in hardware or minor software changes, or is there a major cost associated with improvements? Can the system expand as our processing load increases? We shall evaluate the performance of existing systems we might consider acquiring and attempt to assess how these applications will perform in our environment. Finally, we shall be concerned with the growth path for the software and hardware.

ACQUISITION OF A NEW COMPUTER SYSTEM: MAINFRAMES AND MINIS

Periodically, it is necessary to upgrade a computer system either because more capacity is needed or because technical advancements have produced machines with better performance at a lower cost. The acquisition of a new computer system can be a complicated decision. In this section we describe the computer selection process and offer some suggestions of criteria to be used in the decision.

Request for Proposals

After the need for a new system has been identified, the potential buyer will usually develop a request for bids. The request is sent to various vendors, who are asked to propose equipment. The buyer should attempt to have the manufacturer do most of the work in this process. Table 23-2 shows some of the items that should be included in the request for a proposal.

All present applications should be described in detail in the proposal; we want the vendor to consider these and recommend the best equipment for the workload. Also, plans for new applications should be included. The vendor should specify what type of support will be provided and present reliability data for the equipment. We are also interested in knowing about backup: Are there redundant components in the system? Can a faulty component be isolated while the system continues to run in a backup mode? We also would like to have information about similar installations in the area.

The vendor should indicate the arrangements for demonstrations and describe how the customer can access the proposed configuration to evaluate its performance. Because moving to a new computer system is a major undertaking, the vendor should present a plan for the transition to the proposed system. Are there any special products or services that the vendor offers to ease the transition?

In acquiring a new system, we shall probably also ask for some descriptive material of the type shown in Table 23-3 to obtain a feeling for the type of equipment being proposed. This descriptive information includes both hardware and software capabilities. Finally, the price for the recommended system should be provided in detail, both for hardware components and software.

Performance

The buyer should prepare for testing the proposed machine while the vendor is preparing the proposal. The typical buyer will probably want to include benchmarks and possibly synthetic modules to model the existing and planned workload. Benchmarks are also a very valuable way to indicate the difficulties that can be expected in transition. The buyer can use several existing jobs without changes to see how easy it is to run them on the new system.

Proposal Evaluation

Meaningful criteria should be established for evaluating each proposal from the different vendors. These criteria can include items such as performance, presence of certain software, the availability of special applications packages, the ease of conversion, the response of other users currently using the equipment,etc.

Then the evaluation team should assign a weight to each criterion. It may be possible to eliminate vendors because of one dominant failing, for example, the lack of an applications package that is critical for the evaluators. If it is not possible to eliminate vendors because of some single major failing, then a more formal evaluation procedure is necessary.

One approach that has been used is to assign an interval score to each vendor and to multiply the scores by the weights for the criteria. These weighted scores are then added to form a final weighted total. However, the results are often quite close, and the evaluation team may not have much confidence in a small numeric difference among the vendors. Another alternative is to prepare a brief scenario of how the computer department would function with each alternative system and what transitional activities would have to take place. Then the decision-making body rank-orders the scenarios and chooses the most desirable one.

TABLE 23-3
EXAMPLE OF DESCRIPTIVE PROPOSAL MATERIAL

Hardware	Speed
CPU cycle time	Transfer rate
Memory cycle time and hierarchy	Tracks
Data path	Disks
Registers	Seek time
Type	Rotational delay time
Number	Average access time
Microprogramming features	Capacity
Instruction set	Removable or fixed
Fixed point	Bulk storage
Floating point	Access time
Decimal	Size
Precision	Data path
Interrupt structure	Input-output peripherals
Number	Input-output speed
Type	Reject rate (e.g., OCR scanners)
Priority	Software support
Memory size (each hierarchical element)	
Memory organization	Software
Data	Operating system
Instructions	Job and task management
	Multiprogramming
Special features	Partitions
Parallel operations	Size
Instruction look-ahead	Priority
Multiple processors	Overhead (time and space)
Data channels	Control language
Number	Documentation
Type	Utilities
Transfer rate	Special features
Control units	Compilers
Device assignment	Subset of language supported
Effect on CPU	Extensions to language
Storage devices	File accessing capabilities
Tapes	Storage requirements
Density	Applications programs

Recommendation

Most organizations formally decide on an acquisition as major as a new computer system at a high level. However, most frequently the decision is made on the basis of recommendations from the computer department manager and staff who actually undertake the evaluation. In developing a recommendation for approval, the computer department should present an executive summary of a few short pages, including the reasons for the recommendation. The complete evaluation study can be available as a reference document, but the shorter summary will probably suffice for obtaining approval.

Transition and Installation

Installing a new computer system should be treated just as a systems design project. The overriding goal is for a smooth transition; it is necessary to explain what is happening to users and to have their cooperation. A plan should be prepared showing the schedule and activities that must be undertaken to complete the changeover successfully.

Remember, our goal is to provide service, not to run bigger and better computers! Too many computer departments went from first- to second- to third-generation equipment with no new applications developed during the transition. Users see larger computers being installed, a decrease in service levels during transition, no new applications, and higher bills. Many users found that they were paying more for less service!

OTHER COMPUTERS

The purchase of a mainframe or minicomputer is fairly routine. Even when one is acquiring a computer that will be dedicated to a single software application, the decision is usually fairly easy once the package has been chosen because (1) there are usually relatively few computers for which the package is written, and (2) the vendor has experience knowing what kind of computer should be used, given one's processing demands.

In the category of "other" computers, we must consider microcomputers and specialized computers. For example, a number of computer devices are available for process control and factory automation. Although this area has traditionally been the domain of the engineer, now factory computers are communicating valuable data to other computers that supply information for making decisions on scheduling, raw materials, and production control, to name a few functions.

Personal computers also present a bewildering array of possibilities because of the large number of vendors. The organization is probably well advised to develop a standard, say, to support two or three specific types of personal computers and to avoid acquiring others. The staff can only develop expertise in supporting a limited number of machines. In addition, all the personal computers have the potential for needing to communicate with other computers, so that limiting the number of different computers will eventually help in arranging connections into computer networks.

Decisions for these "other" classes of computers largely depend on the function for which they are being acquired. Many personal computers have been purchased just to run spreadsheet analyses. Factory computers will be chosen for how well they perform a specific task; however, one can still apply some of the considerations for larger computers when considering other types. Specifically, expandability and compatibility along with the ability to communicate with other systems are important. Obviously, the type of software and human-machine interface are also significant, along with vendor support.

A careful analysis of the issues will help to ensure that good decisions are made in the acquisition of all computer equipment. Even relatively low-priced computers have implications beyond their immediate purchase price.

APPLICATIONS PACKAGES

An applications package is a program or set of programs written for use by more than one organization. A number of these packages are for sale or rent by computer vendors and software firms (see Chapter 12).

Considerations and Trade-Offs

The obvious advantage of using a package is cost savings. The package developer expects to sell a number of packages to recover the investment in developing the package; the cost is thus amortized over a number of users. The cost to the developer, though, is usually higher than would be the development of a single application, since the package must be more general so that it can be used by a number of customers. This increased generality makes the package larger, more complex, and often less efficient to operate than an application developed for only a single user. Some of the trade-offs, then, for a package are:

Package generality versus ease of installation and use.

Acquisition and modification cost versus the cost of developing the application within the organization.

The elapsed time to install a package versus the time to develop the application within the organization.

Operating efficiency of the package versus the alternative of a custom application within the organization.

Implementation problems of the package versus those of an application developed specifically for the needs of the organization.

The most serious problem with packages is the need for organizations to customize the programs for their unique situation. (This problem is most severe with dedicated packages like accounts receivable.) Of course, although individual organizations always claim uniqueness, often it is easy to change routine procedures to suit a package. On the other hand, there are legitimate reasons for maintaining uniqueness in the organization.

We have stressed the importance of meeting user needs and obtaining heavy user involvement in the design of systems. Many systems developed on a custom-tailored basis have failed completely or have not met their potential. It seems that packages are even less likely to succeed, because they have a tendency to impose a system on a user. What can be done to lessen the implementation problem of packages?

The package vendors recognize this drawback and generally design packages to allow some custom tailoring. Two ways are often employed for providing this flexibility: the use of modules and parameters. The first strategy is to provide a modular set of programs in the package; the user configures a custom applications package by selecting appropriate modules for a particular set of needs. Little or no programming is required on the part of the user, since the modules are all available from the vendor. Packages also make extensive use of parameters or data values to indicate unique features for a particular user.

Often, the customizing features provided by the vendor of the package are insufficient for an organization. The less expensive packages may have to be accepted as is, but for more elaborate applications the customer often finds it necessary to write custom code to modify the package. Sometimes the modifications are easy and require only the addition of some reports or the alteration of reports already in the package. Code modifications can become quite extensive and may involve rewriting significant portions of the package. One organization uses the rule of thumb that a package will not be considered if it will cost more than 50 percent of the initial package cost to modify it. The important thing to remember is that the cost of a package is usually not just the purchase price; instead we must forecast and consider the cost of modifications and maintenance.

SYSTEMS PROBLEM 23-1

Jack Caradine sat back in his chair and scratched his head as he muttered, "We really opened the flood gates with the ICPC 2 years ago. Now we can't keep up with all the user requests for packages and turnkey systems."

Jack is manager of systems development for Agrequip, a manufacturer of farm implements. Two years ago he helped one plant install a package application called ICPC for inventory control and production control. The package was an example of dedicated application: a small computer and the application were acquired specifically for the inventory and production control application.

Since that time, other users have found out about the system and have requested something similar. These requests have presented relatively few problems, since Jack's staff is quite knowledgeable about the package and is now installing it at three other plants. However, what Jack is concerned about now are the requests for many different types of packages. "They start their own research with package vendors and they don't have the slightest idea of what to look for."

Jack's staff is being stretched to respond to these requests and to evaluate the packages. "Users have gotten the idea that a package is a panacea for any problem," Jack complained. "They don't realize what we have to go through to evaluate and then install a package. Every one we have put in required some modification. Sure, it can be cheaper than doing it ourselves, but the cost is not just the cost of the package; it's the installation, modification, and ongoing costs of taking care of the thing. Also, we rarely find a package with all the same features we'd have put in a system designed as a custom job inside the company."

What kind of policy does Jack need? What procedures for dealing with the explosion of package activities by users would you recommend?

TABLE 23-4
CONSIDERATIONS IN EVALUATING
SOFTWARE PACKAGES

Functions included
Modifications required to package
Installation effort
User interface
Flexibility
Execution time
Changes required in existing system to use package
Vendor support
Updating of package
Documentation
Cost and terms

Criteria

It was recommended earlier that the computer department and the steering committee agree on screening criteria for packages. Many times packages will be considered as alternatives to developing a system in-house. (The computer department will apply these same criteria to packages considered for use primarily within the department.) Table 23-4 lists some possible evaluation criteria for decisions on packages. The major reason for acquiring a package is the function it performs. We want to know how many desired functions are included and what effort would be required to modify the package.

It is also important to consider the user interface, that is, how difficult it is to use the package. How much information does a user have to supply? Is it simple to prepare and understand the input? Is the package flexible, and can it be used if our requirements change somewhat?

The evaluation team is also concerned with how long the package requires to run and how it impacts current operations. Execution time considerations are not as important for a simple application that is run infrequently, but they can be very important for something like a data-base management system. We are also interested in how much present procedures will have to be changed to use the package.

Just as with hardware, it is necessary to evaluate vendor support and the likelihood that the vendor will remain in business. Remember that it does not take many resources to program and sell software packages. Updates and improvements for the package should be forthcoming, so we are dependent on the vendor remaining in business.

With software packages, documentation is vitally important; the computer department staff may have to modify the package and will undoubtedly have to maintain it if errors occur. Guidelines for documentation were presented in Chapter 18, and these can be used to evaluate the documentation for a proposed package. Finally, we have to consider the cost; however, remember that we always underestimate how much it will cost to develop a comparable system ourselves and overestimate the cost required to modify the package!

Decision

In this discussion, we are interested in whether or not a package qualifies for consideration. Many of the criteria in Table 23-5 require analysis of package documentation by the systems analysis staff or programmers. We also should contact present users to answer questions about vendor claims and support. Almost all these criteria are subjective, which means that several individuals should rank a package on each criteria, for example on a 1 to 7 scale. The responses can then be averaged for each criteria and a score developed for the package.

It may be desirable to divide the criteria into essential and nonessential groups. We can insist that a package get a "passing score" (established in advance) on each of the essential criteria to be considered for acquisition. Then we can examine the nonessential criteria to see if the package passes enough of them to be considered.

SYSTEMS PROBLEM 23-2

The bids for a new computer system for Management Advisory Services, Inc. had just arrived. Terry Smith brought the three thick notebooks into his office and began to read. Management Advisory Services is a consulting firm that builds models and decision-support systems for its clients. The firm has used a computer since its founding 10 years ago, but the computer has always been a commercial timesharing system. Now, it appeared that because of the extremely low cost of computer hardware, Management Advisory Services should think about acquiring its own in-house machine.

Currently the consultants with the firm have to learn a number of different systems, because a variety of timesharing service bureaus are employed. Models developed for one customer sometimes are difficult to use again; no real library of systems was being constructed, yet management realized that such a development would be necessary to ensure adequate profit margins in this competitive, service-oriented industry.

Management Advisory Services had held lengthy discussions with three vendors of timesharing systems and had presented the needs of the firm. Now the vendors had all responded with proposed configurations and software. Terry skimmed the bids carefully and noticed immediately that the price differences among the three contenders were almost insignificant. On a more careful reading, he could not find one dominant advantage or major failing of any vendor that would have simplified the decision.

Terry sighed as he realized that a full-scale evaluation of the proposals would now be necessary. He began to make a list of the criteria that seemed important in the evaluation for Management Advisory Services. Can you help him develop the list of criteria? What should Terry do after the criteria have been agreed on by the selection committee?

If a package is acceptable and is the only alternative under consideration, we shall probably acquire it. However, if several packages are available, then the ones that pass the screening test can be compared using ratings or through the scenarios described in the last section. If the package under consideration is an alternative to designing an in-house system, as was the case in the Hardserve example, then use the criteria established by the steering committee to evaluate the package in a comparison with other processing alternatives.

The users, then, help evaluate the package versus a custom-tailored application and make the decision on which would be best. If the user wishes to have the lower costs and faster development associated with the package, then he or she will have to agree that all desired features may not be present. If the decision is for a custom application, the user must recognize that costs will probably be higher than a package and that it will take longer to develop the system. The important thing is for users to make this decision themselves rather than to have it imposed on them by a supervisor or by the computer department. With participation, the user will understand the trade-offs and recognize the reasons for whatever choice is made.

KEY WORDS

Analytic models	Scenarios
Benchmarks	Service bureau
Hardware monitor	Simulation
Hybrid monitor	Software house
Independent manufacturer	Software monitor
Packages	Synthetic programs
Performance evaluation	Turnkey
Plug-to-plug compatible equipment	Unbundling
Remote batch	

RECOMMENDED READINGS

Byte and *Popular Computing* magazines have software evaluations and comparisons.

Martin, J., and L. McClure: "Buying Software off the Rack," *Harvard Business Review*, vol. 61, no. 6, November-December 1983, pp. 32–60. (A good guide to selection and contracting.)

DISCUSSION QUESTIONS

1 What is wrong with the use of simple computer cycle-and-add times for performance evaluation?

2 What is the major difference between monitoring and other types of performance evaluation?

3 Design a series of synthetic modules and experiments for a company that wishes to evaluate the performance of several medium-sized, multiprogrammed, general-

purpose computer systems. The company has 50 percent file processing applications and 25 percent engineering applications. The rest of the work on the system is general business processing.

4 What are the problems involved in using a monitor to tune systems?

5 What are the drawbacks to analytic models and simulation studies for the average computer installation?

6 Why should a computer installation consider the use of applications packages? What are their advantages and disadvantages?

7 In what situations would you expect applications packages to be most satisfactory?

8 What would your reaction be to the development of a set of industrywide synthetic modules to be used in performance evaluation?

9 How would you characterize an existing computer workload for performance evaluation purposes? How would you include consideration for the changes in the workload that might occur in the future?

10 What performance evaluation technique would you use and why if the expected workload in the next 5 years will change drastically from the existing workload?

11 To what extent should different vendors than the one currently supplying your computer be included in bidding for a new system?

12 What are the advantages and disadvantages of mixed-vendor installations? (For example, the computer and main memory are from one company and the peripherals from others.)

13 What factors mitigate against the conversion to a different vendor's computer? How has the development and use of higher-level languages affected this type of conversion? What do you expect the impact of data-base management systems will be on conversion to a new vendor?

14 Make a list of the types of questions and information desired from a survey of other users of computer equipment under consideration for acquisition.

15 How can regular service levels be maintained during the conversion to new computer equipment? What are the dangers of acquiring new equipment?

16 What are the disadvantages of using some weighted score for ranking competing proposals for computer equipment? What advantages are presented by the use of scenarios for describing how a computer department would function under each new alternative?

17 Why is it not a good idea to be a pioneer with new equipment or software? That is, why should an installation wait before acquiring a newly developed computer system component?

18 How can a computer department avoid having to make frequent requests for additional computer capacity? What are the dangers in your strategy? How does the development of a plan for information systems activities affect this problem?

19 Most computer systems can be purchased or rented. What are the advantages and disadvantages of each alternative?

20 Why should applications packages be seriously considered as an alternative to programming and implementing a system? What are the most significant problems with these packages? How can the ease of modifying the package be determined before its acquisition?

21 Compare and contrast the major sources of software; what are the advantages and disadvantages of each?

22 Who should be involved in the decision on new computer hardware? What about software? Does the type of software make a difference?

23 What kind of packages should a computer department acquire for its own internal use?

24 Why do some programmers show a great deal of resistance to applications packages?

25 How can the vendor of an applications package make it more appealing to potential customers?

26 What are the advantages and disadvantages of running batch, on-line, and timesharing on the same computer as opposed to having specialized computers for each application?

27 For some timesharing computers, languages and operating systems are available that were developed by users rather than the hardware vendor. What are the pros and cons of acquiring this software?

28 Some firms have used worldwide timesharing services to install on-line systems. The user of the system does no programming; rather, the application is set up by a systems staff for the user, and the timesharing system is used for its communications and computer power. What are the advantages and disadvantages of such systems?

29 Are there any packages that require no modifications for installation? What types of software do these packages tend to be?

30 Does the decline of hardware costs mean that less effort should be devoted to evaluation? Why or why not?

THE COMPUTER PROFESSION AND ITS SOCIAL RESPONSIBILITIES

THE COMPUTER
PROFESSION AND ITS
SOCIAL RESPONSIBILITIES

In this chapter we conclude the book with the discussion of computer careers and the responsibilities an individual has as a computer professional.

CAREER PATH

We have explored various types of jobs in the computer department throughout this book. On the design and programming side, one can begin as a programmer and develop into a skilled chief programmer. In the past, programming has been viewed only as an interim position, and it had been assumed that the programmer wanted to move on to some other position. Now we are beginning to recognize that programming is a highly skilled task and that we have the equivalent of a senior staff engineer in the chief programmer. Such a career can be highly rewarding, since it combines creative technical challenges with management responsibilities.

These same points are true for the systems analyst; we need highly skilled, user-oriented analysts. The job of the analyst involves diagnosing existing systems and problems, working with decision makers, and designing new systems. The analyst works closely with a variety of people in the organization and can easily move into another department if desired.

Many functional areas of the firm also employ analysts. These individuals interface users and the department to computers and the central computer staff. Analysts in this role help end users work with computers and work on design teams.

In an operations career, personnel can work in different positions. Operations staff members can move into user department positions. Operations personnel have also become programmers and systems analysts.

From a programming, systems design, or operations position, individuals can move into a managerial position in the computer department. There are a number of managerial positions in both the operations and the systems design subgroups of the department. For example, there are usually shift supervisors and supervisors of various subdepartments such as controls, data transformation, etc. On the systems analysis and design side, medium to large computer departments have a manager of systems design and a manager of programming.

For those who aspire to higher levels of management, there is always the position of computer department manager. Now many of the opportunities for advancement from this position are limited. However, present trends suggest that this limitation will not be true in the future. Many organizations are creating separate departments for computers and even vice president of information systems positions. Top management of the organization is beginning to recognize that the computer department manager has exposure to many areas and has gained useful experience in such activities. Thus, it will become natural for computer department managers to move to other managerial positions in the organization if they so desire.

SOCIAL RESPONSIBILITIES

Computer professionals do not work in a vacuum; they and the organizations of which they are members have a responsibility to society. Recently, there has been a great deal of publicity about the misuse of computers and the violations of individual rights through computer systems.

Issues for Public Policy

A committee on computers and public policy of the Association for Computing Machinery (ACM) published a report defining a problem list of issues for computers and public policy. We highlight the various questions raised by this report and update it with current concerns in the discussion below (ACM, 1974).

Home Information Services   The home offers many opportunities for personal information processing services, particularly through the use of two-way cable communications networks for television. It has been forecast that this development will revolutionize all aspects of life from libraries to politics. A number of applications have been suggested, such as an instant national referendum, home-study courses, bank and electronic funds transfers, library and reference hookups, private mail services, personal data storage, and computation and game playing. Experiments are being conducted with these services, and a commercial home-information system is available in the United Kingdom.

Such capabilities raise a number of policy questions. Should an information utility offering this type of service be public, private, or private with some regulation? Are these uses of computers good from a broad public policy viewpoint? Is it possible that such systems would tend to create greater isolation among different groups in society? Another question concerns the basic economics of specific proposals. In addition to economics, we must consider the possibility that people are not really interested in many of the services that might be offered.

If such information and communications capabilities are available, what will be their impact on mobility and personal habits? If these suggestions were ever implemented throughout the country, they might significantly reduce the number of occasions on which people leave their homes.

We also have to be concerned about whether security and privacy can be provided effectively in such systems. Can the owner or operator of an information utility use the information for personal gain, such as conducting marketing research surveys?

Another policy question concerns a capability for a national referendum. Is it desirable to present issues in this manner and ask for public response? Will people become tired of this invasion of privacy and lose interest in the legislative process? It is also possible that such a service would be too expensive, thus disenfranchising certain groups who are unable to afford it. Such a proposal raises the specter of sabotage or of attempts to influence the outcome of elections illegally. How

---

SYSTEMS PROBLEM 24-1

A major metropolitan city in the United States recently compared its payroll against the recipients of welfare. A simple program was used to compare social security numbers from the payroll file with the social security numbers on the welfare files to determine if any welfare recipients were also receiving a paycheck from the city. This check indicated that the individuals were potentially defrauding the welfare system and misappropriating taxpayers' dollars.

The application created concern among some who considered it a violation of privacy. However, the city has brushed aside these criticisms and is continuing with the program. In fact, a new application has been suggested in which an on-line terminal would be used to access a data base of city services. By entering a social security number, an individual at the terminal could find out about any dealings an individual had with the city.

There would be protections; for example, the income tax records of individuals would not be available. However, any criminal, welfare, or other social service interaction with the city would be displayed. The major advantage of such a system would be to centralize data on the individual. City administrators have suggested that the system will make it easier to provide city services and to catch fraud.

The scenario described above is hypothetical; no city has proposed exactly such a system, but it clearly is within the realm of today's technology. What would your reaction be to such a proposal? Would such a system be desirable? If so, what safeguards would you recommend be built into the system?

easy would it be to abuse the information available for the purposes of controlling the population?

Home Computers   One of the fastest growing markets in the United States is home computer sales. Individuals are purchasing personal computers, and elementary and high schools are rushing to keep pace. There have been both successes and failures with home computers; in some instances the devices have been used for a short time and then remain unused. Certainly, a large number of individuals have applications for which the computer is suited, but often the machine is used in this capacity primarily for work. An individual can maintain budgets, keep track of a stock portfolio, and process taxes on home computers. There is no clear consensus now whether there in fact are enough home applications for a significant market potential to exist for computers.

On the educational front, it is clear that many individuals need to be prepared to work with computers in their work roles, if not at home as well. There is great concern that financially better-off schools will be able to buy computers for the classroom and poorer schools will not. Will this trend, if it occurs, condemn a large number of students to a second-class education? Will computer literacy become a requirement for an educated individual?

Educating for Computing   In the section above we raise the question of whether an individual will have to know something about computing to be educated. Regardless of the philosophical question, there is a definite need to educate individuals for the following roles.

End Users   Probably the largest group we consider will be end users, individuals in firms whose primary responsibilities are not in the computer field. These employees need to be able to use computers as a part of their work. The typical professional of the future will have some type of managerial work station, with a powerful microcomputer connected to a network. The local computer will be used to handle tasks that do not require a larger processor, such as word processing, spreadsheet analysis, and similar applications. This user will have to understand something about computers, networks, and different kinds of software.

Computer Professionals   These individuals will work with the technology. The category includes programmers, systems analysts, computer managers, and various clerical staff members. Computer professionals must have an in-depth understanding of technology and its application. Some of these employees will work on the development of hardware and software packages; others will work applying combinations of hardware, packages, and custom programs to the problems faced by organizations.

Interface Personnel   Between the computer professional and the user is an interface staff. These individuals will have functional knowledge of how computers and software work but will not have a command of all the technical details. They will have to be conversant with the kinds of problems faced by organizations and will need to understand business and management.

Our challenge is to provide education and on-the-job training for all these diverse needs. Without qualified individuals, progress in the application of computer technology will be severely retarded.

Computers and Money   Electronic funds transfer systems have been studied extensively during the past decade, and a number of systems have been proposed. To implement such a system, many of the present laws concerning credit and money would have to be rewritten. However, we do not really know the present public attitude toward electronic funds transfer. Questions of privacy are also involved here; for example, information on checks could be potentially useful to different segments of society, or such information could be used for surveillance purposes. The point-of-sale recorders in stores would make it possible to keep track of where a person is at the time of any transaction and thus keep a record of an individual's travels.

Computers and Elections   Computers have been used routinely to predict the outcome of elections and to tally votes. There have also been political candidates who have used computers widely to custom-tailor campaigns to individual areas, ethnic groups, and even individuals. Are the sophisticated computer predictions actually disenfranchising people who live on the West Coast and who will not bother to vote after computer predictions show who has won the election?

Privacy   Certainly one of the most widely debated topics relating to society is the issue of an individual's right to privacy. Foreign governments have suggested placing restrictions on the international flow of information. Many bills and acts have been proposed to ensure the individual's privacy. At what point does the right to privacy come in conflict with other rights? Society certainly has the need and the right to have certain kinds of information that contributes to the general welfare. Demographic information and information on income levels are vitally important in establishing national policy. However, information on wages and financial conditions is considered to be extremely sensitive by most individuals.

Certainly, current thinking is that individuals should have the right to ascertain whether information held about them is correct and to force the correction of errors. There is less agreement on the types of penalties that should be imposed for the misuse of private information maintained in some type of data bank. Other questions arise as to whether individuals should have the right to know who has requested information about them from a data bank. Some countries have become concerned about this trend; for example, Sweden has enacted a comprehensive program to regulate the development of data banks.

A number of solutions have been proposed, and the federal government has passed legislation affecting only federal agencies. There have been suggestions to extend the federal law to the private sector. As it stands now, the legislation requires a large amount of record keeping about the pattern of access to records that contain any personal information. There are fears that the proposals for the private sector may prove extremely costly for organizations. One important issue, then, is what should be the balance between the individual's rights and the burdens and costs of protection and record keeping?

Security Closely related to problems of privacy is the issue of system security. There are many possible threats to the security and integrity of a computer system, particularly on-line systems, where there is widespread access by individuals external to the organization. There have been a number of well-publicized penetrations recently of various computer systems, including a major hospital's on-line cancer research system. Researchers in the field are working on methods of encrypting data so that it cannot be intercepted and decoded by an unfriendly user. Such concerns are very important given the existence of highly sensitive data in on-line data bases. There are also many problems related to the prevention of system failure; individuals and organizations are dependent on many systems, and these systems must remain operational.

Employment Labor leaders have been extremely concerned about the possibility of wide-scale unemployment because of computers. The computer industry is one of the largest in the United States, and it has created hundreds of thousands of jobs. Naturally, the implementation of some information systems has eliminated or modified jobs, though there are few statistics to indicate the overall impact on employment.

It does appear that the continued introduction of computerized robots will reduce employment in manufacturing. The extent to which this effect will be offset by jobs building and servicing robots is unknown. However, certainly increased technology will require a higher-skilled, better-educated work force. There are also implications from the implementation of information systems on the pace of technological change, job security, and the importance of retraining workers when jobs change. Has the opportunity to exercise individual initiative and has the interest of jobs been reduced by computers?

Computer Knowledge There is a widespread lack of understanding in the world concerning the capabilities of computers. Some individuals believe that the computer can do almost anything. Others feel the computer can be used only for performing simple, repetitive chores. What are the responsibilities of the computer professional to help educate the population concerning the actual capabilities and use of computers?

Liability Computer systems are an important part of many business operations. A few companies have already gone into bankruptcy because of errors in processing, and others have turned profitable operations into losses. It is also possible, as one recent scandal has shown, to use a computer to help perpetrate widespread fraud.

There is no way to pinpoint responsibility when a computer system fails. We have stressed that systems design is a creative task; it is possible to have errors in logic and processing that are not caught until actual operations begin. Auditing firms are particularly concerned over the use of computers to process and maintain basic information on the operations of a firm. It is very difficult to audit computer-based systems and to be certain that controls are adequate.

Computers and Communications   One major trend in computing is toward more remote data access and communications among terminals and computers and among networks of computers. This trend raises major policy issues considering the current posture of the government toward communications. All interstate communications are regulated, and a number of private companies are attempting to enter the data communications market. The types of routes given these carriers versus the existing regulated carriers and the tariff structures for communications raise questions of national policy.

Computers and Underdeveloped Countries   Is it possible to use computers to help accelerate the development of preindustrialized countries? If so, how do we transfer the technical expertise required to these countries? It will be necessary to work with the leadership of such nations to develop priorities for applications and to train nationals to carry out the work. What impact will the development of systems have on other aspects of the country's economy?

Computers and Power   We have discussed the fact that computers can change power relationships within organizations. The same trend may occur in society as a whole. Is it possible that through the acquisition of data stored in computer data banks, an organization such as a credit bureau might increase significantly the amount of power that it has over citizens? Is it true that a candidate for national office who cannot afford the use of a computer may be at an insurmountable disadvantage? If there are gross imbalances in power, what can we do about it? How much responsibility does the producer of a tool have for its use?

Complexity and Integrity

Computer systems are becoming steadily more complex. In earlier discussions of controls we have pointed out the rather unfortunate state-of-the-art in reliability and debugging of programs; hardware malfunctions can also reduce the reliability of a system.

Despite steady improvements in hardware and software development techniques, many computer systems do not exhibit sufficient reliability. Are computer systems too complex? Have they grown to the point where people cannot understand and use them adequately?

As computer applications are extended even further and affect more aspects of our lives, is existing technology adequate for the task? Clearly more advanced development and audit and control techniques are needed, but progress has been very slow. Possibly we shall have to resort to extensive hardware and software redundancy in critical systems to improve reliability. Hardware redundancy is

SYSTEMS PROBLEM 24-2

A recent strike in the United Kingdom raised some very serious possibilities for future problems in the world. The civil servants union wanted to strike but recognized that a walkout by the entire union would deplete the strike fund quickly. Instead of a national strike, the union had the data processing employees who were union members strike. Because the government was so dependent on computers for delivering services, this job action by a small number of individuals in the union had the effect that a walkout of the entire union would have had. The advantage for the union was that almost all its members (the members not holding computer-related jobs) were still working, so that the strike fund had to support only a small number of strikers. It was easy to provide the strikers with full pay!

Whereas in other countries the data processing staff may not be as widely enrolled in the same union, it is possible that such a scenario could be repeated in a few years in other places. In the past, we have been concerned with nationwide strikes such as in transportation, energy supplies, etc. that could cripple the economy. The British experience raises the possibility that information processing may become one of these critical industries. We have suggested that the United States economy is becoming more service- and less manufacturing-oriented.

What kind of change in power relationships does this process create in society? What are the long-term implications of our dependence on computer systems? Is national policy needed to deal with this and similar problems?

---

found frequently, but software duplication is more rare. Will we have to program key parts of systems twice using independent programmers and then execute both programs each time one is called?

Possible Solutions

A number of technical approaches have been offered to solve computer-related problems, especially fraud and privacy violations. These techniques and special procedures can help; however, the fundamental issue is one of systems design.

If a system is well conceived and designed then there should be few problems. Below are some questions that systems designers should ask themselves in developing a new application:

1 Is this application a potential threat to anyone's rights? What could go wrong? For example, do the files contain rumors, hearsay information, or unevaluated reports on individuals?

2 Is there a natural disincentive to use the system; for example, does it act to police workers who must contribute the data?

3 Is it difficult for me to use the system; that is, could I fill out the forms, understand the output, enter data through a terminal, or whatever is required?

4 How many ways could I find to defraud the system?

5 If I wanted to misuse the data or the system, how could I get around the procedures that safeguard it? What could I do to misuse the data?

Just as we advocated an independent source of data for testing programs and the design of the system, it is desirable to have independent attempts to penetrate the system along the lines suggested by these questions, to be sure the design is complete.

THE FUTURE OF INFORMATION SYSTEMS

This book has discussed information systems, the computer department, and the organization. What does the future hold for information systems activities? If we follow some of the techniques recommended here to develop successful systems, there should be a bright future for the field.

There is a trend toward supporting more sophisticated decisions as routine transactional systems are implemented and we move into operational, managerial, and strategic-planning applications. Even for very mundane types of processing systems, there is often a significant impact in reducing the drudgery of information processing and enlarging jobs in the organization.

Hardware and software progress during the last 5 years has served to expand the options available for developing a computer-based information system. We can follow the life cycle with conventional development of a custom system, use an appropriate package, employ an applications generator, and/or encourage prototyping and end-user programming. The large number of alternatives creates added complexity in making the decision about what to develop and how to develop it. The skills of the systems analyst are urgently needed to help make the kinds of decisions described in the text.

To some extent everyone in an organization is involved in information processing. While we have a sophisticated technology that is rapidly changing, we are constrained primarily by our abilities to apply and manage it. In information systems we have barely penetrated the surface of what can be accomplished!

KEY WORDS

Alienation

Career path

Chief programmer

Computer professional

Fraud

Management

Misuse of information

Privacy

Personal computers

Programmer

Right of appeal

Social impact

Systems analyst

RECOMMENDED READINGS

ACM Committee on Computers and Public Policy: "A Problem-List of Issues Concerning Computers and Public Policy," *Communications of the ACM,* vol. 17, no. 9, September 1974, pp. 495–503. (An extensive list of computer issues related to society.)

Gilchrist, B., and A. Shenkin: "The Impact of Scanners on Employment in Supermarkets," *Communications of the ACM,* vol. 25, no. 7, July 1982, pp. 441–445. (What do you think of their analysis?)

Weil, U.: *Information Systems in the 80's,* Prentice-Hall, Englewood Cliffs, N.J., 1982. (A forecast of the future and its impact.)

DISCUSSION QUESTIONS

1 Why is the use of a system the responsibility of a systems design team and the organization?

2 Is there such a thing as a right to privacy?

3 Does the presence of computer equipment make it easier to violate an individual's privacy?

4 Is fraud easier with a computer system than with its manual predecessor?

5 What would your response be to a proposal for a national data bank of information on citizens for purposes of social science research?

6 What aspects of a computer profession would you expect to be the most rewarding?

7 Why has research shown (for example, see Mumford, 1972) that frequently systems designers feel a system is best implemented by forcing it on users?

8 What kind of home computer applications would you envision using a television or telephone-type terminal in private residences?

9 What problems would home information systems raise? Do you feel there is a market for this type of service?

10 It has been suggested that an electronic funds transfer system could eliminate "float," that is, the use of money by the purchaser because he or she has not yet been billed for goods or services. Would the elimination of float be desirable? How would an electronic funds transfer system affect the public?

11 In your opinion, would it be possible for a group to utilize computers to rig a nationwide election?

12 Why has computer-aided education been less successful than originally envisioned? What types of educational activities can best make use of this type of computer system? Where might computer-aided instruction be used in the design of information systems?

13 Do computers make it easier to violate an individual's right to privacy? What are the dangers of centralizing all government records on each citizen? What are the advantages?

14 Do employers have a responsibility to retrain workers who might be replaced by a computer system?

15 Why is the public so badly informed about the capabilities of computer systems? Do you feel most problems seen by the public are the responsibility of the computer, the manual procedures associated with the system, or the original systems design?

16 What can be done to reduce the possibility of computer-based fraud causing the failure of a business?

17 How could computers and communications be used to solve some of the pressing problems of society, such as reducing the amount of energy consumed?

18 What priorities should be used by underdeveloped countries in trying to develop computer capabilities?

19 Is it possible that computer systems will become so all-pervasive than an elite of computer specialists will acquire dangerous amounts of power? What factors reduce the likelihood of such a power shift?

BIBLIOGRAPHY

ACM Committee on Computers and Public Policy: "A Problem-List of Issues Concerning Computers and Public Policy," *Communications of the ACM,* vol. 17, no. 9, September 1974, pp. 495–503.

Allen, B.: "Danger Ahead! Safeguard Your Computer," *Harvard Business Review,* vol. 46, no. 6, November-December 1968, pp. 97–101.

Allen, F. W., M. E. S. Loomis, and M. V. Mannino: "The Integrated Dictionary/Directory System," *Computing Surveys,* vol. 14, no. 2, June 1982, pp. 245–286.

Anthony, R.: *Planning and Control Systems: A Framework for Analysis,* Division of Research, Graduate School of Business Administration, Harvard, Boston, 1965.

Auerback Publishers: *Data Communications Management,* Pennsauken, N.J.

————: *Data Processing Management,* Pennsauken, N.J.

Baker, F. T.: "Chief Programmer Team Management of Production Programming," *IBM Systems Journal,* vol. 11, no. 1, 1972, pp. 56–73.

Buffa, E. S.: *Modern Production Management,* Wiley, New York, 1961.

Burch, J. G., F. R. Strater, and G. Grudnitski: *Information Systems Theory and Practice,* 3d ed., Wiley, New York, 1983.

Canning, R.: "The Analysis of User Needs," *EDP Analyzer,* vol. 17, no. 1, January 1979.

————: "Query Systems for End Users," *EDP Analyzer,* vol. 20, no. 9, September 1982.

Chapin, N.: "Flowcharting with The ANSI Standard: A Tutorial," *Computing Surveys,* vol. 2, no. 2, June 1970, pp. 89–110.

Christie, B.: *Face to File Communication,* Wiley, Chichester, 1981.

Churchill, N., J. H. Kempster, and M. Uretsky: *Computer-Based Information Systems for Management: A Survey,* National Association of Accountants, New York, 1969.

Couger, J. D.: "Evaluation of Business Systems Analysis Techniques," *Computing Surveys,* vol. 5, no. 3, September 1973, pp. 167–198.

————, and R. W. Knapp: *Systems Analysis Techniques,* Wiley, New York, 1979.

Crawford, A. B., "Corporate Electronic Mail—A Communication Intensive Application of Information Technology," *MIS Quarterly,* vol. 6, no. 3, September 1982, pp. 1–13.

Davis, G. B.: *Computer Data Processing,* 2d ed., McGraw-Hill, New York, 1973.

Dearden, J., and R. L. Nolan: "How to Control the Computer Resource," *Harvard Business Review,* vol. 51, no. 6, November-December 1973, pp. 68–75.

Dodd, G.: "Elements of Data Management Systems," *Computing Surveys,* vol. 1, no. 7, June 1969, pp. 117–133.

Eliason, A. L., and K. D. Kitts: *Business Computer Systems Applications,* Systems Research Associates, Palo Alto, Calif., 1974.

Filley, A. C., R. J. House, and S. Kerr: *Managerial Process and Organizational Behavior,* 2d ed., Scott, Foresman, Glenview, Ill., 1976.

Fitzgerald, J.: *Internal Controls for Computerized Systems,* San Leandro, Calif., 1978.

———, and A. Fitzgerald: *Fundamentals of Systems Analysis,* Wiley, New York, 1973.

Gane, C., and T. Sarson: *Structured Systems Analysis,* Prentice-Hall, Englewood Cliffs, N.J., 1979.

Gilb, T., and G. Weinberg: *Humanized Input,* Winthrop, Cambridge, Mass., 1977.

Gilchrist, B., and A. Shenkin: "The Impact of Scanners on Employment in Supermarkets," *Communications of the ACM,* vol. 25, no. 7, July 1982, pp. 441–445.

Gore, M., and J. Stubbe: *Elements of Systems Analysis for Business Data Processing,* 2d ed., W. C. Brown, Dubuque, Iowa, 1979.

Haire, M.: *Psychology in Management,* 2d ed., McGraw-Hill, New York, 1964.

Hammond, L. W.: "Management Considerations for an Information Center," *IBM Systems Journal,* vol. 21, no. 2, 1982, pp. 131–161.

Hickson, P. J., C. R. Hennings, C. A. Lee, R. E. Schneck, and J. M. Pennings: "Strategic Contingencies Theory of Interorganizational Power," *Administrative Science Quarterly,* vol. 16, no. 2, June 1971, pp. 216–229.

Hennings, C. R., D. J. Hickson, J. M. Pennings, and R. E. Schneck: "Structural Conditions of Intraorganizational Power," *Administrative Science Quarterly,* vol. 19, no. 1, March 1974, pp. 22–44.

Hoffman, L.: *Modern Methods for Computer Security and Privacy,* Prentice-Hall, Englewood Cliffs, N.J., 1977.

Housely, T.: *Data Communications and Teleprocessing Systems,* Prentice-Hall, Englewood Cliffs, N.J., 1979.

IBM: *Improved Technology for Application Development: Management Overview,* IBM Corp., 1973.

Jackson, M.: *System Development,* Prentice-Hall, Englewood Cliffs, N.J., 1983.

Jensen, R. W., and C. C. Tonies: *Software Engineering,* Prentice-Hall, Englewood Cliffs, N.J., 1979.

Johnson, J. C., K. A. Kozar, and D. A. Ruch: "RAFT: An Information System for Fiscal Analysis," *MIS Quarterly,* vol. 1, no. 4, December 1977, pp. 29–39.

Kanter, J.: *Management-Oriented Management Information Systems,* Prentice-Hall, Englewood Cliffs, N.J. 1972.

Katz, D., and R. L. Kahn: *The Social Psychology of Organizations,* 2d ed., Wiley, New York, 1978.

Katzan, H.: *Systems Design and Documentation: An Introduction to the HIPO Method,* Van Nostrand Reinhold, New York, 1976.

Kay, R. H.: "The Management and Organization of Large Scale Software Development Projects," *AFIPS 1969 Conference Proceedings (SJCC),* vol. 34, AFIPS Press, Montvale, N.J., pp. 425–433.

Kelly, J. F.: *Computerized Management Information Systems,* Macmillan, New York, 1970.

Kolb, D. A., and A. L. Frohman: "An Organizational Development Approach to Consulting," *Sloan Management Review,* vol. 12, no. 1, 1970, pp. 51–65.

Lawrence, P., and J. Lorsch: *Organization and Environment,* Division of Research, Graduate School of Business Administration, Harvard, Boston, 1967.

Leavitt, H. J., and T. L. Whisler: "Management in the 1980s," *Harvard Business Review,* November-December 1958, pp. 41–48.

Likert, R.: *New Patterns of Management,* McGraw-Hill, New York, 1961.

Loomis, M.: *Data Communications,* Prentice-Hall, Englewood Cliffs, N.J., 1983.

Lucas, H. C., Jr.: "Performance Evaluation and the Management of Information Services," *Data Base,* vol. 4, no. 1, Spring 1972, pp. 1–8.

―――: *Computer-Based Information Systems in Organizations,* Science Research Associates, Palo Alto, Calif., 1973.

―――: *Toward Creative Systems Design,* Columbia, New York, 1974.

―――: *The Implementation of Computer-Based Models,* National Association of Accountants, New York, 1976.

―――: *Implementation: The Key to Successful Information Systems,* Columbia, New York, 1981.

―――: *Coping with Computers: A Manager's Guide to Controlling Information Processing,* Free Press, New York, 1982.

McFarlan, F. W., and J. L. McKenney: *Corporate Information Systems Management,* Irwin, Homewood, Ill., 1983.

McFarlan, W. F.: "Management Audit of the EDP Department," *Harvard Business Review,* vol. 51, no. 3, May-June 1973, pp. 131–142.

―――, R. L. Nolan, and D. P. Norton: *Information Systems Administration,* Holt, New York, 1973.

McGregor, D.: *The Human Side of Enterprise,* McGraw-Hill, New York, 1960.

March, J., and H. Simon: *Organizations,* Wiley, New York, 1958.

Martin, J.: *Telecommunications and the Computer,* Prentice-Hall, Englewood Cliffs, N.J., 1969.

―――: *Systems Analysis for Data Transmission,* Prentice-Hall, Englewood Cliffs, N.J., 1972.

―――: *Design of Man-Computer Dialogues,* Prentice-Hall, Englewood Cliffs, N.J., 1973.

―――, and A. Norman: *The Computerized Society,* Prentice-Hall, Englewood Cliffs, N.J., 1970.

―――: *Applications Development without Programmers,* Prentice-Hall, Englewood Cliffs, N.J., 1982.

―――, and C. McClure: "Buying Software off the Rack," *Harvard Business Review,* vol. 61, no. 6, Nov-Dec, 1983, pp. 32–60.

Martin, W. A.: "Sorting," *Computing Surveys,* vol. 3, no. 4, December 1971, pp. 147–174.

Mason, R. E. A., and T. T. Carey: "Prototyping Interactive Information Systems," *Communications of the ACM,* vol. 26, no. 5, May 1983, pp. 347–354.

Merten, A. G., and E. H. Sibley: "Implementation of a Generalized Data Base Management System Within an Organization," *Management Informatics,* vol. 2, no. 1, February 1973, pp. 21–31.

Mills, H. D.: *Chief Programmer Team's Principles and Procedures,* IBM Federal Systems Division, Gaithersburg, Md., 1971.

―――: "The New Math of Computer Programming," *Communications of the ACM,* vol. 18, no.1, January 1975, pp. 43–48.

Mintzberg, H.: *The Nature of Managerial Work,* Harper & Row, New York, 1973.

———: The Structure of Organizations, Prentice-Hall, Englewood Cliffs, N.J., 1979.

Mumford, E.: *Job Satisfaction: A Study of Computer Specialists,* Longmans, London, 1972.

———, and O. Banks: *The Computer and the Clerk,* Routledge, London, 1967.

———, and T. B. Ward: *Computers: Planning for People,* Batsford, London, 1968.

———, and D. Henshall: *A Participative Approach to Computer Systems Design,* Associated Business Press, London, 1979.

Murdick, R. G., and J. E. Ross: *Information Systems for Modern Management,* 2d ed., Prentice-Hall, Englewood Cliffs, N.J., 1975.

Myers, G.: "A Controlled Experiment in Program Testing and Code Walkthroughs/Inspections," *Communications of the ACM,* vol. 21, no. 9, September 1978, pp. 760–768.

Naumann, J., and M. Jenkins: "Prototyping: The New Paradigm for Systems Development," *MIS Quarterly,* vol. 6, no. 3, September 1982, pp. 29–44.

Nie, N., D. Bent, and H. Hull: *Statistical Package for the Social Sciences,* McGraw-Hill, New York, 1970.

Nielsen, N.: "The Allocation of Computer Resources—Is Pricing the Answer?" *Communications of the ACM,* vol. 13, no. 8, August 1970, pp. 467–474.

Nolan, R. L.: "Plight of the EDP Manager," *Harvard Business Review,* vol. 51, no. 3, May-June 1973, pp. 143–152.

———: "Managing Information Systems by Committee," *Harvard Business Review,* vol. 60, no. 4, July-August 1982, pp. 72–79.

Olsen, R. A.: *Manufacturing Management: A Quantitative Approach,* International Textbooks, Scranton, Pa., 1968.

Ouchi, W.: *Theory Z,* Addison-Wesley, New York, 1981.

Parnas, D. L.: "On the Criteria to Be Used in Decomposing Systems into Modules," *Communications of the ACM,* vol. 15, no. 12, December 1972, pp. 1053–1058.

Pounds, W. F.: "The Process of Problem Finding," *Industrial Management Review,* vol. II, no. 1, pp. 1–20.

Savas, E. S.: "The Political Properties of Crystalline H_2O, Planning for Snow Emergencies in New York," *Management Science,* vol. 20, October 1973, pp. 137–145.

Schein, E.: *Organizational Psychology,* 2d ed., Prentice-Hall, Englewood Cliffs, N.J., 1970.

Schroderbeck, P.: *Management Systems,* 2d ed., Wiley, New York, 1971.

Schultz, R., and D. Slevin: *Implementing ORMS,* American Elsevier, New York, 1975.

Semprivivo, P.: *Systems Analysis,* SRA, Palo Alto, Calif., 1982.

Simon, H.: *Administrative Behavior,* Macmillan, New York, 1947.

———: *The Shape of Automation for Men and Management,* Harper & Row, New York, 1965.

Sprague, R., and E. Carlson: *Building Effective Decision Support Systems,* Prentice-Hall, Englewood Cliffs, N.J., 1982.

Stay, J.: "HIPO and Integrated Program Design," *IBM Systems Journal,* vol. 15, no. 2, 1976, pp. 143–154.

Tamir, M., et al.: "DBI: A DBMS-Based Application Generator," *Proceedings of the Very Large Data Base Conference,* Glasgow, Scotland, 1981.

Thayer, R., and E. Hinton: "Software Reliability—A Method That Works," *National Computer Conference,* 1975, pp. 877–882.

Thompson, J. D.: *Organizations and Actions,* McGraw-Hill, New York, 1967.

Tsichritzis, D., and F. Lochovsky: *Data Models,* Prentice-Hall, Englewood Cliffs, N.J., 1982.

Wagner, H. M.: *Principles of Operations Research,* Prentice-Hall, Englewood Cliffs, N.J., 1969.

Walston, C. E., and C. P. Felix: "A Method of Programming Measurement and Estimation," *IBM Systems Journal,* vol. 16, no. 1, 1977, pp. 54–73.

Walton, R. E., and J. M. Dutton: "The Management of Interdepartmental Conflict: A Model and Review," *Administrative Science Quarterly,* vol. 14, no. 1, March 1969, pp. 73–84.

Watson, R. W.: *Timesharing System Design Concepts,* McGraw-Hill, New York, 1970.

Weil, U.: *Information Systems in the 80's,* Prentice-Hall, Englewood Cliffs, N.J., 1982.

Weinberg, G. M.: *The Psychology of Computer Programming,* Van Nostrand, New York, 1972a.

————: "The Psychology of Improved Programming Performance," *Datamation,* vol. 18, no. 11, November 1972b, pp. 82–85.

Whisler, T. L.: *Information Technology and Organizational Change,* Wadsworth, Belmont, Calif., 1970.

Yourdon, E.: *Design of On-Line Computer Systems,* Prentice-Hall, Englewood Cliffs, N.J., 1972.

Zelkowitz, M. V., A. C. Shaw, and J. D. Gunnar: *Principles of Software Engineering and Design,* Prentice-Hall, Englewood Cliffs, N.J., 1979.

INDEX

INDEX

ABOUT THE BOOK

The Analysis, Design, and Implementation of Information Systems, Third Edition, introduces the reader to the most current and practical approaches to systems design. New material stresses communications, data base management, microcomputers, prototyping, generators, and packages. All vital areas of information system design, analysis and implementation are reinforced with a wide array of exercises and problems.

The actual design process is presented through "The Hardserve Case," a concrete case model that is used throughout the book. The case model clearly illustrates the design demands of users, and readers learn about the many trade-offs and alternatives that surface at each phase in the design construction. A meaningful perspective of the whole inter-related computer system is gained through the book's presentation of the conventional life cycle of information systems (study, design, development, operation). The book also includes the behavioral considerations and the organizational theory behind the implementation and design of a system. Actual dialog between users and designers illustrates the importance of good design and the technical aspects of information design are examined in depth so that no redesigning will be needed after the system is completed.

Among the many changes in the third edition are a new section on data communications covering new technological and conceptual developments, and a new chapter entitled Data-Base Management (Chapter 9). New chapters also deal with important alternatives to conventional design such as package programs and prototyping.